SEXUALITY IN THE LEGAL ARENA

Edited by

CARL STYCHIN
DIDI HERMAN

THE ATHLONE PRESS

LONDON

First published in 2000 by
THE ATHLONE PRESS
1 Park Drive, London NW11 7SG

© The Contributors 2000

British Library Cataloguing in Publication Data
*A catalogue record for this book is available
from the British Library*

ISBN 0 485 00409 7 HB
0 485 00609 X PB

Typeset in Garamond by
Aarontype Limited, Easton, Bristol
Printed and bound in Great Britain by Bookcraft (Bath) Ltd

CONTENTS

INTRODUCTION

When academic studies of sexualities experienced a veritable explosion in the late 1980s and throughout the 1990s, legal studies of sexuality initially appeared to lag behind. Moreover, much of the work which was produced was centred on the pragmatic use of legal doctrine to achieve progressive legal change. Such work was important, although legal defeats were far more common than victories throughout those primarily Anglo-American jurisdictions in which legal struggles occurred. In the last few years, however, the legal academic study of 'sexualities' – particularly the interrogation of the legal construction and deployment of sexual identities and practices – has developed at a rapid pace.

Consequently, 'law and sexuality' can now be described in terms of a real diversity of perspectives and approaches; a situation which produces complementarity but also conflict within the academy. On the one hand, there are now many exponents of a positivist, pragmatic approach. These academics tend to assume the importance (and rationality) of law in advancing social change, and they can place tremendous faith in law's rationality. This view also generally assumes the naturalness and coherence of sexual identity categories, and pays little attention to the ways in which such categories are variously socially constructed.

The second trajectory of analysis – in which this volume can be located – encompasses several approaches which might be characterized generally by a more critical, sceptical (but ultimately pragmatic) approach to legal discourse and its relationship to social change. Drawing on a variety of intellectual tools – deconstruction, literary analysis, feminist, queer and critical race theory, post-colonial studies, anthropology, masculinity studies, radical political theory (to name but a few) – this work aims in part to *problematize* both the idea(l) of law and the dominant, hegemonic construction of sexualities. Thus, for example, work of this type might focus upon law's ability to normalize and discipline the sexual subject while, at the same time, recognizing that subject's claim to rights. This approach tends to see sexualities, not as transhistorical, universal categories of identity, but instead as provisional, contested and always produced in relation to other identifications.

The essays in this volume locate these themes in a range of specific political and geographical contexts. Both Jennifer Spruill and Oliver Phillips underscore the role of law as a site for the articulation of connections between post-colonialism and law, and they show how these links are negotiated by southern African lesbians and gays, as well as their opponents. The role of Western categories and definitions of sexuality is highlighted. This point is further developed by Pierre de Vos, who describes a tension between the legal 'fiction' of sexual orientation and the lived reality of South Africans.

Relationships between geographical and sexual identities are explored in other contexts as well. Patrick Hanafin shows the way in which law draws on dominant conceptions of national identity in order to name included and excluded sexual identities in Ireland. This relationship between the national and the sexual is also traced by Emma Henderson in the context of Tasmania, but Henderson also relates the importance of geography to international legal developments, and this international human rights dimension is considered by Wayne Morgan, in a sustained critique of legal positivist analysis. Morgan considers the broader question of whether lesbians and gays should aspire to inclusion in a system of heteronormativity or, alternatively, aim to challenge and destabilize that system.

Heather Brook makes a related point in her analysis of domestic partnership legislation in Australia, finding that, despite the inclusion of same-sex couples, the conjugal relationship of marriage remains stable and undisturbed. Richard Collier strikes a similar note, but he concludes that the heterosexuality of family law may be an increasingly contested, contingent and fluid phenomenon. Collier's essay underscores the political intedeterminacy of current legal developments, and this theme is common to many of the contributions. Claire Young, for example, shows that 'victories' for lesbians and gays in Canadian equality law have been rooted in the sphere of privatized responsibility, and have yet to result in the conferral of universal, public benefits.

In addition, conservative anti-gay responses to lesbian and gay legal claims are analysed by many of the contributors. For example, Jonathan Goldberg-Hiller locates these developments on a wider terrain of backlash against civil rights narratives and their perceived social costs. Similarly, Thomas Kuttner and Rebecca Johnson point to anger directed at minority groups who are identified as the enemies of democracy, and their contribution provides an attempt to find alternative legal arguments which are less susceptible to backlash discourse.

Although such anti-gay rhetoric may display an increased 'sophistication' in that its proponents attempt to avoid blatantly homophobic language, some contributions underscore how those familiar tropes are far from extinct. In this regard, Leslie J. Moran and Derek McGhee's historical analysis of police surveillance of male bodies in London in the 1950s remains highly relevant, as criminal law surveillance of sexual practices continues. Moreover, the construction of the male homosexual as pathological, demonized and murderous, as Derek Dalton shows, continues in legal and cinematic discourse; and that trope, as Adrian Howe demonstrates, ironically is deployed by heterosexual men as defendants in criminal trials through the 'homosexual advance defence' as an excuse for murder.

Thus, what all of the contributors share, in their great diversity, is a willingness to locate legal developments in a wider theoretical, political and social context, demonstrating both the limitations, but also the potentiality, of engagements with law.

There is always a danger that this approach to 'law and sexuality' may be characterized as too remote from the 'practical' legal issues that are faced by, for example, lesbians and gay men. However, we would argue that theory must inform practice, and that law-reform strategies which lack a considered theoretical framework often lead to problematic outcomes. Moreover, many of the essays in this collection neatly bridge theoretical and 'practical' concerns, and many of the contributors locate themselves on both sides of that (artificial) dichotomy.

Another key feature of this collection is its internationalism. These essays embody scholarship from four continents and, in doing so, represent leading work in newly emerging approaches to the study of law and sexuality. For example, the relationship between law and (post-)coloniality is explored by several of our contributors – from both First and Third World perspectives. Themes of globalization, development and cultural authenticity run throughout the collection and, we hope, contribute to comparative, transnational analyses of law and sexuality. Thus, 'law and sexuality' is now a terrain with many competing 'traditions' and these essays provide a snapshot of current developments, drawn from events in numerous parts of the world.

Some years ago, we worked together to produce *Legal Inversions: Lesbians, Gay Men, and the Politics of Law* (1995), a collection that reflected many of the key concerns animating lesbian and gay legal struggles of the early 1990s. We hope that *Sexuality in the Legal Arena* will both complement that earlier work (and others) and, at the same time, represent newly emerging concerns and further reflection on, and from, 'the field'.

PART ONE

NATIONALITY AND POSTCOLONIALITY

INTRODUCTION

The essays which comprise this first part interrogate the ways in which the content, imperatives and norms of law shape subjectivities and subjecthoods in national contexts. Representing work from four nations, the authors' concerns incorporate yet move beyond previous work focusing upon the construction of the lesbian and gay subject in law. For example, these essays contribute to the emerging fields of sexuality and post-coloniality, sexuality and individual subjectivity, and national and regional identities.

Two of the essays focus on the southern African region, a key site in which tensions between national and regional identities, and sexualities, continue to play themselves out. The contrasting experiences of the Republic of South Africa and Zimbabwe are illustrated by contributions from Jennifer Spruill and Oliver Phillips. However, the relationship of territorially based identities and sexualities is certainly not limited to that region. Emma Henderson's contribution demonstrates their deployment in the context of Tasmania, where national and subnational identities have come into conflict with struggles for lesbian and gay legal equality. In this case, law has been deployed at an international level.

Patrick Hanafin's essay looks at nation, colonial constructions and sexualities, but in a European context: Ireland. In this case, transnational law – the law of the European Union – has played an important role in social change in a national culture in which the construction of sexuality has been closely bound up with a colonial history. All of these contributions underscore the importance of recognizing national and regional specificities in the deployment of sexuality, but also demonstrate, at the same time, how similarities and comparisons can be found between different geopolitical contexts.

1

A POST- WITH/OUT A PAST?

SEXUAL ORIENTATION AND THE POST-COLONIAL 'MOMENT' IN SOUTH AFRICA[1]

JENNIFER H. SPRUILL

INTRODUCTION

South Africa's historical colonial status has long been subject to debate, the characterization of the former settler state being complicated by independence from Britain[2] and what the African National Congress ('ANC') even recently referred to as apartheid's 'special type' of 'internal colonialism'.[3] This history produced multiple, imbricating and contradictory 'moments' of anti-colonialism and de-colonization. South Africa's *post*-coloniality is correspondingly contested – its temporality and spaciality being equally as unsettled.[4] And to the extent that the post-apartheid transition is construed as marking a post-colonial shift, the disputed nature of the transformation itself can be added to the circumstances which confound the 'post-colonial' as a redeployment of power across *particular* histories, geographies or subjectivities.

Indeed it is the particularities of time and space which Shohat argues are hidden by the universalizing gesture entailed in 'post-colonial' as a description of a global condition.[5] Shohat also says that 'post-coloniality' masks 'political linkages between post-colonial theories' and the politics of 'anti-colonial ... struggles and discourses'.[6] 'Post-coloniality' in post-apartheid South Africa is caught up in the politics of the anti-colonial imperative to retrieve a pre-colonial past not contaminated by the colonial encounter.[7] The desire to historicize and indigenize post-colonial 'culture' features centrally in a debate about homosexuality and (post)colonialism in South Africa – a debate that re-stages the colonial encounter[8] along axes of sexuality and cultural authenticity.

Within this context I examine new versions of Shohat's questions: 'who is mobilizing what in the articulation of the past, deploying what identities, identifications and representations, and in the name of what political vision and goals?'[9] I am particularly concerned with how 'queer fictions of the [colonial] past help construct, maintain, and contest identities – queer fictions of the [post-colonial] present'.[10] Subtending this process is a discourse of 'love' through which lesbian and gay South Africans ground their identities historically and 'culturally'.[11]

The 'post-colonial' encompasses not only a sense of following a particular historical epoch but also moving 'beyond' particular theoretical paradigms.[12] The multiple registers in which post-coloniality is played out in South Africa about (homo)sexuality envision law, in its capacity as an epistemological regime, as a primary site for the articulation of post-colonialism and sexuality. The post-colonial imperatives for indigenization and historicization combine with liberal rights discourses to condition a colonial history and post-colonial future with regard to 'sexual orientation.'

REAL LOVE AND NATIONAL FANTASIES

The post-colonial imperative to locate and resuscitate pre-colonial tradition dominates the politics of sexuality in southern Africa. South Africa's inclusion of 'sexual orientation' in the equality clause of its 1996 constitution nationalized a debate about homosexuality and colonialism between an ethno-nationalist perspective that sees homosexuality as foreign to Africa and one insisting on the presence of homosexuality throughout African history. Within theories espousing the 'importation' thesis in South Africa, homosexuality has come to signify the colonial and capitalist formations to which 'African culture' was subject. Often accompanied by conservative Christian ideology,[13] this perspective seeks to enforce a culturally authentic heterosexuality uncontaminated by colonization. To that extent it is an anti-colonial discourse concerned with de-colonizing post-apartheid South Africa – by recuperating and enforcing what is portrayed as a pre-colonial, uncorrupted African (hetero)sexuality.

This perspective emerged in South African transition politics in 1987. When asked in an interview by London's *Capital Gay* both Ruth Mompati and Solly Smith of the ANC stated that gay rights had no place in an ANC agenda, because '[lesbians and gays] are in the minority. The majority must rule.'[14] More directly, Bennie Alexander (now !Khoisan X), then secretary general of the Pan African Congress, said that homosexuality is 'unAfrican.... We should not take the European leftist position on the matter. It should be looked at in its total perspective from our own Afrocentric position.'[15] Winnie Mandela's 1991 trial on kidnapping and other charges occasioned a broader, more populist expression of the idea. Some of Mandela's supporters paraded outside the courthouse with placards reading 'homosex is not in black culture'. Indeed, Mandela's defence itself rested on her claim that she was rescuing the victims in the case from the grasp of Paul Verryn, whom she asserted had abused them and lured them into his 'homosexual practices', which were contrary to the boys' 'culture'.[16]

With the emergence of the first post-apartheid constitutional drafts that included 'sexual orientation' in the equality clause, this perspective became a factor in recent regional as well as national constitutional politics. The popular history of this politics is traced to the exclusion of Gays and Lesbians of Zimbabwe (GALZ) from the 1995 Zimbabwe International Book Fair amidst statements by President Mugabe that 'homosexuality is an anathema to African culture.'[17] Letters to South African newspaper editors which supported Mugabe began to appear stating, for example, that 'gayism and homosexuality . . . are not African'[18] and were 'borrowed from the West during the colonial era'.[19] Other southern African leaders, including Namibia's President Nujoma, have since weighed in with their own versions of the import thesis.

Following targeted lobbying during constitutional negotiations, the African Christian Democratic Party (ACDP) was the only party to oppose the sexual orientation clause. Kenneth Meshoe, leader of the ACDP, said:

> [homosexuality] is a lifestyle that is unacceptable to the majority of South Africans, besides the fact that it is unChristian and anti- all religion. It is against our culture as Africans, although we know that there are people introduced to this lifestyle. I'm sure they are an embarrassment to their ancestors. This is a white man's disease that has been introduced into the black culture. This definitely comes from Europe.[20]

Meshoe marks homosexuality historically, geographically and racially as colonial. His particular deployment of this idea defines homosexuality as past and foreign to a post-apartheid South Africa governed by an African majority. The constitutional provision is suspected by many to be the result of European influence and part of the settlement concessions to and reconciliation with 'whites.'[21]

The 'importation' perspective is well documented in the literature[22] and is in some respects unexceptionally another example of the re-articulation of anti-gay animus in the post-colony where the body politic is defined through the ethno-nation.[23] My purpose here is not to critique the many ironies and contradictions of the thesis.[24] Rather, I want to examine the discourses and practices of sexuality and post-coloniality emerging in the field it defines. The search for a pre-colonial past produces inventions of authentic presents that serve to remedy colonial history as well as perceived political weaknesses of the present and future.

The idea of homosexuality as colonial defilement forms an impetus for the emergence of lesbian and gay post-colonial sensibilities. Proponents of gay and lesbian rights reject their exclusion from the new South Africa by a cultural–nationalist solution to colonialism. Their interventions resist the historical, geographic and racial marking of sexuality and rework the idea of colonialism as necessarily defined by the oppositions between foreign and indigenous, past and present.

The National Coalition for Gay and Lesbian Equality ('the Coalition') articulates the most prominent and explicit post-colonial rhetoric. The Coalition serves as an umbrella organization and often speaks publicly on behalf of its affiliates at demonstrations, in the media and in courts. Calling the import thesis a myth, the Coalition states that 'same-sex desire and eroticism is part of every culture in Africa.... The anti-colonial movements re-invented the myth of an "African culture" in which there was no exploitation and oppression.'[25]

Lesbian and gay South Africans directly counter the colonial import thesis by insisting on the presence of gays and lesbians in African 'culture' and history. Some deploy a visibility of African lesbian and gay people at public events and media appearances. For example, on a 1996 *Future Imperfect* television show on gay rights, African members of the Coalition executive were tapped to respond to the import assertion – and Simon Nkoli, founder of the Gay and Lesbian Organization of the Witwatersrand, pointedly appeared in 'African' attire. Zackie Achmat, co-convenor of the Coalition, states that the fact that large numbers of African and 'coloured' men were convicted under colonial sodomy laws indicates that 'white people have [not] brought being gay to Africa'.[26]

Aligning Mugabe's Zimbabwe with Hitler's Germany,[27] the Coalition also suggests that the 'import' objection is inconsistent with a liberationist perspective and is in fact a hypocritical stance for South Africa's leaders. For example, Winnie Madikizela-Mandela reiterated her 1991 trial defence at a 1997 Truth and Reconciliation Commission (TRC) hearing on the trial events. In its December 1997 submission to the TRC concerning her testimony, the Coalition places Madikizela-Mandela's comments within South Africa's history of prejudice, oppression, injustice and violence and aligns the lesbian and gay rights movement with the broader liberation struggle and the interests of human rights.[28] Moreover, activists counter the slogan 'Homosexuality is unAfrican' with 'Discrimination is unAfrican'.[29] And one of the placards at a coalition demonstration against Mugabe read 'No Gay Rights = APARTHEID'.[30] Similarly the Coalition compares Mugabe's statement that 'gays have no rights' with B.J. Vorster's that 'blacks have no rights'.[31] An Organization of Lesbian and Gay Activists' T-shirt reading 'no liberation without gay liberation' also aligned lesbian and gay equality with the national struggle against apartheid's 'internal colonialism'. This undermines the anti-colonial nationalist appropriation of sexuality as the national movement's exclusive domain[32] and suggests that the nationalist movement does not in fact speak for the nation.[33]

In a recent article in *Exit*, a newspaper generally associated with the white gay community, Tim Trengove Jones wrote:

> the histories of gay people are analogous to the histories of formerly colonised ones. Gay experience can, therefore, be illuminatingly compared to that of post-colonial experience. Like the previously colonised, gay people have been positioned by dominant cultural forces ... [and] the movement into liberation involves ... represent(ing) ourselves.[34]

Trengove suggests a transformation in the (anti)colonial opposition but only by way of a parallelism whereby he multiplies colonial binaries.[35] That is, the relationship of gay people to 'dominant forces' is merely analogized to that of colonized subjects, no claim is made to a direct relationship between gay oppression and colonial regimes.

Other analyses suggest a closer nexus to the colonial encounter. The Coalition accuses proponents of the import thesis of themselves assuming the colonial position. They say, 'the idea that homosexuality is alien to Africa was first invented by white missionaries.'[36] An open letter from the Coalition to Mugabe concerning sodomy charges filed against the chair of GALZ stated that, 'Keith Goddard is charged with the common law "crime" of sodomy. A "crime" introduced through colonial conquest.'[37] Likewise, journalist Shaun de Waal says that this anti-gay hostility stems from Christianity – 'a western imposition if ever there was one'.[38]

These ideas resist the reproduction of colonial relations and interiorize their effects. Indeed, Kevan Botha, lobbyist for the Coalition, states '[the ACDP] echo the discarded ideology of apartheid ... it would be a travesty if apartheid in any form resurfaced in ... the new South Africa.'[39] This conversation displaces the relations of colonialism from colonizer/colonized to the internal relations of the post-colony.[40] These post-colonial gay discourses displace Europe as the object of post-apartheid critique and refocus on decentred power relations around sexuality in post-colonial South Africa. This distinctly post-colonial tension between the multiple forms of domination and subalterity left in the aftermath of colonialism confounds anti-colonial binaries.[41] Such internalization 'foregrounds the proliferation rather than disappearance of colonial relations.'[42]

These lesbian and gay rights activists construe the 'colonial' as being less about power and a particular geography, history or subjectivity, than a particular epistemology: the regimentation of the individual by a particular regime of power/knowledge – a regime which is as available to the 'post-colonial' nation as it was to colonial forces. They confront the post-colonial nation with the remainder of the very principles through which it sought liberation. They envision a post-colonial remedy through reconfiguring the boundaries of the colonized individual and the rights-bearing citizen and, as one Pride Parade placard read, claiming a 'Right to Love'.[43]

ANCESTRAL LOVE AND COLONIAL FANTASIES

Recently the Coalition and several lesbian and gay activist/intellectuals have expanded their assertion of apartheid discrimination to encompass an earlier and broader colonial oppression. They disassociate homosexuality from colonialism by specifying an explicit colonial gay oppression and aligning gay and lesbian South Africans with those subjected to colonial power. A new anti-colonial discourse has emerged in the publicity of one of the first cases concerning sexual orientation heard under the new Constitution. South Africa's Constitution preserved the validity of most apartheid-era laws, leaving them subject to legislative reform and judicial review. A High Court petition filed in August 1997 by the Coalition and the Human Rights Commission requested the invalidation of common law and statutory criminalization of male–male sexual conduct. The case itself has become representative of historical gay oppression.

A Coalition rally a couple of weeks before the court hearing began with two Coalition representatives, Mazibuko Jara and Phumzile Mtetwa, anticipating the emergence of lesbian/gay equality and the end of 'more than 300 years of criminalisation of same-sex conduct by various governments from the era of colonisation to apartheid up until now.' The Coalition elaborated on this idea in its 8 May, 1998 press release following the favourable decision in the case:

In the opinion of the Coalition, the judgment stands as a sombre indictment of our intolerant colonial past. During the major part of the 350 years during which these common law offences were part of our law in South Africa, they carried the ultimate penalty of death. Our history records the litany of South Africans who have been drowned in vats in prisons, burned at stakes, hanged on gallows, tortured and banished as punishment for expressing *a sexuality that differed from the heterosexual norm*. The silent suffering of those who have been executed must stand as a constant reminder of the vagaries of intolerance and blind prejudice that use religion as a justification.[44]

More particularly, several gay activist/intellectuals have appropriated a 1735 sodomy conviction and execution as representative of this history. This was portrayed, for example, by Clive van den Berg in an installation entitled 'Men Loving' at the Faultlines art exhibit at the Cape Town Castle in July 1996. The text accompanying his multimedia piece read: 'In 1735 two men were taken into the bay off Cape Town. When the ship was near Robben Island, they were made to "walk the plank" while chained together. They had loved each other. On Friday, May 8, 1996 we adopted a Constitution which forbids discrimination on the basis of sexual preference. Perhaps now loving will be easier.'[45]

The constitutive power of these performative discoveries of a homosexual ancestor oppressed by colonial regimes was confirmed in a *Sunday Independent* article about the sodomy decision which described 'the ignominious end of more than 300 years of legal *discrimination against gay people*.'[46] Even if current lesbian/gay politics of post-coloniality may be more about the impending twenty-first century than the seventeenth, the *Independent* article seizes on the apparent projection of at least some form of 'gay personnage', if not identity, back 300 years into colonial history. This reflects a characteristically postcolonial proliferation of previously subjugated histories.

This move also consolidates sexual identity over time. While exposing the colonial regime of sex as anchored in heteronormativity, this technique also re-affirms the production of the 'homosexual'. Goldberg suggests that an anachronistic ascription of colonial gay identity might be justified by a subsequent politics that makes claims about homosexuality in the colonial order.[47] Despite its possible reifications, this indicates an interruption of Foucauldian genealogies of the European 'centre' by the colonial 'periphery', as suggested by Stoler and others.[48] Current sexual identity politics complicate what Sedgwick argues are supercessionist[49] histories of sexuality – they add new realms of social relations ('race', for example) to the reformulation of sex into sexuality and imply a more dialectical relationship between the discourse of repression and the civilizing mission.[50] Thus, the conversation re-places colonial as well as post-colonial histories from Europe to 'the periphery'.[51]

As well, this emergent post-colonial discourse exploits the now 'common-place'[52] understanding of law as central in the colonizing project. It virtually equates colonial legal prohibitions on same-sex sexual conduct with colonization of the 'homosexual', positing colonial laws as disciplining an eighteenth, indeed, a seventeenth century 'homosexual' body. To be sure, this expands historically the understanding of 'sodomy' prohibitions as symbolic if not in part consti-tutive of gay (and sometimes lesbian) oppression and even subjectivity. In South Africa, both Edwin Cameron's appropriation of Mohr's terminology 'unappre-hended felons'[53] and the text on Stevan Cohen's 1998 Pride Parade poster, 'I'm a Crime',[54] are emblematic of this. Note also that discrimination as such, the concept through which 'sexual orientation' is conceived today, is also projected historically. This is made feasible by the commensurability of identities and forms of discrimination suggested in the equality clause in the implied social and historical parallelism among the enumerated grounds.

As Carusi explains, for anti-colonial cultural discourses of origination like the import thesis, this post-colonial rhetoric assumes the colonial specification of homosexual identity.[55] This identity then serves as the basis for political resis-tance and legal mobilization, which are also aimed at undermining that identity in particular ways. Thus constructed, 'lesbian and gay' South Africans too are subject to the contradictions of colonial identity of the simultaneously 'modern-ist citizen' and 'ethnic subject'.[56] Thus, the pre-modernity of the colonial past is to be remedied with 'modernist' identities – whose historical and social con-stancy bear an uncomfortable resemblance to those of colonial ethnic subjec-tivities. The articulation of a post-colonial identity relies on the construction of a transhistorical, naturalized subject – reflected in the contradictions of identity politics in a regime of individual rights.

LEGAL LOVE AND RATIONAL FANTASIES

In their Heads of Argument in the High Court petition, the Coalition used the colonial history of the laws at issue to discredit them. They argued that the 'peculiar consequence of South African colonial history unnaturally extended the life span of the challenged laws'[57] in that the 1806 British occupation of the Cape Colony 'froze' the common law and precluded adoption of the Napo-leonic Codes which would decriminalize same-sex sexual conduct in the States of Holland in 1811. Petitioners also noted Britain's decriminalization in 1967, long after South Africa's independence therefrom. They said, 'in fact, in the period leading up to the passage of the Sexual Offences Act in England there was an upsurge in official discrimination against gay and lesbian people in South Africa which culminated in the passage of the Immorality Amendment Act, 57 of 1969.'[58] This aligns apartheid with British colonialism and, by effectively removing South Africa from world historical time, emphasizes the insularity of apartheid's particular form of colonialism. The implication that decriminalization under the Napoleonic Codes would have constituted a form of decolonization disrupts the colonial character of later forms of domination experienced by lesbian and gay South Africans, under apartheid for example.

Also in their Heads, Petitioners instructively directed Judge Heher to Britain's Hart–Devlin debates.[59] These debates between H.L.A. Hart and Lord Devlin concerned the proper role of morality in legislation, particularly concerning same-sex sexual conduct. They took place in the context of the Parliamentary debates on the Wolfenden Committee Report prior to Britain's 1967 decriminalization of private same-sex sexual conduct. Published in 1957, the Report is now famous for its recommendation that private, same-sex sexual conduct be decriminalized. In the debates, Lord Devlin made a majoritarian argument favouring the legislation of moral precepts while Hart favoured the protection of a private sphere of conduct.

During the hearing Heher was particularly interested in the relevance of these debates and engaged Petitioner's Advocate Gilbert Marcus in extended discussion about them – basically asking Marcus straight out why Devlin was wrong. Marcus replied that Devlin is not convincing in a constitutional state, referencing South Africa's recent rejection of parliamentary supremacy.

Recall that Heher was to rule on the constitutionality of Roman-Dutch common law and statutory criminalizations of male–male sexual conduct. The most notorious of those statutes were enacted in 1969 as amendments to the Sexual Offences Act to supplement the common law and colonial British statutes enacted in the provinces. However, they were introduced in March 1967 as the political result of the largest, most highly publicized raid on a gay party in one of Johannesburg's northern suburbs.

When Prime Minister Verwoerd's Minister of Justice, P.C. Pelser, introduced these laws in the South African Parliament, Member of Parliament S.J.M. Steyn observed that 'we have found in some of the countries with whom we have been traditionally associated legislation passed recently to exclude private acts voluntarily committed between individuals in strict privacy from the purview of the criminal law. We in South Africa are more conservative than that.'[60] Yet Steyn, wanting to heed changing standards, cautioned, 'we want a moral society; we want the character and fibre of our South African society to be protected against things which are evil and destructive of our character, but at the same time we want to protect the rights of individuals.'[61]

In 1969, following a commission investigation and report on the proposed amendments, a modified version was again before Parliament. At this time, the Minister of Justice assured the Parliament that they did not stand alone in refusing to make 'concessions on the matter'. He noted The Netherlands' refusal to lower the age of consent for same-sex sex and New Zealand's refusal to legalize private, consensual same-sex sex.[62]

In focusing on the Hart–Devlin debates, Heher and the Coalition recovered the reforms of one of those countries with whom South Africa was previously associated. These were reforms rejected at the contemporaneous adoption of some of the laws now under review. Making specific reference to Hart–Devlin in his decision,[63] in a post-apartheid and variously post-colonial South Africa, Heher invoked the debates that were integral to Britain's reforms in order to undo South Africa's stand of 30 years ago. And that stand itself distinguished South Africa from its previous colonial 'associations' during a period when colonialism was contested in different ways. Some propose that underlying the 1960s crackdown itself was an Afrikaner obsession charged with colonial sensitivities that, upon the arrival of young rural Afrikaner boys in the cities, they were preyed upon by gay British men.[64]

Thus, the case rather (ironically?) restores the 'British connection'[65] to remedy anti-colonial measures on the part of the apartheid state which (re)produced colonial epistemologies – a restoration susceptible to exploitation by national movements ascribing to the import theory. Heher's consideration is not a simple precedential reference to British decriminalization. Indeed, both the petition and his decision appeal to the reasoning underlying Hart-Devlin – and not only with regard to parliamentary supremacy. As Wolfenden, quoted by the Petitioners, warned against equating crime with sin, Heher concludes that the 'censure' of the sodomy provisions 'arose mainly from moral objections rooted in religious interpretation' and were intended to prevent subversion of 'the State religion'.[66] In post-apartheid South Africa, the rationality of a secular law and state are to protect the rights of the individual subject in the face of 'religious intolerance, ignorance, superstition, bigotry, and fear.'[67] And applicants called on the court to protect 'warm and stable' (i.e. 'loving') relationships to which counsel referred in argument.[68] This employs the components of the modern culture of legality that ostensibly animated the colonial project – such as rationality, reason and the rights-bearing individual – in the service of reforming colonial and apartheid perversions of them. And these notions of legality are now to be retrieved from the 'metropole' under post-colonial conditions of globalization.

MODERN LOVE AND INDIGENOUS FANTASIES

The rhetoric of the Coalition and certain activists, intellectuals and journalists makes claims, in various forms, to the presence of homosexuality in African history and culture. The degree to which these are strategic co-optations of the black community is a topic of debate within black lesbian and gay settings. The influential leaders in the Coalition and other activist organizations in some ways reflect the 'establishment' of gay rights politics.[69] Some accommodate historically 'apolitical'[70] organizations, and the earnestness of their incorporation of black organizations has been questioned by some.[71] Indeed, the politics of representation within and between lesbian and gay communities in South Africa and between the deployment of post-coloniality by the Coalition and by black lesbians and gays may be read as reflecting the idea of 'post-colonial rhetoric as emblematic'[72] of a form of neo-imperialism. Therefore, 'negotiating locations, identities, positionalities in relation to ... neo-colonialism'[73] is necessary if deployments of colonialism and post-coloniality by 'local elites'[74] are not to lead to uncritical re-inscriptions of colonial modalities and a 'consecration of hegemony'.[75]

I am here concerned with everyday negotiations of Africanness, post-colonialism, and sexuality by African lesbians and gay men themselves.[76] Beyond the rhetoric of activists, intellectuals and lawyers, the self-fashioning of the post-colonial gay/lesbian African subject through practice – the enactment of the post-colonial self – lies at a convergence of the post-colonial as an epistemological and historical transformation.

African lesbian and gay South Africans say that homosexuality, like sexuality more broadly,[77] is rarely discussed in African communities. When it is discussed, African lesbian and gay people may be confronted with a denial that homosexuality exists in African communities.[78] Some are accused of being 'influenced by whites',[79] being 'bewitched by white evil spirits'[80] or being collaborators with white or Western culture.[81]

'The idea that homosexuality is alien to "traditional culture" is invariably dismissed as a myth' by African lesbian and gay people.[82] For gay and lesbian Africans, colonial institutions like industrialization, urbanization, mining and the attendant demands of labour markets radically restructured 'the family' and have hidden the full history of sexuality in African history.[83] And moreover, preserved history is that of 'colonial, white power structures'.[84] 'Secrecy and silence are identified as effective ways of keeping homosexuality out of the public domain.... "If you ask the old people, homosexuality has been there. It's just that it was the community's secret." '[85] Thus, epistemological regimes in society and history are portrayed as hiding a history of homosexuality and contributing to the myth of its non-existence in African 'culture'.

Black lesbian and gay South Africans insist that same-sex sexual conduct has always existed.[86] 'There have always been gay people in African society. They have not always been accepted, but they have been there.'[87] Many cite anthropological[88] and 'oral history' to show 'the existence of homosexuality before colonialism'.[89] Indeed, assurance that the import thesis is not hegemonic is the common assertion that 'the grandparents' stories' attest to the existence of same-sex sex.[90] Donham says that South African black gay identity projects itself 'backward in history'.[91] For black gays, 'gay people have always been present in South African black cultures' but in the 'great-grandmother's time, African traditional cultures dealt with such things differently: "in order to keep outside people from knowing, they organized someone who was gay to go out with you, and they arranged [a marriage of convenience] with another family.... That is the secret that used to be kept in the black community." '[92]

A number of African gays and lesbians presume that informal same-sex sex occurred in the past 'while men were away on "hunting trips"' or among 'co-wives of polygamous marriages'.[93] One report states that relationships between women in rural areas were prevalent while men were away at work in the mines.[94] Another popular assertion is that ritual practices of homosociality and sexuality reflected in institutions like the 'Lovedu Rain Queen'[95] and the practices of those *sangomas*[96] 'who do not sleep with men'[97] are historical predecessors to contemporary homosexuality. This desire to find a pre-colonial gay self may be read as specifying a historical identity by conflating conduct and identity. The general tone of these conversations contends that the conduct in the past indicated the presence of same-sex sexual desire: homosexual desire has 'always existed'.

The class critique central to the national struggle against 'internal colonialism' also figures in South Africa's politics of sexuality. An element underlying many 'import' assertions is a critique of homosexuality as the result of the political economy of apartheid. Highly racialized capitalist structures and excess are read as producing homosexuality. In a 1987 interview, Ruth Mompati stated 'the gays have no problems, they have nice houses and plenty to eat. I don't see them suffering. No one is persecuting them.'[98] In his now infamous statement Bennie Alexander said 'Homosexuality ... is part of the spinoff of the capitalist system'.[99] African lesbians and gays report that, along with accusations of 'white influence', they are also accused of 'being middle class'.[100] An element of this idea points to the 'distortion' of the African family by the system of migrant labour and 'unnatural' sexual practices as emerging from the 'unnatural' living conditions in mine and hostel compounds.[101]

African lesbians and gays now reclaim the male–male sex of mine compounds as a site for the emergence and expression of gay desire. In *After Nines*, a play which chronicles black lesbian and gay history in South Africa, three 'gay ancestors' in the form of spirits, educate a young lesbian ('Lebo') in post-apartheid South Africa about 'her history'. One gay ancestor, a 'natural *skesana*[102] from childhood', recounts leaving his rural home where he was rejected as *stabane*[103] to go to the mines. The compounds, he said, where older miners chose wives at parties and married them in ceremonies, were the place to meet gays in the 1950s. The same ancestor appears to Lebo's grandmother and chastises her for denying knowledge of such practices because her husband had worked in the mines.

This poses a direct challenge to the idea that the mines produced same-sex behaviour – instead they are depicted as a space for the freer expression of a legitimate, pre-existing, presumably indigenous same-sex desire. It also suggests that rather than produce homosexuality, capitalism provided a context in which sexual desire could be more fully expressed.[104] Moreover, rather than African ancestors being embarrassed by homosexuality, as suggested by Meshoe, Lebo says, 'it's not everyday you meet your gay ancestors'.

In a 1991 flyer the primarily black Gay and Lesbian Organization of the Witwatersrand (GLOW) asked: 'where do we, the lesbian and gay community, fit in [to the liberation struggle]? Under present law homosexuality is a criminal act - yet so many of the South African white lesbian and gay community do not feel their – yes – oppression because of white privilege.'[105] Again, this identifies apartheid law as central to gay oppression and frees oppression from any necessary tie to a particular race or class. While this tends to universalize oppression, the historical particularity of South African oppression is reflected in GLOW's insistence that there was to be no post-colonial queer existence without a broader revolution. This was integral to GLOW's critique of the failures of early gay rights movements due to their refusal to associate with the anti-apartheid struggle.[106] And like the Coalition, Simon Nkoli aligned Mugabe's comments with apartheid.[107]

The debate about the cultural authenticity of homosexuality often devolves into an etymological debate around the assertion that there exist no linguistically 'pure' words in African languages to describe 'homosexual'. Import theorists assert, as Epprecht discusses in Zimbabwe, that words making homosexuality explicit were incorporated into African languages from European languages in the late nineteenth century.[108] For example, from the *Future Imperfect* show mentioned earlier, the debate moved significantly into the pages of the *Sowetan* newspaper, where a viewer ridiculed an African representative of the Coalition as displaying 'emancipated ignorance' when she suggested a pre-colonial provenance for the term *sis-bhuti*, a word the viewer argues is a Zulu adaptation of English and Dutch origins.[109] As Epprecht describes in Zimbabwe, lesbian and gay South Africans now appropriate words like *stabane* to show the historical existence of same-sex practices in pre-colonial African cultures. At the Hope and Unity Metropolitan Community Church (HUMCC), a 'gay church' in Hillbrow, Johannesburg, 'gay or lesbian identity [is] proclaimed by naming one self ... "*injonga*"[110].... *Injonga* is an African word that serves to undermine the notion that homosexuality is a Western import, by claiming a specifically African homosexual identity.'[111] Polly Motene says that 'in Tswana, gays are called *kgwete*, which means bold, beautiful, and unique. But in the old days the Twanas [sic] would put men in a kraal to be trampled to death by the cattle if they were found having sex together.'[112]

Black lesbians and gay men also say that it was only after colonialism named 'homosexuality' that the myths about African tradition emerged, and correspondingly that many families tolerate their lesbian and gay children until these children use the words 'gay' or 'lesbian' to describe themselves. Furthermore, it is only by accepting the words 'gay and lesbian', the 'colonial' words themselves, that many African lesbian and gay people report that they can 'find freedom' – but they say that this does not mean that one adopts the colonial culture associated with them.[113]

In contrast to the analogical claim to a colonial ancestor, African lesbians and gays disrupt the (anti)colonial binary by seeking to establish that lesbian and gay people were and are the specified subjects of colonial regimes. While the 'import' discourse produces a pre-colonial heterosexual tradition through a timeless African culture, insistence on the falsity of the claim implies its own timeless South African – this one a naturalized 'homosexual'. But rather than claim a 'false continuity with the past'[114] to recover a sexuality completely uncontaminated by colonization, the self-construction of the post-colonial queer both resists the idea of the West as 'donor' and refuses any contradiction in 'tradition' marked by colonialism. Black lesbian and gay South Africans construct 'fragmented sets of narrated memories and experiences', not 'a static, fetishized phase to be literally reproduced'.[115]

By asserting 'characteristically modern ... identitary forms'[116] black lesbians and gay men seek space to 'express [their] love for each other without anyone raising an eyebrow'.[117] Simultaneously, they don traditional drag at the Pride Parade, exchange *lobola*[118] in connection with marriage ceremonies, and 'chant traditional songs' while handing out gay rights organizations' newsletters in the townships.[119] They refuse a necessary contradiction between 'modernity' and 'tradition' and testify that colonialism and globalization make impossible a return to an original and 'ethnically closed' history.[120]

CONCLUSION

Throughout the post-colonial rhetorics and practices of gay and lesbian South Africans are multiple registers of post-coloniality – and tensions between them. Their discourses construe the 'post-colonial' as 'texts ... practices ... psychological conditions ... concrete historical processes [and perhaps] the interaction of all of these.'[121] Post-colonial gay perspectives reflect colonialism as a 'system of knowledge', 'a system of rule', 'a definitional paradigm' and 'a particular historical moment'[122] – as well as the more specific notion of apartheid as both 'a specific historical logic [and] a mode of identity formation'.[123] Through a particular combination of the historical and the epistemological in the political present, lesbian and gay South Africans expand the subjectivities within colonialism's sight and negotiate the times and places, modes and means of coloniality.

A post-colonial gay present and future, ones that provide both a 'chronological marker' and 'liberating emancipation',[124] require pre-colonial gay origins. The gay perspectives, then, construct gay colonial and indigenous pasts whereby they expand on the binaristic mapping of power relations[125] of anti-colonial import theorists and seek to 'relegate anti-colonial [struggles] to the past'.[126] Lesbians and gay men in South Africa respond to the post-colonial imperative by indigenizing both their identities and the principles on which they claim inclusion in the post-apartheid national imaginary. Their discourses resonate with the ways in which Derrida describes Nelson Mandela's trial testimony[127] – they reconstruct colonialism's identities and appeal to the ideologies that inspired imperialism to remedy their 'dislocated'[128] implementation in South Africa. Simultaneously, they interiorize these identities and ideologies within South African 'culture' and pre-colonial history. These discourses also suggest, as does Derrida, that colonialism's interrelated betrayals of law and identity preclude assigning any singly located source to either.

Thus, according to Carusi, emerges a post-colonial dilemma: while the identities of colonialism's others are constructed through imperialistic subjectivities, those identities form the basis for political action aimed at their own reconstruction.[129] In part the dilemma stems from the stability inherent in the Western notions of consciousness and humanism on which the post-colonial perspective relies for transformative action. It also emerges from the circumstance that the Western notion of heterogeneity underpinning colonialism forms the basis for both ethno-nationalist and subaltern consciousness and identity.[130] Therefore, as Hall argues, the Enlightenment epistemology based in the marking of difference within a universal discursive sphere returns 'in its decentered position'.[131]

This post-colonial 're-enlightenment' produces a tension between the particularity and the universality of colonialism – and its 'successor'. In the South African case, as Norval argues, the universal language of resistance discourses revealed the particularity lurking behind the purported universality of apartheid.[132] Now through the epistemologies of colonialism and apartheid the debate about homosexuality contests the particular times, places and subjectivities through which they were exercised.

The discourses of lesbian and gay South Africans occupy the slippage and contradiction within and between the multiple registers of post-coloniality through which they extend themselves historically and 'culturally'. Similar to During's reading of Derrida's 'Mandela', lesbian and gay South Africans turn to the universals of liberal rights discourses to 'unsettle boundaries and given identities', to direct universalisms 'towards limits and identities that they can not take account of'.[133]

Post-colonial gay perspectives appeal to another form of universality, though – that of romantic 'love'. Lesbian and gay South Africans subsume sexuality and desire within an appeal to a transhistorical, universal 'love' to project an historical and African gay presence – and to gain recognition from a still heterosexualized post-colonial order.[134] To be sure, they assert a right to an authentic love in a post-colonial nation, an historic love for which colonial subjects suffered, a love authorized under a rationalized legal scheme, and seek to express an individuated and identitarian love which is nonetheless traditional. But is this idea as susceptible to the problem of colonial origin as 'democracy', for example? Does the 'romantic ideal of the love marriage' that emerged as the only properly disciplined and managed form of sexuality in European Victorian and capitalist history[135] provide a blueprint for a post-colonial appeal to romantic love? Further politics around sexuality in South Africa will be important to understand new aspects of post-colonialism and sexuality, for example, the capacity of affect within colonial 'deployments of sexuality', extensions of the Christian ideal of love in post-colonial and same-sex contexts,[136] and attendant legal entailments and transformations.

2

CONSTITUTING THE GLOBAL GAY

ISSUES OF INDIVIDUAL SUBJECTIVITY AND SEXUALITY IN SOUTHERN AFRICA

OLIVER PHILLIPS

INTRODUCTION: THE GLOBALIZATION OF LESBIAN AND GAY IDENTITIES

In the 1990s, the sexual activities of people living throughout the southern African region have alternately assumed and been allocated increasing significance as social markers. Botswana, Namibia, Swaziland, South Africa, Zambia and Zimbabwe have all witnessed unprecedented public discussion of the proclaimed rights or declaimed immorality of sexual activities between people of the same sex.[1] Movements calling explicitly for 'lesbian and gay rights' have mushroomed in each of these states, both as a result of governmental derogations of such rights, and as a result of individual affirmations of social identities which deliver these rights.

This proliferation appears to parallel social dynamics elsewhere in the world as organizations calling themselves 'gay' and 'lesbian' can now be found across all continents and in states as different from each other as Japan,[2] Bolivia[3] and Russia.[4] Accounts of the establishment of these organizations suggest a global process of transformation whereby a variety of non-procreative same-sex behaviours become homogenized under the rubric 'gay' or 'lesbian'. These accounts also make clear that, in each case, these 'new' identities are merged into local histories and contexts, so that the end-product has signifiers of local significance while simultaneously providing a strategy for either laying claim to international human rights agreements, or enabling more effective AIDS/HIV preventative work, or simply buying into an expanding market of Western signifiers of 'modern' and bourgeois status, or serving all of these purposes. What is clear is that these identities are not simply imposed through an imperialistic cultural discourse or economic dominance, but they are actively assumed and proclaimed from below, by those marginalized in these hegemonic formations:

> Following the development of capitalism, gay and lesbian identity is dependent on certain material conditions. So accusations that gay and lesbian identity is a sign of cultural imperialism will inevitably contain a grain of truth. Nevertheless, the cultural imperialism model needs to be nuanced by acknowledging that ideas, strategies, and identities are transformed when they are used from below. It may only be the privileged, travelling, cosmopolitan intellectual who recognises these identities as western. And vulnerable groups can mobilise in their own interests the perceived prestige of things western. (Hoad, 1998: 35–6)

Understanding the importance of agency then becomes central in understanding how it is that a boy of 16 years old, working and living on Harare's streets, recognizes only his existential condition, and his relationships of dependence and desire as determining his identity as 'gay' or 'straight'. He assumes such labels and categories interchangeably according to the capital (social and economic) that they offer him in different situations, thereby attesting to the fluid and inherently social construction of these identities for him, rather than to any fixed categorical predisposition (Thomas *Interview*, 1992). In contrast, the educated and privileged President Mugabe sees these definitions as fixed categories between which one cannot slide and as definitive signifiers of cultural imperialism. Indeed, it is this position of privilege which allows Mugabe to define the homosexual as specifically marginal and particularly deviant to Zimbabwean culture, as he implicitly defines heterosexuality as the universal, thereby affirming both the hegemonic ascendancy of heterosexism, as well as his own allegiance to it. But his assertion of a universalism that is specifically heterosexual is predicated on the *a priori* concept of a binary division of hetero/homosexuality. This in itself relies on the psychoanalytic notion of 'a binary sexuality' that is fixed within individuals, and is a distinctly Western European psychoanalytic polarisation of erotic desire as homo/hetero:

> Homosexuality is not a conceptual category everywhere... When used to characterise individuals, it implies that erotic attraction originates in a relatively stable, more or less, exclusive attribute of the individual. Usually, it connotes an exclusive orientation: the homosexual is not also heterosexual; the heterosexual is not also homosexual. Most non-western societies make few of these assumptions. Distinctions of age, gender, and social status loom larger. The sexes are not necessarily conceived symmetrically (Greenberg, 1988: 4).[5]

It is arguable that it is this categorical fixity of definition, rooted in the individual, that has been imported into Zimbabwe, rather than any new activities, and that this has taken place through a multiplicity of variously competing and connecting forces. Mugabe's assumption of (or dare one contend, his colonization by) this binary notion, leads him to deprive the young urban sex-worker of the agency that his fluid sense of self-definition permits. Indeed, while Mugabe employs the category of homosexual as a criterion for exclusion from the polity, that same identity has served as a means of inclusion for many in South African townships (Stychin, 1998: 76). As Neville Hoad points out, 'Claims of authenticity and/or foreignness take place in an extremely vexed representational field' (Hoad, 1998: 36).

This chapter aims to focus on some of the conceptual patterns in law which have facilitated this increasingly fixed conception of sexuality as source of both repression and liberation. For colonial law brought with it a discourse of morality[6] which was very significant in the construction of individual subjects (in possession of a 'sexuality'). Contemporary definitions of criminal liability, social responsibility and human rights are all actively engaged in the promotion of these notions of individual subjectivity. These all develop in a tense relationship to conceptions of power and agency where individual desires and subjectivities are subordinate to lineage and the economics of the family. In this chapter, I want to focus on the development of individualized (as opposed to more 'communal') subjectivities, and trace their connection to the increasing significance of sexuality in the formation of identity in southern Africa.

LAW, CIVILIZATION AND DISCOURSES OF MORALITY

Zimbabwean common law is that which existed at the Cape in 1891 when the British South Africa Company (BSAC) settlers first arrived in Zimbabwe having travelled from the Cape.[7] The Cape had previously been governed by the Dutch and so the common law of the Cape (and subsequently of Zimbabwe) was Roman-Dutch law. The BSAC settled Rhodesia under a charter granted by Queen Victoria which held that in cases concerning 'natives', customary law would apply so long as the particular custom was not deemed to be 'repugnant to natural justice or morality'.[8] It is immediately apparent not only that a whole discourse of 'morality' and law is being introduced, but that the morality of the late Victorian period was equated with notions of 'natural justice'. Unsurprisingly, therefore, sexual relations tended to fall under common law rather than customary law, and various customary practices deemed to be immoral or unnatural were gradually eased into extinction or marginality by the settler administration.

But the settler administration was establishing, a 'natural justice or morality' which had already been promoted as having divine sanction. For prior to the settlers' arrival, the London Missionary Society had blazed the trail for Christianity in the region.[9] It is clear that the work of missionaries had a significant impact on the sexual practices of the people living in the region, and that many

Shona/Ndebele/Tonga ceremonies of circumcision and rituals of initiation were considerably sanitized and in some cases done away with.[10] In many cases, it is not clear what the offensive activities were, but simply that they were 'lascivious', 'immoral' or 'unmentionable vices'.

What is clear, though, is that while no new sexual activities were brought to Southern Rhodesia by the settlers, new offences certainly were. For while the activities would not be new, the definitions of these activities would have been. The whole conception of how those acts that we now understand to be sexual fitted with gender and broader social relations was very different, and remains mediated by the political economy of gender and reproductive relations. The very idea of what acts constitute sex, and what are the implications of sex, are ideas which are culturally construed and contingent.[11] This is most clearly illustrated by Kendall's remarks about the confluences and differences between the conventional existence of erotic relationships between women, and lesbian identities:

> What the situation in Lesotho suggests is that women can and do develop strong affectional and erotic ties with other women in a culture where there is no concept or social construction equivalent to 'lesbian', nor is there a concept of erotic exchanges among women as being 'sexual' at all. And yet, partly because of the 'no concept' issue and in part because women have difficulty supporting themselves without men in Lesotho, there has been no lesbian lifestyle option available to Basotho women. Lesbian or lesbian-like behaviour has been commonplace, conventional; but it has not been viewed as 'sexual', nor as an alternative to heterosexual marriage, which is both a sexual and an economic part of the culture. (Kendall, 1998: 239)

Kendall describes how 'sex' is assumed to require a *koai* (penis), so that erotic activities between two women are not regarded as 'sex' (Kendall, 1998: 233). This would appear to combine with the fact that the establishment of these relationships between women do not require an individual's autonomy from family, marriage and kinship. The relationship is seen as quite distinct from (but supplementary to) heterosexual marriage and so it does not disturb the economic and reproductive implications of heterosexual marriage. This means that the fixed categories which are so much a part of Western European conceptions of sexuality do not reside within individuals, nor even within the relationships between individuals. The only fixity would appear to be the requirement of a *koai* for something to be recognized as 'sex' – and it is this particular fixity which allows the fluidity of all other definitions. It is interesting to speculate whether this requirement is the distancing of potentially procreative sex from non-procreative erotic relations – Kendall does not mention the existence or non-existence of such erotic relations between men, but their existence might illustrate the point further.

This focus on procreative possibilities would certainly appear to have been of considerable significance in Zimbabwe, before the introduction of a colonial discourse of morality; for prior to the arrival of missionaries and settlers:

Illicit sexual acts were only illicit in so far as the partners disrupted kinship relationships. . . . The limits of sexual behaviour were defined by their likely impact on the family, rather than by fixed concepts of 'moral' and 'immoral' behaviour. (Jeater, 1993: 30–31]

In this way, sexual relations were not simply the business of the individuals directly involved, but were conceptualized, negotiated and celebrated by whole lineage groups; they had an effect on the social identity of the entire lineage. They were not conceived as erotic acts separate from kin, but were physically and figuratively constitutive of kinship relations. Whereas, the introduction of a notion of abstract 'moral' judgment separated eroticism further from questions of reproductive consequence, into an economy of desire which gave a social value to each confessed act, and each exhorted repression, so that the sum of these values could be represented in the individual. For this 'discourse of morality' required the labelling and definition of specific acts of what were declared to be 'perversions' residing within the self, rather than a situation where sexual acts were regulated only when they impacted on the broader social context of the reproductive relationships between people.

The arrival of missionaries and settlers brought with it the Judeo-Christian construction of sexual desire as an object of discipline by, and for the sake of, one's self, rather than one's lineage, and introduced the admonishment of personal perversions as predilections to be hidden in private, and shamed in public – in other words, the notion of 'sin'. Crudely put, what had been important prior to Christianity's arrival was who was doing it, and what the reproductive consequences (both social and biological) of their actions were, rather than a prohibitive declaration that inquired into the morality of specific acts. What was important in pre-colonial times was consequential physical activity, rather than a projected cognitive desire to be measured as morality or perversion. This new conception of 'sexuality' which penetrated Shona society was one which was embedded and delivered in a discourse of morality:

Sexuality was not primarily constructed in terms of lineage identity and obligation, and sexual matters were judged on the basis of a set of principles whose concerns were a long way from those of marriage alliance which dominated the African society. Sex occupied the realm of the moral, and was linked to concepts of sin, and of absolute right and wrong. Not only did these occupiers have new ideas about what constituted a sexual offence; they also had different views about whose business it was that such an offence might have been committed. Two concepts in particular, those of 'morality' and 'civilisation', dominated white discussions of African sexual behaviour. (Jeater, 1993: 35)

In the nineteenth century, the concepts of 'morality' and 'civilization' provided a framework for the creation and regulation of a 'sexuality' which went beyond the functional structuring of reproductive relationships, by engaging with a consciousness of the self, centred around self-discipline.[12] With the inculcation of a notion of divine sanction, the consequences of sexual acts became abstracted beyond the regulation of illicit partnerships between lineages, as they came to be loaded with a variety of differing values – of power and perversion – signifying the truth of an individual.

Conjuring fantasy and denial, this location of a metaphysical sex residing within the self was accompanied by the more specific production of individual stereotypes of morality invoking the dangers of disease and the fruits of purity.[13] Out of this combination arose the capacity to alternatively create or censure individual identities through sex, and more specifically through the binary division of homo/heterosexuality. This is a capacity which has come to be deeply embedded in the discourse around sex in contemporary Zimbabwe. To this degree, Jeater would appear to be correct in allocating to the colonial occupiers the role of 'the serpent in the Garden of Eden: they brought the concept of "sin", of individual sexual shame, into societies which had not used the idea before' (Jeater, 1993: 266).

This discourse of morality was central to the civilizing mission of the settlers as it relied on the twin qualities out of which Victorian concepts of a 'civilized' and 'ordered' society were fashioned – repression and discipline. Resting on the Cartesian concept of the mind's rational capacity to cultivate order out of the untamed savage nature of the instinct-driven body, Victorian ideals of 'civilization' pictured the primitive 'nature' of man as embodied in the supposed atavism of 'the native'. They therefore glorified the exquisite pain of denial as constitutive of civilization, and introduced a whole new dimension of sexual morality as a measure of social worth. Add to this the proselytizing of the Christian notion of sin and the introduction of a capitalist economy, and it suggests the development of a consciousness based around the commodification of sex and the erotic regulation of individual desire rather than the prioritizing of procreation and the making of social alliances (see also Phillips, 1997a: 425).

These ideals of order and discipline were not only reflective of metropolitan concerns, but became imprinted more definitively on the lives of the colonized as the colonial (and then neo-colonial) state relied on pathologies and demarcations within both the social body and the individual body to establish itself with increasing efficiency. For the arrival of Christian 'civilization' and colonial authority brought with it not just the notion of individual identity, but also the accompanying techniques and signifiers which produce both stereotypes and the possibility of individualism within the context of the bureaucratic nation-state. Indeed, just as individual identities ironically rely on stereotypes to assert their individualism, so surveillance of individuals is necessary to produce the normative stereotypes required for the patrolling of social margins:

> the distinction between normality and abnormality, between bourgeois respectability and sexual deviance, and between moral degeneracy and eugenic cleansing were the elements of a discourse that made unconventional sex a national threat and thus put a premium on managed sexuality

for the health of a state. Foucault writes, 'Sex was a means of access both to the life of the body and the life of the species. It was employed as a standard for the disciplines and as a basis of regulation.' (HS, 146) Through this new biopolitic 'management of life', sex not only stamped individuality; it emerged as 'the theme of political operations' and as an 'index of a society's strength, revealing of both its political energy and biological vigor' (HS, 146). (Stoler, 1995: 34-5)

In this way, the imposition of an 'anatamo-politics' of the individual body (health and hygiene, work, efficiency, morality, production[14]), as well as a demographic regulation of the social body (land apportionment, pass laws, curfews, compounds, etc.), is significant in that they supply the 'normalizing judgment' which produces self-disciplined 'obedient subjects' (Foucault, 1978: 139–41). This 'obedient subject' is constituted by 'habits, rules, orders, an authority that is exercised continually around him and upon him and which he must allow to function automatically in him' (Foucault, 1979a: 128).

The construction of African customary law and the imposition of Roman-Dutch common law codified the legal constitution of African men,[15] but the real constitution of African people as colonial subjects could only take place through a process which would impact upon both their individual lives and their collective lives. In this way, with a migrant labour system regulated strictly in terms of the sexual division of labour, individual bodies became differently valued, but labour became generally commodified. The creation of a moral discourse was very significant in constituting these individual subjects. With its Christian and medico-scientific elements, it distinguished the sins of erotic sex from the biology of reproduction, thereby furthering the construction of a new distinctive concept of an individual subject in possession of a 'sexuality'. Sex began to be reconceptualized as the location of individual truths, so that ignorance of a 'sexual morality' was seen as one of the primary indicators of the 'savage' status of 'heathen' natives. The inculcation of a moral discourse was considered to be of paramount importance in the development of civilization.

Courts around the world have always found it notoriously difficult to accurately define 'the homosexual' or 'a homosexual act'. The changing faces of the sodomite, and the varied specifications of the bugger, are clear examples of the necessity for this discourse of morality to define and redefine specific acts of perversion. From Roman-Dutch jurists' attempts to define sodomy[16] through to the attempts of the Wolfenden Committee in England to define 'the homosexual' and 'homosexual offences', there is an overriding preoccupation with specifying particular acts of perversion.[17] Roman-Dutch jurists disputed the inclusiveness of 'unnatural offences', ('onkuisheid tegen die natuur') over the last 700 years. During this time, they were at different times construed to include such things as masturbation, sex between people of different races, and sex between a Jew and a Christian. The process of definition which leads into this categorization of 'natural/unnatural' is in itself a very conscious process of deliberation, and is far from being 'natural' in the sense of 'self-evident' or 'given'. Each specific act is carefully considered and judged by the court to be 'unnatural' and enshrined through precedent as an unnatural act. Those on trial will be charged with a variety of acts, each representing a specific and individual breach of what has been defined as 'nature'.

Les Moran's discussion of the syntactical complexities encountered by the Wolfenden Committee demonstrates clearly this preoccupation. Precisely what constituted transgression lay not so much in the identity of a homosexual, as there was 'no necessary connection between the sexual identity that is used to name a category of unlawful act and the sexual identity of the person that performs the act'.[18] What was of more significance was how specific acts came to be relied on as the measure of immorality, both because and despite the fact that it was clear that the commission of these acts did not signify a homosexual identity. But this was the only locus with which the homosexual's 'self' could come close to being identified. For the neat binary division of homo/heterosexual has never been so clearly replicated in activity as it was in ideology.

CONSTITUTING INDIVIDUAL SUBJECTIVITIES

The introduction of this moral discourse in colonial Zimbabwe has thus been very significant in constituting individual subjects. With its Christian and medico-scientific elements, it has distinguished the sins of sex from the biology of reproduction, and so has furthered the construction of a new distinctive concept of an individual subject in possession of a 'sexuality', rather than one person whose existence and partnerships are regulated through his/her relationship to a clan or kinship group. Where previously relationships were regulated according to the collective interests of the group whose continuation was assured both socially and physically through marriage ties,[19] in this new individualized 'sexuality' lies the potential for both the denigration of specific perversions as 'deviant', and the simultaneous normativity of a moral rectitude of individual salvation.

It is this creation of individual subjectivities, with the emphasis on the self, which is contended to be of contemporary significance, as it appears both in the current notions of criminal liability and custodial punishment,[20] as well as the designation of sexual offences, and it is also an integral part of the notion of individual human rights. This emphasis on individual subjectivity provides a thread of continuity between the colonial law's creation of individual subjects bound by their specific proclivities, who are held individually responsible for specific social acts, and the globalization of a notion of human rights which resides in the individual and are often signified through these same proclivities.

As the trace of this thread of continuity, individual subjectivity can also be seen to represent the growth of a particular conception of the individual in society. For implicit in this contention of continuity is the question of 'tradition'. Indeed, cultural tradition is frequently claimed to be under threat from the irrepressible and continuous growth of individual subjectivity as prioritized over lineage, just as 'traditional culture' is also claimed (by the same 'traditionalist' campaigners) to impede the state's ability to invest in individual rights and duties. This is illustrated not just by the contentions that same-sex love is against Zimbabwean tradition,[21] but also by the conflicts over the changing status of women. For when the 1982 Legal Age of Majority Act (LAMA) conferred legal subjectivity on all Zimbabweans over the age of 18 – immediately granting women the unprecedented possibilities of legal subjectivity, with the attendant rights of autonomy – it met with fierce resistance.

Before Independence in Zimbabwe, black women were perpetually legal minors - they had no legal status as adults and were permanently under the authority of a guardian: their father, brother or husband. The LAMA has had extensive repercussions for relations between men and women, particularly as it means that women no longer need the consent of their guardian to marry.[22] While many women continue to operate in a 'traditional' framework whereby they remain under the guardianship of a man, some women make an explicit choice to opt for the individual autonomy which lies outside of that 'traditional' structure. This choice represents a potential autonomy for women and so implicitly jeopardizes the system of customary marriage which involves the payment of bridewealth (*lobola*) to the guardian in exchange for the woman. The assurance of exclusive access to a woman's reproductive system is what makes her a 'good wife', and this assurance, most commonly understood to be signified through virginity, clearly excludes a woman's sexual independence. Thus, a sexually independent woman will not bring her guardian much in the way of *lobola*, and her brothers will in turn not be able to rely on her *lobola* to afford 'good wives'. Furthermore the guardian is often reluctant to invest much in the education of a woman who will not recoup his expenditure through *lobola*. The LAMA has therefore undermined not only men's wielding of officially sanctioned control over women, but also their entitlement to derive economic benefit from them. Elder men's perceptions are that it has fundamentally interfered with their ability to control independent women and their economic and social lives (Seidman, 1984). In view of the kinship relations of production that exist around the marriage of a woman, the LAMA is therefore bound to have a profound impact not just on the lives of those women who choose to exercise their legal subjectivity and lead autonomous lives, but it also brings about considerable changes in the relationships and lives of all the men and women in the extended family.

Resistance to the LAMA amongst men, particularly chiefs and elder men, not only obliged the then Prime Minister (now President) Mugabe to explain its purpose as being primarily to extend the franchise,[23] but also inhibited changes to the institution of *lobola*. In the war of liberation leading to Independence, Mugabe's party ZANU[24] had relied on the participation of a number of women (including as combatants), and the drive of a revolution which promised to liberate women, and the working classes, just as it promised to liberate Zimbabwe from segregation and discrimination. It was recognized that *lobola*'s commodification and inflation had changed it from a traditional bond between lineage groups to a capitalist transaction between men.[25] But when discussion arose around its abolition, and the stable governing support of older men was of more use to government than the disruptive arguments of gender reformers, *lobola* was defended as 'part of the national heritage, an essential element of stable social relations', which should resist 'western feminism . . . a new form of cultural imperialism'.[26]

Similarly, at the March 1998 United Nations Human Rights Committee consideration of Zimbabwe's Report under the International Covenant on Civil and Political Rights,[27] members of the Committee repeatedly expressed their concern with the outlawing of sodomy, as well as other measures and activities of the state which discriminated against or persecuted homosexuals, and they requested a commitment from the Zimbabwean delegation that these measures be repealed. No such commitment was forthcoming on the issue of homosexuality, with the delegation claiming that the government's hands were tied by the social opprobrium for homosexuality which had its origins in local cultures. The delegation suggested that homosexuality:

> was not accepted by Zimbabwe's varied cultures, which had only been introduced to the concept of human rights upon the attainment of independence 18 years earlier. Legislative change was usually effective only when it was culturally acceptable; to that end, much remained to be done in the field of education (UN Human Rights Committee, 1998a).

This argument was not accepted by the Committee, which pointed out that many provisions of the Universal Declaration of Human Rights itself contained revolutionary ideas which had not been supported by many cultures, 'including Western cultures', but which had then helped to transform situations. The Committee concluded by saying that 'education alone was not sufficient; appropriate legislation was also necessary'.[28]

Both the arguments raised against women's autonomous subjectivity, and the decriminalization of homosexuality, defend a particular conception of culture as immutable. Such definitions of 'traditional heritage' choose to ignore the fact that the relative novelty of a Zimbabwean national identity arises from a new political process which relies on modern notions of citizenship within a democratic polity. Proponents of such definitions refuse to acknowledge the impact of industrialization and a capitalist economic system in the construction of individual wage-earners and consumers, as well as the inevitable growth of global dynamics to produce new kinds of cultural interactions and new hybrid identities, agglomerated from a wider variety of sources. Choosing to defend or ignore selective perceptions of 'tradition' is a political process carried out through constructing a consensus around the choices which best serve the maintenance of (the hegemonic) order. The creation of Zimbabwean nationhood, as much as ethnicities, cannot be taken for granted as the ontological evolution that it is popularly taken to be. Indeed, the development of strong notions of 'primal sovereignty' is argued to have been highly instrumental in the colonizing process as a notion of collective identity was emphasized in order to develop a notion of a colonized ethnic subjectivity.[29] Comaroff explains this well in relation to 'the Bechuana':

> Most of the evangelists saw no contradiction, no disjuncture in the discourse of rights, between the register of radical individualism and that of primal sovereignty; indeed, they did not explicitly distinguish them at all. The effort to implant modern, right-bearing individualism might have pointed toward a society of free *universal citizens*, while the conjuring of a primordial Bechuana identity gestured toward the creation of *ethnic subjects*. From their perspective, however, the two things were part of a seamless campaign to rework the indigenous world, one describing that world as it was, the other as it ought to be. The former, in short was a narrative of being, of congealed 'tradition'; the latter, a narrative of becoming, of revealed 'modernity'. (Comaroff, 1997: 225)

The selection of 'empowering' women in the struggle to redistribute power as among free 'universal citizens', followed by its explicit rejection once that notion challenged the consensus of national subjectivity which came to exist between traditional patriarchs and the bureaucrats of the nation-state, is an explicit example of this process of 'selecting tradition'.

What is at issue is not that a selection is made, but rather how that selection is made, and what it represents in a constant process of selecting which customs we value, which we devalue, and which we ignore. We have to accept that we constantly reinvent tradition to suit our contemporary interests.[30] This is how we make law, it is how we make government policy, it is how we produce values and discourse – through the renegotiation and reinvention of tradition.

But who is this 'We'? It is not a neutral term for the collective interests of all people living in a state, but for the interests of those who are in a position to exercise some influence over the process, and have the desire to do so. This question becomes particularly pertinent in examining the assertions of 'traditional' sexual practice, for these practices represent structures of gendered power and social hierarchies. While pre-colonial Zimbabwe may not have had the conception of this 'sexuality' that we have now, it certainly distributed social power through the medium of gender. The introduction of a sexual subjectivity, built around a notion of perversion and predicated on a binary division of hetero/homosexual, will inevitably impact on gender relations (which were never static in any case). While contemporary theorists such as Judith Butler write about the 'performative substance' of gender, and 'the regulatory practices of gender coherence',[31] there is little doubt that the significance of this performance, regulation and coherence was also great prior to the arrival of colonizing settlers 100 years ago. The notion of 'tradition' is a primary modality through which structures of power, and so gender coherence, are defended, melded and asserted.

The specificity of assessment and labelling wrought through the proclamation of tradition is contrasted by a lack of precision in locating tradition in a specific historical time-frame. For the question, 'When was tradition?' becomes usefully revealing when we consider the transmission of sexual values. Were traditional practices those which existed before the arrival of missionaries or afterwards? What happened to the activities sanitized by missionaries? Not all attempts at sanitation succeeded, for some rituals and ceremonies which had been denounced as immoral continued secretly when the missionaries were absent. Did these activities lose their 'traditional' status, or gain the status of 'resistance' – how were they altered? What process determined which practices should be allowed to die, and which to continue?

The pledging of young girls in marriage is now widely recognized as wrong and inappropriate, but it was customary and frequent. Yet few demand its reinstatement as a cultural tradition, as part of the national heritage, whereas homosexuality is castigated and decried as 'against tradition' and by implication totally unacceptable. Besides the fact that research suggests this to be the Christianized tradition of missionaries, rather than the authentic unblemished home-grown tradition that it is made out to be, the question which needs to be asked is what process underlies this selection and labelling of traditions?

Furthermore, it might be pointed out that Christianity itself is not 'traditional' (as it relates to pre-colonial authenticity) to southern Africa, but few Zimbabweans would make the argument that it should therefore be done away with – so how tradition is viewed and when it is given any importance can be significant indicators of powerful interests. Diana Jeater, in writing about the way that the criminalization of adultery deliberately focused on African women, suggested that 'tradition' actually reflects more the present than the past in that 'the past to which the family heads looked back seems suspiciously to reflect the concerns of their present' (Jeater, 1993: 142).

These strategies of present power relations would also appear to be reflected in the process of selection which produces the gendered configurations of 'tradition' mentioned earlier, and which makes the universalization of individual autonomy and subjectivity so problematic. For the promotion of individual rights inevitably conflicts with the proprietorial interests that exist in inherited and historically structured relations of gender power. A measure of individual autonomy is fundamental to one's accession to rights, to liberties and, it is argued, to social responsibilities. For individual legal subjectivity is vital to both claiming rights, and being held accountable for one's actions. The first Native Marriage Ordinance (1901) attempted to protect African women from being forced into marriage, and immediately bestowed on women a measure of potential autonomy from the men who were their custodians:

The African idea that sexual identity was an aspect of lineage membership, and that individual members were answerable to the family group for the uses they made of their sexuality, was undermined at a stroke by the

Ordinance's provision that no woman should be made to marry against her will. The women's rights were given priority over the rights of the lineage....

In effect, the State was usurping the rights of family heads to control the sexual choices of members of their households and lineages. The shift from answerability to the ancestors and the lineage to answerability to the State had major political implications in terms of the authority of 'big men' over the people, presenting client men and women as individuals not necessarily bound by or wholly defined in terms of lineage membership. (Jeater, 1993: 81)

Ironically, this was compounded by the attempts of family heads to use the colonial law to bring women back into their control. In persuading the colonial authorities to pass the Native Adultery Punishment Ordinance of 1916 (NAPO), they specifically prohibited married African women from an act that was permitted for anyone else.[32] What it penalized was not an illicit sexual act, but the specific person of the errant married woman. While this was aimed at disempowering women, it also brought African women's particular social status increasingly within the realm of legal regulation. Implicitly, it constituted in law the criminality of African women's sexual autonomy, and so initiated a partial legal subjectivity. For women were to be treated as legal subjects in that they could be held responsible for committing the offence of adultery, but they did not have the subjective status to be offended by a man's adulterous behaviour. Their individual autonomy was to be limited to the ability to offend, and nowhere else were they to be given any legal subjectivity.

The NAPO was explicitly aimed at controlling women and was clearly intended to empower husbands but, in constituting the criminality of women's sexual autonomy, it implicitly relied on a notion of women's independent action and their specific responsibility. By shifting the source of control from lineage to the state, there was a commensurate shift from the control of lineage-bound relationships, to the control the state exercises over people in their individual capacity which makes them specifically responsible.

For the law (like any form of power) does not just prohibit and control, it does not simply denounce and discredit. It also produces and delivers, and it has the capacity to empower people. It engenders behaviour, it generates ideas and action, it bounds individual responsibility as well as promoting individual capacity and agency and, in so doing, it constitutes individualized notions of identity. Thus, the laws defining sexual offences play a role in giving shape to gender and conceptions of sexuality – they regulate sexual relations between individual people and shape interaction between men and women, and between different men, and different women. They reward certain behaviour and punish other behaviour, and in doing so assess behaviour which fits or does not fit with certain conceptions of masculinity and femininity.

For example, Zimbabwean laws around rape have their origin in the Roman-Dutch laws concerning abduction, and consequently they show a preoccupation with protecting a man's exclusive access to his wife's reproductive capacity, and little concern for the bodily integrity of a woman.[33] Similarly, customary law shared this preoccupation with the interests of men in an undisturbed relationship to a woman's reproductive system. While the law is now showing some more concern with the well-being of women (rather than solely considering the interests of her husband/male guardian), the socio-historical origins of this law are still clear in its impact and in its interpretation; *vide* the difficulty that the law has in protecting women.

THE IMPLICATIONS OF A SEXUALIZED IDENTITY

However, this issue is also interesting when we consider the issue of men who have sex with men, and the manner in which it has arisen in the 1990s. It might appear that the approach adopted towards gay and lesbian rights in Zimbabwe is in complete contrast to that adopted in South Africa where the new Constitution was the first in the world to prohibit discrimination against someone on account of their sexual orientation (see the chapter by Pierre de Vos in this volume). While in many ways this does contrast with Zimbabwe, both situations do share something very striking, and that is the recognition of new identities based around sex. The increasing problematization of same-sex desire is one that must inevitably also speak of different-sex desire, and so must address the question of sexual desire in general. For in defining the homosexual, one implicitly defines the heterosexual. Carl Stychin accurately describes how the erasure of gay identity from the dominant discourse prioritizes the heterosexual subject as 'universal and univocal'.[34] But in order to make this prioritization explicit, in order to assert this universalism as one which is specifically heterosexual, one has first of all to allude to a marginality predicated on the binary division of hetero/homosexuality, and to do that, one has to engage with the *a priori* concept of an individualized 'sexuality'.

Thus, Mugabe has not only been responsible for producing a conception of homosexuality in the Zimbabwean context, but also that of heterosexuality. All those Zimbabweans who have previously not incorporated this notion of a 'sexuality' into their identity, now find themselves blessed with one. By designating others as 'homosexual', Mugabe has automatically emphasized the norm as 'heterosexual', and so many Zimbabweans have come to see themselves as 'heterosexual', where they did not have such a categorically sexual self-consciousness before. This is not to suggest that there was no homosexual or indeed heterosexual sex going on in the past, nor that people never thought about sex. But they thought about it differently outside of this binary division of heterosexual and homosexual, so that the identity of a homo/heterosexual was not one publicly recognized and acknowledged. Through two very different processes, this has now taken place in both South Africa and Zimbabwe.

The inclusion of sexual orientation in the South African Constitution's equality clause has led to the decriminalization of homosexual acts, and also to the recognition and development of particular rights of citizenship for South African gays and lesbians. It has led to a debate around the inclusivity of human rights in which organizations representing lesbians and gay people are able to participate fully and are given relatively equal access to the means of the debate's production. Human rights, legal and constitutional discourse (both popular and intellectual) in South Africa abounds with references which recognize sexuality as a constituent marker of identity and citizenship.

In 1995, President Mugabe suggested that being gay was a 'white man's disease'. This prompted a number of black Zimbabweans who felt themselves to be gay or lesbian to identify themselves as such and insist 'We do exist'. The numbers and visibility of black Zimbabweans identifying as lesbians and gay men has increased considerably since[35] and, unwittingly, Mugabe finds he has been the most effective publicist that the identity and the organization which has been the specific target of many of his attacks (GALZ – Gays and Lesbians of Zimbabwe) has ever had. Indeed, he has introduced the word and concept of a 'sexuality' into a previously virginal public discourse; he has been a virulent propagandist for the whole concept of a binary division, where those boundaries were previously blurred. This is not to suggest that Zimbabwe is now flooded with self-identified same-sex lovers – it is simply to suggest that he has participated in the constitution of a new identity – one that is individualized, sexualized and, in this form, historically marginalized. Further, by publicizing his homophobia, President Mugabe has given an identity to many who were previously ignorant of or uncaring about it. Just as he defines the agenda for the way that much of the country comes to see homosexuals, so he helps define the way people come to see themselves. Whereas they were previously identified through other social markers, now people are also either heterosexual or homosexual and accordingly develop a binary conception of sexuality. This is a conception which can be criticized as limited, in that it concretizes what has previously been fluid and often carries an anticipation of immutably entrenched identities, but it simultaneously allows for an appeal to specific late-twentieth-century notions of rights. In this case, it can be argued that the identity of gay/lesbian has arisen out of a contestation of rights. I would argue that the structure of law is not in itself antithetical to the empowerment of women, as has been suggested by Carol Smart in her book *Feminism and the Power of Law* (1989), and that a rights-based discourse can be helpful. Rights are contested and asserted through challenging existing structures of power rather than simply as ontological givens. Agency is therefore of paramount importance, and legal subjectivity is clearly a precondition of rights. The irony is that this subjectivity may arise through the contestation of its denial – autonomy thereby being produced through resistance.

Just as the South African Constitution has the effect of constituting a gay identity – giving it form and substance, recognition in terms of rights, legal subjectivity - so too does the refusal of these substantive social attributes. Simply put, saying you *do* deserve these rights specifically because you are gay, and saying you *don't* deserve these rights because you are not heterosexual both have the effect of elevating sexuality as a significant constituent of citizenship and identity. What we are seeing is the increasing use, in both countries, of sex as a medium through which more and more people identify themselves; sex as constitutive of people, as an identifier of social and legal subjectivity.

This is a process which has been compounded by the challenges presented to all Zimbabweans with the spread of HIV/AIDS, and interestingly, it is the very heterosexual course of HIV infection in Zimbabwe which has heightened the awareness of the significance of sex in the constitution of the social body. For example, the silences around the sexual which were so deeply embedded in Shona language had to be filled with an articulate currency of anatomical terms and definitions of sexual behaviour. Where previously certain references to sexual practices and relations were spoken only between men or between women, there has had to be a concerted attempt to develop language accessible to all.[36] HIV/AIDS has impacted enormously on how much sex is spoken about, and in what manner,[37] but the vital need to discuss it is constantly challenging the manner in which sex is configured by what are seen to be 'traditional' gender relations. Women are known to be the section of the population most vulnerable to infection, partly on account of their structural position and consequent powerlessness to negotiate safe sexual practices, and partly on account of the gendered silences around sex; it is these factors which figure prominently in the tremendous difficulties in establishing sex/health education classes for women and girls.[38] But nevertheless, the discourse surrounding sex has been considerably affected by the development of HIV/AIDS and related illnesses. The increasing use of language which is so tied into the conceptualization of 'a sexuality' which resides in the individual is of enormous importance. This new currency of language not only renders sexual what may not have been considered 'sexual' before, but also fixes an unspecified fluidity in the concrete shape of definition. Creating terms and definitions inescapably binds and fixes behaviour which might before have been more malleable, removing a potential variety of interpretations, and fitting it into a larger (and binary) discourse around sex as a whole.

In Zimbabwe, with unthinking attempts to encourage sexual abstinence, the discourse around HIV has so far been shaped to emphasize a concept of individual morality constructed around marriage and the notion of fidelity. This has implied a certain elision of individual responsibility, as safety is portrayed as resting on the 'good behaviour' and morality of couples joined in marriage. The notions of individual responsibility within a diversity of chosen lifestyles are sidelined in attempts to discourage sex outside of marriage, and to rely on conventional relationships of monogamous fidelity. The responsibility is seen as shared in that it resides in (presumably monogamous) joint fidelity,[39] rather than the individual and personalized methods of ensuring one's own safety and thereby the safety of those with whom one interacts. Despite the dangerousness of this 'morality' approach in a predominantly polygynous society, its promotion is not surprising in that it dovetails with attempts to conserve 'traditional' gender roles and the importance of lineage. One might tentatively suggest that the notion of individual responsibility (for safe sex or for other issues of health and justice) is something which can only flourish where there is a more developed concept of individual rights and subjectivities. This concept of individual responsibility and rights runs counter to the hegemonic relationships built on an alliance of modern bureaucratic and 'traditional' polygynous patriarchies, which depend on women's lack of autonomy. It is also a concept which can only develop at the expense of those whose power resides in structures which subordinate individual subjectivities in their claim to represent communal interests. Thus, the call to sexual abstinence outside of monogamous married relationships is a call to a lineage-based morality, rather than the potentially 'safer' practice of rooting protection in a notion of individual responsibility. The efficacy of an approach of individual responsibility would require an emphasis on individual rights and individual autonomy, and to proclaim these would be to challenge both a heteronormative notion of fidelity (practised in a sexist manner), and also the 'traditional' subordinated position of women under the power of a male guardian. The recognition of the importance of individual responsibility can only be predicated on a similar recognition of individual rights, and the development of a rights discourse cannot avoid invoking notions of autonomy and so a degree of responsibility for one's self. On the one hand, the establishment of these individual rights and responsibilities presupposes a democratic framework, through which people are able to represent their own interests and account for their own behaviour. On the other, the development of these individual rights and responsibilities might be claimed to be a precondition for the operation of an effective democracy.

CONCLUSION

Foucault wrote much about sex being increasingly invested with power (both as a source of 'oppression' and as a source of 'liberation') within an increasingly bureaucratized and bourgeois state. He wrote about sex being 'originally, historically bourgeois' but inducing 'specific class effects'.[40] This is because, rather than just being perceived as symbolic of life and causative of procreation, sex has come to be seen as the location of some individual truths. It is held to be a veritable treasure trove of dangerous but vital secrets in need of investigation and monitoring. It is seen to call for correction through techniques which render truth rational, engender a discipline of the self, and reveal the subjectivity of an individual desire which locates the person within a social structure of subordination and universal values. Zimbabwe may not be undergoing a rapid process of bourgeoisification at the level of macro-economics, but the increasing urbanization, the quick growth of a middle class, the slow deterioration of old community ties, an incremental commodification, and the growth of individual (as opposed to communal) subjectivities, all suggest a process similar to that depicted by Foucault.

As the certainties which lay behind the old categories of gender identification are increasingly challenged, and the old boundaries of nation states become transgressed by increasing loads of information flowing further and further, so the old categories of power and collectivity become increasingly fragmented. This process of globalization invokes new identities which traverse old boundaries. Whether in Africa, Asia, the Americas or Europe, it is clear that gendered relationships are being buffeted by the newly discovered global titles of identity for what are ancient activities.

These 'gay/lesbian' names for identities might originate in North America and Western Europe, but they have been appropriated by people the world over as they imply a claim to the protection and rights guaranteed under international treaties, and a way out of an almost universal form of marginalization. By proclaiming these identities, people not only lay claim to their corresponding rights, but they also assume a certain level of individual responsibility and autonomy. However, this claim immediately makes them vulnerable to the accusation that they are ignoring their indigenous cultural traditions, by adopting foreign ones. The 'gay/lesbian' identity is now so global that this is an almost inevitable process. It remains to be seen to what extent people adopt and proclaim the identity in such a way that it does not obscure same-sex identities which were accommodated in a local context, and that these local histories augment and help constitute the identity of 'gay', rather than become hidden by it. This process of globalization surfs the electronic wave which accompanies the avaricious multinational spread of the free market, but it entertains a liberal human rights discourse, which carries with it an inevitable growth of individualism. Out of this can spring a more radical pluralism which develops a non-reductive politics of social justice.

Such a radical pluralist approach can be seen to refuse reductionism in that an analysis of the persecution of homosexuals in Zimbabwe, and the contrary extent of their emancipation in South Africa, indicates how sexuality as a whole, regardless of hetero/homosexuality, comes to be a more significant constituent of subjectivity, and so becomes an increasingly constitutive, but certainly not exclusive, ingredient of national identity. The broader lesson learnt from this, is that analysis of one form of categorical oppression can illustrate the need for a politics of diversity, and suggest a platform from which to develop that. Sexual politics can contribute to the reimagining of the nation-state as coalitional and so intrinsically diverse, rather than essentialist.[41] And interestingly, the contrast in these two countries shows us how sexuality comes to constitute identity through its proclamation as much as through its oppression, for it is a process which takes place as much through the assertion of individual human rights, as it does through the denigration of specific stereotypes of individual perversion. It arises from the process of contestation itself.

3

'I'D RATHER BE AN OUTLAW'

IDENTITY, ACTIVISM AND DECRIMINALIZATION IN TASMANIA[1]

EMMA M. HENDERSON

We always pushed that we wanted reform to acknowledge difference in the community. Most who supported us could see it was a diversity issue rather than a sameness thing ... and that's different than elsewhere ... diversity has not been the point elsewhere. Here gay law reform debate in the minds of most people who supported us is a break from a really homogenised past.... [Gay law reform] was a symbol of us ... becoming an interesting diverse colourful [place]. Even those whose support was most shallow ... thought that diversity was the key.[2]

INTRODUCTION

Over the decade 1988–97 the island state of Tasmania experienced the most ferocious and protracted homosex decriminalization battle in Australia. In an area of law reform that has provided a forum for the airing of a wide array of social concerns and panics, the hysteria unleashed by the push for decriminalization was unparalleled and Tasmanian society was ripped apart at the seams as regions set against each other, state and federal government relations broke down, conservatives and conservationists were set against progressives and developers, and sections of established churches set themselves apart from the state and against each other. Situated in the centre of the storm was the Tasmanian Gay and Lesbian Rights Group (TGLRG), a small group of activists committed to changing the nature of the decriminalization debate by making an explicit and very public bid for inclusion within the definition of Tasmanian social identity.

Homosex activism leading to decriminalization in other Australian states and in the United Kingdom and Canada has tended not to explicitly engage with the relationship between legalizing homosex and social change. In fact, in those earlier debates activists struggling for law reform went to great lengths to calm fears that change would be a necessary outcome of law reform at all. They suceeded in this goal by committing themselves to a struggle for privacy – a formal legal right through which homosex would be kept in control by universal disapproval and a reinstatement of the homosex/secrecy nexus which, by virtue of its newly legal status, would become a form of secrecy in which to take pride.[3] In contrast, the activism of the TGLRG was based not on the invocation of privacy but on the need for all Tasmanians to learn about the diverse nature of sexuality and to respect difference within the community; to commit to a new Tasmanian social contract.

This chapter explores the diversity-not-privacy claim, examining the role that the decriminalization struggle had in engendering a discussion about Tasmanian identity, and the extent to which the TGLRG can claim to have succeeded in including 'gay and lesbian' within Tasmanian social citizenship. Beginning briefly with an overview of the role that geography has played in forming Tasmanian identity, I go on to examine the nature of anti-gay organizing following the introduction of the decriminalization issue into Tasmanian politics in the late 1980s. Following the enormously public Salamanca Market protest in 1988, anti-gay organizing in Tasmania embarked upon a campaign aimed at reclaiming Tasmanian space and identity from the dangers of diversity and the invasion of foreign diseases and laws, fears which were arguably exacerbated by the TGLRG decision to take their struggle offshore, to the federal realm of commonwealth government and High Court, and, further away, to the United Nations. The second half of the chapter examines the role that the TGLRG United Nations challenge had in the ultimate success of the decriminalization struggle, and critiques the group's invocation of privacy as a legitimate legal strategy in pursuit of social change.

ON BEING TASMANIAN

Within the often violent parameters of Australian history, the island state of Tasmania is reknown for its bloody and repressive origins – indeed, its role as a penal colony within a penal colony (where the very worst of the convicts were sent as punishment for transgressions in the new colonies), and the savage treatment meted out to its indigenous inhabitants, have attained mythical status within the Australian psyche. The projection of fears and neuroses and guilt onto an 'other' plays an important part in the construction of cultural identities, and it is this role that Tasmania has played in the (re)creation of Australian identity:[4]

> For years they've been saying 'we might not have treated our Aboriginals well but we didn't treat them as badly as Tasmania'.... All those things

that Australians hate about themselves – the inbred nature of our society, and the homophobia and racism and everything else gets projected on to us and if you hate it about yourself and you project it then you hate them.[5]

Mainland Australian media portrayals of Tasmania as the home of extremely conservative, unintellectual, rural, red-necked homophobes throughout the law-reform process were thus not exceptional or unusual,[6] but if mainland mythology claims that there is something different about Tasmania and its inhabitants – that they are not the same as urban mainlanders – it has to be recognized that this claim is even stronger within Tasmania itself. The 'Tasmanian not Austra-lian' theme has huge cultural significance in Tasmania; one has only to switch on the television for 10 minutes to realize that Tasmanians see (or are encouraged to see) themselves first and foremost as local or state, rather than national or federal citizens.[7] As a cultural concept, many Tasmanians argue that 'Australia' denotes an area from southern Queensland through New South Wales and Victoria and then some specific places of beauty such as Kakadu, Uluru, Perth and Adelaide:[8]

Not only was being gay or lesbian in Tas[mania] to be a second class citizen but to be a Tasmanian in the lesbian and gay community in Melbourne or Sydney was similarly to be a second class citizen. Many said they were from Dubbo or Newcastle or Cairns – from anywhere else than from Tas-mania . . . People don't believe us when we talk about this but I remember around Oxford Street one night with one of our petitions just to see what would happen . . . . I remember one person said 'nothing good ever comes out of Tasmania. Like you know I am just really sick of all the Tasmanians who are here' and another said 'if this will stop them coming here because it's more likely that they will stay there, then I will sign it'.[9]
      I don't know a lot about that Tasmanian stuff because I am not from here but I know it's a strong thing. There is a much stronger sense of identity . . . As Tasmanian people we have been the scapegoats and the little bit at the bottom and the ones with the highest unemployment and the baddies with regard to aboriginals and the baddies about the environment and the baddies around gay stuff and all that has helped to forge a stronger sense of being Tasmanian . . . . People from New South Wales don't talk about being from NSW but wherever we go we talk about being Tasmanian . . . . You do get ridicule and the anti-gay stuff was part of that. You go interstate and you speak to the people who supported gay law reform and . . . get ridicule – you know, that you still have those stupid laws.[10]

Geography is central to this sense of difference. As an island, Tasmania is physically removed from the rest of Australia, and the fact of being a space apart has led to movement and a recurrent fear of invasion within the political landscape of Tasmania. Just as religious dissidents moving to Tasmania at the turn of the twentieth century in search of religious freedom caused grave social concern,[11] a century later politicians and social commentators again gave voice to fears that Tasmania was being recolonized, this time by mainlanders seeking an 'alternative lifestyle'. From the 1960s until the early 1980s there came an influx of people looking for a non-cosmopolitan lifestyle, encouraged by the growing Green movement:[12]

> We will be opening the floodgates. Have a look at the power that the conservationists have today; they started in small numbers and they brought down their hordes from mainland states and were able to affect the vote in this state . . . . We have had an influx of people from the mainland, the 'alternative lifestylists', coming over into this State and taking advantage of the situation where we live in a democracy that guarantees them the right to freedom of speech. But they choose not to accept democracy, the rule of the majority – but to take control of democracy through their splinter groups . . . . I will guarantee that the majority of those alternative lifestylists are not homegrown Tasmanians . . . .[13]

That concept of movement, or invasion, has led to reaction: a need to defend and maintain borders. In the same way that British parliamentarians intent on rejecting decriminalization argued passionately that homosex was a contagious European disease that should be stopped at the borders,[14] so Tasmanian conservatives have argued ceaselessly that in order to maintain a true Tasmanian identity, homosex and its accoutrements should be left in Sydney and San Francisco – that homosex is not part of the authentically Tasmanian experience:[15]

> If the grass is greener on the other side of the fence let us extend an open invitation for them to go to the other side of the fence; let us give them a one-way ticket back to those states where they can do what they like. Why do they not go back to those states – where many of them have come from anyway – where decriminalization of homosexuality is a fact, instead of coming here and making us fit into their pattern so that we do what they want to do . . . the same thing is happening in the federal situation where if someone forms a homosexual relationship with someone overseas he can ask permission to come into this country. I say that what we ought to be doing is giving those persons a ticket to the country where their homosexual lovers are so that we do not have to worry about bringing others into this country.[16]

Homosex was repeatedly portrayed as the final frontier during this period. For example, Tasmanian Premier Robin Grey launched an immigration campaign in Sydney in 1988 with a speech in which he welcomed everyone – 'greenies', 'the sick' and Aboriginals – to Tasmania, with the exception, 'but homosexuals, we're not interested in'.[17] The decriminalization debates raised the threat of invasion to new heights: for the first time interstate and federal pressure were brought into what had previously been an exclusively state-based issue. Australia is a federation of states and territories, each of which has its own electoral system and government, with each state enacting its own legislation and legal enforcement systems. The federal government, formed under the Australian Constitution, has specific powers to administer federal matters such as foreign affairs, defence, taxation and so forth. Criminal law falls within the jurisdiction of the states except in so far as state legislation infringes on federal legislation, and it was at this intersection – the involvement of the federal government foreign affairs power to enforce the International Covenant of Civil and Political Rights – that invasion of Tasmanian territory (both physical and political) became a reality. In addition to interstate (every other state and territory had decriminalized homosex by 1991) and federal disapproval and pressure, Tasmania ran the gauntlet of pressure from the United Nations, Amnesty International, and a trade boycott that spread from New South Wales over the whole of Australia and then to the United States and New Zealand.[18] This outside involvement, absent in other decriminalization efforts, adds to and complicates the Tasmanian debates.

ANTI-GAY ORGANIZING AND TASMANIAN IDENTITY

A fascinating and important development in the decriminalization movement in Tasmania was the creation of an anti-gay network which sought – after the proreform stance of the Third National AIDS Conference in Hobart,[19] the Salamanca Market protest[20] and the Greens/Labour election victory of 1989[21] – to reimpose heterosex over Tasmanian citizenship by reinforcing the illegitimacy of homosex in Tasmanian public spaces.

The Salamanca Market protest developed after TGLRG set up a stall at an inner-city Saturday market in Hobart to collect signatures for its law-reform petition after the National AIDS Conference in 1988. The Hobart City Council (HCC) advised the group that their stall was 'political' and 'offensive' and therefore impermissible. Police were used to enforce the ban, arresting stall staff members and supporters for trespass. After a failed attempt to settle the dispute by allowing the TGLRG to keep its stall as long as it did not advertise its cause or actively solicit signatures, HCC officers were given powers to ban whomever they liked from the market for life. They banned those staffing the stall and those media crew covering the incident; photos and videos were taken by the HCC to enforce the ban. Members of the public signing the petition, those who 'looked as if they were going to sign it', those within a certain geographical area around the stall and those who displayed the words 'gay' or 'lesbian' or the pink triangle symbol about their persons, 'known homosexuals' and others were all liable to arrest on the spot; police are alleged to have destroyed signed pages of the petition, to have used rubber gloves when arresting and subsequently processing protesters, to have used homophobic and racist language in addressing and speaking about protestors and, when the Hobart Magistrates Court refused to impose bail conditions preventing protestors from returning to the market, attempted to intimidate Rodney Croome and David Brewer of the TGLRG (who were told that if they left their houses on Saturday mornings they would be arrested for breaching the peace). Over 130 arrests were made before the ban was lifted on 10 December. All charges were dropped when it was discovered that the HCC had failed to specify the market area as a space over which it had control in the government gazette – meaning it had had no power to define who could and could not attend the market in the first place.

The events at Salamanca situated sexuality as contestable terrain within the state: where previously it had been invisible and ignored by the mainstream, the proximity of gay law reform to contestation over goverance and identity in Tasmania became obvious. While the TGLRG and its supporters found the experience of organizing against the oppressive actions of the HCC to be empowering, the gay and lesbian communities were not the only sections of the community to be so affected. Also arising out of Salamanca came a decade of specifically Tasmanian anti-gay activism. Unlike that experienced in the rest of Australia and in the United Kingdom, anti-gay discourse espoused by non-politicians in Tasmania was tightly organized and centralized. And yet, unlike well-organized anti-gay discourse in the United States, Tasmanian anti-gay groups were predominantly secular rather than evangelical Christian-based.[22]

While the state government distanced itself from the Salamanca issue in 1988, declaring it to be a local government matter over which the state government had no authority to intervene, at the same time it immediately banned the use of government resources by gay community groups seeking to implement effective HIV/AIDS prevention education programmes across the state on the basis that, while it did not object to 'safer sex' education, this was not its immediate priority.[23] This 'resource neutral' approach had the effect of forcing such groups to look elsewhere for premises at which to run safer-sex workshops and, in response, the AIDS Council Education Officer sought per-mission to use local government resources in various regions across the state.[24] The reactions to these requests were uneven. In some locations (for example in Devonport) permission was given readily. In other places the requests caused massive controversy. In Ulverstone the request was met with horror and disbelief. Miranda Morris reports that the council meeting at which it was raised 'deteriorated into what one councillor described as a circus'.[25] Rodney Cooper, a councillor who left the Australian Labour Party in the 1970s because of its commitment to decriminalization, asked the people of Devonport to 'keep their homosexual promotion on the east side of the Forth River'[26] and this attempt to keep the gay issue at a spatial distance from Ulverston was the least inflam-matory statement to be made in the ensuing furore.

In June 1989 the Liberal (conservative) government was ousted by a Labour/ Green coalition which had placed decriminalization on its legislative agenda (albeit at the very end). The aftermath of that election witnessed the birth of large-scale anti-gay organizing in Tasmania, as large and (linguistically) violent rallies were held, demonstrating the frustration and anger with which many Tasmanians greeted the potential coalition (between a still unpopular Labour Party and the Green independents who had succeeded in winning a protest vote that was never intended to return the Labour Party to power). The Greens held a commitment to gay law reform, and the Labour Party had had law reform on its manifesto (although it had not been in power since placing it there), and the Salamanca protest had raised the issue of law reform sufficiently in the minds of Tasmanians to make it a flashpoint for a host of frustrations.

When the coalition took office, some of the hysteria that had surrounded the debate abated; the rallies had been extremely heated and the closeness which one rally came to a gaybashing had proved a sobering experience for many. In addition, the existence of other scandals (the attempted bribing of a member of parliament to stop the coalition, for example) led to a cooling of tensions. Nevertheless in Launceston a group of ministers and church leaders met to discuss a joint campaign to support existing laws on homosexual practices and recommended a thorough research project into the issues. They formed a community action group in the north that would oppose decriminalization and examine the issue of a state-wide network to oppose further gay policy initiatives. It was from this meeting that the next phase of anti-gay organizing emerged. First came the formation of FACT (For a Caring Tasmania), chaired by Reverend Robert Beeston, and shortly after that Concerned Residents Against Moral Pollution (CRAMP), a group which met in Devonport and declared itself to be a moral watchdog with no religious or political affiliations.[27] These two groups co-ordinated a series of rallies to coincide with the November 1989 Australian Labour Party Conference. The first, held in Burnie, saw an audience of 600 addressed by the Shadow Attorney General[28] amongst other figures; the second was in St Helens.[29] While the groups were developed as a commitment to the ideal of Christians maintaining a political influence in society, one of the primary targets of hostility at these rallies were the Anglican and United Churches, which had voted in favour of decriminalization at their annual Synods that year:[30]

> communists, fabians, homosexuals and feminists are all involved in politics. There has been a major shift in the church at large over its role in society and it too has a mandate to be involved politically.[31]

Conspiracy was the central theme: the idea that national politics, the bureaucracy and state institutions such as the education system had been infiltrated by homosexual activists who were themselves either from, or encouraged by, influences originating from outside Tasmania. The themes that have been so much a part of conservative rhetoric – about the infiltration of homos from elsewhere colonizing Tasmania with the aim of destroying the family and society – remained dominant. Exploitation – Tasmania being dominated by the world, the mainland, big business, and eventually the state government – was central to the formation of anti-gay strategies, which were tied together by a theory in which the need to maintain a coherent Tasmanian identity against a constantly threatening invasion from above/outside was seen as the primary task. Further, the development of anti-gay enclaves such as Ulverston and Burnie reinforced the idea of the dangerousness of homosex: at a local level leaders argued that some parts of Tasmania were already contaminated and thus less authentically Tasmanian than others – a level of rhetoric which increased the sense of urgency and passion within the debates.

In 1990, the Labour/Green government introduced an AIDS/HIV Preventative Measures Bill into Parliament, which aimed through a variety of methods – privacy of testing results, a testing agency, education and (almost incidentally) decriminalization of gay sex – to reduce the incidence of HIV transmission. While both major parties were in favour of the Bill, the decriminalization provisions proved so contentious that Cabinet could not reach a consensus. As a result of the controversy which surrounded the legislation, Ulverston and Wynyard Councils were lobbied, with the result that they passed resolutions opposing decriminalization, and in turn lobbied parliamentarians to support their views. When the TGLRG offered to meet with Ulverston Council to explain the need for decriminalization in successfully combating HIV transmission, not only did council members respond with hostility, they passed a resolution absolving the Council of any obligation to its lesbian and gay constituents and called on other councils to do the same.[32]

FACT, CRAMP, and another group, TASalert, which formed shortly after the rallies began in 1989, went on to lobby successfully at state level for prohibitions on the teaching of gay sexuality as anything other than deviant in (safer) sex education in community centres or schools, and for prohibitions on condom vending machines in schools. They were also intensely involved in the production of a large volume of publicity material aimed at transmitting their concerns to the wider public.

In the strategies pursued by anti-gay groups in Tasmania there are conflicting images of the state at work: as a concrete monolith captured by the gay mafia in need of exposure and avoidance, and at the same time as open to manipulation and influence – as capable of being recaptured and redeployed. In order to assert their own definition of Tasmanian identity – in which the definition of citizenship was required to be narrowed to exclude gay and lesbian – anti-gay groups engaged in a variety of direct actions aimed at reinforcing fears of the homo as a non-Tasmanian threat. Rejecting homo as a social category which was capable of qualifying for inclusion within Tasmanian society, anti-gay groups, council members and politicians built up a discursive structure in which the homo was constituted as an invasion of the island state, threatening to the unique identity and cultural mores of Tasmanian society, bringing with it new diseases, new social habits and, importantly, new laws designed to circumvent Tasmanian sovereignty.

PUSHING THE BOUNDARIES OF TASMANIAN IDENTITY: *TOONEN v AUSTRALIA*

The extremely hostile reception of the decriminalization clauses in the 1990 HIV/AIDS Preventative Measures Bill[33] led the TGLRG to conclude that the members of the Legislative Council were unlikely to change their positions about law reform in the foreseeable future. In consequence, the group began to develop a strategy which utilized resources outside the parliamentary sphere.

On 26 December, 1991, Nick Toonen, one of the original members of the TGLRG, lodged a Communication with the United Nations Human Rights Committee (UNHRC), in which he claimed that sections 122(a), (c) and 123 of the Criminal Code Act (Tas)[34] infringed the rights of privacy and equality before the law guaranteed by articles 17 and 26 of the International Covenant of Civil and Political Rights (ICCPR). On 31 March, 1994, after a lengthy process of submissions and investigations, the UNHRC handed down its decision, finding unanimously that sections 122(a), (c) and 123 should be repealed as being in breach of the right to privacy and rejecting the justification put forward (indirectly, see below) by the Tasmanian Government that the laws were necessary to defend Tasmania's health and moral codes.[35]

With its human rights reputation at stake in the international arena, the federal government exercised its external affairs legislative power in October 1994 by introducing the Human Rights (Sexual Conduct) Bill (Cth) 1994 into the Federal House of Representatives.[36] The purpose clause of the Bill stated its sole ambit to be the rendering of a state law invalid if it involved an 'arbitrary interference' with the 'privacy' of those aged over 18 years who consented to 'in-private' sexual conduct; it did not make any explicit reference to homosexuality or the Tasmanian Criminal Code, nor did it define the meaning of 'in private' or 'arbitrary'. In the introductory second reading speech, the government made clear that this was a purely technical defence which could only come into effect if an applicable prosecution was initiated. In such a case the defendant could argue to the High Court that the information or charge should be dropped as being an arbitrary interference with privacy.[37] The High Court would have to take into account both the UNHRC *Toonen* decision and direct evidence from the relevant state government as to the necessity and/or desirability for the prosecution, in order to ascertain whether the alleged invasion of privacy was arbitrary or not. The Bill passed into law as the Federal Privacy Act in December 1994, providing a complete defence to any adult (over the age of 18) charged or convicted of consensual, in-private sexual activities. As arguably the Act did not actually invalidate the relevant sections of the Tasmanian Criminal Code, the TGLRG applied to the High Court for a decision as to the status of sections 122 and 123, a case which presented no small difficulty given that no actual justiciable case existed for the TGLRG to bring.[38] Nevertheless, the High Court granted standing, and it was in the face of this on-going pressure that the Tasmanian Parliament finally passed decriminalization legislation in June 1997, days before the High Court case was due to begin.[39]

It is arguable that to some extent the TGLRG exacerbated the promulgation of the anti-gays' 'homo equals anti-Tasmanian' theories through its utilization of the UNHRC and the privacy provisions of the ICCPR. Taking the debate beyond the Tasmanian frontier, placing it in the hands of overseas experts and asking for 'from-above' pressure to be placed on the Tasmanian Government fed into the already existing conspiracy arguments which had been deployed by conservatives to argue that law reform should never have been put on the Tasmanian legislative agenda in the first place. While it was the inability of internal procedures to facilitate reform which had led the TGLRG stepping outside Tasmania, conservatives emphasized repeatedly the failure of the TGLRG to engage in a proper manner with democratic processes.

The appeal to the United Nations was seen as placing illegitimate constraints on Tasmania's democratic system: minorities, once having placed their interests within the system, needed to accept the rule of the majority if it was decided those interests should not be met by society: 'we live in a democracy that guarantees them the right to freedom of speech. But they choose not to accept democracy – the rule of the majority – but to take control of the democracy through their splinter groups.'[40]

The TGLRG continued to state that its aim was to conduct an entirely public struggle where law reform was not so much the ultimate goal but a side effect of genuine, far-reaching social change within Tasmanian society itself. The group has argued that, rather than risk a situation similar to that in Western Australia,[41] the TGLRG was not prepared to lend its support to government-initiated law reform efforts simply on the basis that they were law reform efforts:[42]

> If they [the Government] had ... changed the law in 1988 the level of awareness of gay and lesbian issues would have been really low. There was a level [on which] we didn't want the law changed back then in 1988 or 1992 or 1994 ... just changing the law itself in 1988 wouldn't actually have done anything - because it was symbolic because no one was being arrested and no one was being charged [for private sex]. The amendments that would have provided the defence [were unnacceptable] ... not only would I rather be an outlaw - our approach was that not only did we want the law changed we wanted it done properly – because we knew, and this was partly based on that Western Australian experience that once it was half changed the rest of the change would take ten times as much work whereas now there is nothing to do in terms of the Criminal Code, it's fixed.[43]

That is, unlike earlier law reform groups which fought for decriminalization on any terms, on the basis that illegality was the barrier to positive social change and that decriminalization woud lead to social acceptance and thus to eventual revocation of the legislative compromises (such as anti-proselytizing or unequal age of consent provisions) which had been necessary to achieve the original law reform, the TGLRG recognized that decriminalization removes the impetus for further change.[44] TGLRG would not accept such compromises: it would wait for the social acceptance that would grant full government neutrality in the Criminal Code rather than settle for less.

However, in taking the struggle outside Tasmania into the international legal realm, the TGLRG entered an arena in which the social transformation it claimed to be struggling for was almost irrelevant. The procedure governing the UN challenge existed beyond the reach of parliamentarians and the government of Tasmania: an ICCPR challenge exists between the complainant and its nation state. There is no official voice given to constituent federal states. Thus, although the federal government solicited submissions from Tasmania, it declined to present those arguments or to defend the challenge at all before the UNHRC, instead simply requesting a determination as to whether the disputed laws offended the ICCPR or not.[45] Short of repealing the offending sections of the Criminal Code and thus removing the grounds of the complaint, Tasmania, its people and its politicians could do nothing to facilitate or prevent the proceedings; whether or not the transformation of Tasmanian identity went beyond the purely formal was entirely beside the point.

Adding to the sense of outrage in Tasmania (even for a considerable number of politicians who professed to support the decriminalization cause) was the fact that the UNHRC does not meet in public, is not required to publish the reasons for its decisions, and was at the time made up of a number of members who came from non-democratic countries or countries that retain criminal laws against homosex,[46] as well as five countries who had not themselves ratified the First Optional Protocol of the ICCPR.[47]

Thus, both the federal debates surrounding the enactment of the 1994 Act and the debates held in Tasmania to discuss the *Toonen* decision were almost overwhelmingly opposed to what was painted as an un-Australian/Tasmanian act of foul play: the TGLRG was responsible for abrogating Australian sovereignty and democracy. The federal Act was seen as emblematic of a clash between two essential concepts – the necessity of showing that Australia respected privacy (described by virtually every opposition member as the foundation stone of the federal Liberal and National Party coalition) – and the need to respect and protect the right of individual states to their own characters and autonomy. In Tasmania the call for privacy was overwhelmed by state government arguments about the need to protect the health of Tasmanians: reforming the laws would bring an influx of homos to Tasmanian shores who would bring with them HIV/AIDS, paedophilia and graphic public displays of debauchery and evil, guaranteed to infect Tasmanian children and posing no small risk to adult Tasmanian men.

It is important to note briefly the fact that the TGLRG found itself in the position of having to deploy the juridical categories of 'victim', 'complaint' and 'privacy' in order to bring itself within the boundaries of the ICCPR. Privacy, in particular, being the central platform of the ICCPR challenge, was particularly problematic as it did not fit the systemic harms which the group was trying to draw attention to, and could not, in any case, provide a remedy which would come close to repairing those harms. The group sought to avoid traditional arguments that Tasmanian gay men deserved privacy, instead focusing on the role of state institutions in the perpetration of violence and subordination.[48] However, as the UNHRC decision demonstrates, the group was less than successful in avoiding the problems associated with privacy. The operative part of the decision was restricted to a discussion of the breach of privacy that would occur if Toonen was ever actually prosecuted under the law; just as the Federal Government had not, the UNHRC was not prepared to accept the existence of a link between Tasmania's criminal laws and actual non-prosecutorial-based harms.[49]

Further, the TGLRG recourse to privacy led the UNHRC to a series of precedents from the European Court of Human Rights (where criminal laws in Ireland and Cyprus had been found to breach individual privacy) as the foundation of its decision that references to 'sex' in the ICCPR include 'sexual orientation'.[50] Sexual orientation is not one of the specifically named charac-teristics to which the State is required to remain blind in guaranteeing the rights of article 17, and this was one of the first obstacles which the Communication sought to overcome. Lesbian activists involved with the TGLRG had been concerned to ensure 'immutability' not be used as a platform for reform, and this concern had been strengthened by lessons learned from earlier parliamen-tary debates in the United Kingdom and other Australian states where immutability had allowed politicians to maintain their predominantly hostile attitudes to homosex while still supporting reform. The result was that in drafting the Communication, the TGLRG avoided any discussion of biological or genetic immutability theories as arguments for sexuality being deemed a protected status:

> The women who joined [TGLRG] had mainly rejected the immutability view [and as a result] we have always tried to steer away from having a particular view. The very crude dichotomies that were put forward about born or made, we tried to steer clear of them altogether, we said we just didn't know and that wasn't the point.[51]

The UNHRC disregarded this silence and filled in the blanks itself, using European 'precedent' to decide that reference to 'sex' in the ICCPR includes sexual orientation. There was no necessity for the decision to be made on this basis, and the reliance on those decisions incorporated a simultaneous deploy-ment of tolerance and disgust which the TGLRG had specifically sought to avoid. The reliance on the natural/unnatural binary of homo/het is not surprising in light of the dominance of this explanation for homosex, but the deliberateness with which these grounds were incorporated – at the expense of using as guidelines for the decision the actual criteria in article 17 of the ICCPR (which are not based on biological or genetic grounds) – makes clear the difficulties in assuming that progressive strategies will be heard or followed.

In fact, immutability and disease were incorporated within the strands of the Tasmanian debates rather than distanced from homosex, and the overwhelming need to emphasize the measures taken to protect (boy) children from the seductive impulses of adult homosexuals was as strong in Tasmania and federal Australian parliaments in 1994–7 as it was in the United Kingdom in 1954.

Both the federal and eventual Tasmanian legislation exist firmly within the realms of privacy and constitute attempts to silence homosex rather than to recognize the more complex interpretations of the construction of sexuality which the TGLRG had been trying to achieve:

This bill does not do more than remove criminal sanctions against consenting private adult sexual conduct by homosexuals. It leaves all the other laws in place to protect young people from sexual interference and abuse, and also other people, regardless of age, from unwanted sexual advance and assaults. It changes no law with regard to paedophilia. It repeals section 122 of the criminal code while maintaining beastiality as a crime.[52]

There are strong educational reasons for leaving those sections in place. A considerable majority of people in Tassie understand the consequences in our community from a health and moral point of view of promoting a lifestyle which I think any person in our community would agree is not natural and is certainly not healthy. It is often said that homosexual people ... are that way because they cannot be changed ... There are some things which I believe are not said but quite clearly are natural and other things which are clearly unnatural and I believe that what we are talking about is an unnatural act and one that is prurient to me ... one which is proven to be unhealthy.[53]

We must put in place laws which will democratically protect our society. We need a health education program in schools and more must be done at all levels to discourage people from adopting a homosexual lifestyle ... we need protection for our young people. Steps must be taken to ensure that the protection is in place and that homosexual lifestyles will not be promoted or displayed in the public arena. Although it is denied by the gay and lesbian rights movement that they do not [sic] have an agenda to promote the homosexual lifestyle, I believe that they do.[54]

In addition, it has to be recognized that the TGLRG had no real control over the outcome of the legislation; the success of the reform, when it finally came in 1997, depended on one vote – so unpredictable that the politician concerned declared he literally only made up his mind after listening to all of the debates on the night.[55] It is important also to reflect on just how close (again, one vote) Tasmania came to attaching a preamble to its legislation even more regressive and prohibitive than that which graces the Western Australian legislation.[56]

Finally, there is a strong argument to be made that the public recognition of the validity of TGLRG's claims was somewhat different than what the group intended.[57] It is certainly true that the UN case exists as an example of the TGLRG deploying force rather than persuasive action. The decision acted not by changing the minds of Tasmanian politicians or the public ('if we had started off with the view that politicians were the important focus then we could never have gotten anywhere'[58]) about the value of their arguments – that homosex was a valid alternative or that the discrimination that they sought to expose was illegitimate – but by fostering anxieties about the view of Tasmania from outside:

> I am sick and tired of the snide remarks and the very bad publicity that comes over television programs and radio programs, both state based and nationally based, about the Tasmanians and, snigger snigger, their laws regarding homosexual activity.[59]
>
> Are we going to be viewed as a cultured tolerant and liberal community, or do we reinforce the two-heads, hick image that tarnishes Tasmania's image at the moment...[60]

I would argue that the strong community resistance, for example, to safer sex education, and the exclusion of gay sexuality in the public school sex-education curriculum, are indicators of a failure to substantially challenge many of the prejudices which have made up the bulk of decriminalization debates for the past 40 years. The fact that there remains a feeling in the Tasmanian community that once decriminalization has been achieved the issue of gay law reform is complete is another indicator of this:

> People keep coming up to the market stall now and ask 'what are you still doing here? It's all over now...'. As if the criminal law is the only part of gay liberation.[61]

Although the TGLRG may argue that it would not have accepted legislation such as that enacted in Western Australia, once the matter was taken up on a federal level, the end result was substantially out of its hands: there could easily have been a repeat of the Western Australia legislation – which has not been amended irrespective of the federal legislation. The danger – that legislation is much harder to change once the basic privacy concept has been encoded in law – remains as much the case in Australia as it does elsewhere.

On the other hand, this does not undermine the fact that it is the activism of TGLRG which is, ultimately, to be congratulated for ensuring the inclusion of homo within a new Tasmanian equation. Activists and politicians alike were forced to ask, during the United Nations case and in the aftermath of that decision, whether Tasmania was a state that could make its own laws or one which could have a legislative agenda forced on it unwillingly by outsiders. Should it change its mind about reform simply because the rest of the world was now watching? The issue became how Tasmania wished to be viewed through the looking glass: was Tasmania to be seen as a tolerant and democratic state or as a repressive state intent on hanging on to a colonial past where repression and intolerance of difference had been forced on, and then embraced by, Tasmanian society. Without the constant spotlight of attention directed by the TGLRG and the international and national media, it is doubtful that these questions could have been successfully addressed.

CONCLUSION

Homosex decriminalization debates in other Australian states and in the United Kingdom and Canada have tended not to explicitly engage with the relationship between legalizing homosex and social change. In those other, earlier debates, supporters of law reform argued explicitly on the basis of privacy, a formal legal right that they argued would change nothing at all: homosex would be kept in control by universal disapproval and the compulsory acquisition of privacy/secrecy.

Conservative politicians in Tasmania have argued that going outside for help was fundamentally un-Tasmanian and constituted part of a huge international fabian socialist conspiracy which made victims of all Tasmanians. The TGLRG argued in response that by empowering themselves with whatever tools existed, they were enabling Tasmania to move beyond its historical baggage and to change for the better.[62] They have argued that they sought to do much more than reform the criminal law by invoking privacy; indeed they have argued that they were not interested in privacy at all. And further, they have argued that as a result of their different approach, the furore surrounding gay law reform had very little if anything to do with gay law reform itself, that it was instead about Tasmania making a break with its repressive colonial past and actively embracing social change.

Obviously, making these sophisticated analyses and linking systemic harms to institutional powers is a very important part of an education programme aimed at social change. However, the Tasmanian experience demonstrates the difficulty in having these claims heard. While the group kept a clear focus on law reform as a site for continued conversation, I have argued that the group was not able to escape the seductive power of law reform: the symbolic importance of changing the law was seen to outweigh the potential dangers of engaging in legal processes. Thus, while the eventual legislation in Tasmania was equal to the best yet to be seen in Australia, the debates and the votes show how close the Tasmanian politicians came to enacting legislation that would have made a mockery of TGLRG aims and strategies.

That is, while the group rejected the view that making rights claims within the existing – and widely criticized – category of privacy reinforced traditional decriminalization patterns, arguing instead that by using privacy as a strategic tool it gained access to fora which would otherwise have been denied it, the platform on which the TGLRG hoped to reproduce its case for genuine and far-reaching social change has only been tentatively embraced. The quality of the parliamentary debates is not noticeably more accepting of homosex as a valid, equal and publicly acknowledged Tasmanian social category than those which came before them.

Still, in the final analysis, it has to be acknowledged that Tasmania now has the most progressive anti-discrimination legislation in the country, as well as an equal age of consent. While the actual text of the UN decision did not achieve the link between institutional power and systemic harm that the TGLRG had sought, and while parliamentarians may have 'given in' rather than actively embraced change, it is arguable that the overt linking of homosex to community identity and issues of social transformation is – if impossible to predict – still a worthwhile project.

4

REWRITING DESIRE

THE CONSTRUCTION OF SEXUAL IDENTITY IN LITERARY AND LEGAL DISCOURSE IN POST-COLONIAL IRELAND[1]

PATRICK HANAFIN

INTRODUCTION

The Irish legal imaginary reflects and recalls notions of the Irish national imaginary. Transitions in the conceptualization of the national imaginary will thus be reflected at the level of the legal imaginary. In this chapter I examine why lesbians and gay men have been for so long excluded from full communion with Irish selfhood and analyse the extent to which the legal construction of homosexuality has changed as conceptions of the national imaginary have been transformed. Drawing on the links between legal and literary discourse, this chapter seeks to determine the way in which law draws on dominant notions of national identity in order to name included and excluded identities. As Darian-Smith has noted: 'Law, alongside climate, geography, history and cultural practices, shapes the mythological imaginary of any one nation's ... identity'.[2] The included subjects of Irish law in the post-colonial period have been male and heterosexual.[3] The *grundnorm* that is the Irish Constitution of 1937 was an exclusionary document which enshrined in law the then prevailing notions of a homogeneous Irish self.

In psychoanalytic terms, the Irish self that was posited by the post-colonial elite was pure and clean, expelling what it considered to be 'impure' elements. In this sense, it conforms to Kristeva's notion of abjection, which she describes as the process by which the subject attempts to expel the unclean or impure elements of its corporeal existence.[4] However, the abject can never be fully excluded. It is that element which is rejected but from which one does not or cannot part. Thus, the subject is aware that it is impossible to exclude the abject completely. It is this awareness which leads to the sensation of abjection in the subject. Looking at the national subject created by the post-colonial elite, it is clear that 'impure' elements were to be excluded from the Irish body politic. It was this delimitation of an Irish subject which made possible an Irish sexual identity in the Symbolic. To paraphrase Grosz: 'the abject is both a necessary condition of the subject, and what must be expelled or repressed by the subject in order to attain identity and a place within the symbolic'.[5] McClintock has extended Kristeva's notion of abjection to include within its compass socially excluded groups such as, for example, women, gays and lesbians.[6] It is my contention that the construction by the post-colonial elite of a subject of national self-identification entailed the rejection or expulsion of certain groups from the national family. The result in terms of the notion of a national sexual identity was that lesbians and gay men were marked as being socially abjected groups. This notion of abjection was reflected at the level of the national narrative.[7] The national narrative posited an idea of a pure Irish self, uncontaminated by colonial or other polluting forces. By viewing, as Bhabha does, the post-colonial nation as narrative, one is enabled to go beyond a mere description of political and social institutions,[8] to explore how:

> the nation is articulated in language, signifiers, textuality, rhetoric. It emphasises the difference between the nation as a set of regulations, policies, institutions, organizations and national identity – that is nation as culture ... It offers a perspective that enables us to enter discourses beyond those fixed, static, 'official' ones.[9]

The traditionalist narrative enunciated by the postcolonial elite aimed as Valente has put it:

> at securing a home not only in the sense of a self-determining Irish nation but in the sense of a stable, cohesive, more or less monolithic community organized around a single value and belief system ... an Ireland purged of internal dissonance, not to say difference, as well.[10]

This chapter questions the fiction of Irish sexual identity constructed in the early post-colonial period. It also attempts to draw a parallel between the fictional national narrative encapsulated in legal texts and the representations of lesbians and gay men in literary texts. Declan Kiberd's experiment in linking the literary and the political in an attempt to imagine new conceptions of Irishness provides a preliminary framework for my experiment in linking the literary and the legal as a means of drawing out the ways in which sexuality has been imagined in the emergent Irish state.[11] The link which I want to make is that the literary conception of Irishness provided a powerful anchoring point for the manner in which Irish citizenship was to be imagined in legal terms in the post-colonial state. This occurred as the result of the privileging of a particular literary and philosophical conception of Irishness. Prager has termed this strain of cultural thought the Gaelic-Romantic tradition.[12] The Gaelic-Romantic tradition constructed a version of Irishness in which Ireland's identity:

> was to be found in its rural character. The sanctity of the family was to be preserved, the [Roman Catholic] Church was to remain a central social institution second only to the family, and the farm was to serve as the backbone for a healthy, thriving society.[13]

The foregoing leads one to ask the question, if literary conceptions of the nation can be appropriated in the service of imposing a repressive form of collective subjectivity can alternative literary projections of identity and in particular sexual identity be harnessed to create a more fluid notion of what Ireland means? To quote Kristeva:

> national literature could ... become not the expression of the people's enigmatic intimacy but a charmed space where irony merges with seriousness in order to lay out and break up the changing outlines of the totally discursive being, which, when all is said and done, constitutes the nation.[14]

In this sense, cultural representations of Irish identities are important in dispelling the long-standing myths of an authentic Irish self. As Kiberd has observed:

> the forms evolved by Irish artists ... can be seen as answering questions which have not yet been fully asked in the more conventional political sphere.... Their texts thus become the signposts standing on a shattered road to a future.[15]

Irish societal narration of sexuality has been transformed in recent years. This shift announces itself in the manner in which lesbian and gay voices are represented at the level of legal and cultural discourse. What has been most striking in the Irish context is the presence of legal constructions of homosexuality but the absence of explicit literary engagement with sexual identity, a gap which has only in recent times begun to be filled.[16] In the late colonial and early post-colonial periods, literary representations of homosexuality were largely implicit in the works of writers as diverse as James Joyce, Flann O'Brien, Eva Gore-Booth and Padraic Pearse. One writer in this period who did engage in a more open manner with lesbian and gay themes was Kate O'Brien, although by today's standards her approach may seem subtle not to say coy.[17] Contemporary Irish gay and lesbian writing is more visible and confident.[18] Revisions in the notion of the national subject have led to a situation where the naming of lesbians and gay men as socially abjected groups is itself being reversed.

THE LAW AS (TEXTUAL) PROJECTION OF A
NATIONAL SEXUAL NARRATIVE

The Irish legal imaginary has been influenced by a notion of authentic Irishness which has had the effect of alienating many groups which did not fit into this pre-cast mould. The construction of postcolonial Irish citizenship by the new ruling elite was, to a large degree, a reaction against the colonial construction of Irishness. Ireland, like other colonies, was homologized as a submissive partner in the imperial compact. In this sense, Ireland was visualized as female or effeminate.[19] The colonial narrative of sexuality provided the impetus for Irish nationalists to resist such strategies of representation. This led to the propounding of the ideal of a pure pre-colonial heterosexual state, which had been contaminated by the colonial invader. The late-colonial period following the Labouchere Amendment to the Criminal Law (Amendment) Act 1885 and the trial of Oscar Wilde was one in which homophobia became endemic.[20] In Ireland, nationalists deployed homophobia strategically as a propaganda weapon. In the Dublin Castle 'scandal' of 1884, rumours of a homosexual 'ring' in Dublin Castle, the centre of power of the colonial administration, led the Irish Home Rule MP Tim Healy to write an article in the Home Rule journal *United Ireland* hinting at this 'scandal'. Thus, the colonized attempted to turn the tables on the colonizer by calling into question at the symbolic level the masculinity of the colonial power. As a result, the homophobia of the period became a tool in the hands of Irish nationalists, while making it impossible to equate homosexuality with the nationalist ideal of Irishness. This strain of thinking was to persist beyond colonial times.

The post-colonial elite accepted the Victorian morality of their colonial predecessors and ensured that the legal construction of homosexuality was to remain unchanged, with the extant legislation outlawing same-sex relations, namely sections 61 and 62 of the Offences Against the Person Act 1861 and section 11 of the Criminal Law (Amendment) Act 1885, remaining on the statute books of the new state. This legal model was instantiated in a period when the construction of homosexuality in disciplinary knowledges was being pioneered.[21] The official policy in relation to 'moral' issues in the immediate post-colonial period, being influenced by Roman Catholic dogma, had much in common with the hypocritical Victorian morality which preceded it. A certain idea of the natural was to be upheld and those who did not accord with it were to be regarded as Other. Male homosexuality was represented in legal discourse, albeit in a negative manner. Lesbians were omitted from official discourse and did not even receive the dubious honour of being constructed as criminals. As one Irish politician has observed, the fact that there were no laws against female same-sex relations did not imply that such behaviour was condoned by Irish society. Rather, the 'taboo status of lesbianism functions as an unwritten law, suppressing not only the practice of lesbian sexuality but the awareness of its very existence.'[22]

The patriarchal and homophobic colony was merely replaced in post-colonial times by a patriarchal and homophobic independent state. Yet the new state sought, via the medium of official rhetoric, to distance itself from its former colonial incarnation. The new Ireland was free of contaminating colonial cultural influences. It was born again out of the ashes of anti-colonial and civil wars into a pure uncontaminated state of nature. This rhetoric of the post-independent state configured anything 'unnatural' with the colonial power. What was 'unnatural' of course was dependent on what the Roman Catholic Church, the new arbiter of post-colonial morality, deemed against the laws of nature. Thus, the new body politic of post-independent Ireland was to be heterosexual and God-fearing and always wary of the vile and contaminating practices of foreigners, particularly the British. As one commentator has observed: '[the] Irish nation . . . is heterosexual. Only descent from corrupting, imperial outsiders such as the English (especially the English), could make an Irish person gay.'[23] This heterosexualization of the post-colonial state in the official texts of law and politics was a strategy of disassociation from Ireland's submissive and feminized role in the colonial relationship. It was an attempt to repress the country's past humiliation at the hands of the imperial power, and to reassert the nation's manhood in the homosocial locker-room ambience of interstate relations.

This attempt to be a straight nation could not entirely repress a hidden homoerotic tendency. To control this unruly tendency or sign of post-colonial weakness, the new elite attempted to suppress feminized sexualities in official discourse. From now on Ireland was to be the dominant partner, the patriarch who sublimated all 'unnatural' desires in order to be the model heterosexual state. However, this new model patriarch was riddled with doubts and contradictions, which were manifested in a rage against those he loved. Thus, the repressed patriarch configured with the repressive patriarchal state, preventing the expression of dissonant or disturbing views or of alternative identities. Hofheinz has further elaborated on this parallel between the patriarchal state and the weak patriarch in his study of the powerless patriarch in the fiction of James Joyce. For Hofheinz:

> Joyce's fallen patriarch configures in terms of the Irish Free State because the State institutionalized the patriarchal social philosophy of Catholic Ireland through a long series of prescriptive laws culminating in de Valera's constitution of 1937 . . . . The Free State thereby enshrined as law the predicament that appears again and again throughout Joyce's fiction: Irish homes in which fathers crippled with alcoholism, impotence, and rage beat, neglect, or drive their wives into states of enervation and despair and throw their children to the wolves. Joyce agreed with de Valera that the foundation of Ireland is the patriarchal family, but that concept for him was laced with horror and outrage.[24]

The law therefore acted as an enforcer of an ideal of the heteropatriarchal family unit and imposed a repressed uniformity. Thus, the appellation Free State took on an ironic resonance. The new state created a mythology of Gaelic hypermasculinity as a direct reaction against this perceived trace of colonial effeminacy.[25]

Moreover, the masculine nature of Irish nationalism tended to deny recognition of other groups within the nationalist cause.[26] This creation of liminal groups such as women, gays and lesbians in official post-colonial discourse led to a rather problematic conception of Irish identity. The official construction of Irish identity was skewed along lines of gender, sexuality and ethnicity, thus recreating the colonial moment. The dawn of a new nation was nothing of the sort but a form of colonial mimesis. In fact the liminal groups of colonial Ireland were to become the liminal groups of post-colonial Ireland. The treatment of liminal groups in post-colonial Irish discourse follows McClintock's description of their treatment in colonial discourse:

> the dangers represented by liminal people are managed by rituals that separate the marginal ones from their old status, segregating them for a time and then publicly declaring their entry into their new status. Colonial discourse repeatedly rehearses this pattern – dangerous marginality, segregation, reintegration.[27]

Thus, in the post-colonial period, the new regime created another form of subjection, this time to a native ruling class rather than to the imperial power. The case of Ireland was similar in this respect to other decolonizing states.[28] However, the Irish case differed subtly from other post-colonial contexts. The Irish were literally 'not white/not quite' to use Bhabha's term. They were caught in the double bind of being a metropolitan colony treated with contempt by both the imperial power and fellow victims of colonialism. As Cheng has noted, the Irish were:

> essentialised as racially Other by the English imperial self, but denied the fraternity of victimhood by non-white colonials ... in short, caught in a postcolonial no-man's land, carrying no identity card within the identity politics of postcolonial discourse.[29]

This does not imply that post-colonial discourse is inapplicable in the case of Ireland, but rather complicates the notion of post-colonialism to be applied in the Irish context. As one commentator has pointed out in this regard:

> Ireland's experience of colonialism/postcolonialism does not have to mirror or reflect other countries' experience of this condition. 'Just as the island was one of the first colonies in the modern sense, so we may be witnessing in modern Ireland the conditions for the emergence of the world's first truly postcolonial state.' Ireland does not have to play 'catch-up'; instead Ireland leads the way.[30]

In terms of sexual identity the close relationship of the feminized Irish Other to the male colonial power led to a new puritanism in the post-colonial Irish state. The post-colonial Irish sexual self was to be pure and chaste as opposed to the libidinous and philandering former ravisher. This new asceticism was the basis for the expulsion of all impure elements from the Irish body politic and the creation of socially abjected groups based on sexual identity.

HIBERNIA'S HIDDEN HOMOEROTICISM

The expulsion of gays and lesbians from political and legal discourse was reflected in cultural terms by the marginal position occupied by homoerotic themes in the literary canon. This is not to say that such narratives did not exist but lay hidden in literary discourse. Homoerotic writing existed as a form of oppositional discourse often so subtle as to go undetected. In the works of James Joyce, the issues of sexuality and nationhood are discussed and indeed Joyce was one of the few writers of the late colonial period to treat homosexuality in his works.[31] Even within Joyce's work, treatment of homosexuality is passing. However, as David Norris has noted, the very fact that there are even glancing references to homosexuality in his work is significant in a period when there was widespread ignorance and intolerance of gays and lesbians.[32] The fact that gay and lesbian themes were rare in Irish literature of the early post-colonial period did not imply their non-existence. Thus, even the exemplar of Irish masculinist nationalist writing, Padraic Pearse, wrote homoerotic verse.[33] In his poem 'Little Lad of the Tricks' this undertone is apparent:

Lad of the grey eyes
that flush in thy cheek
would be white with dread of me
could you read my secrets.[34]

In Pearse one can see at the level of the individual the repression of homosexual desire which was to be reflected at the level of the post-colonial state. Other verse forms such as the song poetry of the eighteenth and nineteenth centuries were also a subtle means of expressing same sex desire. Lilis O'Laoire has observed that such song poetry lent itself to communicating encoded homoerotic messages in a society where direct expression of such desire was difficult.[35]

Sublimated lesbian desire was to be found in the works of Eva Gore-Booth. Writing in the late nineteenth and early twentieth centuries against the backdrop of the Celtic Revival in Irish literature, Gore-Booth subverted in a discreet way this tradition by introducing lesbian themes into her reworking of Celtic myths. In her play, *The Triumph of Maeve* she disrupts the traditional reading of the legends of the Celtic heroines Maeve and Niamh in order to create an image of an utopian lesbian encounter beween the two:

For thee Maeve left her kingdom and her throne,
And all the gilded wisdom of the wise,
And dwelt among the hazel trees alone
So that she might look into Niamh's eyes.[36]

This subtle subversion of the Celtic Revivalist tradition is all the more significant as the writers of the Celtic Revival such as Yeats and Pearse were the source
of dominant notions of hypermasculinity and idealized Irishness. This demonstrates that within the context of a homophobic society, the medium of literature
was important for the expression of societally prohibited desires. These writings
thus had a political value reflecting Jonathan Dollimore's point that the representation of homosexuality in literature is always political in that it affects the freedom or otherwise of lesbians and gay men 'who or what they are, or are allowed
to be, even the question of whether they survive or die, metaphorically,
spiritually, and literally.'[37]

CONSTITUTIONALIZING SEXUAL ABJECTION: THE LIMITS OF THE LEGAL IMAGINATION

In post-colonial legal discourse, the idea of an authentic subject of Irish law was
evident. This was particularly so in the Irish Constitution of 1937, which set the
limits of the Irish legal imagination. As Hutchinson has observed, Eamon de
Valera, the primary framer of the Constitution of 1937, 'formulated the
political framework for an autarchic ascetic Gaelic Ireland of rural communities,
whose destiny was to continue the religious mission of its medieval forebears to
a profane world.'[38] This was contained within the framework of a document
whose philosophical basis was heavily indebted to the Natural Law theory of
Thomas Aquinas. As Manganiello has put it: 'In de Valera's new constitution
Irish independence is associated with the Christian redemption, for the constitution embraced in part the theocratic notion of the State.'[39] The constitutional
text conveyed in legal form the framer's conception of the Irish socio-political
imaginary. This process exemplifies how the socio-political imaginary can be
transformed:

> by monopolistic elites into a mystificatory discourse which serves to
> uncritically vindicate the established political powers. In such instances, the
> symbols of a community become fixed and fetishized; they serve as lies.[40]

The centrality of the notion of the heteropatriarchal family unit was enshrined
in the 1937 Constitution. It relied heavily on the national narrative of familial-
ism which was a residue of nineteenth century notions of Irishness.[41] In so doing
it created a hierarchy within the family and between the family and other social
bondings. A disproportionate amount of power was ceded to the father figure
within this model. A paternalistic leader whose traditionalist ideas of society
and the family were translated into public policy governed the Irish national
family. Post-colonial Ireland fits into Kiberd's model of patriarchy which he
defines as 'the tyranny wrought by weak men, the protective shell which guards
and nurtures their weakness.'[42] The conception of the family given constitutional
recognition excluded same-sex relationships and heterosexual relationships not
based on marriage. This metaphor of the ideal family in its double sense, that of

the Irish family as essentialized group identity and as the formal legal arrangement based on marriage, exposes an intolerance of difference. This familial fallacy
shrouded the reality of liminality in Irish society.

In recent years this familial fallacy has been challenged at many levels. One
indication that this model of the family no longer endures is the recent
introduction of divorce legislation. It mirrors the change in the status of the
family in another culturally Catholic region, Quebec, where, as Stychin writes:
'the family as public/national institution has become a site with no essential role
or obvious conditions of membership by which lesbians and gays can be
excluded.'[43]

The practical ramifications of the rather narrow notion of sexual citizenship
reflected in the constitutional text were made explicit in the case of *Norris v
Attorney-General* [1984] IR 36. The plaintiff in this case claimed that the extant
legislation that criminalized same-sex activity was incompatible with the constitutional rights of gay men to equality, privacy and freedom of expression. This
challenge was rejected by the Irish Supreme Court. The majority in the Supreme
Court was not prepared to accept that the rights of individual males to engage in
same-sex activity on a consensual basis was compatible with the ethos of the Irish
Constitution of 1937. The then Chief Justice, O'Higgins CJ, listed a number of
specious and homophobic reasons as to why homosexuals should not enjoy the
equivalent constitutional rights enjoyed by heterosexuals. These reasons included
the unsubstantiated assertions that decriminalization of consensual homosexual
behaviour would lead to a rise in the amount of homosexual activity, that such a
change in the law would weaken the institution of marriage and that it would also
lead to an increase in the incidence of sexually transmitted diseases.

These arguments were supplemented by an even less plausible appeal to
'traditional' constitutional values. This reflected the tradition imposed by the
notion of national narration that infiltrated the constitutional text. However,
the parallel reality of society did not reflect this view. The proponents of the
dominant discourse were blind to this reality. The Chief Justice was of the view
that the adoption of the Constitution did not render inoperative the legislation
criminalizing homosexual acts. He argued:

> When one considers that the conduct in question had been condemned
> consistently in the name of Christ for almost two thousand years and, at
> the time of the enactment of the Constitution, was prohibited by the laws
> in force in England, Wales, Scotland and Northern Ireland, the suggestion
> becomes more incomprehensible and difficult to accept.[44]

These ill-supported conceptions of homosexuality betray a certain wilful
ignorance on the part of the elite on such matters. It also reflected a culture of
the 'blind eye' that was endemic in Irish society. Gay men and lesbians existed
in Irish society but no effort would be made to give official recognition to that
fact save in criminal legislation which ironically gave legal recognition to gay
men, albeit in a negative sense. Thus, as Yoshino notes: 'under this formulation,

homosexuality is regulated through a discourse of ignorance by regulators who do not need to understand it. This can be seen in the way homosexuality often is framed through preiteration: that is, the mention of a term only to dismiss it.'[45] In a newspaper article written some years after the *Norris* decision, O'Higgins, who had then retired from the bench, justified the majority judgment in the following terms:

> The question merely was whether an Act passed by the British parliament in the previous century was carried over into our law as being compatible with the Constitution. But what do you find in the Constitution? You find a whole Pauline tract, the whole Christian Preamble. This is Dev's Constitution. He'd be turning somersaults in his grave if he were told – 'Do you know that your Constitution has been held to prohibit laws criminalising buggery?'[46]

This view prevents the development of the Constitution in line with paradigmatic shifts in society. Rather it imposes a particular moral view on individual citizens. Ronald Dworkin has referred to this model of constitutional interpretation as creating a 'constitution of detail'.[47] Under this model, Dworkin observes, what is created is 'a collection of independent historical views and opinions unlikely to have great unity or even complete consistency.'[48] As a result, one would be confined to a narrow literalist view of the Constitution that is far from dynamic. As Dworkin puts it, such a model would express 'only the very specific, concrete expectations of the particular statesmen who wrote and voted for them.'[49] This model of constitutional interpretation favours the traditionalist national narrative, with its restricted notion of national identity.

Proponents of this model argue that the Constitution as enacted in 1937 recognizes the superiority of divine law and, as such, any legal provisions or constitutional amendments which conflict with the ideals of natural law are invalid, even if they are technically in agreement with the provisions of the Constitution.[50] This approach echoes the view of the American constitutional theorist Walter Murphy, who has argued that the Constitution, correctly understood, expresses a vision sufficiently coherent that amendments that are radically incompatible with that vision may not be regarded as law.[51] The vision of Irish national identity projected by constitutional discourse will be determined by the particular interpretative strategy adopted by the Supreme Court in its deciphering of constitutional meaning. The failure of the Supreme Court to imagine a more inclusive model of sexual citizenship in the *Norris* case demonstrated the limits of the traditional conception of the Irish legal imaginary.

SUB(VERTING) LIMINALITY: RE-IMAGINING THE NATIONAL SELF

The self of post-colonial Ireland is not the authentic Gael of revivalist discourse. The attempt by the elite of the early post-colonial state to impose a notion of

authentic Irishness began to unravel with the growth of groups expressing
alternative notions of Irishness. As Bowman has noted:

> Such processes of division and fragmentation do, after all, assert what
> Laclau and Mouffe refer to as 'the impossibility of society' and threaten to
> set in play the dissolution of the national imaginary and thus the
> disintegration of the nation itself.'[52]

Groups who challenge the so-called homogeneous sense of nationhood are thus
faced with a difficult task. In order to extricate the state from this destructive
search for an authentic self, one must reimagine the national narrative. This
involves reinterpreting the dominant narrative of a perceived homogeneous Irish
identity and allowing groups previously thought of as abject to be accepted as
part of a heterogeneous sense of self. The way in which this process occurs is
redolent of Sunstein's notion of law's 'expressive function.'[53] Law's 'expressive
function' refers to the way in which law expresses social values and encourages
social norms to move in particular directions. However, the values which
law expresses are not necessarily fixed for all time and may change as societal
norms and values change. Thus, when a society experiences a 'norm cascade',
that is, a rapid shift towards new norms, such norm shifts may be expressed in
legal discourse.[54]

The growth of social movements positing new notions of the national
narrative has led to a move towards change in social and legal constructions of
sexuality in Ireland.[55] This process leads to a tropological tension between
traditional models of Irishness and emerging forms of post-national Irish-
ness(es). The failure of the Supreme Court in the *Norris* case to accept the more
inclusive model of Irish sexual citizenship put forward by new social movements
led to an appeal to the European Court of Human Rights. In its decision in
Norris v Ireland (1991) 13 EHRR 186 the Court held that the national
legislation prohibiting consensual sexual activity between adult males constituted
an unjustified interference with the applicant's right to privacy under Article 8 of
the European Convention on Human Rights and Fundamental Freedoms. The
Irish legislature eventually introduced legislation in 1993 which decriminalized
consensual sexual activity between males of 17 years and over. The Act itself, the
Criminal Justice (Sexual Offences) Act 1993, as well as containing provisions
in relation to the decriminalization of same-sex relations between consenting
males, also contains strict provisions in relation to prostitution. This is ironic in
that the Labouchere Amendment was added to the Criminal Law (Amendment)
Act 1885 which likewise contained harsh provisions in relation to the control
of prostitution.

At the level of pragmatic politics, in order to steer the legislation successfully
through parliament, it was necessary to engage in a trade-off with more
conservative opinion. By including in the same piece of legislation more dracon-
ian police powers against sex-workers, the appetite of the moral majority could
be temporarily satiated. At a deeper level, it reflects a more worrying aspect of

postcolonial Irish society. In order for one socially abjected group to win greater legal recognition another such group must suffer. Thus, while gay men have received greater legal acceptance, the status of sex-workers as a socially abjected group is heightened. Therefore, so-called progressive Irish society must continue to have socially abjected groups against which the dominant group identity can define itself. Valente has described this process in the following terms:

> The symbolic surplus embodiment of the subaltern functions as the negative value upon which ... the entire ideological system hangs. On one side, the stereotyping association of various subaltern groups with the abject not only acts as a social sanction on the groups themselves ... but acts additionally as a social threat to other, more privileged groups, discouraging them from approximating too closely those styles of being. In this role, the stereotyping associations enforce the kind of repression that creates and sustains social norms. On the other side, these associations turn the same bodily styles and forms of behaviour into a kind of taboo or fetish and, in this role, they facilitate a certain return of the repressed.[56]

The revision of the legal model of same-sex relations reflects a subversion of liminality. Yet the irony remains that for certain marginalized groups to be included in the Irish legal narrative, another group must be further marginalized. This demonstrates that the liberal sexual agenda is far from being complete in contemporary Ireland. Moreover, the position of lesbians and gay men in the period since the passing of the 1993 Act remains far from ideal. The 1993 Act, while reducing the age of consent for male same-sex relations, remains silent as to the attitude of the criminal law to those males under the age of 17 who engage in same-sex activity. The Act does not specify whether public expressions of affection are included within the ambit of the legislation or whether its provisions apply only to the private sphere. While removing the legal stigma attached for so long to same-sex relations, the Act does not remove from Irish law the extant common law offences of conspiracy to corrupt public morals and outraging public decency. It therefore remains within the discretion of the police as to whether such offences will be deployed against gays in Ireland. In addition to the 1993 Act, other positive legislative changes have occurred. The Prohibition of Incitement to Hatred Act 1989 makes it a criminal offence to incite hatred on the basis, *inter alia*, of sexual orientation. The Unfair Dismissals (Amendment) Act 1993 includes sexual orientation as one of the prohibited grounds for dismissal.[57] However, the process of change is far from complete. While decriminalization is one step towards a more inclusive model of sexuality in Irish legal discourse, other areas such as employment equality and legal recognition of homosexual partnerships have yet to be tackled. Moreover, the fact that the construction of homosexuality in legal discourse has been substantially altered does not imply an immediate transformation in societal attitudes.

BEYOND THE LAW: VOICING QUEER DESIRE

To examine the manner in which legal change does not lead to immediate inclusion in the national imaginary, one must look beyond the legal text to the narratives of those who continue to be constructed as Other. The way in which sexuality is constructed in legal discourse is only part of the story. Bruce Smith has observed that literary discourse enables homosexual desire to be written.[58] Literary discourse allows individuals to voice their desire and, in the process, communicate how the construction of homosexuality by legal discourse affects them. The legal text tells a particular story about gay men and lesbians in a given society. In some cases, it perpetrates a myth about 'deviant sexualities'. The legal story is therefore incomplete and, in many cases, misleading.

The literary text allows for more of the story to be told. Literary discourse fills the gaps in legal discourse, which can only talk of sexual acts. In another sense, literature points the route to political change. Thus, literary texts become 'the signposts standing on a shattered road to a future'.[59] As Smith has noted, it is 'in the nature of moral, legal and medical discourse to deny contradictions by deciding alternatives one way or the other'.[60] Literary accounts mediate between the official ideal and the everyday reality. By looking at literary discourse one may discover the contradictions of law and perhaps find answers that point to a less exclusivist future. Thus, one should not look at the recent legal changes as the apogee of the struggle for the recognition of sexual diversity. Rather, one should note, as Ailbhe Smyth has done, that 'there are indeed many ways in which the everyday realities of Irish life give the lie to the shiny image of progress and modernism'.[61]

One writer who represents an attempt to give the lie to this shiny image and expose the rather flawed reality is the Irish language poet, Cathal O'Searcaigh. O'Searcaigh has appropriated the traditional form of song poetry but has subverted it to express an undisguised homoerotic theme. This, perhaps more than many other developments in Irish gay writing, exemplifies the new model of Irish sexual identity. The traditional tropes and symbols of Irish culture have been recuperated and are now used in a way that subverts their original use, i.e. in repressing sexually dissident groups. Moreover, the use of the Irish language itself is significant in a double sense. Firstly, O'Searcaigh has appropriated the language of the old revolutionary elite, an elite that saw no part in Irish society for the homoerotic voice. Second, the use of what has been, for many years, a moribund tongue to express new and exciting notions of identity is in itself a sign of a society where previously oppressed voices are being heard and alternative stories are being told. The use of gay fiction as a strategy may also have a positive political impact. As one commentator has expressed it: 'The disruptive potential of such writing is in the awareness of historical traditions of homo-erotic writing, and in the conscious use of these traditions to subvert hetero-sexual notions of the natural, the real and the authentic.'[62]

While subverting the traditional models, O'Searcaigh also expresses tellingly the position of the sexually Other in Irish society. Thus, in his poem 'The

Outcast', O'Searcaigh paints vividly and painfully the place of the cultural and
sexual outcast:

> They don't understand the ageing boy
> who composes all night long
> above the hills of Barr an Ghleanna.
> All he does is foolish
> they say below in the pub –
> resembling the white dog
> who gnaws the bone of the moon
> in the small water pools on the road.
>
>   But his songs will yet be
>   islands of hope and shelter
>   in the seas of their darkness
>
> Not for you sadly
>   to turn the peaty earth into good land
>   nor the celebration of Sunday like the rest
>   nor the love of neighbours on the day of tragedy
>   nor the cherishing of woman in the protection of marriage
>   nor the good company of the inn.
>
> For you sadly
>   the indelible mark of Cain
>   smeared on your forehead.[63]

This reflects the rather uneasy tension which still exists between traditional
notions of Irish identity and more inclusive notions of Irishness(es). As Petit has
observed: 'the comparatively recent phenomenon of an organised, "out" gay
consciousness in Ireland has yet to work its way fully through the culture of
Ireland.'[64] This tension is also reflected in contemporary Irish lesbian writing.
The work of Mary Dorcey expresses both utopian visions of lesbian desire and
the reality of homophobia which remains in contemporary Ireland. Dorcey's
story 'A Noise from the Woodshed' portrays the rapture of lesbian love. In this
story, lesbian love moves to the centre of literary discourse. It is not a peripheral
or hinted-at theme of the story. It is a celebration of the reality and normality of
lesbian love. As Anne Fogarty has observed:

> We are asked to recognise the commonplace nature of lesbian desire rather
> than its disquieting otherness. The noise from the woodshed becomes a
> metaphor for the joyous nature of female love and for its unquestioning
> embrace of the familiar and the unfamiliar alike.[65]

This celebration of lesbian desire in the title story of her collection does not
blind Dorcey to the problems of intolerance that lesbians continue to face in
Irish society. In 'A Country Dance', the two lovers become the focus of an

unwelcome homophobic gaze as they dance together in a rural dance hall. However, despite this lingering homophobia, lesbian desire acts as a counter to such threats. As Fogarty observes: '[a]lthough the Irish social world represents a constant threat to the well-being of Dorcey's protagonists, her narratives always open up new spaces of pleasure and fulfilment which coexist with the old, impossible, trivialising places.'[66] Thus, while the homophobic and the homoerotic continue to coexist in an uneasy relationship, one can state that the emergence of queer visibility in Irish culture has had the effect of producing a counter to the overwhelmingly repressive national narrative of an imposed (hetero) sexual identity. The reality of this increased visibility is not a retreat to an imagined homotopia of precolonial times but, rather, a desire to interrogate heterocentric Irish culture in an effort to create an Ireland more accepting of diversity. Such an aim may in itself be impossible, but it is in challenging intolerance and ignorance that shifts in societal attitudes to sexual difference may be effected.

CONCLUSION

The emergence of a gay legal and literary canon in Ireland is in itself part of this writing out of change. As well as the change at the political-symbolic level, the change must be consolidated at the level of ordinary discourse, as it were, by telling stories of ordinary lives dealing with extraordinary obstacles. Thus, the telling of stories both at the legal and at the literary levels contributes to visibility and acceptance. As Eskridge has noted: 'narratives can contribute to law's transformation by aggressively upsetting stereotypes.'[67] This will facilitate a move away from the previously dominant discourse on sexuality. The importance of improving the visibility of gay culture in Ireland cannot be overstated. The old culture of the 'blind eye' is still present at many levels of Irish society and is as resistant to change as ever. Thus, the changes at the level of legal discourse must be consolidated by an increased queer visibility at the cultural level. By portraying the reality of gay lives, individuals can refashion the old stories and (mis)representations of homosexuality in Irish cultural discourse.

At a more general level, this move away from the traditional model of an imposed model of Irishness is conducive to a more inclusive society. As Richard Kearney has observed:

> The 'representative' mode of imagination – where I represent myself as another – may serve to liberate us from narcissistic interests without liquidating our identity. The more people's standpoints I have present in my mind while I am pondering a given issue, and the better I can imagine how I would think and feel if I were in their place, the stronger will be my capacity for representative thinking.[68]

In a similar way, the narrative imagination serves as the precondition for a representative polity, where an inclusive idea of identity is favoured and not a particularistic one such as that to be found in the rhetoric of the founders of the state. The application of narrative identity to the question of Irish sexual identity may lead to what one commentator has described in the following terms:

> A critical fluidity and openness pertains to narrative identity as long as we recognize that it is always something made and remade. Hence, a society that willingly reconstitutes itself through a corrective process of ongoing narrative is as impervious to self-righteousness as it is to fundamentalism. Any temptation to collective solipsism is resisted by the imaginative tendency of narrative to freely vary worlds common to itself.[69]

Irish legal history has reached a point where the idea of inclusion of previously excluded identities is emerging. The rewriting of the legal narrative of sexual identity may be deemed to configure with an unravelling of the traditional narration of Irish identity. In decriminalizing male same-sex relations, the Irish legislature has reflected implicitly the recent 'norm cascades' in Irish society. By linking the law's 'expressive function' to norm shifts in society, the legislature has facilitated the expression of ideals and norms in legal discourse, which mirror more accurately the norms of contemporary Irish society. This move demonstrates that it is possible to replace the previously dominant national narrative of monolithic Irish (hetero)sexual identity by post-national narratives of sexual diversity and that it is possible to represent such narrative shifts at the level of legal discourse.

PART TWO

SEXUALITY AND CRIMINALITY

INTRODUCTION

The essays which comprise this section represent contrasting work in the area of sexuality and crime. All of the authors focus on the relationship between male 'homosexuality' and the criminal law. However, their emphasis is not on the 'traditional' doctrinal issues concerning how positive law has criminalized male same-sex practices, nor on how struggles for gay legal equality historically have focused on the repeal of such laws. Rather, these essays approach the issue of criminality differently.

Derek Dalton's contribution examines the construction of the gay male as a murderous, serial killer, and he weaves recent high profile Australian cases with an analysis of representations of 'homosexual' criminality in film. Adrian Howe's essay, by contrast, does focus on case law, but she analyses the way in which the law of provocation has been used as a defence by heterosexual men accused of violent crime perpetrated against gays. It is ironic that straight men have had some success in using this defence, at the same time that it has proven so difficult to deploy by heterosexual women accused of murdering their violent male partners.

Finally, Leslie Moran and Derek McGhee approach the issue of sexuality and criminality from an historical and geographical perspective, focusing on London. They analyse the ways in which urban space has been used to chart criminal male same-sex activity, as a mechanism for surveillance. Thus, these three essays provide diverse 'takes' on the continuing conjunction of 'sex' and 'crime'.

5

THE DEVIANT GAZE

IMAGINING THE HOMOSEXUAL AS CRIMINAL THROUGH CINEMATIC AND LEGAL DISCOURSES[1]

DEREK DALTON

INTRODUCTION: INDECENT EXPOSURES – TWO FILMIC VISIONS OF HOMOSEXUAL DESIRE

Despite the fact that cinema and law appear to be disparate representational media (encompassing the *projected image* of film and the *written word* of the law), they share a marked degree of complicity in positing the notion that male homosexuality is metonymous with and metaphorical for criminality.[2] They both deploy images and narratives which position a spectator to perceive homosexuality as irrevocably enfolded in the forms and idioms of criminality. In exploring the nexus between law and cinema, I wish to compare the film *Cruising* (1980, dir. William Friedkin) with the film *Swoon* (1992, dir. Tom Kalin). Whilst both films grapple with subject matter equating homosexuality with criminality and deviance, *Swoon* recuperates the homosexual subject from the realm of the pathologized and demonized (depicted archetypically in *Cruising*) and focuses on the integral yet so often overlooked aspect of characterization in films about homosexuality – desire. The stark contrast between the two films thus provides a productive site on which to explore the legal terrain of identity and subjectivity as it is mapped out through cinematic expression.

It has become evident that what we understand to be 'legal' is increasingly porous, signifying a symbiotic relationship between law and popular culture that cannot be ignored. The cultural/legal theorist John Denvir argues that films can be read as 'legal texts' and, like other more traditional legal sources (statutes, common law), films are cultural artefacts open to warring interpretations (like 'law' itself) which can provide worthwhile insights into how the law operates in

Cinema	Film image ⇒	Screened ⇒	Audience
Law	Target of law ⇒ (deviant person) object of law	Text (statute, trial and law report)	Audience (society and other lawyers)

Table 1 *Cinematic jurisprudence*

the world at large.[3] Furthermore, Denvir points out that film often uncovers aspects of law that traditional sources deny and, importantly, that film not only reveals law, it often creates the social reality to which legal institutions adapt.[4]

Consequently, law and cinema, as representational practices, are not so dissimilar as we might first think.[5] Jenni Millbank has presented a persuasive argument for why cinema is jurisprudence. She argues that legal judgments are texts that 'represent, and are themselves often translated back into popular culture in the form of news reports and, sometimes, movies.'[6] This translation of law into film is particularly evident in the film *Heavenly Creatures* (1994, dir. Peter Jackson) in which the screenwriter drew from trial transcripts to construct the filmic narrative that explored how two New Zealand teenage girls, Pauline Parker and Juliet Hulme, murdered Pauline's mother in 1954.[7]

Borrowing from Millbank, I have constructed a schema that details what I term cinematic jurisprudence (Table 1). In relation to a film's narrative, what appears on the screen (filmic images) is somewhat similar to how the law constructs its narratives.

Despite the fact that each discourse utilizes very different media to convey ideas pertaining to various aspects of homosexuality, both law and film deploy persuasive narratives. Film uses celluloid presented as entertainment. Law utilizes the printed text but is also reliant on the oral tradition of common law for the purposes of education, deterrence, retribution and rehabilitation. Furthermore, both discourses rely on the careful crafting of representations to support their particular position. That the two discourses operate in such a similar fashion is highlighted by Rosenberg's view that, in regard to the art of persuasion:

A filmmaker, much like a lawyer marshaling precedents, uses lighting, camera angles, mise-en-scene, and other cinematic devices to create what might be called a 'visual brief' to support his or her chosen ideological position.[8]

CRUISING – AN EXPLORATION OF CINEMA'S LORE OF HOMOSEXUAL DESIRE

Cruising plunges the viewer into the hard core leather 'underground' world of New York's East Village where an unknown killer is murdering gay men and dumping their bodies in the Hudson River. A young police officer, Steve Burns, is sent to penetrate this strange world and identify the killer. He goes 'undercover' by posing as a gay man interested in the leather scene. It is hoped that this will lure the killer to attack Steve, enabling the killer's identity to be revealed (which, not surprisingly, is what eventually happens). The 'undercover' operation is simultaneously an exploration of a homosexual 'underworld' and a study of the detective's search for the killer of gay men. The seeming link between the two elements of the 'undercover' operation is that the victims are identified as gay. Hence, the self-evident assumption that impels the film is simply: if the corpse is gay then one needs to investigate the gay subculture to solve the crime. But the riddle that captures the attention of the audience is the identity of the killer. For *Cruising* is essentially a whodunit.[9] The narrative of *Cruising* attempts to resolve this dialectic of victim and criminal by working to attach a homosexual intention to the dead bodies of gay men.[10] It shall be shown that the synecdochal use of the leather/SM scene (as distinctly separate from the 'normal' world) encourages spectators to read the wilful display of leather as a signifier of sexual deviance that invites, indeed provokes, violence.

In the documentary *The Celluloid Closet* (1996, dir. R. Epstein and J. Friedman) the screen writer Ron Nyswaner (who co-wrote *Philadelphia*) recounts how he and his partner were set upon and bashed in a frenzied attack by several men that occurred just after William Friedkin's controversial film *Cruising* was released.[11] During the unprovoked attack one of the men offered an explanation for the bashing: 'If you saw the movie *Cruising*, you'd know what you *deserve*.' He was clearly implying that the men *deserved* to die violently given that the film is essentially about a gay serial killer who murders other gay men. The explanation for the assault is located in the victim's perceived homosexual identity. Tomsen has noted that many hate crimes perpetrated against gay men in Australia invoke this notion that flaunting a homosexual identity merits assault.[12] What binds the narrative of the film to the phenomenon of anti-gay violence is a structure of representation. That structure is one in which the very display of homosexuality is the cause and justification for attacks on gay men. Therefore, both the film and homosexuality need to be understood as processes/structures of representation.[13]

Friedkin's realization that his film conveyed potently negative images of homosexuality prompted him to add a disclaimer to all prints of his film which read:

> This film is not intended as an indictment of the homosexual world. It is set in one small segment of that world, which is not meant to be representative of the whole.[14]

Yet the filmic images which follow the disclaimer demonstrate that even if the film is only taken to be representative of the 'part', it portrays this part as monstrous and pathologically deviant in the extreme. This is achieved through the deployment of synecdochal images which encourage the spectator to read the 'part' (the violent, bleak SM world of the leather man) as representative of the whole. This is achieved through the deployment of fetishistic images of leather as a potent signifier of deviant homosexuality to the exclusion of other images which might depict other (positive) aspects of the gay world. In *Cruising*, 'leather' operates as a synecdoche through which one reads the part (leather clad men) as representing the entirety of the homosexual world. In regard to the cinema, synecdoche is 'adjectival' in that it shows qualities in characters and operates as a metaphor for their condition. For the spectator, leather triggers a chain of associations that enables homosexuality to be equated with promiscuous sexuality, aggression, violence and danger. There is a causal relationship between leather and desire operating in *Cruising*. Leather functions as a signifier of the wearer's desire for sex with other men.[15] Desire is shown to work through the display of leather. What provokes desire is leather as a sign of violence (and even death). Hence, the sight of gay men clad in tight leather garments dancing together in close proximity sexualizes their appearance. In this sense, *Cruising* encourages spectators to perceive the victims who are murdered as having enticed the killer to 'read' their bodily displays as 'asking for it'; inciting a violent death. Through facilitating such a reading, *Cruising* admonishes gay men by insisting that, in allowing their (homo)sexuality to be made visible, they adopt an appearance that renders them vulnerable. The display of leather is imbued with an insidious veracity – for it decrees that the wearer is not only signalling the 'otherness' of his sexuality, but also that he is offering himself as a potential victim to the murderer at large.

Homosexuality in this film is analogous to vampirism and violence, and the obvious homosexual type appears in the guise of a modern day vampire.[16] This is aided by coding these vampiric characters with clothing of a suitably 'butch' hyper-masculine type (particularly leather gear) which acts as an immediate signifier of homosexuality and danger. The homosexual clubs are presented as dark, cavernous places, visually analogous to the vampire's lair. Steve, an undercover police officer, is frequently filmed descending stairs; plunging himself (and the audience) into the hellish underworld of the hard-core leather bar with its bizarre rituals.[17] And just as vampires can only come out at night, the film frames the men who frequent these clubs (particularly the killer) as requiring darkness in order to survive and operate. Indeed, all the killings occur at night and the refrain from a hard rock song alluding to a vampire searching for prey is heard after some of the murders occur: 'Well it's dangerous out here tonight, but a soul's got to eat'.

In *Cruising*, Stuart, the serial killer at large, is depicted as essentially vampiric in nature. He is shown to thrive on killing new victims in order to survive. In fact, the film's narrative is literally 'death driven' with violent murders carrying the narrative forward. Stuart's modus operandi (which Friedkin modelled on several real life Greenwich Village murders)[18] is centred around him luring his victims to a secluded place where he usually kills them in a fervent stabbing frenzy (the resultant blood linking the crime to vampirism) which is often presented as the culmination of gay sex. This linking of sex and death is not unique to cinematic representations. Discourses of law contain narratives which 'link sex to death and serve as modern parables about homosexuality and the threat of epidemic.'[19]

Perhaps the most disturbing aspect of *Cruising* is its positing of the notion that homosexual sex will ultimately culminate in death. This is often conveyed in the film, though to best effect in the scene where a fashion designer leaves Manhattan as the daylight is fading and drives to a seedy part of the West Village. He is shown entering a booth at a pornographic cinema to engage in sex with the killer. By juxtaposing the image of a gay man deriving pleasure from sex (on the screen within the screen) with the foregrounded image of a man being savagely stabbed to death, a crude equation is conveyed to the spectator.[20] That is, the ecstatic pleasure embodied in gay sex is shown as synonymous with the psychotic pleasure derived by the killer. The two things (murder and gay sex) are presented as equally monstrous. One equates to the other, and further-more, death or being murdered is shown as a natural and inevitable consequence of homosexual acts. In this sense, homosexuality is depicted as a precursory state which predisposes gay men to be victims or perpetrators of murderous acts.

THE FILM AS FRAME: THE FILTERING OF *CRUISING* THROUGH THE AUSTRALIAN LEGAL IMAGINATION

A second process through which meaning is attributed to the death of gay men is highlighted in legal discourse. My attention turns to the ways in which the representational structure inherent in various criminal trials attach homosexual intention to the death of gay men. Such a process sheds light on the porous or symbiotic relationship between law and popular culture.[21]

In an unreported Supreme Court of Victoria murder trial dated 1 September 1998, the idea that murder is a natural consequence of a homosexual sex act was explored in some depth. The defendant, Jamie Koeleman, claimed that killing a 60 year old gay man he met at a public toilet was like 'the Al Pacino movie *Cruising*'. Prosecutor Julian Leckie recited that Koeleman told a friend that he committed the stabbing murder to fulfil himself sexually and that he felt no remorse for the act. It was alleged that the victim, Francis Barry Arnoldt, was performing an oral sex act when the murder was committed.[22] In a secretly tape recorded conversation the accused told an undercover police officer that he 'experienced his most powerful orgasm during the killing'. Leckie said of the film's relevance to the case that 'the theme of the movie appears to be a sexually driven urge to kill'.[23] It was implied in court that the victim was partly to blame for his own death by placing himself in the vulnerable position of seeking to engage in a sexual act with a stranger in a public toilet. A mistrial led to this matter being retried in March 1999.

This retrial resulted in Koeleman being found guilty of the murder by a Supreme Court jury.[24] In sentencing Koeleman to 19 years imprisonment, Cummins J told him that on the surface he had a good character, but that it masked a deep and dark desire.[25] Such a comment adheres to the idea that homosexuality is a duplicitous state where an outwardly 'normal' appearance masks a hidden corruption. The judge spoke of the crime in terms of a sacrificial sexual desire:

> You had a deep desire – a fantasy – and that fantasy involved the sacrificing of another human being to your sexual desires. You decided one night in 1991 to go cruising, to select another homosexual, whose identity and right to life was of complete indifference to you, and to kill that person as part of a self-centred sexual experience by you.[26]

Cummins J recounted that, as Koeleman killed Arnoldt, he said: 'You like this, faggot?' – a comment which is reminiscent of the killer in *Cruising* tormenting his victims with the remark 'you made me do this'. The crime may well have gone unsolved had Koeleman not confessed to a friend after watching the film *Cruising*. In fact, Cummins J framed the confession itself as an aspect of Koeleman's 'continuing desire for excitation', explaining that Koeleman thought sharing his secret might sexually excite his friend.[27] When the friend subsequently informed police an undercover 'sting' operation was set up. In an event that emulated the climactic scene from the film *Cruising*, in which the killer lures the undercover officer Steve into Central Park, Koeleman took an undercover Victoria policeman who he 'believed shared the same warped desires' to the scene of the crime (a park) where he subsequently confessed.[28]

The very admissibility of the film *Cruising* in the Koeleman trials was a contentious issue. In the first trial, McDonald J allowed the prosecution to show the film to the jury in order to help give content and meaning to Koeleman's comments to homicide detectives and a witness that the killing was 'just like *Cruising*'.[29] The prosecution submitted that this reference was a 'simile'; the meaning of which could only be articulated by showing the film in court. Koeleman's possession of a videotape copy of the film on his premises and his comments were imputed to provide a genesis of the killing. In the retrial, Cummins J spoke of a number of 'discrete differences' between the film and the present case.[30] Despite the judge agreeing that it was proper that the prosecution should wish to extrapolate what, in an elliptical way, the simile 'just like *Cruising*' meant, he ruled that the film should not be shown. He said his primary reason to exclude showing the film was not one of relevance, but rather prejudice. Cummins J stated: 'it is a film that raises and inflames questions which are not part of the jury's function: questions of prevention, questions of recidivism, questions of law and order.'[31] Despite saying that *Cruising* is 'a film with significant impact', Cummins J said its screening in court would 'distract the jury from its limited task of deciding the case.'[32]

Most Melbourne newspaper reports attributed the motivation for the crime to an attempt by Koeleman to satisfy his homosexual desires. Indeed, Cummins J said that by killing the deceased during the act of oral sex, Koeleman achieved his very purpose: 'the confluence of sex and killing'.[33] In likening his murderous act to the film *Cruising*, Koeleman, however unwittingly, facilitated a reading of his crime that would be strengthened through comparisons with the disturbing cinematic narrative he invoked by naming the film. Thus, the film and the trials, fiction and reality, intersect to locate homosexual desire as evincing a terrible, murderous potential. In reading about the murder we are not enjoined to imagine Koeleman's stabbing frenzy. Instead we are invited to recall the stabbing scenes in *Cruising* to envisage the horror of the 'real' event. In any event, I would suggest that the distinction between the cinematic image of the homosexual murderer in *Cruising* and the 'real' homosexual murderer in the Koeleman case becomes immaterial. It matters only that they are perceived as indicating the same thing – that homosexual desire is precursory to the act of murder. As Young observes, the failure to distinguish semblance from substance is what 'marks the experience of criminality in ultramodernity.'[34] Such a failure may well account for the filmic murder and the actual murder being taken as the literal measure of the consequences of homosexual desire. In a newspaper report of the retrial of Koeleman, an image of two 'leather' men embracing accompanies the caption 'Murder plot: a scene from the film *Cruising*'. This is an incongruous pairing of a placid, homosocial image with a heading that attempts to ascribe a violent meaning to it. Its absurdity serves to remind us that the linking of homosexual desire to so-called 'plots of murder' obscures a simple but overlooked fact – homosexual desire is intrinsically an expression or avowal of love that is far removed from violence *per se*.

The milieu of the homosexual men in *Cruising* is the seedy subterranean clubs and parks they frequent at night, which is conveyed by the film's depiction of the homosexual's world as dark, bleak and obscured by shadows. In agreeing to go undercover, Steve is told by his Captain that the assignment is dangerous because he must go 'out there' to see if he can attract the killer. Steve replies 'out where?' and is told he must infiltrate the gay leather scene, which is 'a world unto itself'. Thus, the film presents the world as an enclave; one half inhabited by 'normal' heterosexual people, the other inhabited by the 'others' – the easily identifiable homosexual world of the SM clubs and bars.

In a club called 'Precinct 9', Steve is confronted with men dressed as police officers, his unease conveyed by his face registering shock at the sight of giant handcuffs, batons and the shrill sound of whistles blowing.[35] The audience is positioned to identify with Steve in feeling disconcerted and disgusted by this inversion of the 'real' plain clothes cop being confronted with men engaging in deviant sexual practices whilst masquerading as police. Steve is horrified at the sight of a man simulating fellatio with a baton and he is asked to leave the club because of his 'wrong attitude' to 'precinct night'. These men are not police officers, though their appearance (complete with mock uniforms and police paraphernalia like batons and handcuffs) does not immediately belie this fact.

This scene disturbs many viewers because it draws our attention to the role of performativity in collapsing the immediate distinction between what is 'real' and what is imitation. At the heart of this cultural anxiety that decrees that one must not emulate that which one is not, is the desire for predictability and reliability of gesture and bodily performance. These 'mock' police offend because, although they may superficially look extremely 'real', they don't behave like 'real' police.

By cavorting about dancing, embracing and exchanging desirous glances, they fail a presumed test of authenticity. In this sense they are doubly transgressive. They appear to be that which they are not and they behave in ways which contradict their appearance.

These false signs are very troubling to the law because social order is predicated on the ability to accurately identify who enforces the law. This has practical as well as symbolic implications, for reliance upon the appearance of law's agents enables access to the law. These 'pretend' police (who ritualistically appropriate the appearance of the law as part of their sexual culture) deeply disturb the law and its enforcers. This in turn explains the hostility directed by Victoria Police officers at patrons of Melbourne's 'Tasty Nightclub' during a police raid in 1994. In the club, the barmen and DJ were dressed as police; people danced behind prison style bars and a drag queen performed accompanied by six dancers dressed as 'boys and girls in blue'.[36] The subsequent strip searching of 463 patrons and staff exacerbated pre-existing tensions between the Victoria Police and the gay and lesbian community and gave rise to civil law suits from patrons who felt they had been unlawfully searched during the course of the raid.

The murder victims that the spectator witnesses in *Cruising* are all presented as having been lured to their deaths through the promise of sex. *Cruising* suggests that these men are partially to blame because they sought anonymous sex with a stranger.[37] The idea of gay men 'courting' death through a desire for sex is not restricted to filmic representations alone. The law often apportions such blame in circumstances where gay men are murdered. Cases in Australia where defendants utilize the so-called Homosexual Advance defence demonstrate how frequently the law deploys narratives which represent homosexual men as having provoked their own demise.[38] In part this is achieved through judicial inscriptions of the legal fiction of the 'ordinary man' as possessing an added attribute – a violent hatred of homosexuals. In a 1990 New South Wales murder trial, Justice Badgery-Parker implied in his charge to the jury that, by leaving his phone number on the wall at a public toilet, the deceased, 33 year old Mr Johnston, had motivated eight co-accused schoolboys to 'lure Mr Johnston to the scene and assault him not for a desire for violence for its own sake but related to anger at the conduct of homosexuals in the toilet.'[39]

The inscription of a telephone number on a wall is here judicially transcribed as a justifiable invitation to entice a stranger to a toilet and then to violently assault and murder him. Johnston was thus rendered a creature at the mercy of his own lustful desires who, in allowing himself to be enticed to the toilet at night, provoked his own demise. The infamous *Brown* decision[40] reflects a similar logic, whereby gay men are held not to *allow* their desires to be controlled, in their compulsion to engage in SM sexual practices to satiate what Lord Templeman termed their 'sexual appetites'.[41] In exercising their desire (framed as compulsion) to engage in sex, the homosexual is pathologized as addicted to permissiveness both by cinema and law. As Stychin has noted, the ascription of addiction to homosexual attraction allows homosexual men to be blamed for the inevitable result:

> Once he [the homosexual] enters this realm of the forbidden and the transgressive, the compulsion leads to ever-increasing heights of depravity of lust; an escalation that leads ultimately to his self-destruction.[42]

In *Cruising*, the killer, Stuart, is arrested after he attempts to murder Steve in Central Park. The denouement is provided by the Captain who charges Stuart with eight counts of murder. He explains that Stuart's homicidal tendencies were motivated by a desire to obtain approval from his dead father by killing the very people who embodied the thing he most hated about himself – homosexual attraction.[43] Despite the fact that the crimes are solved and the perpetrator brought to justice, we are presented with a new crime scene. A gentle gay character named Ted Bailey who lives in Steve's apartment building is shown lying dead in a pool of blood having been stabbed to death. This development suggests that as soon as one homosexual killer is apprehended another one will take his place. This scene cuts to one of Steve entering a gay bar as twilight is fading to the sound of sinister music. Despite his undercover work having ended, the film suggests that through intimate contact with the gay SM world, Steve has been (reluctantly) seduced into desiring continual contact with a world marked by violence and contagious sexuality. In relation to sado-masochism, bodies and desires conform to a very particular narrative of law and violence. This narrative is one in which *Cruising*, and in which law, through explicit and endlessly accumulated detail, have spoken publicly about homosexual sado-masochism in terms which emphasize its monstrous and contagious nature. Having viewed *Cruising*, the audience is left with the message that not only is homosexuality contagious, it is also inescapably brutal.[44]

Towards the end of *Cruising*, Steve returns to his girlfriend's apartment and the sanctity of the heterosexual relationship is restored. But whilst Steve is shaving in the bathroom we see his girlfriend first admiring and then donning his 'undercover' outfit of a leather jacket and black leather military cap. Like a stain insidiously spreading, the leather formally associated with the gay subculture of the SM clubs has entered the private realm of the heterosexual and domestic bedroom. No longer can the spectator view the world of the leather fetish as relegated to the safety of a contained space (gay clubs); the 'world unto itself' that Steve was sent to investigate. As Steve's girlfriend caresses the leather jacket one is confronted by her proximity to an object that has been associated with danger and death throughout the course of the film. In trying on the jacket she instils an anxiety in the spectator that this may well inaugurate her very infection by the violent, unruly sexuality represented by it. This suggests that the homosexual 'SM/leather' lifestyle is seductive and contagious; threatening to corrupt all the good things in the world that her character has embodied in the film (love, support and stability as idealized in the image of feminine beauty).

Cruising concludes with a scene of a boat traversing New York harbour which takes the viewer back to an almost identical opening scene in which a severed arm from a corpse later identified as gay is found floating in the water. The possibility of a spiralling pattern of homosexual violence (which in turn will seduce more men into this maelstrom of self-perpetuating violence) is conveyed through the law's representation of homosexuality as seductive and contagious.

My readings of the film *Cruising*, and the Victorian murder trial in which the film figured as a signifier of homosexual violence, demonstrate the enduring character of the idea that gay desire is inextricably bound up with risk, danger and the precipitation of death. *Cruising*'s images of multiple gay homicide, and the Koeleman murder trials, distil the essence of homosexual desire into a passion to kill. The film and the trials, reduced to their barest formula, bespeak a terrible equation: gay desire begets death. In the more recent film, *Swoon*, the desire of the two men results in the abduction and murder of a small boy. Yet this film insists that as dreadful as the men's shared bond of criminality may be, it is not the sole or dominant expression of their desire. For in *Swoon* we are presented with a vision that testifies that homosexual desire begets something else: love.

CRIMES OF PASSION: *SWOON* AND THE ADVENT OF THE NEW QUEER CINEMA

In the 1980s, a new style of gay and lesbian-focused film emerged that came to be termed 'New Queer Cinema' to distinguish these films from earlier, more classical gay and lesbian films. The hallmarks of these new films were that they were irreverent, politically informed and, above all, they were crafted to provide pleasure, particularly for a gay and lesbian audience. A central element of much New Queer Cinema was the re-appropriation and reshaping of previously negative ideas relating to homosexuality. *Swoon* exemplifies the New Queer Cinema's quest to deliberately place the sexuality of the characters at centre stage.[45] It also attempts to resist those antecedent filmic narratives, which have represented homosexuality as an essentially deviant state of being.[46] However, at the same time, *Swoon* does not shy away from examining links between homosexuality and criminality. For as director Tom Kalin states: 'we're in a sorry state if we can't afford to look at "unwholesome" gay people'.[47]

Swoon's achievement is that it explores such links whilst emphasizing the desire that binds the characters together. Spectators are repulsed at being exposed to the enactment of the brutal murder of young Bobby Franks; a ferocious act that leaves Richard's face flecked with drops of blood. *Swoon* presents Richard and Nathan as reprehensible criminals bound together in a 'compact' (the term refers to their surrogate form of marriage) which results in the brutal murder of a young boy. Yet the film profoundly touches on the depth of their love in a scene where the spectator sees Nathan grieving after Richard's murder in prison. Nathan howls alone in his cell and is eventually swathed in a crude straightjacket. The inverted 'marriage' has been terminated by an act of violence.

Swoon uses black and white as a sign of history and memory as the spectator is invited to (re)evaluate the mythology surrounding the Leopold and Loeb case.[48] In the first half of the film we are positioned to identify with Leopold through images which equate his deviance with glamour.[49] His homosexuality places him outside the law; yet this works to connect him to the seductively appealing underworld of Chicago which is presented as a world of dancing, frivolity and free flowing liquor (despite prohibition). The second half of the film abandons Leopold's subjectivity as the crime is filtered through various institutional perspectives – psychoanalytic, criminological and legalistic – all of them framed by the film as homophobic discourses.[50]

Swoon (re)evaluates the mythology surrounding the Leopold and Loeb case by presenting the central kidnap and murder as one of many crimes planned by the duo; an extreme outcome of a long and tangled relationship which revolved around the exchange of sex for criminal activity.[51] Yet this relationship is framed by the film as a 'natural' marriage of two people deeply in love. In an opening scene which celebrates their besotted love, the men kiss and exchange rings in a deserted factory enveloped in a bright light which seeps through the rafters. The tenderness and beauty of this romantic scene powerfully suggests to the spectator that this is indeed 'true' binding love.

> Nathan: If I do what you want?
> Richard: I'll do what you want.[52]

This forging of unholy 'marriage' vows inaugurates their shared 'partnership' in crime and reflects the actual findings of the court in the Leopold and Loeb case, in which the judge conceptualized the crime as a contract involving the exchange of crime for sex: 'Leopold acquiesced in Loeb's criminalistic endeavours and received in return opportunities for certain twisted biological satisfactions.'[53]

Yet the film still insists upon a reading that acknowledges that this is a 'marriage' of sorts based on love and desire.[54] The closeness of their 'marriage' is conveyed when Loeb alludes to Leopold's desire for them to be bound together as a 'couple': 'You want to get caught. If you could get pregnant you would.'[55] Nathan then smiles as if to acknowledge the truth of his desire to be bound to Richard as heterosexual married couples are through parenthood. In fact, *Swoon* frames the intense desire of the men to stay together as ultimately offering a motive for their crimes. Nathan's diary testifies to this truth:

> May 23rd 1924: Killing Bobby Franks together will join Richard and I for life.[56]

As such, the murder is framed as a cathartic act which has the power to transcend those worldly restrictions which interfere with their ability to love each other without having to live a life of secretive desire and enforced invisibility. By killing the boy, Nathan believes that this terrible act will unite them and consequently purge his sense of internal conflict. Nathan says as much when he comments on the motive for the killing: 'I wanted to murder the idea of suffering as my condition.' The film demonstrates how both men's prayers are answered through crime. Richard becomes a notorious criminal and Nathan's love for Richard is made public.

The film recreates scenes from the murder trial in which the discourse of law invokes the notion that homosexual desire is distinctly unnatural and abhorrent in comparison to heterosexuality. For example, the prosecutor addresses the court: 'Your honour ... I want to remind this court that the basic motive of this case is the desire to satisfy unnatural lusts'.[57]

This quotation (and almost all of the courtroom material contained in the script) is transcribed from the original trial. As such, *Swoon* re-reads this landmark case against its own inherited mythology, attempting to complicate the easy equation between homosexuality and pathology. The prosecutor calls upon the notion of an aggrieved society in demanding that the men die for a crime which threatens the family unit. Thus, the familiar link is made that homosexuality is a contagion capable of poisoning society: 'In the name of the people of Illinois, in the name of the fatherhood and the womanhood and the children, we are asking for death by hanging. Do not let them go free or allow their spawn to be thrown into society.'

This notion that homosexuality evinces a contagious potential is explored in a scene where the court is cleared of women and children because the judge fears that hearing evidence relating to the defendants' 'perversions' will pollute the minds of these innocents. This ludicrous order forces the female court stenographer to leave the courtroom.

Ironically, it was the 'compact' of these two 'diseased minds' that was invoked by their defence counsel, Clarence Darrow, who called for clemency: 'There is a weird, strange, unnatural disease in all of it [the crime] which is responsible for this deed.'[58]

Thus, the notion of homosexuality, pathologized as a diseased state, was utilized to appeal to the judge to spare their lives. In failing to impose the death penalty, the judge's sentence indicates that he accepted that the diseased homosexual nature of the men predisposed them to kill. However, if the film partially embraces the view that 'disease' was a contributing factor in this crime, the ending repudiates that same linkage. The spectator learns that, immediately after his death in 1971, Leopold's eyes were successfully transplanted to a blind woman; restoring sight to one whose life was lived in darkness. The symbolic association of homosexuality with darkness and evil is disrupted; for here the homosexual is associated with light and the 'goodness' of renewed vision.

In reflecting on the film's title, it is apparent that 'swoon' functions as both noun (a state of romantic ecstasy as depicted in the love the men share) and verb (the process of fainting from horror as invited by the spectator's exposure to the violent murder). Thus, the film can be read as a celebration of homosexual love and an indictment of violent behaviour. To its credit, *Swoon* does not shy away from acknowledging that homosexuality was implicated in the complicated matrix of personal interactions (sexual, intellectual and psychological) which led Leopold and Loeb to murder. But, by emphasizing that the law sought to misconstrue their love for each other as an 'unnatural' desire culminating in crime, the film ultimately rejects this positing of homosexuality as an intrinsically criminal state. *Swoon* holds this tenuous link up to scrutiny and ridicule by presenting the evaluation of homosexuality as disease to be a flawed process. This is best conveyed through the 'slide show' treatise on perversion within the film, where phrenology (a then popular science) is employed to explain why the men are criminally diseased. Some 20 photographs of men and women (including Richard and Nathan) are projected with accompanying diagrams in which behavioural and facial characteristics are matched up. A narrator explains why Nathan and Richard were pathologically predestined to kill:

> Nathan Leopold's criminal nature can be discerned in the contours of his face: the slope of his nose and the tilt of his chin indicate his cunning and deceptive nature. Although he blames Richard Loeb for the murder, his profile proves him a compulsive liar. The patient's sexual pathology can be detected in his abnormally large penial gland. It was this unfortunate imbalance of his sex urges which compelled him to kill without feeling.
>
> Richard Loeb's low sense of self esteem is revealed by the shape of his forehead and the curve of his lips. Due to a subnormal pituitary gland, he was unable to resist the powerful influence of Nathan Leopold. It was this unfortunate deficiency that led him into crime and subsequently destroyed his life.

These phrenological images, drawn in large measure from longstanding anti-Semitic tropes, are presented as serious evidential 'proof' of the defendant's diseased criminal minds (the signs of which can be 'read' from examining facial features). But the film puts phrenology under the microscope (imitating its close study of criminality). *Swoon*'s parody of phrenological investigatory techniques reminds the spectator that such 'scientific' practices are as archaic as the period they are purloined from – the 1920s. Far from being taken as credible explanations for the men's criminality, the slide show functions ironically to position the spectator to perceive the foolishness of this 'science'.

Swoon concludes with a narrator giving a brief account of the last years of Nathan Leopold's life. The audience is told that, in 1956, Meyer Levin fictionalized Leopold's life story in the novel *Compulsion*[59] and that: 'Nathan Leopold tried unsuccessfully to sue Meyer Levin for wilful misrepresentation of his character.' Thus, in addition to often misrepresenting the nature of homosexual desire, here is evinced a situation in which legal discourse legitimizes and endorses the right of another discourse (literature) to misrepresent homosexuality in a similarly unflattering manner.

ACCOMMODATING DEVIANCE, DESIRE AND THE PLEASURE OF EROTIC SPECTATORSHIP

The director Steven Frears recounts how a gay man approached him after the screening of his film *My Beautiful Laundrette* (1986) to thank him for depicting gay people: 'in a perfectly natural way and not as psychopaths or murderers.'[60]

Frears informed the man that his next project, *Prick Up Your Ears* (1987), was based on the life story of Joe Orton, in which Orton's lover Kenneth Halliwell murders him with a hammer. Frears asked him whether he thought the murder should be left out of the film. The man laughingly replied: 'Oh, no, no, no. You must show life as it is. What we want is simply some balance.'[61]

I too would not argue for an evacuation of the link between homosexuality and criminality. What matters is how the link is represented. *Cruising*'s manifest failure to depict gay desire as anything other than a state of being that invites (and deserves) death and violence grossly distorts gay desire. *Swoon* insists that the desire of the two men (evident in their exchange of crime for sex) provides a partial explanation for the murder. As such, the crime is one of passion, indeed it is possible to read the film's murder scene as a declaration of love.

Queer theorist Eve Sedgwick asserts the importance of the axiom that people are 'different from each other'.[62] Acknowledging homosexual difference is a valid and worthwhile thing to do. But the discourses of law and cinema often frame this difference in distinctly negative ways, rendering homosexuality as the deviant '*other*', judged against that which is 'normal', 'healthy' and 'desirable'. Difference is mediated in law and cinema through the construction of categories of normality and deviance that are deployed as powerful binaries of exclusion/inclusion and innocence/guilt. This chapter has sought to illuminate cinema's complicity in deploying representations which link homosexuality with criminality. While law has *desired* the deviant homosexual, cinema also has participated in his social construction. It is not that the discourses of cinema and law project images of how they believe homosexuality is seen that is so reprehensible. Rather, what is problematic is that these discourses often project images of how homosexuality *should* be seen. This is a mythologizing of homosexuality as a negative state of being through the deployment of representations, which enable some spectators to shore up their homophobic beliefs. This is not some haphazard process whereby guilt cannot be attributed. For the law and the cinema are highly crafted discourses. There is always a director (in cinema) and a judge (in law) who, in a variety of ways, have much control over what each medium disseminates – a filmic image or a judgment.

Despite objecting to *Cruising*'s sedimentation of the idea that death, contagion and addiction are inextricably bound to homosexual desire, I do not advocate that cinema should fail to explore the complex relationship between desire and deviance. Various films probe such relationships and explore how criminal and gay desires often co-exist. One such audacious study of deviance is Todd Haynes' cinematic triptych *Poison* (1995). Another film which dares to explore how gay desire can embody impulsive criminal behaviour is Gregg Araki's road movie *The Living End* (1993). However, Todd Verow's *Frisk* (1995) is perhaps a particularly controversial film to deal with the links that are forged between gay sexuality and criminality. *Frisk* plunges the spectator into a world of homosexuality, sadism and insanity, as it explores the psyche of the protagonist Dennis and his compulsion to commit a succession of ritual-like murders. The details of the crimes are conveyed in a series of (love) letters Dennis writes to his friend and occasional lover Julian, and the object of his desire, Julian's younger brother Kevin. In an interview Verow explains his rationale for making a film devoted to the enactment of a gay man's murderous sexual fantasies. He said: 'we really need to concentrate on what makes us unique, what makes us interesting and what makes us dangerous'.[63]

Swoon would seem to be the cinematic embodiment of Verow's credo. *Swoon*'s principal achievement is that it demonstrates that films can deal with the complicated matrix of sexual identity and criminality in a way that accommodates both deviance and desire. Furthermore, such treatments afford gay viewers an opportunity to derive pleasure from the eroticism inherent in these films.[64] One may be repulsed, disturbed, and unsettled by images equating homosexuality with criminality. Yet these reactions do not preclude the possibility that these same images embody a capacity to arouse and excite. Gay viewers of films which represent their sexuality as indicating criminal proclivities may well find such depictions disturbing, but they might also find aspects of these representations alluring, and derive pleasure from being subjected to such 'indecent exposures'.

6

HOMOSEXUAL ADVANCES IN LAW

MURDEROUS EXCUSE, PLURALIZED IGNORANCE AND THE PRIVILEGE OF UNKNOWING[1]

ADRIAN HOWE

Yeah, I killed him, but he did worse to me ... he tried to root me.[2]

It is perhaps unfortunate and unfair that the case of Malcolm Green should be represented ... as having anything to do with homophobia ... it was nothing to do with homophobia.[3]

INTRODUCTION: HOMOPHOBIA AS A PRIVILEGE OF UNKNOWING

The first statement was made by a man to police after killing his friend in a drunken rage. His defence counsel made the second statement in reply to criticism of the High Court's decision to overturn his murder conviction and order a new trial.[4] *Green v The Queen,* decided in November 1997, is the latest pronouncement on the law of provocation by the High Court, the last court of appeal in Australia. I have argued elsewhere that the case represents a new low point in the history of the provocation defence in Anglo-Australian law in that it provides an extraordinarily expansive view of what can count as provocation, at least as far as certain (male, self-identifying heterosexual) defendants are concerned.[5] A man who kills another man, claiming that the dead man made unwanted sexual advances toward him, now has a good chance of successfully pleading provocation. He has an even better one if he can produce a 'sexual abuse factor' such as the one in *Green* – the memory that his father sexually assaulted his sisters. I also argued that the case provides more evidence, for those who still need it, that the law of provocation operates as a profoundly sexed excuse for murder and should be abolished.[6]

To date, the *Green* case has attracted very little commentary. While masculinist scholars may fear being tarnished as gay-friendly or worse, homosexual, if they criticize the decision, feminists are divided about the provocation defence, many of them wanting to retain it for battered women who kill violent male partners. Moreover, having argued for an expanded provocation defence to take account of the circumstances in which women kill, feminists have had to face the paradox of seeing defendants like Green taking advantage of a law reform intended to benefit battered women. Consequently, an eerie, complicit silence surrounds the fact that the *Green* decision effectively condones the incorporation of the notion of an 'unwanted homosexual advance' into pleas of provocation and self-defence in a number of recent Australian murder trials. Within a legal community where it is left to feminists to condemn provocation cases in which women killed by violent male partners are constructed as having 'provoked their own demise',[7] there is hardly a whisper that the much-criticized North American development known as the 'homosexual advance defence' (HAD) now has the imprimatur of the High Court. 'Homosexual advance' and 'homosexual panic' defences still have no formal status in Australia, but few legal analysts appear to care, or even to have registered that now, thanks to *Green*, homosexual men, or more precisely, dead men who allegedly made non-violent sexual advances towards men who subsequently kill them, can also be said, in Australian law, to have provoked their own demise.

This chapter revisits the *Green* case in order to frame a critique around Eve Sedgwick's claim that Western culture has been beset since the close of the nineteenth century by 'a chronic, now endemic crisis of homo/heterosexual definition, indicatively male' and that therefore:

> an understanding of virtually any aspect of modern Western culture must be, not merely incomplete, but damaged in its central substance to the degree that it does not incorporate a critical analysis of modern homo/heterosexual definition.[8]

More particularly, I want to explore Sedgwick's advice about how not to fight homophobia. Most crucially, Sedgwick warns against dismissing homophobia peremptorily as mere ignorance. Far more is at stake. What must be unpacked is the 'epistemological privilege of unknowing', epitomized by the rapist's well-drilled ignorance of his victim's desires, or by the novice's innocence/ignorance of same-sex desire or, more broadly, by Western culture's disavowal of the centrality of the question of homo/heterosexual definition. Sedgwick contends that ignorance is 'as potent and as multiple' as knowledge and that, consequently, the epistemological privilege of unknowing must be scrutinized as carefully as any knowledge claim.[9] Not all would agree that sexuality is 'the most meaning-intensive of human activities' in modern Western culture,[10] especially those whose lives are most intensely affected by highly racialized Western cultures such as that of late-twentieth century Australia.[11] Nevertheless, Sedgwick is surely right to warn of the dangers which attach to dwelling too scornfully on 'the degree to which the power of our enemies over us is implicated, not in their command of knowledge, but precisely in their ignorance.' It is misguided to reify and demonize ignorance, thereby dismissing it as beyond meaningful political engagement, or, at the other extreme, to sentimentally privilege ignorance as 'an originary, passive innocence'. For ignorance is just as politically loaded as knowledge and, in addition, ignorance is attended by powerful 'psychological operations of shame, denial, projection' which require scrutiny. Just as knowledges are now understood to be plural, invested with power and far from having a simple redemptive potential, so ignorance must be pluralised, de-reified and specified. In short, Sedgwick advocates a problematization of ignorance in the field of sexual politics, using a 'deconstructive understanding that particular insights generate, are lined with, and at the same time are themselves structured by particular opacities.'[12]

Sedgwick's conceptualization of a range of particular opacities or 'a plethora of *ignorances*' which circulate as 'part of particular regimes of truth' is an alluring one, providing as it does new ways of analysing homophobic ignorance masquerading as unsexed and ungendered judicial reasoning. Who would not find intriguing her claims that particular ignorances imply, structure and enforce particular knowledges and that this is 'easy to show, perhaps easiest of all today, in the realm of sexuality?'[13] And who amongst critical legal theorists could resist the challenge of testing those claims against judicial pronouncements in a case involving violence, sexuality and questions of homo/heterosexual definition? I have suggested elsewhere, by way of a preliminary comment to my analysis of the controversial UK case, *R v Brown and Others*, that the chasm between judicial and critical approaches to law, sex and sexed violence can only be gauged in light years.[14] In retrospect, that scornful dismissal of the judicial incapacity to grasp the idea of heterosexuality's complicity in sexual violence (or any other theorization of law's violence for that matter), falls into the trap identified by Sedgwick above. That is, I attributed problematic decisions in sexual assault cases to a beyond-the-pale, intellectually stagnant, misogynist ignorance, and the *Brown* decision to an equally dumb, homophobic ignorance. The *Green* case provides an opportunity to redeem myself and deepen the analysis, courtesy of Sedgwick's analytical prodding of the role played by ignorance in literary and, by extension, legal discourses.

The questions to be asked of the case by HAD watchers alert to the perils of demonizing, and thus failing to engage with, homophobic ignorance are as follows. What privilege of unknowing did the majority judges call upon when they held that the trial judge had made a significant error when he directed the jury to have no regard to the appellant's family history of sexual violence – specifically, his father's sexual assaults not on him, but on his sisters? What particular opacity was mobilized by the majority judges which enabled them to recuperate the pain inflicted by a man on his daughters and redeploy that pain on behalf of his son when he killed another man? Compelling critiques of such spurious excuses for men's violence were readily available. So too were critical analyses of the recuperative strategies deployed by dominant groups to channel resistant voices, in this case the voices of survivors of men's sexual assaults, into non-threatening outlets.[15] Yet in a chilling display of recuperative power, the majority judges reconfigured a murderously violent aggressor as a victim of the sexual assaults experienced by his sisters at the hands of his father. No false memory syndrome intervened here to cloud the sisters' stories of childhood sexual assault (as it frequently does when adult women make such allegations). In *Green* a childhood sexual assault narrative was accepted as transparently true and then transformed in the majority decision into a legitimated trigger of lethal violence, albeit one twice removed from the originary violence of the father – no questions asked. Which of the plethora of ignorances operated here? A 'very pointed and well-drilled readerly ignorance', 'a tellingly deployed sexual ignorance', 'a powerful but labour-intensive ignorance?'[16] What specific 'unknowing' mobilized the protective energies of the majority judges towards Malcolm Green and their punitive energies against his victim, Don Gillies? And which one enabled them to disavow their homophobia – to imply what the defence barrister later asserted, namely, that the case had 'nothing to do with homophobia?'

HAD IN AUSTRALIA

The *Green* case is the latest in a spate of recent Australian murder trials in which male defendants alleged that they acted in self-defence or under provocation in response to a sexual advance made by another male. This defence, which has come to be known as the 'homosexual advance defence' (HAD), was argued unsuccessfully in some English cases in the 1950s,[17] and with more success in later cases in the United States, where it has sometimes taken the form of a so-called 'homosexual panic defence'. By the time HAD made an appearance in Australia in the 1990s, it had been subjected to considerable critical commentary, particularly in the United States.[18] Consequently, when Australian analysts set about researching the operation of HAD in this country, they found that the cases had disturbingly 'similar scenarios and outcomes' to those in North America.[19] In most cases, defendants alleging that they killed men who made non-violent sexual advances at them pleaded provocation and were convicted of manslaughter. More problematically, some pleaded self-defence and were acquitted. For example, in the 1992 Victorian case, *R v Murley*,[20] the defendant accepted an invitation to the victim's flat after drinking with him in a hotel. He subsequently attacked the victim, almost decapitating him before robbing him and setting his flat alight. He was acquitted.[21] In a 1993 New South Wales case, *Queen v McKinnon*,[22] a man was charged with murdering a homosexual man. Despite evidence admitted in court that he had discussed the killing with his friends, telling them he had 'rolled a fag', the jury acquitted him, apparently accepting that he had acted in self-defence.[23] The *McKinnon* case, the first of several decisions in New South Wales identified as a HAD murder case, was to become the catalyst for demands for a government inquiry into the use of a victim's sexuality as a defence to violent crimes and, specifically, into cases where juries had acquitted killers of gay men who alleged their victims made advances.[24] Now *Green v The Queen* has become one of the catalysts for renewed efforts, at least on my part and the part of some law reformers, to abolish the defence of provocation in Australia.[25]

If the argumentation in *Green* cries out for analysis, so do the facts. Don Gillies was 36 at the time of his death at the hands of Malcolm Green in May 1993. All we are told of his life is that he was 'unmarried and lived with his mother', who was away for some days prior to the killing. We are also told that he had helped the accused to find work, lent him money and been his confidant. Green was 22, had known Gillies for about 6 years and regarded him as 'one of his best friends' and a mentor. According to Green's record of interview, on the night of the killing, they had watched television and drunk alcohol at Gillies' home in Mudgee. Gillies asked him to stay overnight, saying he would sleep in his mother's bedroom and the accused could sleep in his bedroom. He alleged that later Gillies came into the room, got into the bed and started touching him. Green responded by punching him 'until he didn't look like Don to me'. But Don continued to 'grope and talk', leading Green to hit him again and stab him repeatedly with scissors. The sexual advance had reminded him of 'what my father had done to four of my sisters' and it 'forced me to open more than I could bear'. At the trial he elaborated on this answer, explaining that it meant that he lost control because of thoughts of his father sexually assaulting his sisters and his mother. He also changed the number of sisters assaulted to two, testifying that when he was pushing Don away, he saw 'the image of my father over two of my sisters, Cherie and Michelle, and they were crying and I just lost it.'[26] At the trial, he gave sworn evidence that he had punched the victim about 15 times, stabbed him 10 times with scissors and then banged his head repeatedly into the bedroom wall. The defence argued that the victim had made a sexual advance and that Green had killed him in self-defence or, alternatively, under provocation. Rejecting these defences, the jury convicted him of murder. He was sentenced to imprisonment for 15 years.

Green raised two main grounds of appeal against his conviction in the New South Wales Court of Appeal. First, the trial judge had erred in law in not leaving certain evidence of provocation to the jury—evidence of the appellant's 'special sensitivity to sexual interference' and evidence of his family background going to that sensitivity. Second, the judge had erred in law in his directions as to the meaning of the ordinary person 'in the position of the appellant'.[27] The 2–1 majority judgment confirmed that evidence of the appellant's beliefs about his father's sexual abuse of his sisters would be relevant to the question as to whether he in fact lost his self-control. The majority also found that the trial judge had conducted the trial on an incorrect basis when he ruled that the relevant ordinary person in New South Wales, namely one 'in the position of the appellant,' could have been provoked to do what the accused did. He should have ruled that this ordinary person was provoked to form an intention to kill or do grievous bodily harm. Crucially, however, the majority judges held that any attempt by the defence to emphasize this distinction would simply serve to remind the jury of 'the savagery of the beatings' and 'the terrible things' which the appellant did to the deceased to cause his death. Rejecting the appeal, they said that the jury had properly convicted Green of murder. Indeed, the jury 'could hardly have come to any different conclusion.'[28]

THE HIGH COURT DECISION: THE MAJORITY JUDGMENTS – A TELLINGLY DEPLOYED SEXUAL IGNORANCE?

The High Court gave five separate judgments. Chief Justice Brennan's majority judgment, a masterpiece of a tellingly deployed ignorance of issues of homo/heterosexual definition, provides several insights into the operation of the privilege of unknowing. Reflecting on the defence of provocation's ordinary person test, albeit with its New South Wales legislative gloss, 'in the position of the accused,' the chief justice asserted that juries in that state were required 'to take full account of the sting of provocation actually experienced by the accused'. However, they must not consider 'any extra-ordinary [sic] response by the accused to the provocation actually experienced' for 'extra-ordinary aggressiveness or extra-ordinary want of self-control on the part of the accused confer no protection against conviction for murder.'[29] As provocation did, in his view, confer such protection to the appellant in this case, it follows that the chief justice did not view the homicidal attack as an act of extraordinary aggressiveness. Punching a man's face until it is unrecognizable, stabbing him repeatedly with scissors and banging his head into a wall is not, apparently, an extraordinary response if a sexual advance can be constructed, against the evidence, as aggressive. Further, Green's recollection of and sensitivity to his father's sexual abuse of the appellant's sisters – which he designated 'the sexual abuse factor' – was relevant to the question of provocation:

> The sexual abuse factor was relevant ... because it tended to make it more likely that the appellant was more severely provoked by the deceased's unwanted homosexual advances than he would otherwise have been and thus more likely that he had been induced thereby to lose self-control and inflict the fatal blows and more likely that the appellant was so incensed by the deceased's conduct that, had an ordinary person been provoked to the same extent, that person could have formed an intention to kill the deceased or to inflict grievous bodily harm upon him.[30]

The trial judge had therefore erred in ruling against the admission of evidence of 'the sexual abuse factor' on the issue of provocation. In Brennan CJ's view, a reasonable jury, properly directed, could have had a reasonable doubt as to whether the appellant was provoked in the legally relevant sense, if all the relevant evidence, including evidence of 'the sexual abuse factor' was put to them.[31]

Such a sympathetic reading of Green's testimony was not all that was going for him. The majority judges also relied on the stereotype of the predatory homosexual man, a stereotype so powerful that it overwhelmed the facts in the case, including the fact that no evidence was submitted that Gillies was homosexual.[32] Consider the effect of the stereotype on the narrative provided in Smart J's dissent in the lower appeal court, which was quoted approvingly by Chief Justice Brennan in the High Court.[33] Smart J regarded the deceased's actions, 'as so narrated' by the accused, as 'revolting' and it was 'unreal to suggest that in such a situation the appellant should have got up and walked away.' He was 'being grabbed' and the deceased was making 'very persistent and determined sexual advances'. And, if all this was not 'bad enough', there were further factors to be taken into account, such as the deceased's 'betrayal of trust' and friendship and his 'abuse of his hospitality' demonstrated in his attempt to coerce the appellant into providing him with 'sexual gratification'. It followed that:

> The provocation was of a very grave kind. It must have been a terrifying experience for the appellant when the deceased persisted. The grabbing and the persistence are critical.

And, tellingly:

> Some ordinary men would feel great revulsion at the homosexual advances being persisted with in the circumstances and could be induced to so far lose their self control as to inflict grievous bodily harm. They would regard it as a serious and gross violation of their body and their person. I am not saying that most men would so react or that such a reaction would be reasonable. However, some ordinary men could become enraged and feel that a strong physical re-action was called for. The deceased's actions had to be stopped.[34]

By contrast, the majority judgment in the lower appeal court had inscribed the ordinary person as a moderately homophobic person, presumably a man, who would respond to a homosexual advance with non-lethal blows. Smart J transforms the ordinary person standard into the standard of 'some ordinary men', notably extremely homophobic and violent men with the power and, more crucially, the right to stop sexual advances. While Chief Justice Brennan found Smart J to be in error in his reference to 'some ordinary men',[35] his rights-bearing violent homophobic ordinary man was to emerge triumphant in the High Court.

In the eyes of the chief justice and the other majority judges, the infliction of extensive and brutal injuries was not, apparently, an act of 'extraordinary aggression'. Why not? Because the stereotype of the predatory older homosexual permits the reversal of aggressor and victim. The construction of the sexual advance as 'forceful' can even cancel out retaliation taking the form of 'excessive frenzied acts'. Such is the advantage bestowed by the provocation defence on extremely violent men who are constituted by male judges as ordinary (or understandably violent) men, as opposed to 'extra-ordinarily' violent men. Such is the discursive and non-discursive violence which is organized and legitimated by the epistemological privilege of unknowing. Relatedly, the concepts of aggressor and victim get turned on their head in all the majority judgments. Gillies is constructed as the aggressor, despite the fact that the appellant had hit him in the face so hard that 'he didn't look like Don to me'. Amazingly, Don continued to 'grope and talk' – to persist with the sexual advance.[36] Yet according to Chief Justice Brennan, this could have incensed a reasonable jury. Such a jury might have found 'the real sting of the provocation' in the deceased's attempt to violate the sexual integrity of a man who had trusted him as a friend and father figure and also in his 'persistent homosexual advances'. Resorting to the fictions of the unsexed ordinary person and the ungendered reasonable juror, the chief justice insists that a 'jury man *or woman* would not be unreasonable because he or she might accept that the appellant found the deceased's conduct "revolting" rather than "amorous".'[37] After all, the case was 'not like *Stingel*'.[38] In that case the provoking act was consensual (hetero)sexual activity which inflamed the killer's jealousy, whereas in *Green* 'the deceased was the sexual aggressor of the appellant.'[39]

Impliedly then, the case had nothing to do either with homophobia or gender bias. Yet interestingly, when the chief judge reflected on the Crown's submission that the appellant's reaction to 'the conduct' fell below the standards of self-control of the ordinary person, the ordinary person became 'the hypothetical ordinary *man* in the position of the appellant'.[40] That slippage from 'person' to 'man' illustrates once again the cogency of the observation that law, and the law of provocation in particular, persistently betrays its fiction of a gender-neutral legal personhood.[41] For all of law's grand-standing efforts to endow itself with a gender-less 'truly hypothetical ordinary person',[42] the ordinary person emerges in Chief Justice Brennan's judgment as an ordinary homophobic man who would repel a homosexual advance with blows – and possibly with lethal violence, if he can produce a 'sexual abuse factor' rendering him susceptible to sexual advances. Moreover, the chief justice's token gesture in the gender-neutrality stakes is unconvincing. As if any 'truly hypothetical' objective analyst would believe that a 'jury man *or* woman' would accept that an unwanted sexual advance by a man towards another man was especially 'revolting'.[43] Of course, a jury woman might accept this, if she were properly hegemonized into understanding the homophobia felt by the 'ordinary' man on the receiving end of a sexual advance of another man. Under conditions of masculinist hegemony, such a sexual advance is perceived to be a 'grave' provocation as opposed to a normative or routinized behaviour pattern, such as the unwanted sexual advances made by men towards women on a daily basis. The ordinary standard is that of the ordinary man, and the ordinary woman has very little to do with determining what counts as 'sexual provocation', except in her capacity as provoking victim.[44]

It is precisely an ordinary (read: fiercely heterosexual) man, masquerading as a neutral, gender-less person, who assesses the gravity of the provocation of a homosexual advance on another ordinary man in *Green*. Leslie Moran suggests that law reform and decriminalization have not reduced 'the police need to invest the male genital body as homosexual(ity)',[45] and reform has not alleviated the judicial compulsion to endow that body with a highly sex-specific capacity to provoke lethal violence in would-be happily heterosexual men desperate to ward off unwanted sexual advances from other men.

LABOUR-INTENSIVE IGNORANCE – REASONABLE, RELUCTANT AND HYSTERICAL HOMOPHOBIC JUDGMENTS

If Chief Justice Brennan's judgment can be read as the work of a would-be reasonable homophobe, one firmly committed to the fiction of a gender-less and unsexed ordinary person, Justice Toohey plays the role of the reasonable but reluctant homophobe. He too focused on the meaning of the always fraught objective or ordinary person test – the test requiring that the alleged provocation be assessed by reference to the powers of self-control of the hypothetical ordinary person. This test was to require some pummelling to meet the facts in *Green*, but the majority judges set themselves for the task. For Justice Toohey this involved complicating the already strained rules for applying the objective test in the law of provocation. Here he relied on the observation made in *Stingel* about cases involving a 'particular difficulty' – cases where the existence of an attribute or characteristic of the accused is relevant 'both to the identification of the content or the gravity of the wrongful act or insult and to the level of power of self-control of any person possessed of it.'[46] *Green* was such a case because the appellant's alleged 'special sensitivity to sexual interference' could be relevant both to the gravity of the alleged provocation and also to the level of self-control. Homosexuality was not, of course, relevant to an assessment of the gravity of the provocation. The privilege of unknowing guaranteed a safe opacity on that score.

Another factor complicated Justice Toohey's consideration of the grounds of appeal. The appellant's 'real complaint' was that the trial judge's ruling deprived the jury of the opportunity to hear evidence relevant to the gravity.[47] It was the gravity of the provocation, after all, which was crucial in cases of particular difficulty such as this one. Justice Toohey also found that the trial judge erred in determining that an ordinary person in the position of the appellant could have been provoked to the response to which the appellant resorted, rather than being provoked to form an intent to kill. The trial judge's ruling had put the defence counsel in an invidious position given the excessive injuries inflicted by the appellant. After all, no defence counsel could 'sensibly suggest' to a jury that Gillies' provocative act and its 'high degree of gravity' could cause the legally relevant ordinary person to have so far lost self control as Green did. All that counsel need do was to suggest to the jury that the conduct of the deceased could have provoked an ordinary person to form an intention to inflict grievous bodily harm. Tellingly, 'that was sufficient' and the jurors did not have to subject Green's excessive frenzied acts to the objective test'.[48] Thus did the law of provocation save sensible jurors (and judges?) from having to ponder the excessively frenzied acts of violence of the accused. Somewhat reluctantly, Justice Toohey allowed the appeal, notwithstanding his view that the killing was a 'savage' one.

The third majority judge, Justice McHugh, appears to have had the biggest investment in the appellant's story. At least, his disavowal of homophobia is the most desperate of the three. In his view, the trial judge's errors were so significant that the appellant had not had a proper trial according to law. Justice Toohey was much more circumspect and even the chief justice did not go that far. How then did Justice McHugh come to this conclusion? He began by reviewing legislative provisions on the law of provocation in New South Wales in the context of the leading provocation cases. He determined that in the case at hand, the relevant ordinary person was one:

> with the minimum power of self-control of an ordinary person who is sub-
> jected to a sexual advance that is aggravated because of the accused's special
> sensitivity to a history of violence and sexual assault within his family.[49]

Here he relied on past authority for the view that all of the accused's characteristics, circumstances and sensitivities, including the accused's personal relationships and past history, are relevant in determining the gravity of the alleged provocation. This assisted him in his effort to circumvent the Crown's case that the conduct of the deceased was unrelated to the accused's alleged special sensitivity to sexual assault. According to the Crown, the case involved 'a non-violent homosexual advance' which had nothing to do with Green's alleged beliefs relating to 'incidents of heterosexual sexual assault by his father upon his sisters'.[50] This argument went to the heart of the matter: there was no avoiding the fact that the alleged sexual advance here was a specifically homo-sexual advance. To find for the appellant, the majority judges had to frame their decisions so as to appear sexually neutral in assessing the gravity of a homo-sexual, as distinct from a heterosexual, advance.

Justice McHugh began this difficult task by questioning whether the advance was non-violent. Next, and crucially, he declared that 'the fact that the advance was of a homosexual nature was *only one factor* in the case', thereby abolishing by judicial fiat any consideration, let alone critical analysis, of the centrality of the homophobic prohibition to both Green's lethal violence and to his own reasoning. The following extract must stand as a classic of a labour-intensive sexual ignorance of this prohibition:

> What was more important from the accused's point of view was that a
> sexual advance, accompanied with some force, was made by a person
> whom the accused looked up to and trusted. *The sexual, rather than the*

homosexual, nature of the assault filtered through the memory of what the accused believed his father had done to his sisters, was the trigger that provoked the accused's violent response. Viewed in this light, the conduct of the deceased was directly related to the accused's sensitivity. Indeed, *any* unwanted sexual advance is a basis for 'justifiable indignation', especially when it is coupled with aggression.[51]

McHugh J's attempt to equalize Green's supposedly justifiable indignation at Gillies' advance with the reaction of a woman to a routine unwanted sexual advance made by a man fails through absurdity. His disclaimer that the 'homosexual nature' of the advance was 'only one factor in the case' reeks of the psychological operations of shame, denial and projection which, according to Sedgwick, attend the production and distribution of ignorances pertaining to the crisis of homo/heterosexual definition in Western culture. The spectre of a specifically homosexual advance made by an always already predatory older man looms large over and through his and the other majority judgments. All three are structured by the telling opacities produced by the epistemological privilege of unknowing. And all three display a 'heightened surcharge of the homosocial/homosexual bond' and, virtually simultaneously, a virulent homophobic prohibition by which the homoerotic charge, 'once crystalised as an object of knowledge, is then denied *to* knowledge.'[52]

THE DISSENTING JUDGMENTS – EPISTEM OF THE CLOSET?[53]

There were two dissenting judgments. In a superb black-letter-law judgment, one devoid of social analysis, let alone of a careful attention to the sex/gender questions central to any critical reading of the case, Justice Gummow came to a conclusion diametrically opposed to that of the majority judges. In his view, the legally relevant provocation must be able to induce:

> an ordinary person in the position of the accused, that is to say with the beliefs or state of mind of the accused concerning certain events in his family history, to have so far lost self-control as to have informed an intent to kill the deceased, or to inflict grievous bodily harm upon him.[54]

Justice Gummow could not see how, on the evidence, the appellant had been provoked in this legally relevant sense. He had not been sexually abused by his father and at the time of 'the slaying', he had not seen his father for 7 years. Moreover, this was not a case where the conduct of the deceased was the last episode in a series of provocations which, in that context, proved to be unbearable. It did not, for example, fit the pattern of 'domestic' relationships attended by 'repetitious violence or other abusive conduct of one party towards the other' (read: cases involving women who kill male partners after a long history of domestic violence). As for the homosexual aspect of the case, Justice Gummow had some critical, though hardly damning, comments to make. He observed 'without drawing any conclusion as to any significance this would have had' that this was not a case where the accused had said that his response to the sexual advance sprang from a 'strongly felt aversion' to homosexual sex. No question of 'homosexual panic' arose as it sometimes did in defence pleas in cases of this nature. Accordingly, the trial judge had been in error when in giving reasons for rejecting the prosecution's application that provocation be withdrawn from the jury, he said that there was evidence that the accused found homosexual advances 'repugnant or offensive or insulting' and that such conduct affected him and caused his loss of control. That was not, as Justice Gummow observed, the burden of the evidence given by the accused. Had it been, a different question would have arisen in relation to the relevant ordinary person test and the answer 'may well have been' that given by Priestley JA in the New South Wales Appeals Court, namely, that while the ordinary person may have reacted indignantly or perhaps with blows, the ordinary person could not have been induced by such conduct so far to lose control as to have formed an intent to kill or inflict grievous bodily harm to the deceased.[55]

Impliedly then, Justice Gummow would countenance a 'homosexual panic' plea, but just not in this case. Conceding, yet without condemning, the subject position of a 'mildly' homophobic ordinary person and the existence in the community of strong aversions to homosexuality, he insisted that such a person, even one who found himself (or herself? – Justice Gummow did not address himself to the gender question) in a factual situation where he claimed to have a strong aversion to homosexuality, would have been provoked in the legally relevant sense. The 'ultimate question' pertained to the objective standard of 'a truly hypothetical "ordinary person"'. In his view, such an ordinary person, even one with personal beliefs such as those asserted by the accused with respect to his family history, would not have met that standard. Furthermore, any other construction of the ordinary person which, 'when applied to this case produced a different result, would undermine principles of equality before the law and individual responsibility.' He concluded that no jury, acting reasonably, could have been satisfied that the deceased's alleged provoking conduct was sufficient to 'deprive any hypothetical, ordinary 22-year-old male in the position of the appellant' of the legally relevant power of self-control. In short, the appellant had not displayed the self-control expected of the 'truly hypothetical' ordinary person.[56]

While Justice Gummow refrained from delving very far into the question of homophobia (or should that be: too far beyond the epistemology of the closet?), Justice Kirby's dissent contextualized the case in terms of critical scholarship on the operation of HAD overseas and in Australia. He also included far more details of the lethal attack, including the fact that the victim was 'left on the floor, face-downward, in a pool of his own blood'.[57] His consideration of the post mortem examination facilitated a very detailed account of the 'ferocity and brutality' of the attack, which could be linked to the question of proportionality.

He then moved on to highlight a point downplayed or ignored in all the other judgments, namely that the Crown had not accepted the allegation of a sexual advance by the deceased. Its 'primary case' was that this was a premeditated killing; its 'secondary case' was that even if he had touched the appellant, such conduct could not have amounted, in law, to provocation. It followed that it was unclear whether the jury's verdict was based on the primary or secondary case.[58]

Justice Kirby's judgment differed from the others in still more ways. For example, he observed that Smart J's dissent in the Court of Criminal Appeal, quoted approvingly in the majority judgments, was 'even more forceful in his expression of the alleged provocation' – that is, even more tolerant of homophobic violence – than the defence counsel.[59] Relatedly, Justice Kirby insisted that the case should be understood not only at the general level, in relation to the law of provocation in Australia, but also specifically in the context of 'the particular case of provocation' in HAD cases. He began by embarking on a defence of the Court's insistence on an objective standard for self-control. That standard embodied the principle of equality before the law. Such a principle prevented juries from condoning 'human ferocity' in 'head strong, violent people' displaying a lack of reasonable self-control.[60] Anything less was an affront to 'civilized society'. Further to the question of homosexuality, Justice Kirby took up the suggestion in the Discussion Paper on HAD submitted to the Court by the Solicitor-General for New South Wales that a non-violent homosexual advance should not constitute sufficient provocation to invoke that legal defence.[61] In his honour's view, HAD cases demonstrated the vital importance of the High Court's long-standing commitment to the objective standard. After all, that standard had been upheld in provocation cases 'of a heterosexual character', and equality demanded that it be so applied in a HAD case, especially in the context of research indicating widespread homophobic violence in Australia. In that context, it would be wrong for the law to condone the idea that a non-violent sexual assault, without more, could constitute provocation. It would conflict with contemporary standards. Surely:

the 'ordinary person' in Australian society today is not so homophobic as to respond to a non-violent sexual advance by a homosexual person as to form an intent to kill, or to inflict grievous bodily harm.[62]

It followed that the idea that the ordinary 22-year-old male would lose self-control in such a situation should not be accepted as 'an objective standard applicable in contemporary Australia.'[63]

Next Justice Kirby turned to the appellant's argument that the words 'in the position of the accused' in the Crimes Act modified the objective test so as to require that consideration be given to the appellant's subjective experience when measuring his self-control. The appellant, recall, had wanted to introduce such subjective considerations as the adverse effects of his family history, especially his father's sexual assaults of his sisters, on his capacity for self-control. But the effect of this argument would be to subjectivize the ordinary person test beyond recognition. One could see that the sexual advance may have been a provocative act to the appellant:

It may even have suggested to him assumptions about his own sexuality which he found confronting or offensive. But he was a 22 year-old adult male living in contemporary Australia.[64]

Furthermore, he was wearing clothes at the time of the alleged advance; these clothes were not removed; he was younger, fit and was quickly able to physically repel the highly intoxicated older man and, crucially, he never explained in evidence why he did not simply leave. There was nothing to prevent him simply walking away. It followed that his reaction to the deceased's conduct fell 'far below' the minimum limits on the power of self-control to be attributed to the hypothetical ordinary 22-year-old Australian male in his position. Just as in *Stingel*, the alleged provocation was 'a confronting sexual challenge' and the same standard of self-control is 'demanded by our society' and by the principle of equality before the law, whether the sexual advance be heterosexual or homosexual.[65] Moreover, equality demanded that the same standard of self-control be applied, whether an unwanted sexual advance be made by a man to a woman or to another man. Such equality might revolt some people, but the Court should not signal that an unwanted heterosexual or homosexual advance could found a provocation defence, for that message 'unacceptably condones serious violence by people who take the law in their own hands.' There was 'no way', in Justice Kirby's view, that the appellant's alleged memories of his father's sexual assaults could have induced an ordinary person to kill or inflict grievous bodily harm.[66] But as we have seen, the majority judges found a way, via the privilege of sexual unknowing, to come to just the opposite conclusion.

CONCLUSION

Specific ignorances operated in *Green* which enabled the majority judges to imply what Green's defence counsel-come-polemicist said explicitly, namely, that his client's lethal attack on another man who had made a non-violent sexual advance had 'nothing to do with homophobia' – it was all about the violence of heterosexual men against their daughters and the rage this unleashed in the brothers too young to protect them.[67] These are very powerful ignorances. Witness the failure of the epistemology of the closet operating in the dissenting judgments to withstand the awesome discursive power of the epistemological privilege of unknowing enshrined in the majority judgments. It is all very well for the dissenting judges to assume, as one did, or assert, as the other did, that the ordinary person (read: man) is not so homophobic to kill a man who makes an unwanted sexual advance. But the majority decision demonstrates unequivocally that he may do precisely that. Moreover, it is not only the majority decision that gives the lie to the capacity of the law's objective person to be non-homophobic.

In the Court of Appeal, the majority judgments rejecting Green's appeal also failed to curb the homophobic stereotype of the predatory homosexual male. It is notable that while the majority judges in the lower appeal court took the view that a homosexual advance without more was not sufficient to meet the objective test, they neither excluded nor condemned the idea of a homophobic defence, one based on the notion that a sexual advance by a homosexual man would be repugnant to 'an ordinary person'. Indeed, they indicated that they found the behaviour of the victim offensive and provocative:

> It is easy to see that many an ordinary person in the position in which the appellant was when Mr Gillies was making his amorous physical advances would have reacted indignantly, with a physical throwing off of the deceased, and perhaps with blows. I do not think however, that the ordinary person could have been induced by the deceased's conduct so far as to lose self-control as to have formed an intent to inflict grievous bodily harm upon Mr Gillies.[68]

The ordinary person, in this view, is entitled to ward off a non-violent sexual advance (or is that a specifically homosexual advance?) with physical, but not murderous blows. Does the category 'many an ordinary person' include women? Did the judges mean to suggest that anyone might choose to repel unwanted 'amorous physical advances', or was the 'offensive and provocative' advance he had in mind sex-specific, limited to a sexual advance made by a man to another man? For all the emphasis put on the neutrality of the objective standard in *all* the judgments in this case, it is clear that it is exclusively the latter scenario which dictates the outcome of the decision in *Green*.

Placing their faith in the objective standard, the dissenting judges in the High Court believe that the ordinary person can be judicially inscribed as non-homophobic and gender-neutral, and that the principle of equality, applied to the objective standard, can ensure equal treatment for all sexed identities in criminal cases. Yet the majority judges think they are upholding the objective test when they constitute the ordinary person as a violent homophobic man, one with a right to resort to homicidal rage, depending on his circumstances and family history. Such is the power of the culturally loaded, heterosexist, stereotyped image of the predatory older man and his vulnerable younger male prey. It matters not that there is no evidence, apart from the dubious statement of the killer, that the alleged sexual advance occurred. Nor is a credible narrative required. We are simply asked to believe that a severely injured man, one whose face was bashed to the point of being unrecognizable to his assailant, could and would continue to make a sexual advance on him. *Green* demonstrates that the uncorroborated story told by a young man of a sexual advance by a predatory older man – here a man who was a friend and mentor of his assailant – is one with a great deal of cultural capital under conditions of hegemonic heterosexuality. It is a story told via what Sedgwick calls a tellingly deployed sexual ignorance. But it should be emphasized that this potent ignorance is as profoundly gendered as it is sexed. As Judith Butler points out, gender is accomplished 'at least in part through the repudiation of homosexual attachments', that is, via the prohibition on homosexuality which 'operates throughout a largely heterosexual culture as one of its defining operations'.[69] Gender is performed in *Green* in precisely this way, and the best efforts of *all* the judges to champion provocation law's fictions of an objective standard and a gender-less and sex-less ordinary person cannot obscure the operation of these fundamental subtexts.

Finally, the case provides more evidence for Sedgwick's view that the fight against sexual ignorance, manifested in this instance as homophobia, is 'a fight not against originary ignorance, nor for originary innocence, but against the killing pretence that a culture does not know what it knows.'[70] The polemists who are currently defending provocation to the death in Australia assiduously avoid discussing the *Green* case, and thus the homosexual question, concentrating instead on the older, safer question of whether the defence is 'gender biased'. So far, only Malcolm Green's defence counsel has swaggered into the fray to venture an opinion on the critical issue of homo/heterosexual definition. Refusing the idea that the case had anything to do with homophobia, he has described his client's action of handing himself into police as 'a highly moral and courageous act' and expressed a desire to defend Green 'as many times at it takes'.[71] Such an obstinate sexual incomprehension in someone who has written about miscarriages of justice testifies to the continuing force of Sedgwick's observations that ignorance can be as potent as knowledge and that this is most easily demonstrated in the realm of sexuality. Sedgwick is surely right that the fight against homophobia must be pitched not at the superficial level of a too readily dismissed palpable ignorance, but rather at the killing pretences of those blessed with the epistemological privilege of unknowing in the realm of sexuality. It must be pitched, for example, against the judgments of judges who disavow any knowledge of what they do when they legitimate exculpatory accounts of murderous homophobic violence such as that of appellants like Malcolm Green.

7

PERVERTING LONDON

THE CARTOGRAPHIC PRACTICES OF LAW

LESLIE J. MORAN AND DEREK McGHEE

INTRODUCTION

In a memorandum[1] submitted to the Wolfenden Committee,[2] a government departmental committee commissioned to investigate the law and practice relating to homosexual offences and prostitution in England, Wales and Scotland, Sir John Nott-Bower, KCVO, Commissioner of the Police of the Metropolis, provided the committee with a map of London. This representation of London is bounded by Oxford Street to the north and the Kings Road to the south. Its western edge is Kensington Gardens. Its eastern limit is Westminster bridge and the river Thames. In its detail it is a distribution of familiar urban landmarks such as Hyde Park, Victoria Station, Buckingham Palace, Westminster Abbey, the Houses of Parliament and a complex web of well-known highways and byways. At the same time this London is a less familiar representation. The 'key' to the map draws attention to its novelty and to the terms of its organization:

Location of urinals where arrests were affected during 1953
Importuners   O
Gross indecency   X
Importuners and gross indecency   Ø

Rather than London as a space organized by reference to the retail, business and commercial life in contrast to domestic life or national, and state institutions in contrast to the institutions of the home and the familial, the conditions of possibility of this London are two criminal offences: soliciting and importuning for immoral purposes[3] and gross indecency.[4] The key draws attention to the fact that the boundaries that frame this representation of space are juridical. More specifically this London is a particular juridical space. This is a London made by way of the terms of a specific juridification of the male body. It is a spatial distribution of male bodies in their most intimate interactions. Finally, as a map of the criminalization of male bodies this London is a landscape of male-to-male genital encounters with agents of the law: the police.

The map draws our attention to an aspect of legal practice that has received little attention: cartography. Through the cartographic practices of policing, a familiar London is given unexpected meanings and a different London emerges. Hyde Park is now a bounded space that represents '76 cases of gross indecency'. Victoria Station is no longer a confluence of railway routes and a space of public encounters but a terminal for erotic routes, a site where the most intimate and private genital encounters are performed, the site of an erotic community. Oxford Street and the Kings Road are no longer byways that mark the site of retail and commercial encounters but are now pathways that mark the location of previously uncharted activity: of public intimacy. Rather than routes connecting well-recognized sites of aesthetic, political or national significance, they now connect previously undesignated erotic institutions of the metropolis: urinals.

This chapter is concerned with an analysis of this London as a juridical corporeal/spatial order. The first part examines the cartographic technology of law that generated this map. The second part is concerned with the juxtaposition of the body and space. Here we investigate the role of the body in the juridical cartographic practices through which space is produced. We then explore the specific nature of the space that is central to the production of this London: the urinal. Through an analysis of the corporeal practices of law that are deployed in this space we seek to offer new insights into the nature of legal practice. Finally we will draw attention to some of the problems of reading this map of London in the light of the technologies of law that have produced it.

INSTITUTION/SPACE/OBJECT

Sir John Nott-Bower's memorandum draws attention to various aspects of the technology of juridical cartography associated with policing. First, the name of the institution of policing 'the police of the Metropolis' calls our attention to the intimacy between the police as an institution of law and the production of space.[5] The police, as an institution defined by reference to the 'Metropolis', is an institution of police which produces space in specific ways, in particular through the inscription of a grid of divisions and subdivisions in the form of 'police divisions', 'sections' and 'beats'. These local inscriptions have another significance. They are units and subunits of patrol. As such, these units and subunits of the grid function as a technology of surveillance.[6] The first rule book of the Metropolitan Police clearly documents this aspect of this institution of space:

It is indispensably necessary that he [the police constable] should make himself perfectly acquainted with all the parts of his beat or section, with the streets, thoroughfares, courts, and houses.

He will be expected to possess such knowledge of the inhabitants of each house, as will enable him to recognise their persons. He will thus prevent mistakes, and enable himself to render assistance to the inhabitants when called for.

He should see every part of his beat in the time allotted; and this he will be expected to do regularly. . . .

This regularity of moving through his beat shall not, however, prevent his remaining at any particular place, if his presence there be necessary to observe conduct of any suspected person or for any other good reason; but he will be required to satisfy his Sergeant, or superior Officers, that there was a sufficient cause for such apparent irregularity. He will also attend at the appointed times, to make a report to his Sergeant of anything requiring notice.[7]

From the above, 'the beat' becomes an institution of both space, time and knowledge which actually produces the institution of policing through incessant and regulated surveillance. Through the arrangement of divisions, sections and beats the institution of policing creates the conditions of possibility of producing the metropolis and its population as juridical objects of observation and analysis, a possible representation in criminal law.[8]

Sir John's memorandum draws attention to the importance of this grid in the production of the representation of London as the offences of soliciting and importuning and gross indecency. In the appendix to the memorandum we find these offences organized by way of the contemporary form of the grid. They are tabulated by way of the 22 divisions: 'A' to 'Z' (Division 'O' being absent) that make up the metropolitan institution of the day. Here we also find some detail of the contemporary nature of the practice of the beat patrol. For example, the patrol on 'C' Division took the form of a special two-man patrol. This was deployed every week throughout all the years covered by the memorandum (from 1946 to 1953).[9] In neighbouring 'B' Division where 245 arrests were made, Sir John noted that:

the increase in 'B' Division arrests were due to increased Police activity in that year, increased patrols having been authorised because it was suspected that the situation on that Division was becoming worse.[10]

This comment is of particular interest as it draws attention to the intimate relationship between the surveillance grid, and the production of the landscape and the landmarks that are distributed upon it in the map that is London.

In describing the cartographic practice of law in connection with the offence of gross indecency, Sir John draws attention to the need to recognize that these practices of policing are diverse. For example they may take the form of officers on the beat in uniform or they may take the form of plain clothes operations. In turn these might be ordinary as well as extraordinary operations. Further characteristics of these practices are documented by Sir John in the context of the offence of importuning. For example they might take exceptional institutional form: two men in plain clothes might require special authorization by a senior officer at New Scotland Yard. They might have a special temporal dimension required by the statute which demands that soliciting and importuning for immoral purposes only be an offence if it is persistent. This, he concludes, necessitates a long observation'. He also draws attention to the way the practices of surveillance might be organized by the prerequisites of a specific locus: they 'usually take place in a urinal'. Finally, they might also be particularly problematic. Officers deployed on these surveillance activities, he notes, were only to be employed for a limited duration of time as the work was 'unpleasant' and 'unpopular'.

LEGAL LANDMARKS

The map is the summation of these spatial and temporal techniques and practices. Through their deployment not only is the male genital body produced as a juridical object and a juridical cityscape but they are also implicated in the production of London as the male body in its genital intimacy with other male bodies. However, there is a need to proceed with some caution in reading the map. It would be wrong to conclude that the juridical London presented to the Wolfenden Committee is a representation of juridified male-to-male genital encounters in their totality. It is both much less than that and much more. It is much less than that in that this London is not the space of all 22 divisions. It is London as those divisions where surveillance practices have generated the greatest number of encounters and the greatest number of male bodies. This London is much more than a mere representation of those male bodies and genital encounters. It is also a representation of a surveillance machine and the detail of its operations.

While Sir John's report draws attention to the importance of the institution of the police as a set of distinctive cartographic techniques of surveillance, examination and documentation, it is also important to note that they work within the context of other already existing systems of knowledge that constitute 'London' in other ways. This is apparent in the resort to 'Lavatories (Public or Public House)', 'Parks and Open Spaces', 'Streets and Passages', 'Parked Vehicles', 'Cinemas', 'Garage', 'House' as criteria in the mapping of offences of gross indecency. Each is already a landmark, a designation produced by way of the application of a system of axes that reduce the formidable materiality of space to a more particular signification. Sir John's reproduction of these terms, however, takes place in a specific context. Each landmark is valorized: 'Lavatories 29; Parks and Open Spaces 19; Streets and Passages 4; Parked Vehicles 3; Cinemas 3; Garage 1; House 1'. Each is given a value producing space as the always already nominated space as a particular numerical hierarchy. In doing so each is given a different meaning. Each is connected to a legal nomination, in this instance 'gross indecency'.

CARTOGRAPHY AND THE BODY

In this section we want to examine the relationship between these cartographic techniques of the law and the body in more detail. The reported appeal decision of *Horton v Mead*[11] provides an opportunity to examine this relationship in the context of the metropolis by way of the offence of importuning. The law report records that Horton was watched by two police officers over a period of time, from 11.10 to 11.50 p.m. on 31 May and from 12.05 to 1.00 a.m. on 1 June 1912. The law report describes the incident in the following way:

> At 11.10 he [Horton] entered the public lavatory at Piccadilly Circus and remained there four or five minutes; he then walked to Leicester Square, where he entered the public lavatory and remained for seven minutes; he then walked to Dansey Yard lavatory and remained there three or four minutes; he then walked back to Piccadilly Circus and entered the same public lavatory as before, remaining there five minutes. He then walked in the direction of Leicester Square, but the officers lost sight of him at the corner of Wardour Street at 11.50. At 12.05 a.m. he was again seen to enter the lavatory at Piccadilly Circus, where he remained for a few minutes; he then walked to Leicester Square, where he entered the lavatory and remained a few minutes; he then walked to Dansey Yard, entered the lavatory and remained for five minutes. He then walked to Leicester Square tube station, where he was arrested.[12]

Here the law report records the cartographic technology as one of insistent observation and repeated, searching examination. The repetition and duration of the surveillance operation draws attention to the installation of an institutional incitement to speak of the male body and a determination on the part of the agents of the law to hear the male genital body in its genital relations with other men spoken about, and to cause it to speak.[13] The law report records[14] the way surveillance operates as a machine that proliferates a discourse of a body by way of the accumulation of detail about that body: its perambulations; its territory, 'Piccadilly', 'Leicester Square', 'lavatories'; its gestures, 'he smiled in the faces of gentlemen, pursed his lips, and wriggled his body'. What is not done and not said is as important a detail as what is said and done. 'He did not at any time during this period speak to anybody or touch anybody, nor did he attempt to speak to or touch anybody'. Examination intensifies the surfaces of the body and imprints its difference in the record of the event, 'At the police station the face and lips of the appellant appeared to be artificially reddened, and in the pocket of the appellant was found a powder puff with pink powder on it.' It isolates certain utterances, 'Upon being arrested and told of the charge, persistently soliciting or importuning for immoral purposes, he answered, "Oh dear this is very annoying"'. This insistent observation and examination is concerned with the valorization and intensification of the surfaces of the body and the production of that body as a set of decipherable signs. Through a method of interpretation a body is shaped in law according to schemes of knowledge that normalize and pathologize the surfaces of the body, its gestures and its movements, its territory, its utterances, its interactions, its boundaries.

The law report informs us of another important aspect of the relationship between the cartographical machinery and the body. The techniques of production were put to work to produce this body in law, not as a result of a complaint but despite the absence of any complaint. This is important in various ways. It draws attention to the fact that outwith the machinery that incites, extracts, distributes and institutionalizes a discourse of the male body in its genital relations with other male bodies for the law, Horton's body in general and his body as a male genital body and its desires, had a certain social invisibility and a certain transience, without a fixed or limited reality. Where that which precedes the law and lies outwith the law cannot be brought into the service of the law (the absence of complaint), the law will satisfy its own needs.[15] Thus the court concluded:

> It seems to me on the facts stated in the case that we must of necessity draw the inference that what the appellant did was apprehended by the senses of the persons intended to be solicited.[16]

Horton v Mead draws attention to the way the truth of the body and the truth of the law lies in the phantasy of the body and a phantasy of (public) space generated through the juridical practices of surveillance and documentation performed by the various agents of the law (the police, the magistrate court and the appeal court).

So far, the law report of the case of *Horton v Mead* has provided an opportunity to examine the deployment of a range of cartographic techniques in the production of the body as an object of law. The case is also important in another way. It can be used to examine another aspect of the relationship between these practices and the body: the body as a cartographic technique.

THE BODY AS CARTOGRAPHIC TECHNIQUE

In *Horton v Mead* the success of the surveillance operation engaged in by the police necessitated the presence of police observers; however, these policemen, by necessity, had to be somewhat invisible to their prey. Yet, we learn nothing from the report about the nature of the techniques of the body that generated this invisibility. Sir John Nott's memorandum is perhaps of assistance here. His reference to the deployment of plain clothes police officers in the investigation of offences draws attention to one technique of the body that produces its invisibility. It is to this particular technique that we now turn.

Law reports and evidence of police practices documented by homophile organizations suggests that the body as invisibility might take many forms. The body may be rendered invisible by way of its location. It may be outside the immediate place of the genital encounter. The police might observe looking under a locked door, or over the walls of cubicles, or by way of 'glory-holes'

(holes in the wall that separates one toilet cubicle from another).[17] They might be rendered absent by being situated in secret cupboards with spy holes or more remote (yet proximate) by way of the use of video cameras and fibre-optic technology.

The techniques change when the body is deployed by way of plain clothes police operations. A rare documented example of these corporeal practices is found in a Metropolitan Police report of a surveillance operation that deployed plain clothes officers in public lavatories now preserved in the Public Records Office, London. It relates to an operation on 25 August 1933 mounted in 'M' Division of the Metropolitan police undertaken by two officers, PC 528 and PC 565, based at Tower Bridge Station. The report of PC 528 records the operation in the following terms:

> At 11-15pm. on the 24th. August 1933, I was on duty in plain clothes, accompanied by P.C. 565 'M' Division . . . , keeping observation on the public lavatory situated at the junction of Fair Street and Tooley Street, Bermondsey, in consequence of complaints having been received of indecent behaviour by male persons, when I saw two men enter the lavatory, they remained there until 11-35pm. I entered the lavatory and the two men then walked out. A short time later the prisoner . . . , entered the lavatory and went to the stall immediately opposite the one in which I was standing. In about a minute later P.C. 565 'M' . . . entered and stood in the stall nearest the entrance which was between the prisoner and myself. After a short time the prisoner left the stall in which he was standing and came round towards me stopping near the stall on my left hand side. I then saw P.C. 565 . . . move round towards the stall which the prisoner had left. Two other men then entered the lavatory, one of them behind P.C 565 . . . and came around to the vacant stall directly on my left, the other men remaining near P.C 565 . . . The prisoner then said to me 'Will you give me a light please?' He then walked behind me and took up a position in the stall immediately on my right, which P.C. 565 . . . had previously occupied. After a few minutes the prisoner made a half-turn towards me, stretched out his left arm and placed his left hand on my person and commenced rubbing it. I immediately took hold of his left arm, his left hand still being on my person. I said to him 'I am a Police Officer and I am going to take you into custody for indecently assaulting me'. He said 'Not me, you have made a mistake'.[18]

The accused was charged with two offences: indecently assaulting PC 528, contrary to (as it then was) section 62 of the Offences Against the Person Act 1861, and a second offence of indecency under a London County Council Bye Law, 20-3-1900.[19]

While this document refers only to one operation it would appear that the police surveillance performance described in this document was not an isolated one. The record notes that since 21 June 1933 similar operations had produced

four arrests for indecent assault, a fifth man had been found guilty of importuning and sentenced to 3 months hard labour and three men had been found
guilty of indecency under the London County Council Bye Law. Appendix C
of the Sir John's memorandum tabulates the productivity of this particular set of
surveillance techniques in the late 1940s and early 1950s: average number of men
per week specially engaged against the number of arrests per year. He noted that
the number of officers deployed in these 'special exercises' varied from 3 in 1946
to 7.4 in 1953. Arrests varied from a high in 1949 of 441 to 188 in 1946.
Appendix 'B' of his memorandum draws attention to the fact that most arrests
took place in 'B' and 'C' Divisions. These statistics suggest that these practices
of the body were of some importance in the production of the criminalized
bodies and landscape represented through the map of London appended to the
memorandum.

The details of the police operation performed by PC's 528 and 565 catalogue
a range of bodily practices as cartographic techniques of policing. In general
they take the form of an elaborate choreography of the body. They include the
deployment of particular modes of the body (silence), the use of specific
sartorial codes and a resort to a complex set of rituals. Far from being remote
from the technology of surveillance, these practices of the body have a compulsory quality. In order for the police to have access to these encounters between
men, it is essential for the police to 'act' their bodies in a performance of
'availability' which allows them to disappear as agents of the law, to become not
merely men but 'insiders'.[20] The failure of the police to perform these movements, codes and complex rituals successfully would have at best suggested that
they were unavailable or at worst that they were policemen. This would have led
to the cessation of all activity and thereby to the failure of surveillance. This
performance results in the policeman 'passing' as an 'insider', a fellow-pervert
who can therefore inhabit the urinal and thereby undertake surveillance and
make arrests. The police technique of surveillance, as participant observer, performing the role of a 'fellow-pervert', is central to the production of knowledge
that is manifest in Sir John's map of London. Performing the perverse body
is a condition of the possibility of the practices of police observation, analysis
and representation.

BODY/SPACE

In this section we want to examine the specifics of the relation between the
'pervert body' of the police and the generation of space. This body of the police
is performed in a specific location of the public urinal. Our particular concern is
the nature of the relationship between the body and the public and the private
in this space. The 'public' of the urinal is in the way it is designated as a place
outside the home, as a place of strangers and thereby as a place outside the
private. However, at the same time, this place is also designated in various ways
as the private. The private of this public (convenience) is represented in the idea
that the urinal for men is a place that is elsewhere, where men 'retire' from the

public realm, a space of both men and women. The private is also expressed in this place as a site designated for the performance of certain intimate and personal functions of the body: urination and defecation. However, these aspects of the private are co-extensive with the public of the urinal. The urinal appears as both public and private.

Laud Humphreys[21] has drawn attention to the place of the body in the constitution of the public/private of these places. His work focuses upon the corporeal performances of men who utilize these spaces for erotic encounters with other men. The corporeal practices recognize the public of these places and at the same time work to sustain and reproduce the private of the space. These are performances whereby the body is acted or worn as a cultural sign,[22] a sign of availability, of being an initiate.

Through the corporeal practices of policing in 'plain clothes' the police are implicated in the production of the private of this public space. In the moment of their revelation they re-install the public of private encounters.

The official report of the police operation documents the spatial and corporeal characteristics of this space and body in a particular way. The references to police names, numbers and terms such as 'prisoner' seek to constantly remind us that we are reading of the presence of the police and thereby of the 'public' nature of the space and the events. As such the 'private' of these places and the place of the police in the production of the private of that public place is erased. But this is only a partial success. The report documents not only the distance between the police and the events and the 'absence' of the police from this site but it also records the 'private' of these activities in which the police take part. In the performance of the body the police draw and redraw the line of public/private, first, in order to create the possibility of division and second, in order to impose a division in the naming of that place and that body as public.

The public/private of the space and the bodies within that space draw attention to the ambivalence of this space and the corporeal practices that generate this space. This ambivalence is of particular significance. It draws attention to the particular nature of this space. David Bell[23] has described this ambivalence as being simultaneously an insecure privacy and a selective publicity. Here the male genital body is positioned and deployed on the actual 'slash' of the private/public split,[24] in this sense the public urinal can be described as a 'gap between ordered worlds',[25] a liminal space which in turn produces liminal personae which Turner describes as 'threshold' personae.[26]

This liminal zone has specific qualities.[27] It is an already discursively confused space which blurs the point of definition at which the private becomes public and vice versa. It is a public, private boundary in oscillation.[28] These 'threshold' people – both the police, the juridical subject, and the other men, the juridical object – occupy a position through their use of space that is, to a degree, invisible to the dominant culture. Bell describes this position in terms of tension, that is, a tension between the public space of citizenship and the private space of intimacy.[29] In the context of the legal persona the 'threshold persona' of the agent of law is a tension between the subject of order and the object of disorder.

In this light Sir John's map of London's urinals might be read as a representation of the landmarks of male-to-male genital encounters that are markers of both Bell's sites of tension, as well as being markers of the cultural limits of the uses of public spaces.

LAW, LIMINALITY AND THE CARNIVALESQUE

In this liminal zone the juxtaposition of transgression and assertion is not only characteristic of the one who is the object of law's interest but is also characteristic of the agent of law. It is to this aspect of the practices of law in the liminal space of the urinal that we now want to turn.

In this liminal space law appears not so much in the guise of the mind, as rules and reason but as a choreography of the body, a set of sartorial codes and a collection of erotic gestures. In this in-between place of the urinal the male homosexual as an object of law, a sign of disorder, is imitated by the subject of law, the very medium of right order, the agent of law. Here reason is replaced by passion and legal practice becomes an erotic practice. The truth of the homosexual as disorder is destroyed in the parody of homosexual as the mask of order.

These inverted relations are reminiscent of practices associated with the carnivalesque.[30] In the carnivalesque, to a degree, life is turned upside down. The laws, prohibitions and restrictions which determine the system are suspended. The hierarchical system and the forms of fear, awe, piety and etiquette are suspended. That which is usually distant is proximate. A new inter-relationship is performed.

This instance of the reconfiguration of the law within the carnivalesque is important in various ways. Carnival is an ambivalent ritual. On the one hand it draws attention to the inevitability of law as order and hierarchy and simultaneously on the other hand it points to the capacity of law to be a site of creativity, of change and of renewal. The idea of another law and another order is immanent from the very operation of the law. Law within the parameters of carnival draws attention to law as a medium not of fixity but of change. However, this possibility within law and law's carnivalesque participation are disavowed in the report of the police constable and in the law report. In these documents only the hierarchy, the distance, the monolithic is documented. The jolly relativity of law and legal practice is systematically erased.

CONCLUSION

Sir John's map of London demands that we rethink law and legal practice. Our analysis of the map has been an attempt to think the law, and expose the law as being Other. Rather than law as a system of rules and reason and officials engaged in the deployment of those rules and reason the map draws attention to legal practice as a practice of map making and set of techniques of space, surveillance and recording concerned with the production of space as a particular social order. The map also draws our attention to the need to think the relationship between the law and the body in different ways. The body cannot be reduced to an object of law, it is also a technique of law. That is, the techniques of producing this perverse London actually eradicate the distance between the perverse and the norm.

This mapping of the metropolis is also a mapping of a body, especially the body's (re)division into public and private. At the same time these cartographic practices produce a very specific, and impoverished representation of London and the male body. While the map represents a certain fixity, Horton's case draws our attention to the mobility in gender performance and the difficulty of containment. The problem of containment is also made in the drawing of boundaries. While the map locates designated sites of male erotic relations, at the same time other male encounters remain unrepresented. The bounded space puts them in a new shadow.

While the juridical surveillance machine might be implicated in the division of public and private, it also works within the parameters of an already existing public/private division. So, for example, the offence of buggery is rarely produced by way of the surveillance machinery described above as the act tends to take place by way of another division of the public/private which produces domestic space. Finally, the map draws our attention to another aspect of these landmarks: the startling distance, yet the simultaneous propinquity, between different, imbricated landscapes. The legal landmarks inscribed on the map can be described as markers of the limits of the moral economy of (good) citizenship.[31] By producing and representing a map of these transgressions, Sir John's map facilitates a reading of these 'invisible' transgressions of the limits, values and morals of the normative culture made by male-to-male genital encounters at specific sites in London. This mapping of London can be described as a representation of an unrepresentable danger from 'within'[32] the cultural space of London. From this perspective, knowledge of the geography of the landmarks becomes knowledgeability which legitimates actions which in turn legitimate the knowledge base.[33]

PART THREE

PARTNERS AND FAMILIES

INTRODUCTION

The essays which comprise this part focus on partnership and family law issues. While existing scholarship in this broad area has tended to focus on the 'pros' and 'cons' of 'gay marriage', or upon making (usually in the American constitutional context) legal arguments in favour of same-sex spousal recognition, these essays have a different focus. The emphasis here is on theoretical questions to do with legal strategizing, identity, privatization and the sociality of heterosexuality.

Jonathan Goldberg-Hiller's essay begins this section with a spatial exploration of the relationship between status and contract in same-sex domestic partnership and marriage debates. His interest is in how these debates illustrate broader issues concerning national citizenship. Heather Brook's contribution focuses on similar 'partnership' developments – this time in Australia. Brook interrogates the 'sexual performatives' of marriage/partnership discourse and concludes by reflecting on the relative intractability of heterosexual performatives despite lesbian and gay legal 'victories'.

Claire Young's essay provides a detailed examination of the effects of winning 'spousal rights' in Canada – in this case, inclusion in a taxation benefit scheme. Through exploring the court's construction of 'public' and 'private', Young questions to what degree the legal case she examines really is a 'success' for lesbians and gay men. Finally, Richard Collier's contribution represents a newly emergent concern in law and sexuality studies: the construction of heterosexuality in law. Through examining developments in UK family law and policy, Collier unpacks the myriad ways in which law and heterosexuality shape, reinforce and, at the same time, destabilize each other.

8

'MAKING A MOCKERY OF MARRIAGE'

DOMESTIC PARTNERSHIP AND EQUAL RIGHTS IN HAWAI'I[1]

JONATHAN GOLDBERG-HILLER

INTRODUCTION

Concern about marriage for same-sex couples in Hawai'i has mushroomed from the local to the national in the blink of an eye. The state-wide panic in Hawai'i following *Baehr v Lewin* (1993)[2] and *Baehr v Miike* (1996)[3] – holding that the state's refusal to grant marriage licenses to three same-sex couples violated the state constitutional ban on gender discrimination – has already led to a national 'Defense of Marriage Act' (DOMA) permitting states to ignore such marriages, constitutional language to the contrary notwithstanding.[4] What is all the more curious about DOMA, as well as the numerous state-wide attempts to restrict and preempt the Hawai'i courts, is that same-sex marriages don't yet exist. What do now exist, and what have successfully moved across jurisdictions in just as quick a manner – if more stealthily and with less associated panic – are domestic partnerships which provide some of the material benefits of marriage to those unable to marry by force of law (see Briggs, 1994; Christensen, 1998; Speilman and Winfeld, 1996). However, a growing political opposition to public and private domestic partnership agreements has made them remarkably visible today.

The recent convergence of public concern about these two policy innovations – same-sex marriage and domestic partnership – raises important questions which frame this chapter. What accounts for the changing political reception that marriage and domestic partnership receive? What can this politics of status tell us about the struggle for rights and citizenship, and about other strategies for social change? I argue in this chapter that contemporary debates over domestic partnership both reveal and construct a shifting tectonics of political space. Today, the vilifications of gays and lesbians that once characterized counter-discourse to rights demands have shared the agenda with arguments

about 'special rights' and about the limited capacities of states, political econ-
omies and societal institutions to continue the pluralist division of space on the
basis of legal right (Currah, 1997; Herman, 1994: 112ff; Herman, 1997: 28-59;
Patton, 1995, 1997). Indeed, discourse about the rights of gays and lesbians is
now only tangentially about the gay body and gay practice. By implicating the
place of courts and the limits of legal discourse it operates as a transformative
metonym for the body politic, a spatial arrangement contributing to a growing
scepticism and uncertainty about the costs and payoffs of rights strategies and
civil rights narratives (Bower, 1997; Connolly, 1991; Herman, 1994; Phelan,
1995; Schacter, 1997; Stychin, 1995; Vaid, 1995).

This chapter examines the discourse about domestic partnership in order to
map some details of this emerging space and the possibilities of progressive legal
mobilization within it. I present this changing terrain through an analysis of
debates over the meanings of the legal form of domestic partnership agreements
which I characterize as a discursive tension between status and contract. In contrast to the modernization thesis which approaches the evolution of individualist
contractual rights as an inevitable unfolding of liberty at the expense of status,
and in departure from dialectical theories which understand a functional relationship between the meanings of the legal form and economic or social relations,
I see the emerging discourse about the legal form as only loosely referential,
essentially plastic and unstable, and deeply implicated in the shifting boundaries
of political space and citizenship, and the uncertain strategies of legal mobilization within them. These discourses about the legal form also have important
material effects – beyond their significance for state competence –which further
explain their instability (see also Butler, 1998; Patton, 1997: 4). Significant here
are the hollowed meanings of economic contract and client status now that the
institutions of wage regulation, collective action, and redistribution preserved by
collective bargaining in the Fordist period have begun to wane.[5]

I explore these themes at further length below. I turn first to a theoretical
discussion of the legal form in order to highlight the distinctive genealogies of
citizenship which inhere in notions of contract and in status. In the following
section I draw from public testimonies and interviews with activists engaged in
the domestic partnership and marriage controversies in Hawai'i in order to show
how these discourses have been woven into the domestic partnership and same-
sex marriage debates. I demonstrate how the legal and political arguments in
this controversy have articulated an inconsistent and indeterminate relationship
between status and contract. In a final section, I examine the implications of this
indeterminacy for strategies of legal change which privilege domestic partnership as a prelude to a more inclusive citizenship for lesbians and gays.

THE RISE AND FALL OF DOMESTIC PARTNERSHIP

In April 1997, amid popular protest and legislative manoeuvring to derail the
marriage case, the Hawai'i legislature passed the nation's first state-wide domestic

partnership legislation. Hastily cobbled together and passed in an eleventh-hour conference committee facing a constitutional deadline, the legislation was a concession to appease the Senate which had qualms over a constitutional amendment that would wrest jurisdiction from the courts over the definition of marriage and lodge it securely in the legislature.[6] This compromise is inscribed in the language creating this new legal status. The Reciprocal Beneficiaries Act[7] (RBA) affirms that 'the people of Hawai'i choose to preserve the tradition of marriage as a unique social institution based upon the committed union of one man and one woman'[8] at the same time that it acknowledges that:

> there are many individuals who have significant personal, emotional, and economic relationships with another individual yet are prohibited by such legal restrictions from marrying . . . . Therefore, the legislature believes that certain rights and benefits presently available only to married couples should be made available to couples comprised of two individuals who are legally prohibited from marrying one another.[9]

The statute goes on to enumerate the contractual benefits and obligations to which reciprocal beneficiaries are entitled,[10] noting that they 'shall not have the same rights and obligations under the law that are conferred through marriage.'[11] The distinction between marriage status and RB status is reflexively understood in this language as a political difference. How might we understand this distinction and the compromise intended here? What is meant by the image of a people defending its status prerogatives against those whose evolving forms of social attachment are seen as needs to be recognized by independent statute?

Domestic partnership managed to avoid the political contrast with marriage for many years. Since the *Village Voice* first established a policy of extended benefits in 1982 – what they called 'spousal equivalents' – as a consequence of bargaining with one of its labour unions, the number of private companies granting benefits has rapidly expanded to more than 300 today.[12] Private companies and their unions paved the way for public agencies, universities and entire jurisdictions to follow suit. Large cities such as New York, Atlanta and Chicago now have domestic partnership arrangements for public employees and San Francisco mandates that private contractors with the city offer domestic partner benefits to their employees, and extend any public discounts for married couples to domestic partners on an equal basis. Lambda Legal Defense and Education Fund estimates that nearly one out of every four firms (23%) employing 5000 workers or more provides health benefits to non-traditional partners, and over 50 cities and counties and five states provide domestic partner benefits to their employees.

Since the national reaction to the Hawai'i marriage case, controversy has grown, most noticeably in Hawai'i itself, San Francisco, and in the case of Capital Cities/Disney, whose extension of benefits in 1996 led to a boycott by conservative Christian groups. Nonetheless, opposition has only infrequently

succeeded in overturning such benefits.[13] Arguments against domestic partnership have predominantly taken two forms (Briggs, 1994: 758). As in the case of
Disney, conservatives have reacted against what they have understood to be a
kulturkampf (see Sullivan, 1998); in the words of one conservative activist, '[b]y
offering same-sex benefits, companies take the position that homosexual unions
are morally equivalent to traditional marriage.'[14] In a second line of attack, it is
contractual obligation more than cultural status which has led to some employer
opposition. Ross Perot articulated this line when he became the first CEO to
roll back domestic partner benefits: '[This] has nothing to do with homosexuality. If we made this benefit available to everyone living together in the
same apartment the cost would be through the roof.'[15] In both cases, whether
the concerns be for the social status of legal status or for the obligation
of contract, there is an expressed anxiety about the limits of such policies. What
connects these two concerns?

The advent of domestic partnership in the 1990s suggests to some (both
empirically and normatively) a gradual evolutionary approach to equal rights for
gays and lesbians beginning with decriminalization of sodomy – and the
elimination of the status of the 'homosexual' – and ending, someday, in full
citizenship symbolized by equal rights to marriage (see Coleman, 1995: 545–7;
Sunstein, 1994; but compare Christensen, 1998; Wolfson, 1994). This legal
odyssey hearkens back to the early modernist ideas of a gradual elimination of
status relationships in favour of social regulation by contract. Sir Henry Maine
owns this citation with his argument that:

> [t]he word Status may be usefully employed to construct a formula
> expressing the law of progress .... All the forms of Status taken notice of in
> the Law of Persons were derived from, and to some extent are still coloured
> by, the powers and privileges anciently residing in the Family. If then we
> employ Status, agreeably with the usage of the best writers, to signify these
> personal conditions only, and avoid applying the term to such conditions
> as are the immediate or remote result of agreement, we may say that the
> movement of the progressive societies has hitherto been a movement *from
> Status to Contract.* (1917, 100; emphasis in the original)

Status, in this view, denotes persons bound into a social order, their obligations
and legal duties constricted by their position within familial, occupational and
religious institutions. In contrast to the expected submergence of the rational
will to the normative authority of the social unit in status relationships, contract
connotes a world view in which the accretion of social obligation is dissolved in
the autonomous intentional arrangements of the marketplace (Feinman and
Gabel, 1990: 375). Driven by the interests of *homo economicus,* 'every person
becomes man in the abstract ... every subject becomes an abstract legal subject'
(Pashukanis, 1978: 120–1). Society is made to shed its pre-conscious obligations, 'Man [is] the primary and solid fact; relationships [are] purely derivative'
(Robert Nisbet quoted in Bergman, 1991: 174).

Viewed from the modernist assumption of a growing contractualism, domestic partnership reflects a move toward social recognition of purely intentional arrangements based upon mutual understanding. Those corporate and governmental plans (such as Hawai'i's RBA) that are gender-neutral – that is they don't discriminate based on the sex of the partner and thereby include non-married heterosexual couples or even non-sexual partnerships in this status – acknowledge the inventiveness of social choice (and the movement toward contract) perhaps more than plans which limit benefits to gay or lesbian partners. This evolutionary/contractualist perspective might also be bolstered by recognition of the innovations in marriage law itself which have retained marriage as a dubious status with fewer social interests – hence, less obligation – than in its earlier incarnations. For example, unmarried cohabitation is no longer illegal, marriage is more easily dissolved, the legal significance of bastardy has declined along with its social condemnation, fornication and adultery are rarely prosecuted outside the military, penalties against homosexuality have been expunged or remain unenforced, and racial barriers to marriage have been eliminated. As marriage has assumed a more intentionalist character in this view, 'heterosexual marriage superficially appears to retain its central position in the social order [but] in reality, it has been largely undermined by the rise of the pure relationship and plastic sexuality' (Giddens, 1992: 154; see also Luhmann, 1986).

The policy consequences of this perspective are seen as a search for 'a new model of status[;] how we might use status in a way that is sensitive to both the egalitarian ideal and the pluralistic character of contemporary family life' (Regan, 1993: 118). In the words of one same-sex marriage advocate in Hawai'i:

Gone is the barbaric idea of a wife who is by law the property and completely under the control of her husband. Now a wife is an equal partner with her husband, both in fact and under the law. We call for further enlightenment.[16]

For many advocating this 'silent revolution' (Jacob, 1988), it is understandable why domestic partnership laws in combination with loosening legal bonds on marriage itself might be seen by some gay rights activists as 'a logical next step as the process of law reform continues' (Coleman, 1995: 545), especially because these social policy reforms are anchored in the popular legitimacy of legislative action and not adjudication.[17] For Richard Posner, the mature development of domestic partnership laws such as exist in Scandinavia constitutes 'in effect a form [of] contract that homosexuals can use to create a simulacrum of marriage' (1992: 313–4). In this view, contract has now become the sole basis of status.

This modernist and, indeed, realist perspective has significant explanatory limits, however. While the availability of domestic partnership surges, and as marriage is gradually hollowed out of its unitary legal character, marriage as a status concern has become culturally magnified, dominating state and national politics. Since the prospect of legalized same-sex marriage in Hawai'i, 48 states

have considered bills to restrict marriage to heterosexual couples; 29 of these
have been enacted as of this writing. Oklahoma, Ohio and other states are
considering the lead of Louisiana which has instituted a 'covenant marriage'
status designed to restrict rights to divorce for any:

> one male and one female who understand and agree that the marriage
> between them is a lifelong relationship.... Only when there has been a
> complete and total breach of the marital covenant commitment may the
> non-breaching party seek a declaration that the marriage is no longer
> legally recognized.[18]

Indeed, the politics of status today demonstrates an 'evanescent anxiety' over the
disappearing vestiges of status obscured by the expansive presence of contract.

For some observers, this growing anxiety over status is less a harbinger of
something new as much as it represents an inevitable dialectical reassertion
of the need for authority and legitimacy amid social change:

> Status and contract are both representative of a social need: status represents
> the need for legitimacy in legal adjudication; contract the need for formal
> legal categories which transcend the substantive issues of the particular case.
> In times of social change, the need for formal categories is preeminent
> because a stable and unbending legal referent is necessary to regulate
> dynamic social relations.... Status considerations return to ameliorate the
> effect of social change and bolster the formal legal categories with substan-
> tive considerations of justice. (Bergman, 1991: 216; see also Pound, 1909;
> Unger, 1987: 70)

This dialectical account of the movement between status and contract has
explanatory affinities for broader economic forces impinging on social change.
It helps explain why a limit to contract was reasserted earlier this century when
individualism was recognized to dangerously increase state and corporate power
(e.g. the rise of the legal labour union and the traditional family regimes that
higher wages produced; see Gabin, 1990) and why global economic needs for
flexible specialization involve an attack on the ideology of unions as well as
tolerance and support for newer forms of social and marital relationships (see
Stacey, 1996).

While the dialectical approach accounts for the security that status relationships can provide in a changing world, its functionalism assumes a clear corres-
pondence between social needs and legal instruments. I argue, however, that
despite the distinctive genealogies of status and contract and the forms of
subjectivity, security and society which they comprehend, functional theory is
confounded by a discursive uncertainty permeating the debates over domestic
partnership. Status and contract today are rhetorically entangled one with the
other, simultaneously and equally valorized by all parties to these debates, making

the very categories of the legal form discursively unstable and increasingly mutually interdependent. As I will illustrate later in this chapter, domestic partnership agreements are identified by some opponents as signs of illegitimate social status in one breath and castigated for extending obligations of contract in the next, while for proponents it is the possibility of contractual duty which signifies social acknowledgement and marks the status of citizenship. Haunting this uncertain referentiality is both the mobilizing fantasy of marriage between same-sex couples (see Hughes, 1998), and the uncertain significance of the contract relations (including marriage) to the political economy.

What I believe limits the dissonance in these debates are new and exclusionary languages of sovereignty and new practices of statecraft, fresh articulations of political spatiality within which support for equal rights and limitations of marriage and domestic partnership are made to echo melodiously. Donzelot has explored the historical roots of this tactical collusion, a 'harmony between the order of families and the order of the state' (1979: 25) which is once again a dream of new sources of power. When Ross Perot restricted benefits for the gay and lesbian partners of all his new employees, he maintained '[i]t has nothing to do with gay rights[;] it has everything to do with fairness and equity' (Myerson, 1998). This paradigmatic equation between the denial of rights and strengthened ideals of a democratic sovereign only balances because of this new power produced in the imagination of marriage as the privileged and official form of family–state relations.

If, as I am arguing here, contract and status have now become distinct discursive categories for common legal objects which help produce understandings of state sovereignty, what characteristics differentiate the two categories in these debates? In this chapter I use contract and status to indicate different subjectivities and the political theories and economic realities in which they are embedded. Contract explicitly interpellates an abstract identity such as the juridical self or the worker self. These identities are imagined to lie in parity within the contexts of democratic equality (e.g., blind justice or the market) and to encourage negotiated and egalitarian family relations. Status, in contrast, is a gesture toward the whole, socially integrated self (paradoxically understood as a necessary legal fiction). Since the whole is always limited by the social horizon, status presumes an implicit social boundary. For this reason, where contract assumes a democratic legitimacy, status relationships are often defended in republican or communitarian ideology based on a notion of respectable citizenship imbued with social values over and above legal rights.[19]

These democratic and republican traditions play off each other with evident political consequences in these debates. Cloaked in a republican mantle, legal status gains *social* status in its articulation of boundaries by contrasting itself to the limitless democratic character of contract. This contrast is present in other political venues but its impact is modulated by the political economy. It may be less significant for labour unions whose declining influence militates against a demonstration of the contribution their particular legal status makes to the universal conceptions of the social and economic good, than it is for such elite

legal/social statuses as corporations on whose increasingly unchallenged economic hegemony marriage as status is modelled. Nonetheless, just as identity
imagined through the lens of contract is diffracted by these particular conditions,
so too does status fail to articulate the universal since the social horizon is an
open boundary, never fully articulated. As Weitzman observes in the context
of marriage:

> The marriage contract is unlike most contracts: its provisions are unwrit-
> ten, its penalties are unspecified, and the terms of the contract are typically
> unknown to the 'contracting' parties. Prospective spouses are neither
> informed of the terms of the contract, nor are they allowed any options
> about these terms. In fact, one wonders how many men and women would
> agree to the marriage contract if they were given the opportunity to read it
> and to consider the rights and obligations to which they were committing
> themselves. (Quoted in Robson and Valentine, 1990: 528)

As Pateman has argued, these 'repressed dimensions' (1988: ix) of marital status
run in two directions. The explicit abstractions of the marital relationship have
their counterparts in the unarticulated dimensions of status in the democratic,
contractarian tradition.

This cultural repression permits competing discourses about the necessarily
ambiguous legal form to have unpredictable, but significant consequences.
Marriage can be articulated in the terms of social status when it is defended in
republican or communitarian language designed to firm social boundaries by
narrowing legitimate conceptions of the common good. But, marriage can also
be articulated as contract: as a series of discrete obligations democratically available to citizens capable of demonstrating their abstract capacities to rationally
assume such responsibility. Compounding this categorical slipperiness are transformations in the economic foundations of capitalism which alter traditional
meanings. The replacement of contract with ersatz post-Fordist discourses of
flexibility (Esser, 1996), adversarial bargaining relations with corporate 'team'
and 'family', and worker-as-producer with worker-as-consumer (Amin, 1994;
Casey, 1995) – all within the context of growing social inequality and economic
scarcity (Oliver and Shapiro, 1995) – has further obscured the distinctions
between status and contract, and made the meaning of the social contract
available for revision. Contract today can become a sign of economic profligacy
endangering the common good as much as it can remain a marker for the limits
of the sovereign body. Domestic partnership, particularly the legal form that it
has assumed, has become enmeshed in these debates as I show in the next
section of this chapter.

A SOVEREIGN PARTNERSHIP

In this section I examine debates over the legal form of domestic partnership.
I look particularly at the case of the RBA in Hawai'i since that law was historically

developed as a bulwark against the marriage case, thus intensifying the increasingly common types of discourse I am interested in here. But Hawai'i is uniquely situated for this type of study for other cultural reasons. Hawai'i has long been celebrated – and celebrates itself – for its tolerance and openness which sustains its romantic image. Since the end of the plantation era, Hawai'i has been a true ethnic melting pot where inter-racial relationships have become the norm rather than the exception. This social tolerance is reflected in the law, which has little cognizance of status exceptions. For example, Hawai'i has no anti-sodomy law. It has its own constitutional protection for equal rights on account of sex. It prohibits discrimination based on sexual orientation in public and private employment. And it has the *Baehr* case which would extend marriage to gay and lesbian couples. How the RBA reinforces, or works against the grain, of this cultural and legal logic is therefore of significant political importance.

Contract and status have had a peculiar and ambivalent relationship throughout the history of liberal thought. On the one hand, the discourse of contract is central to the liberal imagination of sovereignty, for contract presumes the subjectivity essential to liberal authority. For John Locke, contract is the basis of authority when it provides for a stable currency, a growing economy, and ultimately a means of protecting individual wealth and security through mutual agreement:

> And this *puts men* out of a state of nature *into* that of a *common-wealth*, by setting up a judge on earth, with authority to determine all the controversies, and redress the injuries that may happen to any member of the common-wealth; which judge is the legislative, or magistrates appointed by it. And where-ever there are any number of men, however associated, that have no such decisive power to appeal to, there they are still in the *state of nature.* (Locke, 1980 [1690]: 48)

In Locke's theory, then, contract eliminates the vestiges of many earlier social obligations, building new forms of social intercourse and authority based on self-interested acts of will. On the other hand, contract in Locke's account also signifies an important status relationship, here envisioned as the distinction between membership in the commonwealth and the civic virtues of restraint on which it rested, and the non-identities of the state of nature. For Kann (1991) this Lockean ambivalence is the origin of enduring American liberal and republican traditions.

Feminist theorists have shown that marriage, for Locke, retains a similarly ambivalent relationship to contract (see also Grossberg, 1985). Marriage retains this pre-political flavour, an island of 'paternal right' in a sea of 'political right' (Pateman, 1988). It also marks the limits of community by institutionalizing the flow of property to successive generations. Nancy Fraser has questioned whether social and economic organization should continue to be seen as more than an enduring double dynamic of contract and patriarchal status. In the present, 'post-socialist condition' gender dynamics are ambivalent, subjectivity constructed both by the legal meaning of contract and the materialism of the market:

> Even as the wage contract establishes the worker as subject to the boss's command in the employment sphere, it simultaneously constitutes that sphere as a limited sphere. The boss has no right of direct command outside it.... In those arenas which are themselves permeated by power and inequality, the wage functions as a resource and source of leverage. For some women, it buys a reduction in vulnerability through marriage. (Fraser, 1997: 230)
>
> Gender inequality is today being transformed by a shift from dyadic relations of mastery and subjection to more impersonal structural mechanisms that are lived through more fluid cultural forms. One consequence is the (re)production of subordination even as women act increasingly as individuals who are not under the direct command of individual men. Another is the creation of new forms of political resistance and cultural contestation. (Fraser, 1997: 234-5)

My goal below is to further examine this political resistance and cultural contestation. Rather than limiting the impact of status, as Fraser seems to suggest, status returns in a manner that Locke might understand, even if in a form he might not recognize. While these new dynamics are unique, they are not 'merely cultural' (Butler, 1998), but remain connected to the discursive dynamics of the modern political economy.

This is revealed in the phenomenological impressions of the threats posed by the political demands of gays and lesbians by anti-rights activists:

> Hawai'i has been changing a lot. Quite frankly, people are saying, not for the better. We have more crime. People aren't as nice.... I grew up here ... we used to keep things unlocked. You never worried about churches being broken into. Now we have rectories that have bars on the windows. The poor rectories. It's not like there's anything in them. This is not Philadelphia.... On top of that, the economy stinks. I think people are saying, wait a second, someone's determining social policy. Someone's determining what Hawai'i's going to look like. It ain't us. We are not benefiting.... At a certain moment I think people started to think, wait a second. The gays aren't just asking for protection of housing and employment.... We're OK with that. But now you want us to redefine marriage for you? Wait a second. You said you weren't going to do that.... I think people really started to feel that they were out of control. They're not asking for a few things and we'll give a little, and get a little. They want everything. This is really it.[20]
>
> There's just something really special between me and my husband.... How do we preserve society the way it is? I guess, when people see our

culture going through a lot of changes, they're saying we need to draw the line somewhere. They're trying to draw it in other social issues. Gun control and things like that. Well, we need to draw the line here, too. I guess it's one way of society saying: this is where we're going to stand for now.[21]

The fear that gay and lesbian demands for rights are responsible for individual perceptions of being 'out of control', demanding 'everything', is met by efforts to 'draw the line'. This desire to recreate secure social boundaries inside of which democratic sovereignty is re-imagined is challenged by the loss of usual status markers by which gays and lesbians were previously 'contained' (Fortin, 1995). Without a spatial location, a history, and a nation – all sovereign boundaries around which many modern-day status markers cohere – once gays successfully challenged homosexuality's status as a medical psychopathology in the early 1970s, they were more free to 'expos[e] the range and variety of bounded spaces upon which heterosexual supremacy depends, [to] see and conquer places that present the danger of violence to gays and lesbians, to reterritorialize them' (Berlant and Freeman, 1993: 205).

This boundary challenge has novel phenomenological and legal components, especially since legal rights for gays and lesbians have been secured without a 'protected class' status.[22] Rights provide the requisite subjectivity for contract, and the basis for social recognition within the status of nation. As Marx once characterized this notion:

The state abolishes, after its fashion, the distinctions established by *birth*, *social rank*, *education*, *occupation*, when it decrees that birth, social rank, education, occupation are *non-political* distinctions; when it proclaims, without regard to these distinctions, that every member is an *equal* partner in popular sovereignty and treats all the elements which compose the real life of the nation from the standpoint of the state. (Marx, 1978 [1848]: 33, emphasis in original)

Against this liberal background it is common to hear in response to supporters of *Baehr* who see 'the first legal decisions establishing that gay people are also protected by the Constitution',[23] that protection for gays' citizenship rights is not in question. As one conservative activist told me, 'we're not anti-homosexual at all. They have every right under the Constitution that you and I ... anybody has,'[24] rights legitimately acknowledged by Hawai'i's anti-discrimination statutes. Instead, it is the articulation of status differences based on the extension of these rights which recreates security and resists the realization of the imaginary world that rights gains help produce.

One way that this status is constructed is through self-positioning. Attempts to prevent same-sex marriage are best fought out in the rational middle of the road, eschewing obstacles of passion. 'On this issue in particular, and a lot of these hot button issues, it's the extremes that are a problem. They tend to define

the issues. Extreme right and extreme left. Neither one I find very desirable'
(Alexander). For this reason, the main conservative opponents distance themselves from religious labels: 'It became very difficult for us to publicly say, "Yes,
we have religions that are supporting us"; . . . it's not something we've gone and
said to the community.'[25] This positioning works well in an island community
feeling the threat of social change. Even in an economy that depends upon
global tourism, it is the imagination of the extension of the political community
to outsiders and the mixing of cultural with political citizenship which helps
reproduce status boundaries:

> We wanted [a group] that was non-religious. That was kind of ordinary,
> middle of the road people. People that live here. Because the polls . . .
> showed that those who supported same-sex marriage were those who were
> from outside. The most recent moved here tend to be Caucasian. The
> Orientals and those who had lived here were those most opposed to same-
> sex marriage. Even the Hawaiians were overwhelmingly against same-sex
> marriage. So we wanted something that would represent us . . . . We wanted
> it focused on what was really an issue for Hawai'i. We wanted us to have
> a word. Not the courts. And to a certain extent, not even the legisla-
> ture. We wanted them to represent us the people, the middle, the silent
> majority. (Alexander)

The imagination of a bounded community pursuing a reasonable, centrist
course, responsive to threats to individual and collective security is furthered by
legal arguments contrasting contract to status. The RBA serves as a unique and
ambivalent handle in this regard. In as much as the RBA establishes an ersatz
'marriage' equivalency, the two statuses appear as competing estates threatening
to erase the significance of their differences. As one attorney voiced the problem
with this equation, 'domestic partnerships are the means of conferring preferred
status upon homosexual couples, but without calling it marriage. It will thereby
dilute the significance of marriage.'[26] This dilution stems from the ways in
which the RB relationship is unavailable to heterosexuals able to marry:

> If a reciprocal beneficiary does not include qualified unmarried people,
> then opposite sex unmarried couples would again be disadvantaged, and
> reciprocal beneficiaries would be elevated above parents and placed closer
> to married status in the [social] hierarchy.[27]

However, because the Act is not limited to gay or lesbian couples but recognizes
any two life-partners – even partners residing out of state – it can also serve as a
metaphor for a loss of rational boundaries threatening republican restraint and
its benefit to economic health:

> The reciprocal beneficiaries, that pretty much gives [recognition to] couples
> . . . not necessary gay couples but people that are not permitted to

marry.... Apparently this has opened a unique can of worms. Because [now] we're only limited by our imaginations. That's probably not what the legislators intended when they did it.... But it just goes to show you what happens. [We're] in enough trouble with the economy that it would just put another nail in the coffin. (Kurtz)

Where do you draw the line in this whole area?... What if two brothers live together or a mother and a son live together or a daughter and three sisters – all these combinations? It could be devastating to our economy because many times ... when there are those kinds of rights ... the abuse is unbelievable. (Paul)

I think people see a limit is being crossed when the absurd starts to become possible. (Alexander)

Formless, this new status threatens to escape democratic control.[28] On the social front it may consume the newly established middle ground: 'the [RBA] is a foot in the door for homosexual activists to achieve their ultimate goal – societal acceptance of homosexuality on an equal basis as heterosexuality.'[29] The result is a loss of self-recognition in the very forms of the political debate. In reference to the November ballot amendment to wrest control of the *Baehr* decision, one activist remarked:

In the old days, when you said marriage, the popular assumption was a man and a woman are getting married.... When I read the Amendment statement [I'm lost. It says] 'Opposite sex couples.' Believe it or not, opposite-sex couples is a real stumbling block for people. That's normal folks. It seems strange for something to be worded as opposite-sex couples. We're used to hearing same-sex couples. We've heard same sex-couples for three years. And now opposite-sex couples seems odd. (Kurtz)

Since RB status is really like contract, lacking any natural social boundaries, it may engender its own necessity and the involvement of the legislature with further severe consequences for individual security:

The language and effect of this bill is to establish a category which is parallel to marital status in all but name. It gives certain rights and benefits to this status which can be added to, each year, on an incremental basis so that eventually what we know as 'marriage' may become a subset of this status. We realize that this is not the intention ... but unfortunately, due to the structure of this bill we think that this end is virtually unavoidable. (Alexander)

Courts are not immune to this expansionary logic. As one social worker testified about the RBA: 'a court which can find a right to homosexual marriage in our

Constitution can also be expected to stretch reciprocal relationship statutes beyond any intentions we can presently imagine.'[30]

This vulnerability to political institutions is also obtusely mirrored on the part of gay rights' proponents. For some, the RBA is 'a right step in several directions' in part because it might 'escape the politically laden phrases such as marriage and domestic partnerships',[31] thereby ensuring a more rational debate over civil rights. Yet, for many proponents, the productiveness of this debate is in question for the very reasons that conservative opponents mistrust the judicial and legislative processes. 'Domestic partnership as suggested leaves open a Pandoras [sic] box of judicial decisions about who qualifies.'[32] Where opponents to domestic partnership see status, many gay rights supporters see the legislature as only able to provide contract, and insufficiently at that. For these activists, the RBA is a 'feeble attempt at providing far too few rights to the gay and lesbian community in lieu of granting them full and equal rights provided in state sanctioned marriage', and in this regard the meaning for citizenship is second-order, no better than 'allowing Rosa Parks to "have a seat in the back of the bus" '.[33] As one activist accused the legislature, '[o]ut of the entire supermarket of rights and benefits, you've served up four cans of soup. That's four more than we had before, but it's not a balanced diet. It's a measly meal on a placemat of fear.'[34] It is the contrast between full marriage rights, precluded by the proposed amendment, and the limited scope of the RBA, which demonstrates for these activists that domestic partnership is discriminatory.

With different valances, the mistrust of how political institutions handle issues of status and contract tends to foreclose domestic partnership options for opponents and proponents of equal status alike. For gay rights advocates, the avoidance of institutional uncertainty ultimately demands the affirmation of equality by unconditionally upholding the ruling of *Baehr*. Conservatives ignore the mutual unhappiness with the RBA, resurrecting it as a Frankenstein demanding increasingly more legislative appeasement. This helps make the case for the direct involvement of the people to reclaim their threatened sovereignty by means of a constitutional amendment restricting marriage to heterosexual couples. Yet, for conservatives, the multiplicity of legal statuses projected in these images of the RBA and domestic partnership movement still demands that 'traditional' marriage be differently valued, that the state be held accountable for its preferences.

In order to make the claim that the RBA is a status of a different sort – and not, qua status, equal to the status of marriage – the idea of domestic partnership is rhetorically contrasted to (fictive) claims for marriage status. The model for this argument was advanced by Governor Pete Wilson of California in 1994 when he refused to sign Bill 2810 which would have established domestic partnership. He wrote then:

> We need to strengthen, not weaken the institution of marriage. In virtually every culture, marriage has been deservedly celebrated as a relationship demanding commitment and unselfish giving to one's family – especially

to one's children. Government policy ought not to discount marriage by offering a substitute relationship that demands much less – and provides much less than is needed both by the children of such relationships, and ultimately much less than is needed by society.[35]

Despite the *Baehr* (1996) trial decision finding no merit in these reasons to prefer marriage over other partnerships, the RBA has become the rhetorical substitute to demonstrate the continuing necessity of such a preference. Much as Governor Wilson has suggested, marriage is distinguished for its social connotations, especially the expectation of responsibility and 'restrained citizenship' (Kann, 1991: 15) which it is supposed to signify:

I think it's problematic ... creating this whole new category of law that leaves undertones of sexual categorization without a clear distinction between why we benefit certain relationships and why we don't. I think it's problematic. The better way to do it, which I agree is more complicated, which is why the legislatures want this quick, is to look at the different benefits and decide which ones could be extended and which one should be extended and which ones ought not to be ... to do the hard work. (Alexander)

[Traditional families] tend to build a stronger society. And produce a citizen that we would like to see.... Fragmented families or new families have shown that [they don't] produce the strong individuals that you need to hold society together. In a society like the United States, we have a lot of personal freedom but with it comes a lot of personal responsibility. [You must] be willing to give up personal gratification for the betterment of the society. (Kurtz)

Public arguments make it clear that the legal form of RB status signifies this lack of responsibility and lowered social value of these newer relationships:

I note that this bill [RMA] does not appear to confer any fees or costs on the reciprocal beneficiaries it seeks to embrace. Clearly, parties to marriage receive no such freebies. Therefore, as written this bill appears to discriminate against those who are permitted to marry.[36]

One opponent of San Francisco's Proposition S, which would have created limited domestic partnerships in the late 1980s, echoed the same concern:

The draft ordinance states that 'domestic partnerships' are relationships which can be minimally defined by six-month periods. The ordinance does not see 'domestic partnership' as entailing any of the manifold legal rights or duties created by marriage; rather domestic partnerships 'create no legal rights or duties from one of the parties to the other.' Thus domestic partnership in the proposed ordinance seeks to provide domestic partners all of the public benefits of marriage while imposing none of the legal obligations of marriage.[37]

The anxious equation of legal status with social status, the expressed fear that 'equal economic benefits [for gays and lesbians are] merely a first step; [t]hey will not be satisfied until they have equal social, religious and economic status with heterosexual couples',[38] is modified by arguments about the legal form these status relationships take. This rhetorical positioning uses the relative openness of domestic partnership status laws – both the undefined nature of the relationships they cover and their incompleteness which is yet to be perfected by future legislatures – to make a contrast with marriage and draw a limit. In the logic of status, it is those legitimately burdened with the responsibility for community who must take in hand their political responsibilities and reconstruct their own security at the ballot box. Majorities are crucial in this *realpolitik*, but so are sovereign discourses about law and its relationship to cultural values.

One important aspect of the debates about the cultural status of legal status is that the social advantages which accrue to heterosexual married couples do so because they represent an authentic sovereignty. Rather than the social contractarian imagery of individual equal rights predating the social body, it is society and its status relationships which provide the basis for the reconstituted political body delimited by adherence to the norms of heterosexual status. This rhetorical inversion is deeply layered in that law is invoked to substantiate the original claim for status, but status is then fetishized as the solitary claim for law, able to redeem law:

Part of the problem [since the *Baehr* case] relates to Hawai'i's Constitution which was changed at the last Constitutional convention [to include equal protection on account of sex]. By doing that, I guess it was really us, we the people did that ... whether unwillingly or intentionally, we did that. We essentially opened the door for the court interpretation that we got. Now in retrospect we're going, wait a minute, that wasn't what we meant.... You have law and justice ... and justice should be interpreted culturally. (Kurtz)

I think ... implicit in some of the desires to redefine family is that for anything to be legitimate it has got to be recognized by law. And I would say, well, no. I mean, law has to recognize those things which are necessary for the common good and for the basic protection of individual rights. Which, of course, is always in connection with the common good I am not defined just by my rights as a human being. I am defined also by my responsibilities. To other individuals, to myself, the environment, to the community, to institutions within the community as well. (Alexander)

The idea that rights are dependent upon proof of the common good inverts the usual argument that gays and lesbians are seeking 'special rights'. To the contrary, it is heterosexuals who deserve special rights, particularly the special status of marriage.

CONCLUSION

The idea that the demand for equal rights threatens popular security is reproduced through a re-imagination of sovereign political space. Domestic partnership has played a mediating role in this new cartography by modulating the debate over equal rights to marriage, permitting new arguments about the limits to equality and the power of status to reconstitute the political body. Central to this reactionary response to domestic partnership is the articulation of a slippery interface between status and contract. When domestic partnership is argued to be a fair source of protection for lesbians, gays and others who have no benefit of marriage, languages of contract are tactically deployed, depicting now the material danger of an unfettered extension of obligation amid economic needs for restraint, later the open horizon of legal status demanding social limits to reclaim political space and reconstitute a more authentic social contract. When domestic partnership is argued to be a status equivalent to marriage or when it is argued to be a stepping-stone to full participation in citizenship for gays and lesbians, heterosexual status is conflated with citizenship by again playing off the legal form: the apparent cost-free nature of new legal statuses or their ersatz quality due to their open membership. Reinforced by the convergence of liberal contract theory and by republican and communitarian ideologies, equality and status differences are reimagined to reinforce new majorities and a resilient sovereignty.

The elections in November 1998, demonstrated the force of this new mapping of political space when, after a hard-fought multi-million dollar campaign which dominated all other state-wide contests, nearly 70 percent of the electorate voted for a Constitutional amendment intended to derail the *Baehr* case. The day following the election, the Democratic Governor, re-elected with the slimmest of majorities in a race in which both he and his opponent supported the amendment, declared his intent to revive the domestic partnership law as a sign of his party's (belated) commitment to equal rights. The reaction by anti-marriage activists was immediate. The chair of the Alliance for Traditional Marriage condemned those trying 'to make a mockery of marriage':[39]

It's a sad day for democracy in Hawai'i. Just one day after the people made it absolutely clear that we don't want same-sex marriage, the Governor declares that he will push for legalization of same-sex marriage in the legislature, but in the disguise of a different name; same-sex union or domestic partnership. This is an outrageous attempt to undermine the will of the people.[40]

One outraged citizen echoed:

I voted for [the Governor] and the marriage amendment so I'm bummed. Throughout the campaign [he] said he was against same-sex marriage. Then one day after the election, he says he wants a domestic partnership law. Any idiot knows this is just another name for homosexual marriage. . . . Governor, you betrayed 70 percent of the people. . . . Shame on you.[41]

The Governor's response was equivocal. As his communications director explained:

> [The] Governor . . . supports domestic partnerships, which are by no means the same as same-sex marriages. Domestic partnerships extend such rights as hospital visitations and shared insurance benefits to people who have formed long-standing domestic relationships. A domestic partnership law will not place such relationships on a par with traditional marriages. By asking next year's Legislature to create a workable domestic partnership law, [he] is working to provide equal rights for everyone without altering the institution of traditional marriage.[42]

That domestic partnership can be portrayed as a compromise, one able to preserve the status of traditional marriage while providing 'equal rights for everyone', suggests the cultural interplay of contract and status will continue to define a political space in which the denial of citizenship for a few can be made in the name of citizenship for all.

How to tactically exploit such paradoxical terrain is unclear. Debate within the rights advocacy community now turns on whether to seize the Governor's initiative to gain increased partnership benefits without a signifier of equal citizenship, or to continue litigation against the amendment in opposition to a sovereign super-majority. These unsatisfying options were narrowed when the Hawai'i Supreme Court ruled in 1999 on the final appeal of the *Baehr* case, dismissing the marriage option on account of the amendment and remaining eerily silent on the underlying issue of equal protection. Several months later in early 2000, the legislature silently tabled remediation of the RBA. In the complex and indistinct discursive interplay of status and contract, one certitude must soon prevail: the strategic hope for expanded citizenship based on domestic relations law is a labyrinthine dead-end.

Perhaps what has been experienced in Hawai'i may encourage a deconstruction of the very terms of citizenship, revealing its exclusiveness, privilege and ultimate indeterminacy in both its democratic and republican guises. As Shane Phelan (1998: 1) has pointedly noted, '[t]he political goal of equality cannot be achieved without thorough examination of the structures of thought and society that have made political equality seem scandalous.' That interrogation, she demonstrates, is likely to make alternative conceptions of citizenship based on republican ideas of work, tropes of reasoning and passionate bodies, and on democratic notions of abstract rights, face the same problems of exclusion encountered by a politics of access to marriage and domestic partnership. Progressive struggle now is likely to have to work on the interstices of these various legal and political discourses. As an example, individual security and collective recognition may advance less through a direct engagement of marriage rights in courts and legislatures, than through ancillary struggles which make access to health care, shelter and the like, independent of domestic status. This interstitial politics – although difficult – might best revalue the sovereign discourses of contract and status that have themselves made a mockery of marriage.

9

HOW TO DO THINGS WITH SEX[1]

HEATHER BROOK

INTRODUCTION

In his seminal lectures, How To Do Things With Words (1962), linguistic philosopher J.L. Austin posits that sometimes saying is doing. In the utterance 'I christen this ship . . .' a ship is launched; in the judge's utterance 'I sentence you . . .' the criminal is condemned; and so on. In this chapter, I want to take a leaf out of Austin's book to suggest that sometimes 'doing it' is saying, too. Sex-acts can 'say' all sorts of things. I want to argue that conjugal sex has an important recent history: in matrimonial law, sex acts are invested with specifically heterosexual imperatives and injunctions. I will show how married bodies are inscribed with and reiterate what I call 'sexual performatives' – that is, how we 'do things with sex' in much the same way as we 'do things' with performative utterance. Using J.L. Austin and Judith Butler as theoretical springboards, the immediate aim of this chapter is to contextualize current debates on same-sex marriage.[2]

At present, various strategies are being mooted to regulate gay and lesbian relationships. The most popular (or at least the most obvious) options include ending the debarment of gay and lesbian couples from existing marriage and/or *de facto* relationships law, or creating entirely new 'partnerships' legislation. Each option comes with differently weighted political subjectivities and effects. My main argument in this essay is that matrimonial law, with all its heterosexist inscriptions, helps to constrain and construct subjectivities – that is, our identities (who we are) and our capacities (what we can do). The crux of my argument is that the identities and capacities of husbands and wives are very different from those of 'domestic partners'. At the heart of this difference is sex; and, in particular, the (hetero)sexual performatives of marriage and matrimonial law.

The argument is organized into four main sections. In the first of these, 'Words and deeds', Austin's work on performative utterance serves as a useful starting point. From here, I will present an abbreviated exposition of Judith Butler's development of 'performativity'. Butler's theory of gender performativity has drawn extensive feminist commentary and critique concerning the constitution of sexed subjectivity, but these critiques will not be canvassed here.

Rather, in the second section of the chapter, 'Governing performing subjects', I will suggest that our identities and capacities as subjects depend on the various and political means by which performative transformations are *authorized*. After all, anyone can say 'I sentence you to 10 years imprisonment', but the performative consequences of sentencing (that is, the infliction of punishment upon the person sentenced) will not 'work' unless the words are spoken by a judge in a courtroom at the end of a trial.

The third section of the chapter, 'The conjugal body politic', uses Australian matrimonial law to illustrate the corporeal performatives of marriage. Here, I will argue that sexual performatives – that is, sex acts which impart legal meanings and consequences – have operated to constitute a unified conjugal body. This conjugal body is reminiscent of coverture – that supposedly archaic practice by which husband and wife become one person at law, that one being the husband (Blackstone, 1765). Though coverture has been challenged by various feminist reforms, I will contend that its (hetero)sexual performatives remain a key trope in marriage and (to a lesser extent) marriage-like relationships.

I will turn, finally, to the legal regulation of gay and lesbian relationships in one Australian jurisdiction. In this section, 'Regulating same-sex/ual relationships', I will suggest that it is reasonable to conceptualize the Australian Capital Territory's Domestic Relationships legislation as a strategy of subversion. However, even though the ACT legislation can be understood as a tactic of iterative and subversive mimicry, it has not delivered a homosexual citizen-subject whose status and capacities are comparable to those produced in the heterosexual performatives of marriage. The subversive potential of 'legitimate' same-sex relationships is limited by the absence or incompleteness of a properly authorized basis from which homosexual performatives might succeed on the same terms as certified, heterosexual performatives. In other words, subjects imbricated in homosexual performatives are constituted as different from those imbricated and inscribed by heterosexual performatives. What's more, part of the basis for this different, less privileged political subjectivity is inscribed in law. I conclude that there are two options for reforming and redressing the injustices suffered by gay and lesbian couples in the government of relationships, both of which relate to political subjectivities and their performative capacities.

WORDS AND DEEDS

Austin: Doing Things with Words

Austin's theory, at its simplest, is that we 'do things with words' when we use performative utterances. He says:

(1) the performative should be doing something as opposed to just saying something; and
(2) the performative is happy or unhappy as opposed to true or false. (Austin, 1962: 132)

Examples of performative utterances include naming ('I christen this ship *The Titanic*'), promising ('I promise to come and see you'), betting ('I bet Phar Lap will win the horse-race'), declaring (as when a cricket umpire declares 'No ball'), sentencing ('I sentence you to ten years imprisonment'), and so forth. In each of these cases, 'the issuing of the utterance is the performing of an action' (Austin, 1962: 5) and may thus be understood as 'performative'.

One of the most oft-cited examples of performative utterance is the saying of wedding vows.[3] To be lawfully married, parties are required to make certain ceremonial utterances: the 'I do's and 'I now pronounce you' (etc.) of wedding ceremonies.[4] Austin posits that for a performative utterance to succeed, however, it must be made in accordance with any number of cultural conventions: 'Speaking generally,' said Austin, 'it is always necessary that the *circumstances* in which the words are uttered should be in some way, or ways, *appropriate*' (Austin, 1962: 8, his emphasis). Such circumstances determine whether a performative utterance is authorized or not.[5] A television soap opera wedding between two characters, for example, does not result in the marriage of the two actors reciting their lines – even though they may replicate the correct ceremony precisely. Under Australian matrimonial law, soap opera marriage is null and void according to regulations concerning identity, authority and intent. Austin's interest in performatives was entirely (or at least largely) concerned with matters peculiar to linguistic philosophy, but his approach may, as we will see, be applied much more broadly.

In a discursive milieu, it is quite possible to understand *all* utterances as performative. At least, whatever we say, our words are imbricated in webs of knowledge and power, uttered and understood against cultural conventions of linguistic and discursive intelligibility. Latter-day theorists have adapted and extended Austin's work in interesting directions – the most notable development being Judith Butler's work on gender performance (1990) and hate speech (1997).

Butler: Doing Things with Austin

Butler's redeployment of J.L. Austin is difficult to define concisely. Her work is, in her own words, 'dense or difficult to read or theoretically rarefied' (Butler, 1992: 85), and draws on a number of influential philosophers such as Foucault, Wittig and Kristeva to develop arguments which exceed the scope of this chapter. For present purposes, a diminishing simplification is necessary and, I hope, forgivable.

Butler argues that embodiment is discursively informed; that gender is both inscribed upon and performed through the body. In a sense, she seems to figure bodies *as* utterances: that is, she suggests that bodies are both discursively informed and discursively productive. 'We do things with language, produce effects with language, and we do things to language', she says, 'but language is also the thing that we do' (Butler, 1997: 8). She contends that gendered and sexed identities are constituted in the repetitive performance of social norms; norms which police and construct 'compulsory heterosexuality' (after Rich,

1980). After Foucault, she posits a subject which does not precede its social construction in any essential way: 'There is no "sex" to which a supervening law attends; in attending to sex, in monitoring sex, the law constructs sex, producing it as that which calls to be monitored and is inherently regulatable' (Butler, 1996: 64). Butler's deployment of performativity comes, in the first place, from her reading of Austin through Derrida and other contemporary theorists. She draws, from this reading, a space in which to interrogate what we might call self-discourse, or ways in which subjects deploy 'I' in identificatory processes. Butler's contention is that, in the variously successful and imperfect renditions of performative utterances, the norms and conventions through which they are understood are reinforced or contested. 'Performativity', says Butler:

> is thus not a singular 'act,' for it is always a reiteration of a norm or set of norms, and to the extent that it acquires an act-like status in the present, it conceals or dissimulates the conventions of which it is a repetition. Moreover, this act is not primarily theatrical; indeed, its apparent theatricality is produced to the extent that its historicity remains dissimulated. (Butler, 1993: 12)

In the potential for the failure or partial failure to perform utterances or speech acts 'correctly' (that is, according to conventionally established norms), discursive fields of social contestation are identified. In this way, says Butler, 'change and alteration is part of the very process of "performativity"' (1995: 133–4).

Butler argues that gender performance proceeds as iterative mimicry without reference to any 'original', or prior, standard. In *Gender Trouble*, she uses drag as an example or illustration of her notion of gender performativity (1990: 136–9). While she celebrates the subversive potential of drag, Butler means to expose the material referentlessness of gendered identity: no person ever actually inhabits or performs gender perfectly, for the standards of 'correct' gender performance are not fixed, but float in a perpetual reconstruction of symbolic or psychic binaries pitting heterosexuality against non-heterosexuality:

> *[G]ender is a kind of imitation for which there is no original*; in fact, it is a kind of imitation that produces the very notion of the original as an *effect* and consequence of the imitation itself. In other words, the naturalistic effects of heterosexualized genders are produced through imitative strategies; what they imitate is a phantasmatic ideal of heterosexual identity, one that is produced by the imitation as its effect. (Butler, 1991: 21, her emphasis)

Butler's theoretical fascination with drag has seen a certain misreading of her notion of performance. In her contention that 'gender ... produces on the skin, through the gesture, the move, the gait (that array of corporeal theatrics understood as gender presentation)' (Butler, 1990: 28), some have understood Butler to be figuring gender as a kind of vast costume box from which one might whimsically select the significatory accoutrements of one's preferred gender of the day (Butler, 1992: 83)

Butler defends her position against precisely this sort of criticism in *Bodies That Matter* (1993), taking up Austin's distinction between perlocutionary and illocutionary utterances in ways that are not especially relevant to the present discussion. Her focus directs attention to the constitutive operations of gender performativity, but relates more to psychic identifications than to the political mechanisms of transformation. Some performatives have relatively fixed meanings and consequences; others, like dress-ups, are much more fluid. To illustrate the point with a mundane example: my consumption of breakfast cereal might be utterly imbued with performative inscriptions. The advertising message of the brand, for example, or my understanding of dietary discourses might see me constituting, embodying, 'performing' my breakfast routine against norms of self-care: I might eat Weet-Bix because 'nine out of ten nutritionists recommend it', accomplishing a performative of 'health' as I eat. If I switch tomorrow to Fruit-Loops, the change in my performative construction of my embodied self is unlikely to be self-evident, and (barring spills) is unlikely to be proclaimed in any overt resignification of my identity. In any case, my consumption of Weet-Bix might be entirely unrelated to brand-name discourses: perhaps I avoid exposing myself to advertising; perhaps I select whichever cereal happens to be on special at the time of my weekly trip to the supermarket.

By contrast, if I marry tomorrow, a great deal would seem to change: the bank manager might be more likely to approve my application for a loan; my employer might be less inclined to promote me; I might adopt my husband's name and apply to have all my identificatory papers and cards altered; I might begin to recognize myself – the way that my being is constituted in all manner of everyday activities – as fundamentally altered. Above all, I might find myself *interpellated* differently, even to the point of being called by a new name. There is a clear difference in the constitutive and conventional weight of these performatives: marriage is far less subtle in its identificatory or subjectifying results. This seems to me to point to the need for identifying how performative weights and consequences vary. We can begin this task by theorizing performative subjects within specifically regulatory contexts.

GOVERNING PERFORMING SUBJECTS

J.L. Austin's subjects 'do' as they 'speak', yet retain some prior ontology: that is to say, Austinian subjectivity assumes a doer prior to the deed (Butler, 1997: 24). In Austin's ontology, performers of utterances and the illocutionary force of their utterances are conceptually separate: subjects enter, already complete, into the transactions of utterance. His subjects are relatively discrete: their capacities to make 'happy' performative utterances depend largely on *already fixed* cultural conventions and ascriptions (Butler, 1997: 24–5). Butler's subjects, on the other hand, are intimately involved in establishing, sustaining or indeed subverting the conventions which render various bodily performances intelligible. Drawing from philosophers who argue the inseparability of identity and discourse, Butler argues that there is no doer before the deed. Rather, subjects simultaneously construct and are inscribed by discourse. In this sense, every utterance is performative, and every action is discursive: saying is doing, and doing is saying. Butler's entwinement of actions and discourse destabilizes the separation of subjects and their discursive transactions, but retains the transformative referentiality problematized by Austin.

Austin's subjects are figured as regulated by rules of law, while Butler's are governed through the regulatory operations of norms. In the realm of marriage and relationships regulation, Austin's subjects become married only according to fixed legal conventions: they must make the performative utterances of marriage according to prescribed laws, and the effects of a wedding ceremony are intricately rule-bound. Butler's subjects, however, might 'perform' marriage by adopting the normative conventions of a husband-and-wife relationship, without necessarily fixing those norms in law. To put it another way, Butler's subjects might be 'married' by virtue of their adoption of certain relationship behaviour which is generally understood as conjugal, whether or not they have made the performative utterances of wedding.

This is not to suggest that Austin's bride and groom are governed, while Butler's are not, or that Butler's subjects supersede Austin's. On the contrary, both are governed (in different ways), and both may exist simultaneously. Under Australian marriage law, most people marry by performing wedding utterances, but this is not the *only* sense in which people may be understood as 'married'. The Australian Department of Social Security, for example, assesses welfare entitlements according to a long list of normative criteria in order to determine whether a claimant should receive welfare entitlements as a 'single' or 'married' person. Austin's husband and wife are unequivocally married according to performative utterances inscribed by rule of law, while Butler's may be deemed married, or not, according to assessments of the couple's day-to-day performance of their relationship against a set of normative calculations.

I have oversimplified both Austin's lectures and Butler's extension and adaptation of his ideas. Both move into linguistic and philosophical nuances outside the scope of my present undertaking. I want to confine my thoughts to one small aspect of both Austin's and Butler's positions as they apply to the particular instance of marriage. In Australia, as I have already indicated, marriage can be constituted by more than one means – one can be 'married' in several senses. Butler, after Derrida, describes the conventions through which performatives accomplish their ends more or less successfully ('happily' or 'unhappily') as *repetitions* (Butler, 1997: 165, n 3). I want to suggest, albeit tentatively, that the Butlerian approach does not adequately distinguish the varying weights attaching to performatives associated with different inscriptions of *government*. Butler does try to 'offer an account of the social power of the speech act that takes into account its specific social iterability and the social temporality' (Butler, 1997: 166, n 3). However, Butler's attention is focused on a more general theory of performativity, and anchors her discussion to hate speech, censorship and psychoanalytic theory. In fact, the regulatory context of what remains 'unspeakable' in marriage – that is, the potential performative utterances and sexual performatives which might be transacted between gay and lesbian couples – is very *concretely* tied to the political subjectivity of its (speaking) subject.[6]

Butler's theory of citationality – that is, that performatives are accomplished as citations of law, and understood as cultural iteration – does not address marriage as such. Her approach may, in any case, offer a useful way to understand what is happening as people marry, but there is some slippage in her explanation. On the one hand, it is clear that marriage vows are necessarily citational. The words which must be spoken in order to effect a wedding are precisely stipulated in law.[7] On the other hand, Butler's conceptualization of performatives as iteratively inscriptive evokes a layer-upon-layer construction of subjectivity which somehow diminishes or de-dramatizes the performative of certified marriage as an immediate, interpellative, discursive shift. This slippage makes it difficult to understand how marriage-*like* relationships are different from actual, certified marriage. If the same effects accompany *de facto* relationships as marriage, what is the nature of the (political/legal) distinction between the two? Do *de facto* relationships merely mimic the performative effects of marriage – can we conceptualize *de facto* performativity as the citation of a citation? What of 'domestic partnerships' legislation? Would the regulation of gay and lesbian relationships under such legislation construct same-sex couples as mimicking *de facto* relationships – as a citation of a citation of a citation? And, in any case, what difference does it make?

Performative weights and consequences vary; the cultural conventions buttressing performatives are established or consolidated through various claims to authority. For performatives to succeed, that is, to work *as* performative utterances, they must be authorized (Butler, 1997: 33, 151).[8] As Austin notes, (in a rather offhand manner):

> the person to be the object of the verb 'I order [you] to . . . ' must, by some previous procedure, tacit or verbal, have first constituted the person who is to do the ordering an authority, e.g. by saying 'I promise to do what you order me to do.' This is, of course, *one* of the uncertainties – and a purely general one really – which underlie the debate when we discuss in political theory whether there is or is not or should be a social contract. (Austin, 1962: 28–9)

While Butler does turn her attention to certain aspects of law and political legitimation, neither she nor Austin is, strictly speaking, terribly interested in the politics of government. But, in the case of marriage at least, the authorization of marriage – these days through law and the state – seems crucial to its performative eclat. A cohabiting couple may be deemed 'married' according to governmental norms or policies, but its parties are not married in precisely the same sense as if they had performed wedding utterances. Though the day-to-day effects of their cohabitation may be identical (or at least very similar) in either case, *their capacities as subjects are differently inscribed*. If Butler's subjects somehow superseded Austin's, a 'commitment ceremony' – in which the performative utterances of wedding were exchanged between two men or two women – would *be* a marriage: there would be no difference between a play-acted and a bona fide marriage. My concern, then, is to examine how various performances of marriage carry different political import through their regulation in law.

As noted above, Butler theorizes the conditions or conventions of performativity as iteration. This carries her development of performativity away from Austin's central concern: namely, to identify what distinguishes performative utterance as a peculiar, particular type of linguistic expression. In the case of marriage – and perhaps other types of performative utterance (which never-theless remain outside the scope of this chapter) – performatives effect *discursive transformation*.[9] Perhaps the most appropriate example or metaphor of perfor-mative utterance (absent from the literature, as far as I can tell), capturing precisely the transformative effect of a happy performative, is the magician's fiat 'Abracadabra!' Its utterance announces transformation (the rabbit has turned into a flower, the Jack of Spades disappears) and ('happily', suspending disbelief) we understand the transformation to have been effected *as* a performative utterance – by the power of the magician's word. At the same time, however, we realize that the success of the magician's 'Abracadabra!' involves much that we cannot see. It's all done with mirrors, the way the cards are stacked, surreptitious substitution, or *something* going on underneath that curtained table. This cultural sleight of hand is a crucial component in what I would call the *politics* of performativity.[10]

THE CONJUGAL BODY POLITIC

The key discursive transformation in wedding performatives is the production of a complex conjugal body. This transformation is starkest under the ostensibly archaic law of coverture, which decreed that, upon marriage, husband and wife become one person at law, that one being the husband. Blackstone's oft-cited commentary declares that: 'By marriage, the husband and wife are one person in law: that is, the very being or legal existence of the woman is suspended during the marriage, or at least is incorporated and consolidated into that of the husband' (Blackstone, 1765, as cited by Parker *et al.*, 1994: 308). Coverture is generally understood to have been extinguished by the passage of the English Married Women's Property Act in 1882, and the enactment of this legislation has been rightly celebrated as one of the earliest and most important feminist victories for women – or, at least, for white, propertied women.[11] But coverture is far from finished with: the idea that the uttered and corporeal performatives of marriage accomplish a discursive transformation of bride and groom remains current.

Consummation as a Sexual Performative

In Australian matrimonial legislation, sex – *having* sex – operates performatively. The Matrimonial Causes Act 1959 (parts of which remain in force as the Marriage Act 1961) stipulated a number of ways in which sex could accomplish a performative of conjugal unity. Where the validity of a marriage was called into doubt, the question of whether the marriage had been *'consummated'* or not – that is, whether the bride and groom had performed a certain type of sexual intercourse – was pivotal. Consummation 'finalized' the performative utterances of wedding, and was very precisely articulated in law as a particular corporeal practice. While sex in general can be understood as a range of actions and behaviours, consummation refers to one specific type of sex which was legally invested with meaning such that it, rather than other sexual acts, came to stand as 'sex' as such, or as *all* sex.[12] The notion of consummation, then, is a corporeal yoke linking law and marriage.

Consummation is defined in case law as *vera copula*, or 'the true conjunction of bodies' (Hambly and Turner, 1971: 96, 98). For consummation to be deemed to have occurred, the penis must penetrate the vagina, and must ejaculate – inside or outside the vagina. There is no need for the sex to be procreative, nor is there any reference to mutual gratification. A marriage could be declared invalid where the failure to consummate resulted from an unforseen but permanent incapacity, but if the failure to consummate was deemed wilful, it constituted a ground for divorce.

Under the Matrimonial Causes Act, then, a specifically heterosexual kind of sex is understood to constitute a necessary precondition of conjugal unity, and is crucial to the accomplishment of a bona fide marriage. Along with the performative utterance of wedding vows, the corporeal union of what we might call 'consummative' sex established a conjugal body whose elements were not in any straightforward way the autonomous individuals of liberal political theory. Husbands and wives could not be compelled to testify against each other in (non-matrimonial) legal proceedings, could not sue each other in tort, and could not be convicted of conspiring with each other – on the rationale that one cannot by definition conspire with oneself.[13] Husband and wife continued to be known by one name (the husband's), and a husband could not normally be known to have raped his wife. The bodily mechanisms of heterosex constituted husband and wife as one conjugal body – as 'one flesh'. But the corporeal performativity of conjugal sex did not end with the 'happy' performative of consummation.

Condonation as a Sexual Performative

To obtain a divorce under the Australian Matrimonial Causes Act, one party to the marriage had to prove the other's matrimonial offence. There were several absolute bars to divorce, however, one of which was the *'condonation'* of the matrimonial fault constituting the ground for divorce. Legal commentary stipulated that condonation:

involves three elements. A matrimonial offence is condoned when the innocent spouse (1) with knowledge that a matrimonial wrong has been committed, (2) forgives or remits the matrimonial offence, and (3) reinstates the offending spouse in the matrimonial relationship. (MacDougall, 1966: 295)

In most cases (and at least until 1965, when the bar was amended slightly), a single act of marital intercourse would amount to the second and third parts of MacDougall's definition of condonation. That one act, or those few minutes f corporeal merger, was enough to reconstitute or reiterate conjugality. For example, if a woman were to discover that her husband had been having an affair, the wife could petition for divorce on that ground. If, however, at any time between her discovery of her husband's adultery and the case being decided in court, the wife were to have sex voluntarily with her husband, she would be said to have *condoned* her husband's adultery – that is, to have forgiven him the offence and to have reinstated him as her husband.

While a husband could not ordinarily be judged guilty of the rape of his wife, her consent to sex would figure again once a matrimonial offence occurred. Under the Matrimonial Causes Act, married parties' consent to marital sex is irrevocable for the duration of the marriage, but a husband's right to have sex with his wife – his 'conjugal rights' – could be rescinded or revoked by legal sanction only against *his own* commission of a matrimonial offence. The same is true for wives. Married parties' agreement (usually understood as tacit rather than explicit) to allow each other sexual access could thus be said to be conditional yet personally irrevocable: only a husband could create the conditions under which his wife's consent to conjugal sex could be revoked; and, similarly, only a wife could create the opportunity for her husband to revoke his consent. And only an 'innocent' spouse could file for divorce. It is difficult, given the transformative and unifying operations of sexual performatives in marriage, to conceive of husband/wife subjects as exercising autonomous agency or individual 'will' – at least in relation to each other.[14]

It is reasonable to understand condonation of this specifically sexual type as a sexual performative in two senses: in Judith Butler's sense – that is, as constitutive of sexual and gendered identity through repetitive self-performance (Butler, 1990: 145); and in its earlier meaning established by Austin – that is, accomplishing something by the social investment of an action with something more or besides its 'face value' (Warnock, 1973). Having marital sex after the discovery of a matrimonial offence assumed a meaning by convention very much additional to or apart from the more everyday meanings having sex might usually have implied. By political–legal convention, where marital sex amounted to condonation, it re-performed the marriage *as* marriage by re-performing consummation – by iteratively performing conjugal sex. Just as consummation initialized the corporeal unity of husband and wife, condonation, as the continuing performance of consummative sex, *re-performed* the marriage: corporeal unity repeatedly re-established *legal* unity.

Tracing Conjugal Sexual Performatives

The conjugal body politic of the Matrimonial Causes Act is constituted as a not-individual entity replete with traces of coverture. Its components are by definition one man and one woman, and its union is effected through uttered and sexual performatives. Though the means by which the union may be dissolved have changed, its constitution has not: under its legislative stable-mate (viz. the Marriage Act 1961) certified marriage continues to be accomplished through performative utterance explicitly codified in law, along with scattered sexual and normative performatives. The subjects of certified marriage continue to constitute themselves as complicit in a historical tradition of promising: as each couple utters its 'I do's, it reiterates a relation of ostensibly mutual corporeality which has historically privileged men.

Some of these privileges have been undone: it is no longer acceptable for a husband to rape or beat his wife, for example. However, as feminist lawyer and scholar Jocelynne Scutt (1995) makes plain, laws against marital rape and domestic violence remain conceptually tied to their legal ancestors. In a recent trial concerning rape-in-marriage, a South Australian judge attracted feminist wrath for appearing to condone the acceptability of the husband's 'rougher than usual handling' of his wife.[15] Scutt shows how his comments were consistent with a 1967 divorce ruling on the constitution of 'matrimonial cruelty', in which the presiding judge – finding that the husband's behaviour had *not* amounted to cruelty – said:

> The common law has invented that useful fiction, the reasonable man, as the yardstick ... by which conduct may ... be measured. But the law of divorce recognizes neither the reasonable man nor the reasonable woman. The litigants in the divorce court are people, and being people, are expected to behave unreasonably. This Court refuses to accept any standard of conduct against which behaviour can be measured ... [according to the 'reasonable man' test]. The relationship between husband and wife is too close and intimate to be tested by arbitrary standards. ... The issue of cruelty can only be determined after a review of the whole married life of the parties and the making of an assessment of their characters. ... The same conduct may amount to abominable cruelty in one set of circumstances; to the enjoyable rough and tumble of a happy married life in another ... (J. Selby, as cited in Hambly and Turner, 1971: 207–208)

It is clear that, despite feminist legal reforms transferring matrimonial offences into criminal law, judges (and others, of course) continue to understand marriage as a unifying relation whose subjects are neither the 'reasonable men' nor the autonomous individuals of jurisprudential and liberal political theory. Rape-in-marriage and domestic violence are qualified as such – they are understood as *different from* 'ordinary' rape and assault.

It would be wrong to conclude that one might avoid the anti-feminist seal of certified marriage by refusing a wedding: the accomplishment of certified marriage is effected not simply in the utterance of vows, but also through the cultural conventions which ratify their performance as 'happy' or successful. So long as most (or perhaps even *some*) people continue to marry under present legislation, these contextual inscriptions are reinforced as they are reiterated, and can no more be avoided or ignored as could felons perpetrate crime 'outside' the cultural context of law and its police. Conjugality is, in this sense, unavoidably inscribed on the body politic.

With the passage of the Australian Family Law Act in 1975, the conjugal body politic of coverture gave way to *consortium vitae*. The matrimonial unity of husband and wife was cleft: with the abolition of fault-based divorce, each party to marriage could now revoke, at will, her or his own consent to continue the marriage. (Recall that, under the Matrimonial Causes Act, spouses could revoke their marital promise only upon the other spouse's commission of a proscribed matrimonial offence.) This reform – supported, for the most part, by feminists and their allies – saw the regulation of marriage shift from rule of law (namely, fixed prohibitions and penalties administered through judgment) into a more governmental mode. The ongoing marriage 'contract' was no longer constituted against a set of fixed prescriptions and proscriptions, but could be negotiated almost entirely at will. Marriage law moved into a new phase, into a more specifically *liberal* rationality of government; one whose subjects were largely, necessarily, self-regulating.[16] Though the performative utterances of wedding continue to accomplish marriage, its cultural conventions have been partly refigured through new procedures for dissolution. In Australia, where divorce is premised on proving that a marriage has suffered irretrievable breakdown (as evidenced through 12 months separation), marriage has become negatively defined through a set of norms whose absence lends weight to the assertion that separation and marital breakdown have in fact occurred in any given case.

In the case of *de facto* relationships, these norms operate positively, in lieu of the performative utterances of wedding. In both cases (certified marriage and *de facto* relationships) sex continues to operate as a performative – as accomplishing, by cultural convention, some discursive transformation additional to or apart from its occurrence in fact. Under present law – in much the same way as condonation operated under the Matrimonial Causes Act – separated spouses who have sex with each other offer an opportunity for either party to dispute that their separation is complete, with its corollary inference that the marriage may not in fact have irretrievably broken down. In the regulation of *de facto* relationships, sexual relations between a cohabiting couple signal more than any other indicator that the relationship is indeed 'marriage-like'.

Sexual acts by and between married people have clearly had legal meanings between and beyond subjective desires, pleasures or duties. It is as if every time a married couple rattles the bedsprings, it iterates the sexual performative of consummation, which sustains, in turn, various vestiges of coverture and its historically masculine privilege. Marriage is, in this sense, a specifically corporeal relation: a relation whose cultural conventions are socially and subjectively imputed to the *sexual* relationship, the sexual performatives, of conjugality.

The project of deciding if or rather *how* same-sex/ual relationships are to be regulated needs to be understood against this background. Certified marriage continues to operate as a corporeal, sexual, performative, but, thanks to vigorous feminist reforms, the unity of the conjugal body politic has been cleft. By 'cleaving', I mean not just the separation or prising apart of coverture (although this is certainly evident), but also what might be called 'Wonderbra' cleavage: that is, the pushing together and increasing visibility of elements formerly less distinct. This cleavage of unity in the conjugal body politic, then, is neither complete nor 'clean': regulations governing *de facto* relationships, for example, did not replace or supersede matrimonial law. Rather, various means by which relationships might be regulated overlap, giving rise to what some commentators describe (in appropriately corporeal metaphor) as the 'limping marriage', in which the same two people might be understood as married for certain purposes but not others.[17] Just as the introduction of 'Ms' as a personal title for women has failed to completely supersede 'Miss' and 'Mrs', being a *de facto* spouse carries meanings apart from, and relative to, being a bona fide husband or wife. The primary and politically preferred model remains certified, performative marriage, and its glory is still entirely heterosexual. With every passage of new relationships legislation in Australia, the same sorts of statements concerning the purported social value of marriage – always meaning certified, performative marriage – were aired. From the 1950s through to the 1990s, politicians have continued to laud and champion marriage as the foundation and bulwark of good society and great nationhood. It is against this political backdrop to the matrimonial scene that debates about the regulation of same-sex/ual relationships must be viewed. As yet, the only Australian State or Territory to pass legislation 'recognizing' same-sex relationships (that is, to grant rights and responsibilities comparable to heterosexual relationships) is the smallest jurisdiction, namely, the Australian Capital Territory (ACT).

REGULATING SAME-SEX/UAL RELATIONSHIPS

The Domestic Relationships Act (ACT) 1994

Introducing the Domestic Relationships Bill, the ACT Attorney-General, Terry Connolly, summarized it as follows:

> The Bill provides that, where a person has lived in a domestic relationship for two years, that person may apply to the Magistrates Court or Supreme Court for adjustment of property rights in relation to property which is in the possession of the other person on the basis of the applicant's contribution to that property. A domestic relationship includes not only those who live in traditional [*sic*] de facto relationships but also relationships where one party at least provides a personal or financial commitment

and support of a domestic nature for the material benefit of the other. *Whether there is or has been a sexual relationship between the parties is thus an irrelevant consideration.* (Connolly, 1994: 1117, my emphasis)

The Bill was drafted in the first place as *de facto* relationships legislation – hithertofore absent from the ACT law books. However, the man/woman definition of '*de facto* relationship' was removed because, as the Attorney-General described it, 'this was considered an unnecessary distinction on the basis of gender' (Connolly, 1994: 1119). The Act thus 'recognizes' gay and lesbian relationships, yet this recognition is nowhere rendered explicit in the Act. Its relevance to lesbian and gay couples seeking legal recognition of their relationships is, however, made clear in the Hansard reports of the bill's passage.

The Domestic Relationships Act 1994 (ACT) attracted very little debate in Parliament (and even less in the press), belying lesbian and gay lobby groups' fears that the political will for such legislation would be lacking (LGLRS,[18] 1994). On the contrary: the debate in the ACT Legislative Assembly was especially calm and convivial. There were hearty congratulations on both sides of the House when the bill was quietly passed. Politicians across the party spectrum agreed that the legislation was timely and necessary. But they agreed, too, that the bill was not so much about recognizing lesbian and gay marriage or relationships as it was about recognizing *individuals* in such relationships. Bearing in mind the issues raised earlier in this chapter concerning conjugal bodies politic and individuality, this is an important qualification. In congratulating the Assembly on its manner of dealing with the bill, the (then) ACT Attorney General, Terry Connolly, said:

> The issue could have been played in a divisive manner to split the community, to inspire fear and loathing, to divide community sector against community sector. It was all there for the picking. People could have gone off on a sort of homophobic gay-bashing exercise; there could have been rhetoric about undermining the sanctity of the family. This could have been portrayed as a radical and dangerous piece of reform.
>
> [I]t is a credit to this community and this parliament that we have been able to run a debate on this issue and to run it sensibly; to talk about extending access to justice and the ability to enforce a right, instead of racing off on a tangent about gay marriages and about condoning gay marriages... (Connolly, 1994: 1810)

The debate, such as it was, included only mild concern that the Bill under consideration might in some way erode or devalue marriage. The Assembly took pains, however, to reassure itself that the Bill was *not* about same-sex marriage. At the same time, though, the Assembly prided itself on passing 'landmark legislation' which, it was widely held, put the ACT at the vanguard of progressive relationships law precisely *because* it was the first (and as yet, only) Australian jurisdiction to 'recognize' gay and lesbian relationships. How is it possible for a bill to be debated as 'about' and simultaneously 'not about' marriage-like same-sex relationships? To answer this, we need to reconsider the Act against aspects of the regulation of marriage developed throughout this chapter.

It is clear from the Attorney General's speech that the notion of gay and lesbian marriage continues to be understood as threateningly divisive. The ACT government was willing to recognize individuals in gay and lesbian relationships only as corporeally distinct – only as far as it could put the meaning of marriage as a sexed, corporeal merger to one side. It could recognize individuals in lesbian and gay relationships only as long as marriage itself, as a site and technology of a governmental concern with the heterosexual regulation of men and women, remained undisturbed. To put it bluntly, ACT Parliamentarians could think about individuals in lesbian and gay relationships as long as they could avoid talking about those individuals having not-so-individual sex. As the deputy Prime Minister of Australia put it, '[Homosexual people] are entitled to full protection under the law *as individuals*. That is a far cry and a quantum leap from according full legal recognition to same sex couples' (*Canberra Times*, 11 September 1995, emphasis added).

This is not to suggest that the enactment of the Domestic Relationships Act was a pyrrhic victory. On the contrary, gay and lesbian couples were granted legal relief previously denied them against grave and hurtful injustices. Further-more, the Gay and Lesbian Legal Rights Lobby could take some comfort in the fact that this new legal regulation of same-sex/ual relationships was not forged on the anvil of heterosexual marriage's misogynist history. What remains troublesome, however, is the way sex does or does not operate in different sorts of relationships law. The governmental determinations of Marriage-Act mar-riage work to construct political and legal subjectivities as sexed and sexual, and this sexed citizenship is a site which, however problematically, renders the autonomous individual of liberal political theory corporeally ambiguous.

While (in the ACT at least) gay and lesbian couples may exercise legal rights as individuals in their relationships with their partners, they may not choose from the *range* of relationships legislation that currently exists to the extent granted to heterosexual couples. Gay and lesbian couples can neither marry nor be accorded the status of *de facto* marriage. On the other hand, heterosexual couples wanting to escape the governmental calculations of conjugality may find the web of relationships legislation heterosexually sticky. It is difficult, for example, for a woman to live for any length of time with a man with whom she has sex without becoming, in the eyes of the law, his wife – regardless of her willingness to occupy that subject position. Even so, gay and lesbian couples cannot really make a personal choice to *reject* certified marriage because that choice is simply not available in same-sex relationships.[19] It would seem that homosexual couples cannot choose marriage, while heterosexual couples can't escape it.

Conjugal bodies politic offer simultaneous threats and promises. The promise is that the abstract individual of liberal political theory and law may be destabilized or even replaced by a configuration of subjects engaged in corporeal relations with each other and bearing certain responsibilities for each other by virtue of those relations. The threat is that it is the regulation of heterosex, especially, which has been deployed to inscribe political subjects as other than individual, constructing and reiterating sex-gender differences which have historically privileged men. If same-sex marriage were to be recognized *as* marriage, the heterosexual logic of the conjugal body politic might be shaken, but perhaps only as it risks reinforcing sex – or certain *sorts* of sex – as performatives inscribing the governmental regulation of bodies. Whether the potential benefits render the risk worthwhile must remain, at least for the time being, something of a moot point.

Queer Marriage?

As noted above, Judith Butler argues that gender norms are sustained through iterative gender performance. Rejecting the notion that gender performance is in any sense expressive of a biologically determined sex (Butler, 1988: 528), she argues that 'gender is in no way a ... locus of agency from which various acts proceed; rather, it is an identity tenuously constituted in time – an identity instituted through a *stylized repetition of acts*' (Butler, 1988: 519, her emphasis). Butler argues further that the normative weight of iterative gender performance might be challenged through imperfect repetition, or in subversive parody which both mimics and displaces. With respect to *marriage* and its heterosexism, what might constitute its parodic subversion?

Sarah Zetlein asks, and answers, almost precisely the same question in her 1996 article 'Lesbian Bodies Before the Law'.[20] Exploring the interplay of queer theory and the legal recognition of lesbian relationships, Zetlein argues that '[a] queer approach to marriage involves "theatrical militancy" to blast its (usually hidden) shaky foundations'.[21] She goes on to suggest that this is 'already occurring in cultural representations' (Zetlein, 1994: 72). Zetlein finds examples of parodic representations of marriage in magazines, art, television programs, and at the Sydney Lesbian and Gay Mardi Gras. She concludes, optimistically, that the lesbian who would parody marriage is 'laughingly defiant' (1994: 75), imitating historically heterosexist traditions as she displaces them. Though her position is decidedly seductive, I would suggest that the subversive potential of such cultural representations is much more limited than Zetlein allows.[22] While her approach is deliberately and self-consciously theatrical, it is nevertheless vulnerable to a misreading which has also plagued Butler: namely, that gender – or in this case, marriage – is performed through its accoutrements or props (Butler, 1992: 83). As suggested above, this misreading is facilitated by Butler's emphasis on identity as a crucial, primary category, and her (and her commentators') relative neglect of the social conventions which must prevail for the successful accomplishment of performative utterance.

As I have argued throughout, various performatives constitute marriage: performative utterance continues to play a crucial role in certified marriage but, more recently, the day-to-day performance of spousal norms has become just as important. The performative common to marriage as it has been constituted in Australia through the Matrimonial Causes, Marriage, Family Law and De Facto Relationships Acts, is sex – or, more precisely, heterosexual intercourse. In this respect, marriage law has steadfastly refused to accord gay and lesbian relationships the same status as heterosexual marriage. Zetlein suggests that legislation of the kind enacted in the ACT is potentially its queerest strategy, because, she says, 'It refuse[s] a neat line between gender, sex and care' (1994: 66). Perhaps she is right. Certainly the prospect of a relationships law *not* dependent on sex and sex-roles is alluring, and may signal an especially attractive option for those for whom the vestiges of sexual coverture have been most pronounced.

However, in the ACT, the operation of the Domestic Relationships Act has been anything but queer. It was not enacted as a result of gay and lesbian lobbying, and it was not debated as the legitimization of same-sex relationships. As yet, there has been only one reported case under the Act, and this concerned the division of joint property between a man and a woman in a defunct *de facto* relationship. Anecdotal evidence suggests that the Act is being deployed most often to resolve property disputes between adult children and their parents. Reading the Act's silence on sex as a positive (as Zetlein does) is, I think, prematurely optimistic, and forecloses a more menacingly homophobic interpretation. In other marriage legislation, (*hetero*)sexual performatives help to constitute a valorized conjugal body, which in turn is partly constitutive of identity: the married citizen receives societal reward as a valued subject, and these rewards are clearly tied to heterosexual imperatives. Gay and lesbian sex, however, remains steadfastly 'unspeakable' in the ACT legislation, as it does elsewhere. In a way, then, the corporealities of gay and lesbian relationships are simply effaced, or rendered invisible yet again.

CONCLUSION

We still do and say things with sex. Despite the benefits women have accrued though attempts to erase coverture by negating the performative effects of conjugal sex, we should not be too hasty to reject the possibilities conjugal bodies may hold for theorizing political subjectivities. In the complex subjectivities of conjugality, embodiment has *figured* – corporeal, sexual interaction has figured – as politically relevant. While we might want to erase the vestiges of coverture, or remove its heterosexual imperative, we can nevertheless see marriage as a space where embodiment has always 'counted' in establishing political subjectivities, where we recognize liberal individuality as a fiction, and where what we do, as other-than-individual people, carries the weight of embodiment, and embodied interaction.

We need to contextualize same-sex marriage debates in the specific histories of relationships legislation. We need to recognize the political weight attaching to the uttered and sexual performatives of marriage: subjects who promise in particular, sexually loaded ways are celebrated and valorized; subjects who take on the discursive transformation of marriage are *politically preferred*. In that these transformative effects have subjugated women in the past, they have been rightly challenged and to some extent destabilized, but may yet carry some potential for figuring political subjectivities – even *liberal* political subjectivities – as other-than-individual.

Under the Domestic Relationships Act, subjects in relationships are figured as *individuals*: as such there is no conjugal body under construction. Gay and lesbian relationships may be regulated through governmental rationales, but marriage and its performatives (both uttered and sexual) remain steadfastly hetero. The move towards individuality for conjugal subjects seems consistent with a feminist trajectory away from coverture: as each new piece of Australian marriage legislation is enacted, the legal ties binding wife to husband seem to loosen. But (with the exception of the Family Law Act 1975, which replaced most of the Matrimonial Causes Act 1959) successive Acts do not *supersede* their predecessors. Though relationships other than certified marriage have become more acceptable, certified marriage continues to sit at the head of the relationships table.

In the ACT, gay and lesbian relationships are governed through domestic relationships legislation, yet are by no means accorded the status of marriage. As noted earlier, politicians were careful to insist that the legislation was *not* about recognizing same-sex relationships as such: the Domestic Relationships Act, they insisted, is *not* about homosexual marriage. It is, however, about extending access to justice to individuals in gay and lesbian relationships. This double move is facilitated by the effacement of sexual performatives. In certified marriage, the conjugal body secures its unity through sexual performatives: in certain circumstances, having sex inscribes and regulates the conjugal body through legal means. But in the Domestic Relationships Act, sex has no legal meaning – rather, it is officially irrelevant. The possibility of a *homo*/sexual performative is thus swiftly foreclosed.

Unless gay and lesbian couples have the option of marrying a same-sex partner, the choice *not* to marry – the choice to *reject* marriage – is incoherent. Fears that same-sex marriage might begin to 'normalize the queer', sounding, as Judith Butler warns, 'its sad finish' (Butler, 1994: 21) are unfounded. It is by no means clear whether same-sex marriage would normalize (some) gay and lesbian relationships, or whether it would in fact operate to queer marriage itself. After all, marriage is not a fixed and inflexible institution: its meanings and experience are culturally and temporally diverse. Butler's own logic (by which hetero and homosexual identities are perpetually reconstructed in floating opposition to each other) suggests that 'normalizing the queer' could never extinguish queerness, but merely signal its reconstitution (Butler, 1997: 14). In my opinion, there are only two options for remedying the injustices caused by the failure of governments to 'recognize' gay and lesbian relationships. The first would require the sexual performatives of (heterosexual) marriage to be effaced. (Having) sex would become, as it is in the ACT Domestic Relationships legislation, governmentally 'irrelevant'. However, the cultural and legal conventions yoking sex and marriage are so entrenched that this effacement is unlikely to be easily accomplished. The second option is to authorize non-heterosexual performatives: that is, to allow gay and lesbian couples to marry on the same terms as heterosexual couples, and to endow homosexual performatives with the same transformative and political effects as the historically heterosexual performatives of marriage. Perhaps this second option is as politically implausible as the first. I am not sure whether the result of victory, in either case, would be worth the cost. But I am convinced that the fight itself is worthwhile.

In this chapter, I have not addressed the current crop of scholarly and other literature on the regulation of same-sex relationships.[23] Despite the current scholarship's reliance on such staples of political discourse as 'rights', 'justice' and 'equality'; and despite these debates' recognition of marriage's largely heterosexual history, the (predominantly American) literature on same-sex marriage fails to take adequate account of the corporeal operations of marriage, particularly its (hetero)sexual performatives and their political significance. Contextualizing the regulation of same-sex relationships in the trajectory of Australian marriage legislation, however, exposes these operations. Unlike other marriage legislation, the ACT's Domestic Relationships Act obviates the legal conventions of sexual performatives, thus foreclosing the possibility of a homosexual performative. Instead, discourse about the ACT legislation constructs those subjects in lesbian and gay relationships as *individuals*. While this treatment seems doomed to iterate homosexual marginalization and exclusion, the playing down of sexual performatives is nevertheless consistent with changes wrought by governmental regulation of relationships over the last 30 years or so. Perhaps this complete effacement of sexual performatives comes as a condition for *any* legal recognition of gay and lesbian relationships. The ACT's Domestic Relationships Act is certainly better than nothing, and offers important avenues of protection and redress for gay and lesbian couples. However, if the price of this 'recognition' is to maintain a homophobic silence, or to continue to render gay and lesbian sex unspeakable, it is won against an iterative reinforcement of heterosex – and *only* heterosex – as a politically, culturally, performative shibboleth.

10

'AGING AND RETIREMENT ARE NOT UNIQUE TO HETEROSEXUALS'

ROSENBERG V CANADA[1]

CLAIRE F.L. YOUNG

INTRODUCTION

In Canada, as elsewhere, the struggle by lesbians and gay men for spousal status continues with mixed success. One notable step forward occurred in the spring of 1998 when the Ontario Court of Appeal decision of *Rosenberg v Canada (Attorney General)*[2] (hereinafter *Rosenberg*) was released. This decision has been heralded as symbolizing 'a new era in the struggle for lesbian and gay equality'.[3] In *Rosenberg*, the court held that the words 'or the same sex' should be read into the definition of spouse in section 252(4) of the Canadian Income Tax Act,[4] for the purposes of the registration of pension plans. This ruling effectively extends entitlement to survivor benefits under occupational pension plans to the partners of lesbians and gay men who die while covered by the plan. *Rosenberg* is a ground-breaking decision for several reasons. It is the first case in which the government of Canada conceded that a provision of the Act discriminated against lesbians and gay men in contravention of section 15(1) of the *Charter of Rights and Freedoms.*[5] The decision also means that Canada is the only country in the world that includes lesbians and gay men in the definition of spouse in income tax legislation, albeit only for the purposes of the Act's application to occupational pension plans. The decision has also acted as a springboard for the extension by the province of British Columbia of full pension benefits to lesbians and gay men employed in the public sector and a review of the issue by the province of Quebec. From a practical perspective, the decision will improve the economic security in retirement of some lesbians and gay men by ensuring that those in spousal relationships with an individual who has an occupational pension plan receive benefits on the death of that individual.

In this chapter, I review briefly the political and legal background to the decision. I discuss the case in detail, and then consider the implications of the decision for lesbians and gay men. While the decision is obviously a very important step forward in the battle for equality being waged by lesbians and gay men, I wish to sound a note of caution about some of the potential consequences. These include concern about the possibility that the definition of spouse in the Act will be further amended to include lesbians and gay men for all income tax purposes and not just the pension provisions. As I shall discuss, such a measure requires careful analysis of its consequences. A second concern is a trend emerging in recent cases involving the entitlement of lesbians and gay men to 'spousal' benefits currently accorded to heterosexual couples. As I shall demonstrate, the benefits that we are winning, either through the courts or political action, which lead to legislative change, are those that are rooted in the private sphere. That is, the courts and legislatures in Canada have, to this point in time, resisted conferring on lesbians and gay men the more universal and public benefits such as entitlement to the Old Age Security (OAS) spousal allowance and survivor benefits under the Canada Pension Plan (CPP). Such plans are considered to be the 'public' part of the Canadian pension system because the OAS is universally available to all persons over 65 and the CPP is a mandatory earnings-related public pension. If, however, the benefit is one that is provided by the private sector, such as the private family or the private market, courts and legislatures have been more willing to extend entitlement to those benefits to lesbians and gay men. Closely tied to this point is the issue of cost. Are courts being influenced by the potential cost of remedying the discrimination when considering whether it can be justified under section 1 of the Charter,[6] and is that one reason for the fact that challenges to discrimination on the basis of sexual orientation with respect to more public benefits have not been successful?

THE BACKGROUND

Before discussing *Rosenberg*, it is helpful to consider the context in which this litigation took place. In Canada, the late 1990s have seen a significant amount of litigation and political action with respect to lesbian and gay issues. There have been victories and defeats in both arenas. In the provincial legislative fora there have been mixed results. For example, Bill 167 was introduced by the Ontario government in 1994. That bill proposed to redefine 'marital status' and 'spouse' in 56 pieces of Ontario legislation by removing any reference to opposite sex, thereby giving lesbian and gay couples the same rights and obligations as heterosexual couples.[7] The bill was defeated on a free vote in the legislature. On the other hand, British Columbia amended the definition of spouse in the Family Relations Act[8] to include lesbians and gay men for the purposes of spousal support, child support and access.[9] The province also amended the Adoption Act[10] to permit two same-sex partners to apply to adopt a child or one lesbian or gay man to adopt the child of their partner, although it is interesting to note that the partners do not have to be 'spouses' to do so.

There have also been mixed results in the courts. As I shall discuss, successes have tended to come when the benefit sought is one located in the private sphere. These include, for example, entitlement to spousal support[11] and child support[12] from one's ex-partner. They also include entitlement to employment benefits based on spousal status such as travel allowances and health and dental benefits. Successful cases before human rights tribunals include *Leschner v Ontario*[13] and *Moore v Canada*,[14] both of which form an important backdrop to *Rosenberg*. In *Leschner*, a human rights tribunal upheld an Ontario government employee's claim to the extension of insured employee benefits (including health benefits) and survivor pension benefits to his male partner. What is especially interesting about this ruling is that the board of inquiry ruled that if the federal government did not amend the definition of spouse to include same-sex couples, then the Government of Ontario must 'create a funded or unfunded arrangement outside of the registered pension plan to provide for equivalent survivor benefits and eligibility to persons living in homosexual conjugal relationships with employees as provided to persons living in heterosexual conjugal relationships with employees outside marriage'.[15] Until the *Rosenberg* decision, the establishment of a separate plan which did not receive any of the tax benefits that I shall discuss was the only manner by which employers could extend full pension benefits to their lesbian and gay employees on the same basis as they are enjoyed by heterosexual employees.

In *Moore*, the Canadian Human Rights Tribunal found that the federal government's refusal to give 'spousal' benefits (including health and dental benefits but not pension benefits) to its lesbian and gay employees on the same basis as they were given to its heterosexual employees offended both section 15(1) of the Charter and the Canadian Human Rights Act. Five months after this ruling the federal government quietly released a technical tax interpretation which stated that, as a result of the ruling in *Moore*, any private health services plan that was provided by an employer and that applied to both heterosexual and same-sex couples could qualify as a private health services plan under the Act.[16] This interpretation effectively extended the tax advantages associated with such a plan to lesbian and gay couples. Important as this concession was, it is limited in its application and, most importantly, it does not affect the definition of spouse in the Act.

In contrast to these decisions was the defeat in *Egan v Canada*.[17] This case involved a claim by a gay man to the spousal allowance under the Old Age Security Act[18] (OAS Act). The appellants argued that the definition of spouse in the OAS Act violated section 15(1) of the Charter on the basis of sexual orientation because it did not include lesbians and gay men. Although the Supreme Court of Canada held unanimously that sexual orientation is an analogous ground of prohibited discrimination under the Charter, and held by a 5–4 majority that there was a breach of section 15(1), the majority of the court also held that the discrimination could be justified under section 1. Sopinka J, who had found that there had been discrimination in contravention of section 15(1), joined the dissenters on that issue to uphold the discriminatory legislation under section 1. In so doing, he accorded a high level of deference to the government because the issue was one of a social and economic nature and concluded his judgment by stating that '[g]iven the fact that equating same-sex couples with heterosexual spouses, either married or common law, is still generally regarded as a novel concept, I am not prepared to say that by its inaction to date the government has disentitled itself to rely on s. 1 of the *Charter*'.[19]

THE TAX CONNECTION

What is the relationship between pensions and the income tax system? The answer is money. Private pensions such as occupational pension plans are heavily subsidized by the tax system. Tax systems are not merely revenue-raising instruments. They are also massive spending programs, a fact acknowledged by the Canadian government, which publishes tax expenditure accounts each year detailing the cost of funding all those programmes subsidized by the tax system. Tax expenditure analysis recognizes that any departure from a normative tax system (a system that consists only of the basic elements required to raise revenue) by way of measures such as income exclusions, deductions, credits or tax deferral is a tax expenditure. That is, rather than delivering a direct subsidy for a particular activity or endeavour by way of, for example, a direct grant, the government delivers the subsidy through the tax system. Occupational pension plans, referred to as Registered Pension Plans in the Act (RPPs), are heavily subsidized by the tax system. In the case of RPPs the subsidy is two-fold. First, the contributions made to the plan by both employers and employees are deductible in the computation of income,[20] and, second, all income earned in the plan accumulates on a tax-free basis in the plan,[21] which allows tax to be deferred until the contributor receives the pension. Taken together, the value of these tax breaks is huge. In 1998, the value of the deduction and the deferral was estimated to be over $18 billion, making it the single largest tax expenditure in that year.[22]

In order for a plan to qualify for the preferential tax treatment and be registered under the Act a pension plan must meet certain criteria.[23] One of the criteria is that survivor benefits may only be paid to a spouse within the meaning of the Act. Section 252(4) of the Act defines spouse as a person of the opposite sex who cohabits with the taxpayer in a conjugal relationship and who has so cohabited for 12 months, or who is the parent of a child of whom the taxpayer is also a parent. Lesbians and gay men are therefore not spouses for the purposes of the Act. Consequently, if an RPP provides survivor benefits to the partners of lesbians and gay men, it will be deregistered and will not qualify for the tax subsidies. The options for employers who wish to include their lesbian and gay employees in the RPP with the same coverage as their heterosexual employees are limited. The only way to accomplish their goal while maintaining the registration of their RPP is to set up an 'offside' plan for their lesbian and gay employees, as was ordered in *Leschner*. The offside plan will receive no tax breaks and the extra cost must be borne by the employer and its lesbian and gay employees. One example of such a plan is the one established in 1994 by the Ontario Public Service Employees Union for its lesbian and gay employees. OPSEU subsequently applied for and received leave to intervene in *Rosenberg*.

Prior to the Ontario Court of Appeal decision in *Rosenberg*, the issue of entitlement to survivor benefits was the focus of several cases before human rights tribunals. In *Laessoe v Air Canada*,[24] a gay Air Canada employee sought survivor benefits for his partner under the Air Canada RPP. The tribunal denied the claim in part because, in the tribunal's opinion, Air Canada could not provide those benefits while the tax and pension legislation remained unchanged. Unlike *Leschner*, where the tribunal ordered the employer to set up an offside plan, the tribunal in *Laessoe* took the position that it was up to the federal government to make the appropriate changes to the Act. Likewise, in *Dwyer and Sims v Metropolitan Toronto*,[25] William Dwyer sought, among other benefits, survivor benefits for his male partner. The Board of Inquiry refused to order the employer to provide an 'offside' plan. The court in *Rosenberg* would resolve the issue.

THE TRIAL DECISION

The case was brought by Nancy Rosenberg and Margaret Evans, two lesbian employees of the Canadian Union of Public Employees (CUPE), and by the National Secretary-Treasurer of CUPE, on behalf of the union's members and employees. CUPE has an occupational pension plan for its employees which includes a provision for survivor benefits. The plan provides that, if an employee covered under the plan dies, the spouse of that employee will receive a benefit for surviving spouses of two-thirds of the pension benefit of the deceased employee. In 1992 CUPE amended the definition of spouse in its pension plan to include same-sex partners and sought a ruling from Revenue Canada (the federal government department which administers the Act) as to whether or not the department would accept the amendment. Revenue Canada refused to accept the amendment because the new definition of spouse in the plan was not in accord with the definition in the Act. At the Ontario Court (General Division), the applicants argued that the refusal to accept the amendment to the plan discriminated against them on the basis of sexual orientation in contravention of section 15(1) of the Charter and that the discrimination could not be saved by section 1. As mentioned, the government conceded that the definition of spouse in the Act, as it applied to RPPs, infringed section 15(1). Therefore the issue for Charron J was whether or not that discrimination was justified under section 1. The Attorney General argued that *Rosenberg* could not be distinguished from *Egan* and therefore section 1 did apply to save the provision. Charron J agreed that she was bound by *Egan*, stating somewhat cryptically that '[t]he facts and the issues are too closely related. My own views on the matter are irrelevant.'[26]

THE APPEAL

Given the importance of the issues in *Rosenberg*, it is not surprising that several applications for intervenor status were made to the court. By the time the case was heard intervenors included the Canadian Human Rights Commission, the Coalition of Equality Seeking Groups (the Equality Coalition), the Ontario Public Service Employees Union, the Foundation for Equal Families, and William Dwyer[27] all supporting Rosenberg *et al.*; REAL Women[28] and the Evangelical Fellowship of Canada supporting the Attorney General. The issue before the court was the application of section 1 of the Charter and, in particular, whether or not *Egan* was determinative. The main thrust of the appellants' argument was that *Egan* could be distinguished on the basis of a contrast between public and private benefits. In *Egan* the issue was the extension of direct social welfare benefits (the spousal allowance) while *Rosenberg* involved private non-governmental employment relations.[29] The appellants also argued that, while the cost of extending the spousal allowance to lesbians and gay men was an issue in *Egan*, that was not so in *Rosenberg* because there would be no cost to the government of allowing the amended plan to be registered under the Act.[30]

In arguing that the discrimination was justified under section 1 the respondent took the position that the Ontario Court of Appeal was bound by *Egan* and that *Rosenberg* could not be distinguished from that case. The Attorney General also drew on the 'novelty' point of Sopinka J, stating that the definition of spouse in the Act for the purposes of its application to pensions had only been amended recently to add common law heterosexual couples, and that equating same-sex couples to heterosexual spouses was still a novel concept.[31] The Attorney General also argued that the criteria established in *R v Oakes*[32] were met and therefore section 1 applied to save the provision. In this case the objective underlying the provision of survivor benefits was to provide economic security in retirement for the elderly and, in particular, elderly women. This objective was of sufficient importance to warrant overriding the protection from discrimination afforded by section 15(1). The goal was one of pressing and substantial importance. Further, the means chosen to accomplish this goal were proportional because they were rationally connected to the objective. The tax subsidy aided the vast majority of those identified as being in need, namely elderly women in 'traditional relationships'.[33] The measures adopted minimally impaired the right to equality of those excluded from the definition of spouse. The Attorney General also raised the issue of cost, which had not been argued at the trial level. He argued that expanding the group entitled to survivor benefits would increase the cost to federal pension plans, although the factum does not elaborate on why this would be so.[34]

At the time *Rosenberg* was argued in October 1997, *Vriend v Alberta*,[35] another section 15(1) case involving discrimination on the basis of sexual orientation, was on its way to the Supreme Court of Canada. The issue in *Vriend* was the omission from the Alberta Individual Rights Protection Act (IRPA)[36] of protection against discrimination on the basis of sexual orientation. Vriend had been dismissed from his job as a school teacher because of his sexual orientation and he sought to have 'sexual orientation' read into the Alberta human rights legislation in order to bring an action against his former employer. The Supreme Court of Canada found that some provisions of the IRPA did contravene section 15(1) and were not saved by section 1 and the remedy was to read 'sexual orientation' into the IRPA. Although *Vriend* was argued after *Rosenberg*, the Supreme Court released its decision in *Vriend* before the Ontario Court of Appeal handed down its ruling in *Rosenberg*. One can speculate that the Ontario Court of Appeal was waiting for the Supreme Court to rule in *Vriend* because of that decision's relevance to the issues under consideration in *Rosenberg*.

In *Rosenberg*, the Ontario Court of Appeal unanimously held that the discrimination could not be justified under section 1 and that the words 'or same sex' should be read into the definition of spouse in section 252(4) of the Act, as it applies to the registration of RPPs or amendments to RPPs. Abella JA wrote the decision. While noting that it was 'understandable' that Charron J felt bound by *Egan*, Abella JA described the analysis in *Egan* as 'only one branch of a divided guidance that has emerged from the Supreme Court'.[37] She determined that the section 1 analysis in *Vriend* was very different from that employed in *Egan* and concluded that it was 'no longer necessary or even appropriate to decide whether the motions judge was correct in applying the s.1 result in *Egan*'.[38]

The key issue in *Rosenberg* was whether, when determining if there is a pressing and substantial objective justifying the Charter infringement, it is the objective of the statute or section itself, or the objective of the infringing limitation in the statute or section, that is the focus of inquiry. That issue, the court said, had now been resolved by *Vriend*. It is the objective of the infringing limitation in the section that is relevant. In *Rosenberg* the Attorney General had argued that the objective of section 252(4) was to encourage voluntary workplace arrangements for retirement and that this objective was pressing and substantial. The Court of Appeal agreed but stated the objective of the section was not the issue before the court. Rather, the issue was the objective of the infringing limitation, namely the exclusion of lesbians and gay men from the definition of spouse in section 252(4) of the Act. It was this exclusion that had to be pressing and substantial in order for the infringement under section 15(1) to be justified.

The Attorney General had also submitted that the pressing and substantial objective of survivor benefits was to provide a measure of economic security for women in traditional relationships. Abella JA responded by noting that these benefits are also available to men, and she described the Attorney General's objective as being an 'explanation' of the omission of lesbians and gay men from the definition of spouse and not an objective. In this context she said:

Aging and retirement are not unique to heterosexuals, and there is nothing about being heterosexual that warrants the government's preferential attention to the possibility of economic insecurity. It cannot therefore be a pressing and substantial objective to single out for exclusive recognition, the income protection of those older Canadians whose sexual preferences are heterosexual.[39]

Section 1, therefore, did not apply and the appeal was successful. Even though it was not necessary to go further, Abella JA embarked on an analysis of the second part of the *Oakes* test and considered whether or not the means used to satisfy the alleged objective were proportional. She found that there was no rational connection between protecting heterosexual spouses from economic insecurity on the death of their partners and denying the same protection to lesbians and gay men. In this context she addressed the argument of the Attorney General that the government could address equality issues on an incremental basis. She took a firm line on the issue of whether time was an appropriate factor to consider when giving lesbians and gay men the same rights to survivor benefits as heterosexual spouses, stating:

> Courts do not operate by poll. They are required to make a principled decision about whether a constitutional violation is demonstrably justifiable in a free and democratic society, not about whether there might be a more propitious time to remedy it.
>
> Governments necessarily prefer to rely on perceived majoritarian wishes; courts, particularly in the enforcement of minority rights, are necessarily obliged to override them. Waiting for attitudes to change can be a glacial process.[40]

Abella JA also addressed the issue of cost. On a factual basis she found that there would be no cost to the government of including lesbians and gay men in the definition of spouse in the Act. Rather, there would be a tax windfall for the government as a result of such action. In fact, that analysis is correct only if one is considering the impact of including lesbians and gay men in the definition of spouse in the Act *for all purposes* and not just with respect to the impact on pension plans. As I shall discuss later, there would be no tax windfall in the latter case. Whether or not the remedy sought in *Rosenberg* would have resulted in an increased cost for the pension plan or the federal government in terms of more tax subsidies was not, however, a crucial point. Abella JA confirmed, relying on the judgment of Lamer CJ in *Schachter v Canada*,[41] that cost is not a constitutionally permissible justification for discrimination under section 1.[42] It is interesting to note that the court made no reference in the *Rosenberg* decision to the argument, made by the appellants, that *Egan* could be distinguished because it was about entitlement to public government welfare benefits while *Rosenberg* involved private non-governmental employment relations.

SUBSEQUENT EVENTS

In May 1998, a month after *Rosenberg* was decided, the Nova Scotia government announced that it was extending pension benefits to all gay and lesbian public employees on the same basis as those benefits were provided to heterosexual employees.[43] In early June 1998, the Reform Party of Canada (a right-wing party that forms the official opposition) introduced a motion in Parliament declaring that courts should not be able to alter federal legislation and criticizing the *Rosenberg* decision.[44] The motion also called on the federal government to appeal the decision. While some Reform MPs cast their concern as being one about judicial activism, others took a different approach. Reform MP Grant McNally said that failure to appeal *Rosenberg* would create 'a domino effect on 40 pieces of legislation in this country, all of which strike at the heart of the definition of spouse and in fact at the definition of marriage', adding that 'marriage is the fundamental cornerstone of any society'.[45] In late June 1998 the federal government announced that it would not appeal the decision[46] and on the same day the province of British Columbia unveiled legislation that gives the same pension benefits to lesbians and gay men in the public sector as are available to its heterosexual public sector employees.[47] In March 1999 the federal government announced that it would extend survivor benefits provided by the federal civil service pension plan to the partners of its lesbian and gay employees.[48]

SOME CONCERNS ABOUT THE FUTURE

Clearly *Rosenberg* marks a huge step forward in the fight for equality being waged by lesbians and gay men. For many, it means that they can now aspire to some form of economic security in retirement, whether as a direct result of the decision or because of provincial legislative action. Nevertheless, in this part of the chapter I raise some concerns about the potential impact of this decision in a broader context. I also consider the limitations of the decision in terms of its application to equality issues that are outside the framework of the private pension system.

One concern is that, while the remedy in *Rosenberg* is limited to the definition of spouse in the Act as it applies to pension plans, there is now considerable pressure being exerted from several quarters, including lesbian and gay individuals and organizations, to include lesbians and gay men in that definition as it applies throughout the entire Act. For example, gay M.P. Svend Robinson has introduced a private members' bill to amend the definition of spouse in section 252(4) of the Act, the result of which would be to include lesbian and gay couples for all purposes under the Act.[49] A gay male couple in British Columbia has filed a statement of claim arguing that Revenue Canada's refusal to allow one of them to claim the marital tax credit in respect of the other discriminates against them on the basis of sexual orientation in contravention of section 15(1).[50] The remedy sought is the inclusion of same-sex couples in the definition of spouse for all income tax purposes. The Foundation for Equal Families, a lesbian and gay activist group, commenced legal action against the federal government arguing that the term spouse in 58 pieces of legislation, including the Act, discriminates against lesbians and gay men contrary to section 15 of the Charter because it applies only to persons of the opposite sex.[51] The remedy sought is the extension of the term 'spouse' to include same-sex couples. One consequence of this law suit is that rumours are afoot that the federal government will introduce sweeping legislative amendments to extend spousal status to lesbians and gay men. In January 1999 the *Globe and Mail* newspaper (self-described as Canada's national newspaper) ran an article headed 'Ottawa to enshrine same-sex rights' in which it quoted a government source who stated that 'the government has to deal with this [discrimination against same-sex couples in federal legislation] sooner or later. It's unavoidable'.[52] Nevertheless, when the Prime Minister was questioned about this news report, his response was a very cautious 'I don't know if legislation is needed'.[53] Clearly change is in the air, a result both of intense lobbying by lesbian and gay individuals and groups and the litigation losses incurred by the federal government in cases such as *Rosenberg*.

My concern is that, while recognition of lesbian and gay relationships is central to attempts to achieve equality for lesbians and gay men, changes to the definition of spouse to include lesbians and gay men must be considered on a statute-by-statute basis. The implications of such change may not always be positive. My focus in this chapter is the tax context and, as I have demonstrated in other work, including lesbians and gay men as spouses for all purposes of the Act can be highly problematic.[54] There are two particularly unfortunate consequences. First, any such action will result in a considerable tax grab by the federal and provincial governments. When the definition of spouse was amended in 1993 to include heterosexual common law spouses, the Department of Finance estimated that the change would result in increased tax revenues over a 5 year period of $9.85 billion.[55] The bulk of the increased revenue is attributable to the rules that require the combining of spouses' income for the purposes of the refundable tax credits.[56] This requirement results in the overall reduction in the value of tax credits owing to taxpayers because they are no longer treated as individuals.

Second, it is important to realize that, if the definition of spouse is amended to include lesbians and gay men, the burden of increased taxes and loss of tax subsidies will not be borne equally by all. If the 'advantage' of being included as a spouse under the Act is determined by reference to tax dollars saved, then the lesbian or gay couple in a relationship in which one partner is economically dependent on the other will benefit from being included as spouses under the Act. This is because the Act provides certain tax advantages to those who are in relationships with a person who has little or no income. There may also be a benefit to the couple in which both partners have high incomes, such as the opportunity to each own a home that qualifies for exemption from capital gains on disposition. Conversely, it will be the low-income couple, in which each partner earns approximately the same amount of income, that will suffer the greatest disadvantage, primarily because their income will be combined for certain purposes, thereby reducing their entitlement to certain tax credits.[57] These class implications are an important factor to be considered before embarking on any change to the definition of spouse in the Act. Given that women tend to earn less than men and have lower incomes, there may also be significant gender implications, with lesbians more likely to suffer a greater disadvantage than gay men. Furthermore, the requirement to combine incomes for the purposes of calculating entitlement to the child tax credit is likely to have a more detrimental impact on lesbian couples than gay male couples. Lesbians are more likely to have their children living with them and the credit is given to the primary caregiver of the child, usually the mother.

One might argue that if lesbians and gay men seek entitlement to rights such as pension benefits then they should also accept the responsibilities that attach to those rights. In this case it presumably would be the responsibility of same-sex couples to be treated as spouses for all purposes of the Act, which, as I have discussed, would result in more taxes payable by many lesbians and gay men. That argument is fallacious in the case of survivor pension benefits and the income tax system. *Rosenberg* is about access by lesbians and gay men to pension entitlement on the same basis as that enjoyed by heterosexual couples. The only connection between survivor pension benefits and the tax system, other than the registration requirements, is the tax subsidy given for contributions to private pension plans and the sheltering from tax of income accumulating in the plan. Those subsidies have always been available to all contributors to pension plans, whether in a spousal relationship or not and whether the taxpayer is heterosexual, lesbian or gay. Including lesbians and gay men in the definition of spouse for the purpose of the registration of pension plans does not change this state of affairs. The result of *Rosenberg* is that lesbians and gay men may now receive survivor benefits, but there is no increased cost for the federal government in terms of the tax subsidies provided to RPPs, as tax deductions or sheltering of income in the plan that flow to taxpayers by reason of this increased access to survivor benefits. Therefore it cannot be said that lesbians and gay men are now receiving a benefit for which they must pay. They have been paying and continue to pay the same cost as heterosexuals who contribute to these plans, but they have just not been entitled to the same benefits.

The enthusiasm generated by success in *Rosenberg* is somewhat tempered by the realization that this decision only directly affects RPPs provided by an employer to its employees. The decision does not affect public pensions such as the OAS spousal allowance or survivor benefits under the Canada Pension Plan. This result is consistent with a trend that has developed with respect to lesbian and gay claims for equality. The benefits being acquired tend to be situated in the private sphere. For example, legislative successes such as the redefinition of spouse in the B.C. Family Relations Act,[58] to include lesbians and gay men for the purposes of the payment of child support and spousal support, place increased reliance on the private family to provide for the economic welfare of those who require financial support on breakdown of their relationships. Similarly, cases such as *M v H*,[59] which added lesbians and gay men to the definition of spouse in the Ontario Family Law Act for the purposes of spousal support, and *Buist v Greaves*,[60] where the non-biological parent of a child was ordered to pay child support, are cases where the right secured is one provided by the private family. Other cases such as *Kane v Ontario (Attorney General)*[61] have been about benefits delivered by the private market. In that case a claim by a lesbian to a death benefit under an insurance policy after her partner had been killed in a motor vehicle accident was successful, even though the definition of spouse in the policy referred only to opposite-sex partners. *Rosenberg* was also firmly rooted in the private sphere. The case was about a private pension plan, albeit one that was entitled to a tax subsidy. But such a plan relies on employers (the private market) to provide the plan and to make contributions on behalf of employees, and the survivor benefit sought by *Rosenberg* is one that is accessed through the private family.

Why have the successes been ones that are in respect of benefits or rights that operate primarily in the private sphere? One might speculate that the perceived cost to the state is one reason. In *Rosenberg* Abella JA took care to declare that cost was not a constitutionally permissible justification for discrimination under section 1. Indeed, she was clear that cost–benefit analyses were not appropriate tools to apply to equality issues because the costs of remedying discrimination 'will always appear to be more fiscally burdensome than beneficial on a balance sheet'.[62] But this approach is not one that has been taken on a consistent basis by the courts. In *Egan* Sopinka J talked about balancing competing interests and the basis for his section 1 analysis was that *Egan* was about socio-economic policy. The costs of extending benefits and the government's limited resources were central to his reasoning. As he said, '[i]t is not realistic for the Court to assume that there are unlimited funds to address the needs of all'.[63] In *Vriend* Iacobucci J distinguished *Egan* by noting that in *Egan* there was concern about the financial impact of extending benefits to a previously excluded group while 'including sexual orientation in the IRPA does not give rise to the same concerns.'[64] The role of the relevance of cost in determining whether or not discrimination may be justified under section 1 is unclear. It has been suggested that 'recent human rights jurisprudence and legislation warn against assuming that cost, from the perspective of denial of equality rights, will safely continue to be largely irrelevant'.[65]

CONCLUSION

In conclusion, *Rosenberg* is a case of significant impact. In successfully challenging the heterosexist definition of spouse in the Act, it has made inroads into legislation that is increasingly being used to deliver social and economic programs through tax expenditures. Despite this success, the unanswered question is whether the decision can be applied either in the courts or as a tool for legislative reform in a manner that goes beyond its narrow application. The true test will be the future challenges to the discrimination that lesbians and gay men encounter with respect to the more universal state-delivered benefits such as survivor benefits under the Canada Pension Plan, where alleviating such discrimination will result in an increased cost to the state. One hopes that the uncertainty demonstrated by the courts about whether cost should be a relevant factor in considering whether discrimination can be 'saved' under section 1 of the Charter will be resolved in a manner that recognizes that discrimination should be eliminated. Any cost that may be associated with its elimination is one that should be paid because of the benefit that accrues to society as a whole from such action.

STRAIGHT FAMILIES, QUEER LIVES?

HETEROSEXUAL(IZING) FAMILY LAW

RICHARD COLLIER

INTRODUCTION

This chapter presents an exploration of the 'heterosexuality' of 'family law.' It seeks, specifically, to unpack some aspects of the discursive construction of heterosexuality as a social practice within the context of debates taking place in the field of family policy in Britain. In relation to issues of divorce reform, the meaning of parental responsibility, child care and, more generally, an ascendant political discourse of 'family values', it will be argued that the complex and contingent relationship between (hetero)sexuality and the idea of the 'social' is at present undergoing a profound shift; and that, in this process, questions of gender, sexuality and 'family life' are themselves being politicized and rendered problematic in some frequently unpredictable and contradictory ways. The argument presented seeks to focus on the interplay of pleasure and resistance in an exploration of what will be termed the discursive 'heterosexualization' of the legal subject. Within the conditions of late modernity the underlying normativity of a gender regime/order which had hitherto framed the encoding of the 'familial' as, *a priori*, heterosexual within family law is itself, I shall argue, in some key respects now being subverted and called into question. Heterosexuality, for so long the taken-for-granted epistemic context in which discussion of family law has taken place, appears increasingly as a contested, contingent and fluid phenomena. What follows begins from the premise that the very idea of the heterosexual 'familial' social subject, no less than the concept of heterosexuality itself, has been discursively produced by relations of power, constituted by the productive work, not of one discourse, but rather a plenitude of discourses.[1] In disturbing the dualisms through which heterosexuality is presently being (re)constructed within debates around family, law and social change, this chapter seeks to move the debate around sexuality and the legal arena 'beyond heterosexuality' in an exploration of what it means to speak of both the gendered subject and the sexed body in/of family law.

SUBVERTING HETEROSEXUALITY? THEORETICAL AND POLITICAL CONTEXT(S)

The relationship between gender, law and the family has produced a vast literature much of which, though by no means all, has sought to engage in a conceptual and practice-based critique of law from a range of feminist perspectives (see, for example, Fineman, 1995; O'Donovan, 1985, 1993; Smart, 1984; Smart and Brophy, 1985). Yet notwithstanding the now well-established nature of this 'gender' frame of analysis, and of critical discussion of the legal construction of such familial(ized) categories as motherhood (Diduck, 1998; Fineman, 1995; Fineman and Karpin, 1995; Silva, 1996) and fatherhood (Collier, 1995; Wallbank, 1997), it continues to be rare to speak specifically of the *heterosexuality* of the 'family' and of 'family law'. This may, in part, be due to what appears to be the tautological nature of the relationship. Marriage in Britain is, after all, an institution reserved for 'biological' men and women and can thus be seen as the institutional embodiment of heterosexuality (Section 11(c) Matrimonial Causes Act 1973). Within social and political theory more generally little attention has been given to *theorizing* heterosexuality as a historically, culturally specific concept (Richardson, 1996). Thus, although heterosexuality is clearly deeply embedded in accounts of social and political participation, and is 'of the essence' to the institution of marriage (and thus, it could be argued, to popular understandings of what constitutes a 'family'), it is rarely acknowledged or problematized in these terms. The broader 'heterosexual frame' or 'matrix' (Butler, 1990) of family law and family policy, as it were, has been largely unspoken and taken for granted (Carabine, 1996a). When sexuality is discussed in the context of family policy in Britain it continues to be taken as a 'handy euphemism' (Stychin, 1995) for discussion of the relationship between lesbian, gay and bisexual issues and the law/legal subject.

It is notable, therefore, how in recent years there has occurred, across disciplines, some 'significant attempts by both feminists and proponents of queer theory to interrogate the way that heterosexuality encodes and structures everyday life' (Richardson, 1996: 1). For some, indeed, the study of heterosexuality *in its own right* has emerged, in the words of one text, as 'a new research agenda' (Richardson, 1996; Steinberg *et al.*, 1997; cf. Maynard and Purvis, 1995; Wilkinson and Kitzinger, 1993). A central concern within this scholarship has been to recognize and redress the profound impact that ignoring, taking for granted or otherwise excluding heterosexuality as a distinct and historically contingent concept has had on the historical development of social theory more generally. Thus, the relationship between heterosexuality and social policy (Carabine, 1996b), schooling (Prendergast and Forrest, 1997), heterosexuality and psychoanalysis (Hollway, 1995a, b, 1993, 1996; Samuels, 1997), crime (Collier,

1998), masculinity and femininity (Robinson, 1996) and feminist and men's movement politics (Collier, 1996; Jackson, 1996; Segal, 1997) have each been subjected to critical analysis via an explicit 'heterosexuality' problematic. And yet, and by stark contrast, any engagement with heterosexuality and *legal* studies or, my concern in this chapter, with the 'heterosexuality of family law', remains relatively rare and undeveloped.

A number of diverse disciplinary and political influences underscore this emerging 'heterosexuality turn', each of which is worthwhile briefly unpacking with a view to charting the potential analytic utility of the concept of hetero-sexuality for developing an engagement with sexuality in the family law arena. There have been (at least) four clear strands to the recent emergence of hetero-sexuality as a research topic within the social sciences, each of which raise particular questions about women, men and 'family life'.

Feminism and the 'heterosexuality question'

Firstly, and perhaps most significantly, heterosexuality can be seen to have (re)surfaced within the context of a long-standing debate within Western feminism around questions of epistemology, praxis and standpoint in relation to the politics of sexual orientation. A recurring theme within an, at times, heated conversation about the relationship between feminism and heterosexuality, has been the meaning, indeed, the very possibility, of 'heterosexual feminist' identity/ ies (see further Brown, 1994; Hollway, 1993, 1995a, b, 1996; Johnson, 1997; Kitzinger and Wilkinson, 1994; Ramazanoglu, 1994, 1995; Segal, 1994, 1997; Smart, 1996a, b; Soper, 1995; Swindello, 1993; Thompson, 1994; Young, 1993). In the almost 20 years since Rich's (1981) influential identification of 'compulsory heterosexuality' a vast array of terms – heterosexism, heterocentric, heterocentric logic, heterosexualist imperative, heterosexual matrix and so forth – have been widely used within feminist scholarship to denote aspects of the multifarious oppressions, injustices and prejudices associated with the social and economic hegemony of a normative model of the familial as embodied in the legal institution of marriage.

On one level this feminist (re)problematization of heterosexuality within a range of texts during the 1990s can be seen as part of a broader critical engage-ment in social theory with 'the previously unquestioned centre'; that is, an attempt to reconceptualize normative categories in and against which particular social groups have been historically judged and, invariably, found wanting. More generally, and as part of the broader 'liberalization of heterosexuality' which has marked the latter half of the twentieth century (Hawkes, 1996: 105), the political, social and cultural impact of feminism's critique of heterosexuality cannot be underestimated when assessing and contextualizing the uncoupling of sex from marriage and reproduction. This has followed the increased avail-ability of contraception and, in particular, the challenging by women – both theoretically and in practice – of the 'long established and insidiously effective construction of [hetero]sexual pleasure' as male-defined and male-centred (see further Segal, 1994). Contested ideas of family and family life have, of course, been central to such debates around sexual practices, sexuality, contraception and reproduction, as well as to the history of feminism as a social movement more generally.

Queer theory and (hetero)sexual performativity

A concern to transcend the implicit assumption of a fixed, unitary and confining notion of heterosexual identity within social theory has led some writers, both feminist and otherwise, to draw on a range of postmodern conceptualizations of the subject and subjectivity in seeking to critically engage with the discursive construction(s) of heterosexuality. This work has involved an attempt to open out a 'politics of heterosexuality' to very much the same kinds of questions of fluidity, contingency and, indeed, possibility which have more traditionally been associated with aspects of queer politics and theory. And what has emerged from this now rich and diverse body of queer theoretical scholarship on subjectivity, corporeality and the (instability of) gender(ed) identities is an, albeit sometimes implicit, theorization of the heterosexual subject itself as a fluid 'performative practice'; that is, an understanding of being 'straight' in which the idea of the 'gendered self' *per se* is conceptualized as a series of constantly shifting practices and techniques (Butler, 1990, 1993; Probyn, 1993). Within that strand of political–theoretical work on sexuality and identity informed by different variants of queer theory and gay and lesbian legal studies (Auchmuty, 1997; Butler, 1990, 1993; Cooper, 1994; Herman, 1994; Herman and Stychin, 1995; Robson, 1992; Sedgwick, 1994; Stychin, 1995; Warner, 1993; Wittig, 1992) the very idea of there *being* a (hetero)sexed subjectivity, a distinctive process of being 'sexed' as heterosexual – as having, or rather obtaining or 'taking up' a heterosexual sensibility – has itself been seen as a process not merely defined by private sexual acts but as 'a public process of power relations in which everyday interactions take place between actors with sexual identities in sexualized locations' (Bell and Valentine, 1995: 146; see also Hollway, 1996; Smart, 1996a, b). Thus, within the 'heterosexual problematic' emerging from queer theory, and at the interface of feminist and queer scholarship more generally, it is no longer simply counter-hegemonic or subordinate sexualities which are thought of as 'marking' their bearers in some way. The 'straight sensibility' of heterosexuality, and the radical instability of the hetero–homo(sexual) distinction itself, have each become meaningful objects of concern in critical analyses of how sexual borders are patrolled and constructed, sexual identities assigned and sexual politics formulated (Robinson, 1996; Waldby, 1995).

Sociological accounts: heterosexuality as a 'reflexive project of the self'

In highlighting the way in which heterosexuality 'has ceased to be a fixed terrain, interlocking gendered desire and institutions of lifetime marriage or long-standing monogamy' (Hawkes, 1996: 106), there is some overlap and common ground between these feminist and queer theoretical engagements and those accounts of heterosexuality which have emerged from a rather different strand of contemporary social theory. Drawing in particular on the influential work of Giddens (1991, 1992) and Beck and Beck Gernsheim (1995), the disengagement of heterosex from marital monogamy has been explored to some rather different ends. Certainly, this work could not always be described as being 'pro-feminist'.[2] Nonetheless, the 'new sociology' of the family (see further Smart and Neale, 1997) has been seen by a number of writers as sharing with aspects of contemporary feminist thought a concern to integrate insights from new theories of the body, corporeality, desire and identity. And in so doing it has, in particular, sought to highlight the increasingly heightened commodification and political problematization of heterosexual desire and pleasure more generally within late modernity.

What has emerged from each of the above strands of scholarship is something of the increasingly contested nature of the concept of heterosexuality within social theory. Whilst it is recognized that heterosexuality continues to be constituted as normative, as an ethically 'correct' social practice, recent sociological work has pointed out how the proliferation of expertise associated with all aspects of daily life has itself made the 'complex diversity of choices' (Giddens, 1991: 80) involved in 'being straight' an increasingly problematic enterprise. Indeed, the material structural conditions of late capitalism are themselves seen as having given rise to new channels of communication, knowledge and experience about heterosexual practices which have themselves promoted new and diverse heterosexual identities and subjects, new ways of 'doing' heterosexuality. It is in this context that the ideas of 'lifestyle choice' (Giddens, 1991: 5) and 'reflexive project of the self' have been seen as having become vital elements in the shaping, and even creating, of both individual and collective senses of a (hetero)sexual 'self' in society. Without in any way negating the powerful cultural and legal injunctions which continue to work *against* the taking on of a gay or lesbian identity, the idea of the 'heterosexual lifestyle' has thus itself become something which can no longer be assumed (if it ever could) to be unproblematically 'inherited' by 'heterosexual' individuals. It is, rather, something defined by a range of consumer choices, created in the context of a multiplicity of choice. An overarching 'matrix' (Butler, 1990) of 'compulsory heterosexuality' (Rich, 1981) may be experienced as continuing to frame such 'choice', to the degree that, for some, it could be seen as no choice at all. However, a key concern here has been to present heterosexuality, not as a fixed, homogenous or unchanging concept, but as an *interdiscursive* construction; as something which transcends the public/private dualism of liberal legalism and encompasses instead a multiplicity of parallel worlds of workplace, family, friendships, body regimes, sexual practices and relationships. As an object of knowledge and 'subject of power', the heterosexual body, no less (or no more) than the queer body, has been disengaged from the certainties of hitherto 'categories of givens', not least, of course, about what constitutes a 'normal' family life.

Cultural reconfigurations: heterosexuality and the 'crisis' of 'the family'

Each of these strands address something of the theoretical and political influences informing the present reassessment of heterosexuality within gender and sexuality scholarship. It is, finally, and by way of drawing together the above points, important to recognize also some of the broader ways in which questions of family and family law reform have become central to a range of popular cultural accounts which have sought to address economic and social change in terms of shifting 'gender relations'. A concern to reappraise social relations between women and men has become one of the most pressing, discussed and contentious (if frequently obtuse) questions within the *fin de siècle* cultural landscape. Traversing numerous media and academic texts, some recurring questions have become the staple fare of television, newspaper, magazine, radio and film explorations of the parameters of 'family' and 'family life': what is happening to men and women's 'traditional' social 'roles' in Western societies, whether in relation to employment, sexuality or 'family practices' (Morgan, 1996)? What, in particular, is happening *to* (and within) 'the family'? Is it in 'crisis', a point of breakdown, or is it being reconstituted, redefined and remodelled in new ways? Is it as powerful as ever, whilst simultaneously embracing more and more people within its familial web (Midgley and Hughes, 1997)? Do 'families need fathers'? Do, increasingly it would seem, families need men at all?

That each of the above are questions about (among other things) heterosexuality and heterosexual social practices tends, for much of the time, to be overlooked in such conversations. What *cannot* be ignored, however, is the present cultural and political purchase of these questions. Of course, concerns about the relationship between family and ideas of sexuality, sociality, citizenship and social order cannot be confined to debates about law. They are, nonetheless, issues central to, indeed they are at the heart of, contemporary family law policy. Within a broader debate, a whole range of issues pertinent to family law reform have been constituted as attesting to the profound transformation taking place within heterosexual social relations at the end of the twentieth century. Economic, cultural and technological changes (not least around new reproductive practices) have each, in different ways, problematized the way in which adaptations, forms of attachment and subjective commitments are being mobilized towards modes of belonging and integration such as legal marriage and the heterosexual 'family'.

In the remainder of this chapter, and by way of brief illustration simply of the *kinds* of questions that can usefully be asked about heterosexuality and family law, I wish to unpack some of the ways in which family law policy is itself (re)constituting a number of categories through which the idea of the heterosexual social subject has, historically, been encoded as familial. In seeking to 'heterosexua*lize*' family law, I shall focus on just one aspect of contemporary debates around parenting and law in the UK. Although its origins lie in a political context predating the election of the Labour government in May 1997, this issue has nonetheless come to have a central significance within current thinking around family policy: the relationship between men, children and the meaning of parental 'responsibility'. I shall, before concluding, proceed to assess some of the analytic strengths as well as weaknesses of reconceptualizing hetero-sexuality as an analytic tool when critically approaching changing configurations of sexuality and gender in the legal arena.

'HETEROSEXUALIZING' FAMILY LAW: MEN, THE 'NEW FAMILY' AND FAMILIAL RESPONSIBILITY

At the present moment there exists a proliferation of legislation and policy initiatives around the family and 'supporting families' in Britain. This itself raises a number of important questions about the power of law within a norma-lizing society (Ewald, 1990), not least in relation to the shifting relationship between legal and non-legal forms of knowledge and expertise. It also raises the questions of *why* and *how* a particular 'problematization' (Rose and Valverde, 1998) of fathers and fatherhood is presently being articulated, and what this tells us, not just about the contours of the changing family, but also about the status and meaning of the heterosexual(ity) (of) family life. What, more generally, are the implications of the increasingly fragmented/fragmenting family (Smart and Neale, 1997) for the legal regulation of divorce, child support, inheritance, housing and welfare provision? What, ultimately, do these very shifts in hetero-sexual social practices mean for the development of law and family policy at the end of the twentieth century?

Family values, law and government: the example of making the 'father figure'

Over the past 20 years (at least) there has occurred a widespread reconsideration of the place of men within the family in which the position of the father and fatherhood has assumed a central and contested role. At the present moment a profound cultural and legal re-appraising is taking place of the relationship between men and children *per se* in which a rethinking of 'the father figure' has been a central concern (Blankenhorn, 1995; Burgess and Ruxton, 1996; Burghes *et al.*, 1997; Dench, 1996; Mitchell and Goody, 1997; Westwood, 1996). These uncertainties around fathers and fatherhood are further reflected in, and illustrated by, the way in which a range of social and legal policies in recent years have focused on the issue of fatherhood (Burgess, 1997). The legal rights and responsibilities of unmarried fathers (Lord Chancellor's Department, 1998), the enforcement of men's provision for child support, the perceived need to encourage men to be active parents in the post-divorce family (Smart and Neale, 1997) and to *be with* their children (Collier, 1999) – to 'care for' as well as 'care about' them – are just some of the areas which have assumed an increasingly high profile in debates about the possibilities, and the limits, of law in the regulation of social life.

How are we to make sense of these developments in terms of engaging with the heterosexuality of 'family life'? The perspectives or 'ways of seeing' provided by functionalism, the public/private divide, postmodern or familialist accounts and autopoesis remain perhaps the most prominent of the diverse theoretical frameworks through which family law has been approached within legal scholarship (see further, by way of overview, Dewar, 1996, 1998). Feminist legal scholarship, however, can be seen not just to have 'mapped onto', or to have 'drawn on', but to have profoundly developed and progressed theoretical thought in relation to each of the above perspectives in the way in which it has explored that aspect of the relationship between legal and family practices so often passed over in 'malestream' accounts: that is, a critique of law in terms of *power* and *sexual difference*. It is certainly tempting to interpret the major family law reforms of the recent period – the Family Law Act 1996, Child Support Act 1991 and Children Act 1989 – as having involved the promotion of a 'new' kind of heterosexuality, more in tune with contemporary demographic changes, cultural shifts and changing gender ideologies. By drawing on feminist, queer and sociological engagements with heterosexuality, as outlined above, it is possible, however, to ask a number of rather different questions about such reforms.

Heterosexualities, family practices and sexed subjects

Let us be clear. At the present moment a clear correlation is being made, almost universally it would seem, between 'supporting families' and 'supporting fathers'. Parliamentary debates, ministerial statements, government documents and numerous policy reports in Britain bespeak this need to make the father figure in social life.[3] And, in so doing, a number of 'core values' or assumptions have been seen to underpin a belief in the desirability of a 'new democratic' 'socially integrated' family. These values circulate around a political belief that 'autonomy' liberates the individual (something of a key motif within what has been called 'third way' political thought: Giddens, 1998): the values of emotional and sexual equality, of mutual rights and responsibilities in relationships, a negotiated authority over children and, of particular importance to debates around fatherhood and law, co-parenting and lifelong obligations to children. Each of these values would appear, on the surface, to be both positive and desirable. And yet it is possible to raise a number of questions about how they are presently informing the current direction of family policy when seen from within a broader frame of heterosexual family practices.

On one level what we are dealing with here is a question which has become central to recent feminist scholarship around the philosophy of care and caring (Sevenhuijsen, 1998): how does an abstract 'ethic of obligation' relate to the 'ethics of care' *in practice*, that is, in the 'day-to-day' lives of women and men when seen through the prism of gender? The parenting ideal central to the new family policy clashes, in a number of respects, with what research suggests is the continuing disjuncture between the rhetoric surrounding, and the realities of, the contemporary parenting practices of men and women (Social Focus on

Men and Women, 1998).[4] Without in any way underestimating the economic imperatives of capitalist societies, as mediated in national governmental contexts, experience across jurisdictions suggests that it is by no means clear that men assume a greater share of child-care responsibilities even when specific public provision is established (for example in the form of parental leave arrangements). Notwithstanding evidence which suggests some men do experience real difficulties in combining paid work with child care and other commitments (Oerton, 1996: 178; New Ways to Work, 1995), there would also appear to exist a considerable reluctance on the part of many men to change. Indeed, empirical research suggests that many men's embrace of domestic roles may be, at best, a reluctant response to circumstances beyond their control, not least the demands of their women partners (Gerson, 1993). This point is of considerable importance when it is recognized how current legislative interventions have themselves been premised on a number of assumptions about the relationship between gendered identity and family practice in which the deep-rooted and psychologically complex nature of heterosexual social relations has tended to be routinely effaced. This point requires clarification.

In terms of the discursive structuring of parenting as a sexed (as different) experience, the dominant notion of gender neutrality sits uneasily with the nature of heterosexual relationships which, empirical studies of motherhood, fatherhood and 'family life' suggest, tend to entail differential experiences for women and men (Arendell, 1995; Day Sclater, 1998, 1999; Day Sclater and Yates, 1999; Smart and Neale, 1997; cf. Bernard, 1973). This itself can be seen to relate to the way in which the gendered nature of caring inescapably brings with it social and political meanings of masculinity/femininity, motherhood and fatherhood, which do not play out in the same way for men and women in relation to dominant understandings of familial 'commitment'. Indeed, male heterosexuality can itself be seen to have been configured historically not so much by a connection *to* the familial as by a *dissociation* of men from, in a number of respects, 'the family' (Collier, 1995). That is, heterosexual masculinity has itself been historically institutionalized within dominant understandings of both family and working life via a distancing of men from those material practices associated with 'caring for' (as opposed to 'caring about') within the everyday living out of the 'dependencies' which, in Fineman's (1995) terms, inevitably mark the familial sphere.

None of the above is to argue that women are somehow inherently or biologically more 'connected' or 'relational' than men. It is, however, to question the complex, contingent and contested nature of an overarching frame of heterosexual relating in which men and women have been positioned differentially within the material, cultural and emotional discourses surrounding ideas of 'family life'. Approaching parenthood as a material, embodied practice in terms of sexual difference involves surfacing how a range of gendered experiences of parenting are themselves discursively produced and 'lived' in everyday family practices (Brown and Day Sclater, 1999; Day Sclater, 1998, 1999; Lupton and Barclay, 1997). And, from such a perspective, what becomes clear is how men's parenting practices have historically been constituted via the making of certain assumptions about issues such as paternal presence/absence, heterosexual marriage, economic status, emotionality and the nature of sexual difference/ontology. Although the law may be seeking to reconstitute the relationship between men and children in a number of ways, other economic, cultural, social and legal discourses continue to position men as social agents who are, if not effectively free, then as at least dissociated in a number of important respects from a range of familial, emotional and material encumbrances in relation to children and 'family life'. Moreover, in the complex renegotiations taking place around the formation and dissolution of these heterosexual attachments, it would appear to be in relation to men's and women's differential relationship to/with children that these sexed *as different* negotiations of heterosexual gendered subjectivities are being experienced in a particularly acute form. This itself is unsurprising, given the way in which an acceleration in the intensity, purchase and currency of emotions centred around the idea of the 'fragmenting' (private) heterosexual family has itself come to assume a central significance in contemporary understandings of how women's and men's experiences of the 'social' are grounded in the first place.

There remain other, internal, contradictions in the way in which present family policy is conceptualizing heterosexuality. On the one hand, heterosexual marriage continues to be central to the privileged and enforced foundational imperative of family law (Reinhold, 1994). Indeed, it is a heightened support for the institution of heterosexual marriage which underscores the divorce law reforms of Part II of the Family Law Act 1996. The 1998 Green Paper 'Supporting Families' virtually ignores the needs of heterosexual cohabitation, let alone same-sex cohabitation, by similarly conceptualizing law reform in terms of 'strengthening marriage'. Yet, at the same time, and in theory at least, both gender-neutral parenting and the 'new fatherhood' are themselves 'divorced' from this heterosexual frame in a number of respects.[5] Within the privileging of active parenting envisaged in the legislation, and in the context of large-scale family restructuring away from marriage, the combination of an ontology of sexual difference, hierarchy and normative heterosexuality – the trinity historically central to the discursive con-stitution of father-presence as socially desirable – is itself displaced as the door is opened to readings of 'transformations of intimacy'. Such transformations *cannot* be confined to changing contours of heterosexuality and, importantly, embrace forms of 'confluent love' which do not have to be heterosexual (Giddens, 1992). Indeed, it could be argued that the 'space' of the heterosexual family is itself now being fractured and reformed as a different kind of space, open to new possibilities and new familial subjects (cf. Smart and Neale, 1997: 182).

TAKING HETEROSEXUALITY (AND LAW) SERIOUSLY?

We have seen above how a range of discourses in the area of family law reform continue to reproduce a notion of the heterosexual subject as familial and as familial*ized*. In the context of late modern social formations, however, I have argued that this is a process of heterosexual*ization* which would itself, in a number of respects, increasingly appear to be contingent, fluid and uncertain. It is necessary at this stage to push the argument a little further in order to think through what it means to engage with the relationship between heterosexuality and law more generally, in seeking to develop an understanding of the relationship between sexuality and the legal arena.

Within dominant gender discourse a particular familial ideology has been supported by, indeed, has been embodied by, law. Whether this familial ideology is termed heterosexist, heterocentric or heteronormative, as it has been within a range of counter-discourses, it remains unquestionably powerful, pervasive and brutally unforgiving of those who do not ascribe to its social and sexual codes. Yet it is also possible to argue that it is, at the present moment, somewhat paradoxical that the very (sexual) identity politics and discourses of resistance which have historically sought to name oppressive 'straight' practices and beliefs should have themselves brought about a questioning, challenging and undermining of the analytic unity of (hetero)sexual subjectivity itself. In theorizing the social subject as an always/already discursive artefact, contingent, in process and unstable, queer theory has fractured the hetero/homo(sexual) binary and pushed both hetero and gay and lesbian identities to the status of nothing more than (at most) a temporary association with a particular desire and/ or social identity. And in so doing, and just as queer theory has utilized a notion of the sexed subject in some strategic, pragmatic ways, it becomes possible to see how ways of 'being straight' might be something deployed in particular ways and to particular discursive ends. Heterosexual bodies, heterosexual identities and practices are not, in short, pre-given, pre-discursive artefacts; they cannot be taken for granted, whether in dominant political discourse or in ostensibly critical accounts of family law.

Yet it has, at times, been a particular kind of heterosexual social subject which has been brought into being by *both* dominant and counter-discourses. There is a profound danger in ascribing to a social institution or practice such as law any homogenous, fixed and/or unchanging qualities. The ideas of 'family' which have been historically constituted as a heterosexual(ized) phenomenon, for example, have presented a description, a list of attributes encoded as 'heterosexual', each of which conjure up powerful images about social relationships (and certainly not just about sexual/bodily practices).[6] What is actually being discussed in many accounts of heterosexuality is, in effect, a range of popular ideologies of what constitutes the ideal or actual characteristics of complex social relationships between men and women. What frequently remains unclear, however, is the relationship between these structured relationships: 'how many structures are needed to think this series of relationships? . . . is structure simply the outcome of prior practice, albeit constrained practice, how does practice produce, and continually reproduce, something as systematic as the gender order?' (Jefferson, 1994: 15). Depicting or dismissing law as somehow essentially or irredeemably 'heterocentric' in nature is, by itself, to fail to address 'the theories or institutions [of law] as such, [and] the significance of . . . statements *within their specific discursive contexts*' (Brown, 1990: 47, my emphasis). What such depictions of law as inherently, inescapably heterosexual, heterosexist and so forth, do tend to do, however, is to conflate, by reference to a preconstituted definition of the ideological or cultural meanings of heterosexuality, a number of beliefs about sexual practices, identities and value systems. It has been a common tactic within much critical sexuality scholarship to see a range of (preconstituted) 'heterosexist' beliefs as somehow intruding 'into the "sacred" realm of theoretical or institutional practices' (Brown, 1990: 48–9). And yet, in making this argument, both social theory and specific practices and institutions (not least those associated with family law) are themselves seen as being linked together in a systematic unity of shared assumptions, as, variously, 'heterocentric' or, in a variant, 'masculinist' embodiments of 'the heterosexuality of law'.[7] Heterosexuality itself, arguably, is conceptually imprecise; distilling, as Hearn (1996) has put it in discussing masculinity, a broad range of activity in the social world into one neat word. It is certainly unclear how it relates to understandings of culture, something particularly evident within strands of both feminist and queer theoretical scholarship.

CONCLUSION

The starting point for this engagement with sexuality in the legal arena has been a belief that the concept of heterosexuality has been, and remains, largely unexplored within the field of family law and legal studies. I have sought to surface just one aspect of the way in which the development of present family policy has involved what I have termed a reconfiguration of heterosexual familial subjects. Heterosexuality, as a marker of a particular social identity (to feel oneself to be, to be seen as 'straight'), has been produced and sustained by discourses of sexuality and gender which have been historically interwoven and rooted within the dualistic configurations which have pervaded liberal legal thought. What is all too clear from contemporary debates about divorce, 'family values', parental responsibility and the quality of 'family life' more generally, is the way in which questions of ethics, justice and social value continue to be articulated within a political and legal discourse in ways which reproduce dominant gendered assignations of male/female attributes in a hierarchical manner. Moving beyond those traditional concepts through which the very idea of the familial has been constituted – heterosexualized categories such as fatherhood and motherhood, wife and husband – may itself be, as Fineman has argued, to 'forge social and political meanings that are corollaries to the challenges presented by single mothers ... to raise questions about, perhaps challenge the whole conceptual basis of the 'private' family and to recognize the need for systemic societal reform to address inevitable dependencies' (Fineman, 1995: 205; see also Fineman, 1991). At the present moment such a project appears, if not unthinkable, then certainly far away. The private(ized) family, the 'family as society' and the 'society as familial', far from being an increasing anachronism, are themselves experiencing a resurgence within a dominant political discourse in which individual choice, free will and 'normality' have become barely questioned touchstones of debate.

On one level, therefore, there is perhaps little cause to be optimistic about the advent of the 'democratic' model of the 'new family' at a moment when the gender(ed) pains of contemporary heterosexuality remain only too clear to see: in the prevalence of interpersonal violences, the physical and psychological sufferings lived out and experienced by so many women and men day-to-day in the name of 'normal' family life; in the patent contradictions and ambivalence – indeed, the blatant hypocrisy – of societal attitudes to divorce, as witnessed in ongoing debates around the implementation of Part II of the Family Law Act 1996 (Day Sclater and Piper, 1999); and in the now familiar narrative of marital breakdown and reconstitution, the dominant discourse of familial crisis and reformation which simultaneously acclaims each new union as social (if not sacramental) bond whilst equating the end of an individual marriage with the end of 'family life' *per se* (Smart, 1997; Smart and Neale, 1997). Far from reducing conflict between men and women, present family policy might itself be serving to heighten and exacerbate the divisions only too evident within an increasingly prevalent rhetoric of the 'sex war', a gendered discourse through which, it would seem, increasing numbers of both women, and in particular men (Arditti and Allen, 1993; Berotia and Drakich, 1993; Collier, 1996; Day Sclater and Yates, 1999), are seeking to make sense of their 'family' lives – and of their heterosexualities – at a time of rapid social change.

And yet, notwithstanding the above, it is possible to end on a more positive note. Perhaps something new is being born at the turn of the twenty-first century, as social and economic changes open up new possibilities, new ways of 'being' straight (Segal, 1994; Smart, 1996a, b). Far from simply mirroring the familiar (familial) crises within the gender order which marked the previous *fin de siècle* (Showalter, 1992), it is possible that what we are presently witnessing is – albeit to degrees, and albeit in certain contexts – no less than the detaching of (hetero)'sex' itself from 'gender'. And as the hitherto dominant sex/gender distinction is itself called into question, the parameters of the 'familial' are themselves being questioned and made permeable by the demands of those who have hitherto been excluded from this heterosexualized familial domain. The clearly contested and problematic, but seemingly unstoppable, processes of the familial*izing* of, not just single mothers and gay and lesbian parents, but of all those previously outwith the patriarchal family, attest not so much (or not just) to a growing liberalism around sexuality and a weakening of the hold of Judaeo-Christian morality. It also bespeaks a re-appraisal of heterosexuality itself as a normative 'performative project of the self' in a context in which, within the sexualized and sexually obsessive popular cultural formations of advanced capitalism, what was once 'behind closed doors' is now rendered 'public' in a particularly powerful, unsettling (and yet perhaps strangely reassuring) way.[8] Sex – hetero/homo/bi – is not simply on the front page of every newspaper, on television, video, satellite and cable, beamed down into almost every home and potentially filtered through the Internet into more and more locations (the child's bedroom, the school, the library, the university). Sexual identity has become, as Foucault (1979b) observed, that through which we speak of *and become* ourselves, the Truth of our beings. And it is in this context, I have argued, that the diverse practices which presently constitute 'the familial' are being transformed, fragmented and reconstituted. Family practices *have never been*, notwithstanding their legal classification and moral injunction via marriage laws, simply confined to a particular conjunction of penis and vagina (Collier, 1992; O'Donovan, 1993; Segal, 1994: 318). From this perspective, and in recognizing the diversity and psychological complexity of human sexuality, the 'heterosexual family' does not need to be *made* queer, or to *be* 'queered'; it has always been, to adopt a definition of queer itself, a most transgressive, fluid and performative of social practices.

PART FOUR

THE POLITICS OF RIGHTS

INTRODUCTION

To this point, a number of essays have raised questions about 'rights'. This section focuses more directly on the politics of rights, but moves beyond the now well-explored question of 'are rights good or bad?' Rather, the contributors here are concerned to follow and analyse particular case studies of actual rights struggles (from Canada, South Africa and the international human rights context), drawing from these to consider wider questions about strategy and goals in particular contexts.

In their essay, Rebecca Johnson and Thomas Kuttner advocate a widening of lesbian and gay legal strategies in Canada; in particular, they urge a return to what is usually perceived as part of a conservative, anti-gay rhetorical arsenal: appeals to constitutional tradition and history. Pierre de Vos also explores a constitutional theme by reflecting upon the South African experience of 'constitutionalizing' sexual orientation rights. Finally, Wayne Morgan concludes this section by injecting an activist, expansive and inclusive agenda into the traditionally bounded field of international human rights law.

12

TREADING ON DICEY GROUND

CITIZENSHIP AND THE POLITICS OF THE RULE OF LAW

REBECCA JOHNSON AND THOMAS KUTTNER

Just as the constitutional choices we make are channelled and constrained by who we are and what we have lived through, so too they are constrained and channelled by a constitutional text and structure and history, by constitutional language and constitutional tradition, opening some paths and foreclosing others. To ignore or defy those constraints is to pretend a power that is not ours to wield. But to pretend that those constraints leave us no freedom, or must lead us all to the same conclusions, is to disclaim a responsibility that is inescapably our own. (Laurence Tribe[1])

INTRODUCTION

In the second half of the twentieth century, many struggles for justice and equality have been conducted on the terrain of rights. One dimension of the struggle has involved attempts to draft and constitutionalize various rights-granting documents.[2] A second dimension has centred on the legal interpretations to be given to the resulting texts.[3] Both types of struggle have produced contradictory and conflicting results. While activists have sometimes managed to harness equality rights discourse to advance their claims, some have noted that these positive moments have been coupled with many other moments where the discourse of equality has been deployed in ways that have dismantled legislatively won social victories.[4] Some writers have suggested that an excessive reliance on rights discourse has led to an impoverishment in democratic fields of politics.[5] Others, without suggesting rights are meaningless, have argued that rights are simply incapable of resolving difficult problems of social injustice.

Bakan, paraphrasing Marx, articulates the problem by commenting that the material inequities of the world cannot be fought simply by fighting the phrases of this world.[6]

While rights discourses alone have not been enough to shift the phrases of this world, they have nonetheless played an important role in attempts to displace both harmful frameworks of meaning and material inequities. There are, however, constraints on what rights discourse can do, constraints that vary according to the history and tradition of the contexts in which they are employed. In the quote above, Tribe suggests that those seeking to harness the discourse of rights in the cause of social justice have been up against not just textual limits, but limits imposed by history and tradition. For lesbian and gay activists, one of those limits has been the role played by dominant heterosexist frameworks of meaning, frameworks that are difficult to displace/replace.[7] The existence of such constraints and limits need not lead to rights cynicism or a rejection of rights discourse.[8] It should, however, encourage activists to take heed of Tribe's comment that history, while closing off some paths, opens others. As Hans argues, 'if our region of choices is severely limited, and if our effectiveness within the fields of play differs considerably, then surely the question of choosing is paramount.'[9] In order to make choices about legal strategies to use, we must have a good sense of the contexts in which those strategies will be deployed, and of the ways in which history and tradition both close off and open up new avenues. The challenge is to be continually searching for additional paths and alternative forms of argument. And, as Hans argues, 'Any understanding of the nuances of the embedded condition of the world is based on the notion that there are always at the very least a number of possibilities.'[10]

Without suggesting that rights discourse is ineffective, we argue that it is only one of a number of possibilities, and that it is important to continually search for additional paths and additional choices. Since activists are not autonomous from the fields in which they work, these possibilities will vary according to each country's history and tradition. In this chapter, we seek to illustrate the search for additional paths – for multiple ways of using law to advance progressive social change in a society steeped in a tradition of an exclusively heterosexist model of human life.

To explore some of these possibilities, we will use the Canadian case *Vriend v Alberta*,[11] and discuss the arguments made at the Supreme Court hearing by the Intervener, Canadian Association for Statutory Human Rights Agencies (CASHRA).[12] CASHRA, while supporting a claim based on equality rights, also made arguments tapping into older paths in Canadian constitutional history. These arguments raised questions about parliamentary supremacy, federalism, the implied bill of rights, citizenship, constitutional conventions and the rule of law. The strategy was to invite the court – an inherently traditionalist institution – to re-explore its own constitutional traditions that predated modern rights discourse, and to discover there powerful support for a vision of a society capable of shedding its heterosexist atavisms. We will begin with a discussion of the *Vriend* case, explore some of the (typically Canadian) potential limits to the traditional equality rights argument, and then discuss some of the possible routes around these limits, routes located in an evolutionary approach to Canada's constitutional text, structure, history and tradition.

THE CASE

In the early 1990s, Delwin Vriend, an employee of a small fundamentalist Christian college, was fired because he was gay. Vriend sought the assistance of the Human Rights Commission. There, he was told that sexual orientation was not a prohibited ground of discrimination under Alberta's human rights legislation. Indeed, the Commission had been directed by the government not to accept complaints based on sexual orientation, and thus could do nothing for people who were refused housing or employment because they were gay or lesbian.

Nor was Vriend entitled to bring a common law action based on tort. The Supreme Court of Canada had already held that there was no private law tort of discrimination in Canada. Issues of discrimination were to be dealt with under human rights legislation rather than before the courts.[13] Indeed, the decision not to recognize a private law tort of discrimination was based in large measure on assumptions about the legislator's preference for specialized human rights agencies as the most suitable vehicles to deal with discrimination in the private realm. In this case, given the refusal of Alberta to add sexual orientation to the list of prohibited forms of discrimination, Vriend was denied any legal avenue to pursue his claim.

Vriend then challenged the constitutionality of Alberta's human rights legislation. He argued that the government's failure to include sexual orientation as a prohibited ground of discrimination in the Human Rights Act was a violation of the guarantee of equality contained in section 15 of the Canadian Charter of Rights and Freedoms.[14] The text of this section provides:

> Every individual is equal before and under the law and has the right to the equal protection and equal benefit of the law without discrimination and, in particular, without discrimination based on race, national or ethnic origin, colour, religion, sex, age or mental or physical disability.

On its face, section 15 does not appear to prohibit discrimination on the basis of sexual orientation. However, in early interpretations of the section, the Supreme Court focussed on the text's open-ended language, and concluded that the list of prohibited grounds was not closed.[15] Section 15 provided protection for other groups suffering invidious discrimination, as long as those groups were analogous to the listed groups. After more than a decade of litigation, the Supreme Court concluded in *Egan* that sexual orientation was analogous to other prohibited grounds of discrimination.[16]

It was the Charter's section 15 guarantee of equality that formed the central backdrop for the *Vriend* case. The case worked its way to the Supreme Court, where more than 15 different groups were granted intervener status.[17] For the most part, the arguments supporting Vriend were rooted in modern rights discourse - that Alberta had violated section 15 equality rights by excluding gays and lesbians from human rights protection.[18] The equality claim is an important one, but there are limits to the utility of a Charter equality claim. We focus on three.

POTENTIAL LIMITS OF EQUALITY DISCOURSE

First, the section 15 guarantee of equality is not absolute. According to section 1 of the Charter, a government may violate equality rights as long as the violation is 'demonstrably justified in a free and democratic society'.[19] The Court has struggled with the question of justification. This struggle has been particularly problematic in the context of gay and lesbian litigation. The reasons in *Egan* illustrate the problem. Though the entire Court concluded that sexual orientation was (in the abstract) protected by section 15 of the Charter, section 1 was used to justify the denial of pension benefits to same-sex couples.[20] According to Sopinka J, sexual orientation was a newly recognized form of discrimination, not universally acknowledged as invidious. Governments should thus be allowed to take slow or incremental remedial steps.[21] Building on a line of cases which bow to legislative allocation of social and economic benefits, he found the discriminatory impact of the legislation on gay and lesbian couples to be justifiable in the context of limited funds, and government attempts to remedy poverty for some heterosexual couples. In short, for Vriend, even if sexual orientation was protected in general under the Charter, there was the risk (and a real one, based on the jurisprudence) that the Court would simply conclude as it did in *Egan* that the violation could be justified at least in the short term, and perhaps indefinitely.

A second potential problem came in the guise of section 33 of the Charter, the much debated 'notwithstanding' clause. According to this section, a government found to be in violation of the guarantees included in sections 2 and 7–15 of the Charter can re-enact that law in derogation of Charter rights. All that is required is a majority vote in the legislature. This clause was part of the compromise necessary to obtain the support of the majority of provinces to the entrenchment of the Charter. Some writers see the clause as a necessary safety valve for democracy while others see it as a failure in rights protection.[22] Certainly, outside Quebec, the political costs to a government invoking the clause are high, and it has been used very rarely.[23] Nonetheless, during 1998, the government of Alberta suggested it would invoke the clause in support of its position in the *Vriend* case. There was a real possibility, even if Vriend were to win his section 15 Charter claim before the Supreme Court, that Alberta might use section 33 of the Charter to re-enact the discriminatory legislation.[24]

But there was a third and perhaps even more troubling problem, one located in a strong vision of parliamentary supremacy within Canadian federalism. In short, there was the suggestion that Alberta, rather than extend protection to gays and lesbians, would rather revoke its entire human rights regime. Here, a brief word on Canadian constitutional history is in order. It was only in 1982 that Canada entrenched the Charter of Rights, a document which articulated limits on governmental action. Prior to 1982, the discourse of constitutional law was dominated by concerns with the nature of parliamentary supremacy in a federal state. The Canadian Constitution Act, 1867 (or, The British North America Act as it was known until 1982) was explicitly based on the British model. Indeed, the Preamble to the Act said, 'the Provinces . . . have expressed their Desire to be federally united into One Dominion under the Crown . . . with a Constitution similar in Principle to that of the United Kingdom'. Under the Canadian system, the word was thus Parliamentary Supremacy, albeit a supremacy modified by the doctrine of federalism. In Canada, the world of legislative power is divided between the federal and provincial governments. The issue for constitutional discussion was less one of limits on government, than it was the question of whether or not the correct level of government was legislating.

We will return to this history later in the chapter, but at this point it is important to know that, in the Canadian regime, human rights generally is a matter of provincial jurisdiction; each of the provinces has enacted its own human rights legislation. Alberta argued that, according to section 92(13) of the Constitution Act, 1867, it had complete jurisdiction over civil rights in the province – it was free to enact (or not enact) a human rights regime as it wished. Since it was free to enact nothing, surely it should also be free to enact a limited regime of human rights protection. One-half of the argument had already been dealt with by the courts. Having decided to legislate, Alberta would be bound to do so in accordance with the provisions of the Charter.[25] But the more troubling spectre was this: could the province put itself back in compliance by simply repealing the human rights act *in toto*?[26]

So, while Charter based equality rights discourse opened up some avenues, they were not avenues completely free from risk. The question was then, were there any additional ways of approaching the problem, ways that might circumvent some of the risks listed above? If, as Hans put it, there are always at least a number of possibilities, what might some of those possibilities be? In its intervention at the Supreme Court, CASHRA attempted to sketch out three alternative routes based on evolutionary approaches to Canada's own constitutional history. These alternatives required a re-walking on (and a reworking of) the 'Dicey' ground of parliamentary supremacy and the rule of law. The first alternative was rooted in federalism and civil liberties, the second in an expansion of citizenship, and the third in constitutional convention.

FEDERALISM AND CIVIL LIBERTIES

The first path involved an equality argument rooted in the Canadian history of federalism. CASHRA argued that the Charter and the Constitution Act, 1867 had to be read not as 'two solitudes', but in an integrated fashion. Vriend's appeal engaged not only section 15 of the Charter, but issues central to the Canadian constitutional order in its entirety: the relationship between fundamental rights and legislative authority. Indeed, in the legislative supremacy argument made by Alberta in defence of its legislation, the constitutional order first established by the Constitution Act, 1867 was firmly engaged. Foregrounded by CASHRA was the notion that the division of powers is a principal characteristic of the Canadian political unity, with legislative sovereignty, the rule of law and civil liberties the informing values. Under this constitutional order, CASHRA asserted, the seeds of equality protection were sown well before 1982. Even in the absence of section 15 of the Charter, courts had laid the groundwork for equality-based protections. This argument made explicit the claim that the past informs the present, and that the tension between fundamental rights and legislative authority must be determined with reference to the entire body of constitutional doctrine and history.

Reference to Canada's constitutional history reveals that, despite the absence of any constitutionalized rights-bearing documents, courts have found constitutional devices to extend a measure of protection to fundamental freedoms and civil liberties. Often, the doctrine of federalism served as the device to protect civil liberties. Given the classic Diceyan formulation of parliamentary supremacy on which Alberta heavily relied, it is interesting that our Courts have had recourse to the federal principal as a source of entrenched liberties – for Dicey himself doubted the integrity of the doctrine in the context of a federal state.[27] Perhaps implicitly drawing on that doubt, in one case the Supreme Court struck down provincial legislation which restricted free and public discussion in the press.[28] In another, it struck down provincial legislation which interfered with freedom of religion.[29] In yet a third, the Court invalidated provincial legislation which targeted communists and bolsheviks.[30]

In each of the three cases, the legislation in question was provincial. Thus, the narrow legal question was not whether civil liberties were generally immune from government incursion, but only whether provincial governments had the authority to affect such liberties. However, there were suggestions by some of the judges in these cases that civil liberties might indeed be beyond the reach of not only provincial governments, but also the federal government: even Parliament itself was not free to abrogate the right of discussion and debate.[31] In coming to this conclusion, the judges adverted to the (judicially developed) doctrine of an implied bill of rights. The Preamble of the Constitution Act, 1867 (they claimed) imported into the Canadian constitution a series of constitutionally buttressed implied rights.

In the development of this theory, courts had focussed on the right of free and public discussion, said to be 'the breath of life for Parliamentary institutions' in the *Alberta Press* case (1938); on freedom of religion as articulated in the *Jehovah's Witnesses* case (1953); and on freedom of speech in the *Padlock Act* case (1957). While some argue that civil rights arise only from positive law, Rand J once argued that freedom of speech, religion and the inviolability of the person, are 'original freedoms which are at once the necessary attributes and modes of self-expression of human beings and the primary conditions of their community life within a legal order'.[32] CASHRA argued that, as with the case of freedom of speech and of religion, so too with that of equality before the law. Equality comprises a necessary attribute and primary condition of community life within the Canadian legal order, and should be beyond the reach of the Legislature of Alberta. Certainly, there was a tradition in the courts which accorded civil liberties supremacy of place over legislative sovereignty. At its strongest, this tradition held that civil liberties were beyond the reach of either level of government.[33] However, even in its weaker formulation, civil liberties were immune from incursions by provincial governments.

Taking this approach to equality, CASHRA argued that Alberta's discriminatory approach to human rights protection was constitutionally suspect on federalism grounds. The advantage of such an approach is that it avoids issues related to the justification of discrimination under section 1 of the Charter. In addition, it sets a new/old framework within which to address equality issues, one with which Canadian courts are familiar. But the argument presents hurdles of its own which need to be overcome. First, what is the informing constitutional value which will trump Alberta's exclusion of gays and lesbians from the protective embrace of its human rights legislation? Second, if we are correct in our analysis, is there a remedial avenue open to the plaintiffs in light of the doctrine of parliamentary supremacy which still informs our federalism? We turn to each of these issues.

CITIZENSHIP AND THE CANADIAN CONSTITUTION

CASHRA's second argument changed the focus from equality to citizenship. Here was a concept deeply entrenched in our constitutional order. Interestingly enough, Dicey did have something to say about citizenship and federalism. According to him, a condition of federalism itself was a 'body of countries (such as the Provinces of Canada) so closely connected ... as to be capable of bearing, in the eyes of their inhabitants, an impress of common nationality.'[34] That impress is the institution of citizenship, an institution at the base of our federal system itself. The argument here was that the actions of the Alberta government eviscerated any notion of a common citizenship, and thus could not be countenanced.

The case law supports such an argument. The roots of the argument lie in the early parts of the century. Canada, a developing industrial state, was making extensive use of underpaid immigrant labour. For all sorts of complex reasons (including economic pressures, rapid expansion, industrialization, moral panic and simple racism), provincial governments were passing legislation placing various restrictions on Chinese immigrants. In one of these cases, the Privy Council struck down a British Columbia statute preventing people of Chinese origin or descent from working in mines.[35] The Privy Council saw the right to work as being a fundamental piece of what it is to be a citizen. To restrict the employment opportunities of Chinese Canadians was to interfere with their rights as citizens. Citizenship, they held, was something of a national character, reserved to the federal parliament to regulate. The provinces had no authority over this area. The scope of rights available to the naturalized citizen was a matter to be exclusively determined by the federal government pursuant to its section 91(25) British North America Act powers over 'naturalization and aliens'.[36]

The thread of this argument was picked up again mid-century. The Court determined that legislative authority over citizenship generally (citizenship not being explicitly listed as a head of power in the Constitution Act, 1867) was something which lay 'at the foundation of the political organization of Canada'.[37] Thus, they said, it fell within the residual powers of the federal government. Parliament's power to determine the rights of naturalized citizens was extended to include all citizens of Canada. The Court concluded that a province did not have the power to prohibit a citizen from working within that province. As Rand J stated, the province could not divest the citizen of their right or capacity to remain in the province and engage in work there. '[T]hat capacity inhering as a constituent element of his citizenship status is beyond nullification by provincial action.'[38] In short, Alberta does not have the power to interfere with the right or ability of gay and lesbian Canadians to seek work in the province of Alberta.

In the context of *Vriend*, the legislation in question does exactly that. By excluding gays and lesbians from having recourse to the human rights code, Alberta authorizes private bodies to refuse employment and services to gays and lesbians. They can be denied jobs and denied housing with impunity – an impunity that is not available for denials based on other historical grounds of invidious discrimination like race, gender and disability. Such a denial obviously has a negative impact on the capacity of gays and lesbians to seek work in the province. Alberta argued that it was simply doing its best to mediate between the demands of equality and religious freedom. This certainly mis-stated the issue. CASHRA argued that, in any pluralistic society, it is inevitable that there will be deep differences, even clashes, between individuals and groups over differing moral values. This is simply an aspect of life in a modern liberal democracy. The human rights regime is one which is designed to mediate just such conflict. In common with that of other jurisdictions, the Alberta legislation specifies contexts in which one right will take precedence over another, providing for instances where conflict will result in justifiable discriminatory treatment. By failing to include sexual orientation as a prohibited ground of discrimination, Alberta sought to exclude gay and lesbian citizens from access to the forum designed to mediate conflicts rooted in differing moral values. Surely this compromises the notion of equal citizenship.

Under the simple doctrine of federalism, the Province is prevented from legislating as it has done in this case. Although the above argument does not require any reference to the Charter, it opens up an additional avenue of relief under the Charter, quite distinct, indeed far removed from equality discourse. This is because the centrality of citizenship and its attributes to the federal union established by the Constitution Act, 1867 is now buttressed by the guarantee of mobility rights entrenched at section 6 of the Charter. CASHRA argued that the Court had stressed that inasmuch as 'Citizenship and nationhood are correlatives', their relevance goes beyond the economic ordering of the State to the very essence of the relationship of citizen to country. The external indicia of the economic union and national economy forged by the Constitution Act, 1867, rest on the footing of a national identity in which each citizen is entitled to participate by moving and taking up residence in any province and pursuing there the gaining of a livelihood.[39]

Expulsion, banishment or exile from Canada was always beyond the reach of the Legislature of a Province. Section 6 of the Charter now renders it beyond the reach of the Parliament of Canada. If external expulsion, banishment or exile is so constitutionally proscribed,[40] then *a fortiori* is this the case internally. Legislative denial of the right to pursue the gaining of a livelihood in a province violates that proscription. Here, the Legislature of Alberta would condone a decision of its residents to deny to a gay or lesbian citizen of Canada the right to pursue the gaining of a livelihood within the province. As CASHRA put it, the Court could not view with equanimity the passivity of the Legislature of Alberta in addressing discrimination against gays and lesbians within the Province in a century which has witnessed the despoliation, deportation and mass murder of an entire people, first stripped of their civil status. Alberta's action was all the more disturbing and ironic given that it occurred in the context of a statutory regime significantly retitled from The Individual's Rights Protection Act to the Human Rights, *Citizenship* and Multiculturalism Act (emphasis added).

In short, CASHRA submitted that gay and lesbian citizens of Canada have the right to move to and take up residence in the Province of Alberta and to pursue there the gaining of a livelihood. That right inheres in their status as Canadian citizens and is a necessary attribute of citizenship which lies beyond the jurisdiction of the legislature of Alberta to impede. It is moreover, a right accorded Charter entrenchment, lying as it does at the core of Canadian nationhood. The failure of the Legislature of Alberta to include sexual orientation as a prohibited ground of discrimination in its human rights legislation violated the citizenship rights of its gay and lesbian residents and could not withstand constitutional scrutiny.

LIMITS TO PARLIAMENTARY SUPREMACY?

As already noted, the government of Alberta was relying on a very strong notion of legislative sovereignty in support of its legislation. The province, they argued, had power over civil rights, and this power was absolute: they could do whatever they wished. Rather than attack Diceyan principles head-on – a dangerous tactic with a judiciary still drinking at its well – CASHRA urged a contextual re-reading of the received wisdom. It argued that the government of Alberta had relied on a misreading of Dicey. Certainly, Dicey did assert that, legally, the sovereignty of Parliament was the 'dominant characteristic of our political institutions'. And the vision of sovereignty asserted by Alberta was one that Dicey himself referred to as 'the despotism of the King in Parliament'. But

Dicey had also argued that this notion of absolute sovereignty was little more than a fiction, and that in reality the powers of Parliament were 'not unlimited'. Rather, Dicey argued that the law of the Constitution was in fact constrained by what he termed 'constitutional morality'. This morality, captured in consti-tutional convention, creates a series of internal and external limits to the unrestrained exercise of power. This allowed Dicey to assert that 'speaking generally Parliament would not embark on a course of reactionary legislation.'[41]

In the Canadian context, with its hybrid written and unwritten constitution, the Court has also acknowledged the importance of constitutional conventions. Though these are not justiciable, courts will take cognizance of constitutional conventions which 'form an integral part of the Constitution and of the constitutional system'. Indeed, these 'may be more important than some laws', ensuring as they do 'that the legal framework of the Constitution will be operated in accordance with the prevailing constitutional values or principles of the period.'[42] CASHRA argued that access by gays and lesbians to the protective embrace of human rights legislation throughout the country has, by convention, attained the status of a binding constitutional norm. The precedents for such a conclusion are many.[43] Thus Diceyan constitutional morality would constrain the Legislature of Alberta from denying to gays and lesbians access to the protective embrace of its human rights legislation.

This more subtle appreciation of Dicey mirrors the growing recognition in the common law world – even in those jurisdictions which still hew to the doctrine of parliamentary supremacy – that there is indeed a 'higher law', a higher order to which judges must bow if the integrity of the constitutional order is to be preserved. A principle proponent of this understanding of the doctrine is Lord Cooke of Thorndon, formerly President of the New Zealand Court of Appeal, who has asserted that some common law rights '[l]ie so deep that even Parliament cannot override them.'[44] And again elsewhere speaking extra-judicially:

> [I]t may be that there are some values so fundamental in our society that it would be the court's duty, if Parliament ever did go to such extraordinary lengths, to say that it has gone beyond what you might call the 'social contract.'[45]

The momentum of what we might term a reformed doctrinal orthodoxy in our understanding of parliamentary supremacy is compelling, particularly given its confluence with modern rights discourse.

This new understanding of the strength of convention to rein in the un-bridled exercise of parliamentary supremacy interlocks neatly with a central tenet of Canadian Charter doctrine, namely that it is only public (i.e. governmental) activity which attracts Charter scrutiny.[46] This is the understanding our courts have of section 32 of the Charter – the Application clause –although this drawing of a bright line distinction between the public and the private spheres has been sharply criticized by some commentators.[47] The important point here for our purposes is that in drawing that dichotomy, both the theorists[48] and the judges[49] place heavy reliance upon the existence of provincial human rights regimes to vindicate equality claims in the private sphere. It would be counter-intuitive then to simultaneously assert a government discretion to repeal human rights legislation, and so abandon the private sphere to the perils of invidious discrimination by the citizenry. The result generally could well be then what it was under the particular legislation under review in *Vriend*: open hunting season on gays and lesbians in Alberta.

RETURNING TO THE *VRIEND* CASE: WHAT DID THE COURT DECIDE?

In the end, a unanimous Supreme Court decided the case in favour of Vriend, using traditional equality discourse: Alberta's refusal to include protection based on sexual orientation violated the Charter's guarantee of equality, and the discrimination was not justifiable in a free and democratic society. Eight of the nine judges determined that the phrase 'sexual orientation' should be read into the legislation's list of prohibited grounds of discrimination.[50] Immediately following the decision, there were a few threats to invoke the notwithstanding clause in support of the legislation, but in the end Alberta accepted the Court's decision. Lesbian and gay Albertans would no longer be denied access to provincial human rights forums.

Vriend won his case. Justice was done. Of course, as Charter sceptics might point out, a victory like this may not be completely satisfying. Consider what was won, and what was not. Many years of struggle culminated in a legal declaration that those encountering discriminatory treatment based on their sexual orientation should have access to human rights forums. Vriend did not win the substantive right to be free from discrimination and he won only the procedural right to have his case heard before a specialized human rights tribunal. In front of such a tribunal, Vriend would still have to confront the argument that his right to be free from discrimination had to be tempered by other societal rights and interests. Would a tribunal conclude that heterosexuality was a bona fide occupational requirement in a fundamentalist Christian college? Could fundamentalist colleges steeped in a tradition of homophobia impose the requirement of heterosexuality on their employees, and discriminate against gay and lesbian citizens? The *Vriend* case can rightly be seen as a success because it affirms that gay and lesbian citizens can no longer be denied access to the forums in which society struggles to resolve the conflict of rights and interests. However, as gay and lesbian litigation has revealed, there are still hurdles to jump. It is still unfortunately necessary to challenge societal views that gay and lesbian citizens are less valuable to society, and that heterosexuals deserve superior treatment because of their greater importance to society.[51]

In this chapter, we argued that there are constraints on what rights discourse can do. CASHRA invited the Supreme Court to resolve the issues in *Vriend* by drawing on an invigorated understanding of the court's own traditions concerning citizenship, federalism and parliamentary supremacy. Regrettably, the Court did not take up this invitation, and did not confront the challenge presented by the public/private distinction in the face of strong public support for discriminatory conduct. Rather, it gambled on its reading-in power coupled with a sense that Alberta would not go so far as to repeal the legislation *in toto* in response to its remedial activism. Naturally, we do not decry such activism in these circumstances. However, we do caution that attempts could well be made in the future to negate the effect of the judgment by a government intent on satisfying the will of an oppressive majority.

We also note that equality discourse, though it may be able to provide the same end results as the approach proposed by CASHRA, has become increasingly susceptible to discourses of backlash. Certainly, the fallout of the *Vriend* case illustrates this backlash. *Vriend* has been at the centre of public debates about the excess of rights rhetoric, and the illegitimacy of so-called judicial law-making. The case is held up time and time again as an example of the evils of judicial review – of illegitimate judicial interference with democratic process.[52] Those concerned about the limits of judicial review under the Charter do not necessarily support the exclusion of gay and lesbian citizens from full participation in society. However, the critique of rights-based review does provide an avenue for the anger of those opposed to Charter rights in general, and angry in particular with minority groups who would use the Charter to demand equal treatment. These minority groups have been portrayed by some as the enemies of democracy. The approach suggested by CASHRA, while also providing gay and lesbian citizens with access to the human rights regime, may have minimized the backlash by avoiding the currently hazardous grounds of Charter rights based judicial review. While there would still have been segments of the public upset with the result, their fury would have had to emerge via discourses of federalism, the rule of law and parliamentary supremacy. Such discourses, since they do not so easily allow for the portrayal of minority groups as the enemy, may leave less room for backlash against these groups.

The Court in *Vriend* did not adopt the Diceyan approach, but we assert that these alternative arguments were in no way superfluous or a failure. Here, we agree with Martha Mahoney, who says, 'In law and politics, we need to choose terms of discussion and forms of legal challenge for their capacity to mobilize consciousness, not solely for their potential success.'[53] Arguments such as these assist in sketching out the realm of possibilities. Whether or not they were used by the Court in this case, their articulation opens up ways of thinking about progressive social change and the role of legal discourse.[54]

And so, we end where we began. The constraints of text, history, language and tradition are real. But these constraints do not leave us with no freedom, and cannot absolve us of the responsibility to make choices. Movements for social change confront a horizon which is constrained by context, but which is also a horizon of possibility. Part of the lawyer's task is to continually re-think the elements of text, structure, language, history and tradition – to articulate as many alternatives as possible, to open the field of not only what can be argued, but also of what can be thought. Constitutionally entrenched equality rights, while undoubtedly of great importance, are not the only vehicle for progressive social change through law. It is also possible to take evolutionary approaches to legal argument, to keep an open mind about strategy. The material reality of injustice can be attacked using the discourses of equality, but also using discourses of federalism, parliamentary supremacy, citizenship and constitutional convention. The challenge is to claim the responsibility that is ours, the responsibility to understand the nuances of the embedded condition of the world, to explore the boundaries of possibility, and to search for multiple paths towards a more inclusionary society.

13

THE CONSTITUTION MADE US QUEER

THE SEXUAL ORIENTATION CLAUSE IN THE SOUTH AFRICAN CONSTITUTION AND THE EMERGENCE OF GAY AND LESBIAN IDENTITY

PIERRE DE VOS

[R]ather than ask ourselves how [for example] the sovereign appears to us in his lofty isolation, we should try to discover how it is that subjects are gradually, progressively, really and materially, constituted through a multiplicity of organisms, forces, energies, materials, desires, thoughts etc. We should try to grasp subjection in its material instance as a constitution of subjects.[1]

INTRODUCTION

Towards the end of 1997 the South African *Mail & Guardian* newspaper carried a report on the wedding of Polly Motene, an executive member of the Gay and Lesbian Organisation of the Witwatersrand (GLOW), and Robert Poswayo, a former policeman. In the breathless style of a journalist striving to sound both amused and amusing, one of the newspaper's journalists reported as follows:[2]

The *lobola* [bride price] had been paid. The blue and white striped tent was up. And as good old tradition dictates, the bride was three hours late. But when she emerged from her Meadowlands home in Soweto last Saturday, she was worth the wait. Polly Motene wore a flowing pants-suit in lime green. A silk scarf tied just so. A vest. And black leather Crocket and Jones brogues. Her macho groom, Robert Poswayo, wore bottle green. In double breasted suit he was led by a bridesmaid down the dusty pavement to fetch his bride as one of Soweto's first gay street weddings got under way.... The couple met [in 1996] in Cape Town. Motene was everything Poswayo, a former police officer, was looking for after his female girlfriend had ditched him. Says Motene: 'He told me he had been separated from his partner for two years and he was in pain. I was the one who made the pain fade.' After a whirlwind courtship, they found a flat to buy in Yeoville, near Johannesburg's city centre, and exchanged rings. Motene chose a twirly woman's wedding ring, Poswayo's was all male with a chunky band and a single diamond.

But it was not all smiles for the wedding couple. All the nitty-gritty wedding plans had been left to Motene and he had forgotten to confirm the priest:

Motene looked close to tears. She gripped the hand of her husband-to-be and gave it a reassuring clench. They decided the wedding should continue; they would return to do the spiritual thing. 'Which means I'm not going to throw my bouquet,' says Motene.

The report on the wedding day of Polly Motene and Robert Poswayo speaks volumes about the emergence of a complex and dynamic discourse on homosexuality and homosexual identity in South Africa in the wake of the inclusion of the sexual orientation clause in South Africa's 1994 constitution. This discourse builds on a variety of existing understandings and conceptions of sex, race, gender and sexual orientation in the society. Yet, as I shall argue in this chapter, the emerging discourse does not merely mimic existing ideas and concepts but is in the process of transforming the discourse(s) in a variety of ways. At the same time this transformation is, at least partly, due to the intervention of the constitutional text. To support this argument I shall contend that the constitution – as an instrument and a technique of power – has productive force and therefore continually contributes to the (re)production of sexual identities in South Africa. In particular I shall contend that the 'constitutionalization of homosexuality' has affected the way in which the discourse on homosexual identity has emerged in South Africa and that this constitutionalization of homosexuality is reflected in the way gay men and lesbians constitute themselves and are constituted by others.

It is, of course a fiendishly complex and difficult topic with which to engage. Several important questions suggest themselves from the outset. How does one begin to establish a causal connection between the sexual orientation clause and what goes for a public discourse on homosexuality in South Africa? How does one begin to show that changes in this discourse are taking place? Indeed, how does one begin to talk about such a problematic and opaque concept as homosexual identity when such an identity is less a matter of final discovery and more a matter of continuous reinvention?[3] Moreover, how does one talk about homosexual identity in the South Africa context in which it seems to be in constant and vicious interaction/intersection with racial, gender, class, ethnic and language modalities of (other) discursively constituted identities?[4]

As I poured over press clippings, pamphlets and the odd court case, I was convinced of only one thing, namely, that the inclusion of the sexual orientation clause in the constitution has lead to a quantitative explosion in the discourse on homosexuality in South Africa. Since 1994 the coverage in newspapers and magazines and on television and radio has increased dramatically and, although much of it has been tied to the legal fight for equal rights, it is impossible, really, to say conclusively how this affected and continues to affect the way in which we see ourselves and how others perceive us.

Nevertheless, I will take my cue from the story of Polly and Robert in an attempt to explore three contentions related to the construction of homosexual identity through constitutional rights. These are, first, that the sexual orientation clause in the constitution is implicated in the production of gay and lesbian identity in South Africa; second, that the most obvious way in which it has contributed to the constitution of gay and lesbian identity is through the opening up of a space in which the traditional Western narrative of 'coming out' can be enacted (or acted out?); and, last, that this does not in any way imply that a more or less unified gay or lesbian identity is emerging in South Africa in the post-apartheid era.

HOMOSEXUAL IDENTITY IN SOUTH AFRICA

When President Robert Mugabe of Zimbabwe made a stinging attack on homosexuals at the official opening of the 1995 Zimbabwe Book Fair after the organization Gays and Lesbians of Zimbabwe (GALZ) attempted to join the other 239 exhibitors at the fair, he verbalized a strongly and widely held belief in sub-Saharan post-colonial Africa about the 'true' nature and origin of homosexuality.[5] At the root of many of these attacks is the commonly expressed belief that homosexuality is an un-African concept brought to Africa by the colonizers, a concept which has been flourishing due to the capitalist system.[6] In this view, homosexual practices amongst Africans are a product of colonial exploitation and individuals who take part in such practices are therefore 'wayward children' who need to be chastised.[7] As Stychin demonstrates, this 'colonial contamination model' is an insufficient account of the role of same-sex practices and identities in South Africa.[8]

Yet, in the light of Michel Foucault's contention about the historically contingent and constructed nature of homosexual identity, the argument that homosexuality – as an identity category – is 'un-African' is not that far-fetched. As Foucault showed convincingly, homosexual identity is the product of medical and legal discourses in Europe towards the end of the nineteenth century and, in that sense, is a European social construction.[9] The long tradition in which a Eurocentric analysis of sexuality tended to interpret same-sex practices that occurred in many cultures (including in Southern Africa) through the lens of the (European-originated) constructed category of homosexuality – as if the latter was a universal and a-historical concept that could be applied without distinction[10] – is therefore problematic. This does not mean that same-sex sexual practices did not occur before the imposition of the European classification system of sexual identity. On the contrary, there have been many reports of pre-colonial same-sex relations in various parts of Africa, the most prominent being the report of anthropologist E.E. Evans-Pritchard on age-structured homoerotic relationships between older men and younger males of the Azande tribe.[11]

But because the emergence of homosexual identity is historically contingent, it means that the emergence of a discourse on homosexuality in South Africa would not follow the same historical trajectory as its European colonial antecedents. Not only is the periodization different, but the social process also transforms the discursive character of sexual relations in a different way. The central role of missionaries in the process of colonial conquest, the rise of the colonial state as the new sovereign power on the subcontinent, and the interest of the mining houses sometimes contested but mostly colluded in the formation of institutions to regulate the distribution of discipline on the bodies of all its subjects.[12] It is therefore impossible to speak about homosexual identity in South Africa without reference to colonialism, which effectively constructed the 'native' as sexually depraved.[13] Here the role of 'Protestant imperialism', particularly that of the Methodist missions, played a crucial role during its 'civilizing' process. As Comaroff and Comaroff demonstrate, the encounter between religious imperialism and the African people in Southern Africa was a dynamic process in which each culture came to define itself in relation to the other.[14] Thus, 'African tradition' – also regarding sex – was deeply influenced by this process. One could say that it was the missionaries who brought sex and sexuality to Southern Africa.

This makes it difficult, probably impossible, to talk of homosexual identity in South Africa as a monolithic, describable, stable concept. Most probably, different homosexual identities were and still are produced by a unique set of power relations and apparatuses in the context of colonialism, capitalist development and racial domination.[15] While many men and women in South Africa may engage in same-sex sexual activities, not all of them would identify themselves as 'lesbian', 'gay' or 'bisexual' and, in fact, to see sexuality only in terms of these identities would serve:

> to misrepresent Africa as statically monocultural, to ignore the richness of differing cultural constructions of desire, and in suggesting such a totalised notion of African culture, one simply replicates much of the colonial discourse on African sexuality.[16]

The implication of this insight is that we must be careful not to frame homosexual identity in Southern Africa as a universal category, without recognizing its historical and cultural specificity. When we talk about sexuality, we thus cannot accept that all of us share an understanding of sexual identity or even of what acts can be termed sexual and which ones not. At the same time this does not mean, as African nationalists like President Mugabe claim, that black people in Southern Africa stand to be corrupted by decadent Western notions of sexuality. Rather, as Phillips argues:

> the corruption that has been 'imported' is not the homosexual act, but rather the growth of the bourgeois notion of sexuality as constitutive of social truths, and the concomitant need to declare and control these truths through such categorical mechanisms as hetero/homosexual dichotomy.[17]

I believe the fact that this bourgeois notion of sexuality has not yet firmly taken root in South Africa is one of the main reasons why there was relatively trouble-free passage of the sexual orientation clause into the Constitution. Only time will tell whether the continued bourgeoification of South African society will lead to some form of backlash against the inclusion of this clause or whether its inclusion will be further legitimized. However, the question now is how the incorporation of a sexual orientation clause in South Africa's 1994 Constitution will continue to contribute to the understanding and conception of the sexual identity of sexual minorities in South Africa.

THE PRODUCTIVE FORCE OF THE SOUTH AFRICAN CONSTITUTION

In 1994 South Africa became the first country in the world to include an explicit ban on discrimination based on sexual orientation in the judicially enforceable Bill of Rights of its Constitution.[18] This was followed by the inclusion of a similar clause in the 1996 Constitution,[19] in article 9(3), which states:

> The state may not unfairly discriminate directly or indirectly against any-one on one or more grounds, including race, gender, sex, pregnancy, marital status, ethnic or social origin, colour, sexual orientation, age, disability, religion, conscience, belief, culture, language and birth.

Today, more than 5 years after the sexual orientation clause was first taken up in the Constitution, the legal battle to translate this constitutional promise into more tangible legal results has only just begun. Although there have been notable early constitutional successes, it is unclear to what extent the courts will give effect to the constitutional injunction against discrimination based on sexual orientation.[20] However, the inclusion of the sexual orientation clause in the South African Constitution is significant, not only because of the changes it is likely to bring about in laws and regulations and has already brought about in such laws, but also because it will ultimately affect the public discourse on homosexuality and will change the way in which gay men, lesbians and other sexual minorities come to view themselves and how they are viewed by others.

In support of this argument I argue – contra Foucault – that the law, far from diminishing in importance, is increasingly encroaching on all aspects of life in modern society. Foucault's impoverished conception of law leads him to consistently undervalue the importance of law in general, and human rights in particular, in a modern constitutional state. Because he contrasts his conception of law as command with the rise of disciplinary power, it sometimes seems as if he suggests that disciplinary power is in the process of supplanting the law as the site for the exercise of power. However, I would argue that law, particularly human rights law, has become an important terrain on which the battle for and against domination and subjection is taking place. It is thus imperative that any individual or group wishing to become engaged in any meaningful way in this 'war of domination' should attend to law as an important site of struggle.[21] I thus reject Foucault's narrow conception of law as command in favour of a view of law as both an instrument and an effect of power in modern society. Foucault himself reiterated that law, like the disciplines, is not somehow outside or above power but is implicated in power relations. Law is therefore an instrument of power. But power is productive: it produces reality; it produces domains of objects and rituals of truth; it produces the individual and the knowledge that may be gained of her.[22] Furthermore, if we accept the productive nature of law, it implies that the law itself, in all its manifestations, potentially has a disciplinary and normalising effect. If law produces the discourse of power/knowledge, it surely also (re)produces and circulates another, similar kind of discourse of knowledge and truth, namely a discourse of 'discipline'. I believe the law perpetually and increasingly seeks those discourses which provide the knowledge and truth of a 'disciplinary society' or a society of normalization[23] –that is the knowledge of normalization, abnormalities and control.[24] In other words, the law is acting more and more as a norm, and legal institutions are increasingly incorporated into a continuum of apparatuses (medical, administrative, and so on) whose functions are mostly regulatory.[25] Such a view rejects Foucault's rhetorical equation of the law with sovereignty or with the repressive aspect of power in favour of a view that emphasizes the disciplinary aspects of the contemporary exercise of legal power.[26] In such a conception of law, the possible effect (both oppressive and emancipatory) of legal rules and concepts and court judgments goes far beyond the immediately repressive, regulatory, empowering or emancipatory.

The legal discourse, and particularly the discourse of constitutional rights, can therefore be both an instrument and an effect of power, but also a hindrance, a stumbling block, a point of resistance and a starting point for an opposing strategy. Discourse transmits and produces power; it reinforces it, but also undermines and exposes it, renders it fragile and makes it possible to thwart it. In the same way, silence and secrecy are a shelter for power, anchoring its prohibitions; but they also loosen its hold and provide for relatively obscure areas of tolerance. If the creation and proliferation of 'the homosexual' makes possible a strong advance of social controls on this group, it also makes possible the formation of a 'reverse' discourse: homosexuality can begin to speak in its own behalf, to demand that its legitimacy or 'naturality' be acknowledged, often in the same vocabulary, using the same categories by which it was medically disqualified.[27]

This insight allows us to look at the role of law – and particularly of the constitutional law of rights – in a different way. Far from seeing the law merely in negative terms, one discovers how the legal discourse can open up the body to speech and to practice. One sees that the legal discourses surrounding sexual orientation allow all the players to participate in the construction of their own sexual orientation identities, and to make themselves available for interpretation along this register by others.[28] Thus, the role of law – including the constitutional law that signals the protection of individual rights – in constituting persons by providing a forum for their conflicts over *who they shall be understood to be*, is not only symbolic but also deeply material, even though it involves not physical force but the more subtle dynamics of representation.[29] Put differently, the constitutional protection against discrimination based on sexual orientation forms part of a complex web of power relations that, in effect, produces the 'reality' of identity and thus contributes to the perpetual (re)invention and negotiation of sexual identity by all of us. And this identity can operate either to discipline and subjugate those who take it on or to whom it might be assigned, or to provide a space within which emancipation becomes possible. This process can thus be both oppressive and emancipatory in nature.

THE SOUTH AFRICAN CONSTITUTION AND 'COMING OUT'

The most obvious way in which the constitutional ban on discrimination based on sexual orientation has contributed, and clearly continues to contribute, to the (re)constitution of gay and lesbian identities in South Africa is through the opening up of a space in which the traditional Western narrative of 'coming out' can be more readily played out. The multiplication of the discourses on homosexuality engendered by the inclusion of the sexual orientation clause in the Constitution has assisted in the creation of a legal and social space in which coming-out rituals are facilitated and, perhaps just as important, in which it becomes possible to reflect the narratives of these rituals in the media and in popular culture. How has this happened?

First, the inclusion of the sexual orientation clause in South Africa's Constitution has clearly led to a quantitative explosion in the discourse on homosexuality on the legal as well as the social front and has led to a radical increase in the use of words such as 'homosexual', 'gay', 'lesbian' and 'sexual orientation' in public discourse.[30] Nowhere is this more apparent than in legal discourse. By 1994 the word 'lesbian' had only been used once in a reported case[31] by a South African court. At that time there had only been two articles published about homosexuality in legal journals.[32] Since then, words like 'homosexual', 'homosexuality', 'gay', 'lesbian', 'sexual orientation' and, really, even 'moffie', have been popping up everywhere – a large number of articles have been published in law journals in recent years dealing in some way or other with issues of sexual orientation and gay and lesbian rights.[33] There has also been a proliferation of articles in the popular press surrounding homosexuality. An indication of this is that the number of articles gathered by the most prominent clipping service in South Africa, under the title 'homosexuality', more than doubled each year between 1994 and 1996.

Second, this dramatic increase in the references to homosexuality, in both popular and academic media, is particularly significant because such representations are increasingly being linked to the discourse of rights and equality in general, and with the constitutional protection afforded on the basis of sexual orientation in particular. It is not surprising that every single one of the legal academic articles dealing with sexual orientation mentioned the section of the Constitution which deals with sexual orientation and equality. That is, after all, only to be expected from any half-competent or ambitious academic. More interesting is the prevalence of talk about the constitutional protection of gay men and lesbians in the popular press. The story of Polly and Robert is an excellent, but by no means isolated, example.[34] The journalist explicitly links the public wedding to a campaign to legalize gay marriage, which, in turn, is linked to the sexual orientation clause in the Constitution:[35]

> Their very public wedding highlighted a new campaign to legalise gay marriages. Such unions remained illegal even though South Africa's Constitution is a world leader in enshrining the freedom of sexual orientation.

Pastor Tsetse Thandekiso, approached for comment, made the same point in a different way:

> No more than a handful of churches will marry gay couples, but demand is growing, says pastor Tsetse Thandekiso of Hilbrow's Hope and Unity metropolitan community centre, another church which would marry gay couples. He puts gay couples through premarital religious counselling prior to the wedding ceremony. 'I bless, I teach, I advise. We marry people in church because we believe we have the right to do so, and the government is going to be forced to do it.'

Pastor Thandekiso thus argues that the government is going to be forced to recognize same-sex marriages, not because of the pressures of the democratic process, but because the equality clause in the Constitution requires it to do so. The implication here is that public enactment of a same-sex wedding forms part of a process in which gay men and lesbians are claiming their constitutional right to equality. In other words, the presence of the constitutional protection makes this public demonstration or coming out possible.

The causal link between the constitutional protection based on sexual orientation and the public coming out of individuals is even more explicitly stated in the narrative of the formation of the South African Lesbian and Gay Police Association.[36] In the middle of 1997 a group of mostly white police officers came together to form this organization in order to 'help support police officers who are too scared to come out of the closet'. According to one of the leaders of this organization, Sergeant Dennis Adriao, who admitted to his superiors that he was gay shortly after he was named the force's officer of the year, the hardest part of being gay was coming out of the closet. He pointed out that his parents kicked him out of the house when he told them that he was gay.[37] It must have taken considerable courage for these police officers to come out as gay men and women in the South African Police Services, an organization which used to have a reputation, not only as a brutish enforcer of apartheid, but also as an institution with an aggressive, macho culture, infused with sexism, racism and homophobia.[38] The organizers of the police task force expressly linked this newly acquired confidence to the advent of the equality clause in the South African Constitution. Furthermore, they claimed that it would not have been possible for them to establish such an organization in the Police Service without the protection afforded gay men and lesbians in the Constitution. Sergeant Andre Collins of the Flying Squad in Pinelands explained:[39]

> A year ago many police members were dismissed if they revealed their sexuality. Now, with the equality clause in the new Constitution, that should all change.

At the time this statement was made, the sexual orientation clause had been in place for more than 3 years. Why then did Sergeant Collins contrast what had happened a year previously with his present situation? He evidently still believed that a member of the police service could be dismissed for revealing his or her sexual identity, but, as he had become acutely aware of the constitutional protection against sexual orientation discrimination, the safety net of constitutional protection (as he perceived it) made it possible for him to act in a way as if the law has already changed.

This leads us to a third important point, namely that the coming out narratives represented in the popular press are not, by and large, constructed as liberatory acts *per se*. One finds no sense, here, that the act of coming out is viewed as enabling its participants to emerge from a state of servitude into a state of freedom; no conception, either, of the Constitution as a magical document with the power to completely transform our lives and make us all free and happy homosexuals, respected and revered in our communities and immunized against verbal and/or physical assault. More often than not, these narratives represent a different kind of coming out, a coming out, I would argue, in the Foucauldian understanding of such a term. In this view, the act of coming out does not liberate one in a traditional liberal sense of the word. It does not immediately free one from all forms of marginalization and oppression. Instead, the act is understood as something which exposes oneself to a different set of dangers and constraints. As Halperin has pointed out, in as much as coming out thus understood is a release from a state of unfreedom, that is not because coming out constitutes an escape from the reaches of power; rather, coming out puts into play a different set of power relations and alters the dynamics of personal and political struggle. Coming out, then, is an act of freedom, not in the sense of liberation, but in the sense of resistance.[40] And I would argue that these acts of resistance are important acts by which we are constituted and by which we begin to constitute ourselves. By this I do not understand coming out as a process in which one admits the truth about oneself to the world. On the contrary, the coming out is part of the process of perpetual reinvention of the self.[41]

Thus Sergeant Collins' tentatively expressed hope that all will change in the South African Police Service implies that it may not change and that trouble might be brewing ahead. The comments by his colleague, the decorated officer of the year Dennis Adriao, showed that the latter was also very much aware of the problems that coming out might bring on. He mentioned how his parents threw him out of the house when he came out to them and off-handedly added that it 'took three months for them to come to terms with it – and then only up to a certain point'. The same mixture of courage and apprehension can be detected in the comments of Polly Motene on his public wedding ceremony. The article reports as follows:

> Motene, an executive member of the Gay and Lesbian organisation of the Witwatersrand, is a long standing gay activist from the ranks of township activists who have for years lobbied civic organisations and the African National Congress branches for gay rights. 'I was nervous about what the reaction of the community would be,' he said. 'I didn't wear a white dress. I wore a suit because I wanted the community to see this man-to-man wedding.'

In other words, the wedding ceremony was, in a way, a 'coming out' ceremony to the community. But Motene clearly does not conceive of the 'coming out' (or, at least, does not *merely* conceive of it) as a public revelation or an announcement of the 'truth' about his same-sex relationship and about himself. He also, and I think more importantly, conveys the understanding of this ceremony as a 'coming out' in the sense of a challenge, as an act of resistance, as a further step in the continual (re)invention of himself, a renegotiation of his place – indeed, his identity – inside the community from which he comes. The fact that this resistance is explicitly linked to his activist background, his fight for gay rights and the possible constitutional challenge to the ban on same-sex marriage, suggests that the constitutional ban on sexual orientation discrimination is playing an important role here in the battle over how Polly Motene conceives of himself and how he relates this perception to the way 'the community' might perceive him. Of course, exactly what this perception might be is another matter altogether.

QUEERS, MOFFIES, DYKES, MANVROUE OF HOMO'S[42] –
WIE EN WAT IS ONS DAN?

It would be tempting to conclude, even speculatively, that the constitutional protection afforded people of various sexualities in South Africa should be seen as a more or less unifying force from which a distinctive homosexual identity for all South Africans is slowly emerging. Such a view would be in line with the 'Rainbow Nation' rhetoric which became popular in the wake of the first democratic election in South Africa. This rhetoric aims to produce and perpetuate the idea that all South Africans share a common bond that brings us together as a 'nation', despite any differences between us. If one accepts this line of argument it would suggest that a more or less unified gay or lesbian identity is emerging in South Africa despite differences of race, sex, class, gender, religion, language, culture, etc., and that this is at least partly the result of constitutional protection. In this mythology, the various gay and lesbian identities forged in the colonial and apartheid eras are seen as giving way to a Rainbow identity shared by all men and women who feel emotional and sexual attraction to members of their own sex.

There is, of course, some evidence of the colonizing effect of a Western-style gay identity which has been accelerated with the advent of the 1994 Constitution. If we accept the argument that the subject – including the homosexual subject – is at least partly constituted by juridical power, then this formation of language and politics that represents homosexuals as the subject of the (legal) liberation of gay men and lesbians is itself a discursive formation and an effect of a given version of representational politics. It then seems logical that the emerging subject of gay liberation is, in fact, discursively constituted by the very political/legal system that is purporting to facilitate its emancipation.[43]

However, one cannot conclude that this emerging subject is a stable and unified one that should be accepted (or even enthusiastically embraced) uncritically in the name of 'gay', 'lesbian' or 'queer' liberation. Drawing such a conclusion would be problematic because, as Butler points out, juridical subjects are invariably produced through certain exclusionary practices that do not 'show' once the juridical structure of politics has been established. Thus, the political construction of the subject proceeds within certain legitimating and exclusionary aims, and these political operations are effectively concealed and naturalized by a political analysis that takes juridical structures as their foundation. In effect, the law produces and then conceals the notion of a subject before the law in order to invoke that discursive formation as a naturalized foundational premise that subsequently legitimates that law's own regulatory hegemony. Once such a category is firmly established, it becomes a potential tool for legal and social control and/or exclusion. Hence in South Africa a move towards a Western-style gay identity might invariably produce a homosexual identity that is viewed as a white, male identity, thereby marginalizing or even negating the experiences of white women and black men and women. In the South African context such a result would be doubly problematic because it may potentially operate to erase or at least to obfuscate – not only in the legal sphere, but also in the social sphere – many of the other identity categories to which an individual potentially may be attached. Where individuals are attached to identity categories which are very strongly associated with oppression under apartheid – such as race, colour, gender – it may be potentially disempowering for individuals to be identified as gay if this will mean that they will not also be seen as black men, or more particularly, black women. It is therefore imperative to challenge the idea that the discourse of rights is in the process of producing a more or less stable, monolithic – if uniquely South African – homosexual identity. In any engagement with rights discourse, it must be stressed that sexual identity is not always constituted coherently and consistently in different historical contexts and because sexual identity intersects with racial, class, ethnic, gender and regional modalities of discursive constituted identities. As a result it becomes impossible to separate out sexual identity from the political and cultural intersections in which it is invariably produced and maintained.[44]

This insight is significant for a more nuanced understanding of the coming-out processes described above. Recall that I have argued, first, that coming-out is seldom if ever understood as a liberatory process in the sense of an escape from power, but, on the contrary, is seen as a resistance to power, a *political act*, and second, that such resistance is in some way part of the process of how we see ourselves, of how we are constituted and how we begin to constitute ourselves. Then, surely, within such a framework the economic, social, cultural, historical or any other significant context in which we find ourselves, must play a role in the construction of our identities. The immediate future in South Africa, with its new Constitution, its 'Rainbow Nation vibes' and its democratic order, will be different from that in England, India or Zimbabwe. While it is in the nature of such processes of resistance, of coming out, of continual constitution of ourselves and our constitution in the web of power relations, that it will contain exclusionary practices, these exclusions will differ depending on the specific aspects of our history, our sexual, cultural, religious, racial, linguistic or any other identity as a site (or sites) of resistance. And the aspects we choose to focus on in any such a process might be revealing about the way we see ourselves and how we are seen by others. Here I am not suggesting that, somehow, we can escape all these forces, these fields of power. Rather, we are, I believe, entangled in a complex web of power relations from which we can never escape. In the coming-out process, in the constitution and reconstitution of our identities, we are therefore, to some extent at least, beholden to our own racial, sexual, gender, cultural, social, religious or other identities. One's personal history and situatedness is therefore part of the tangled, complex, unstable and ever-changing nature of identity formation. It is therefore highly problematic to accept the given and rigid boundaries between various identities, as 'slippages' invariably occur. Thus, for example, a lesbian in South Africa can never be accepted as merely a lesbian, but is always also a black or coloured or white lesbian, poor or rich lesbian, Afrikaans, Zulu or Xhosa lesbian, butch or femme lesbian and so on. This is not to deny that the constitutional discourse also operates as a form of power and that it will have a strong influence on the formation or reconstitution of sexual identities and will aim to produce a discourse around a stable Western-style homosexual identity. Rather I contend that there will inevitably be a tension between the homogenizing constitutional discourse on homosexuality and the lived reality of individuals. The danger exists exactly in the fact that this tension will not be recognized and the constitutional discourse on homosexual identity will be accepted as the final and natural one, thus silencing all those very real identity differences between individuals.

I will attempt to explain my point with some examples. In almost all the reports in the popular media I have come across in which black South Africans have talked about themselves as gay or lesbian, the particular so-called 'African context' within which they found themselves and from which they see themselves as 'escaping' in one way or another, is stressed.[45] Many of the stories relate how difficult it is, within 'African culture' to be accepted when one comes out of the closet. In one such report on black lesbians, Thembi Mandla, a member of a black lesbian group called Nkateko, is quoted as saying:[46]

> There are gender stereotypes [in African culture]. Women are not valued as highly as men. A woman is expected to conform and is silenced into a wife-and-mother role. As a woman ... you have no say in terms of sexuality.

She also indicates that class is a problem, as the poorer you are, the harder it is. 'White lesbians do not face the same problems. They do not have to grapple with African culture.' In this passage Thembi Mandla suggests something about how difficult it is to be gay as a woman, but more particularly, as a black woman. Her comments reflect a deep understanding of the tension which arises between her constitutionally sanctioned identity as a lesbian, and her identity as a black woman. Thus, she asserts her identity as a black lesbian, even as she is talking about how she is fighting the prejudice of black culture. In doing so, she is not seeking to escape from the fact that she is black, or that she is a woman. On the contrary, by identifying, class, race and gender as issues in her constitution as a lesbian, she is involved in a process of resistance against the traditional rigid identity categories to which she had been assigned in the past. There is more than one way to be an African, she seems to suggest, and there is more than one way of being an African woman. In the process of perpetual reinvention, she thus demonstrates the lack of borders between these categories.

CONCLUSION

The inclusion of an explicit sexual orientation clause in South Africa's post-apartheid Constitution will no doubt have a major impact on the way the discourse on homosexuality and homosexual identity develops in South Africa into the twenty-first century. Not only has its inclusion led to an explosion in the discourse on homosexuality in South Africa, it has also provided a space within which it has become easier for men and women who experience emotional and sexual attractions for members of their own sex to come out of the closet and take on some kind of homosexual identity. However, this process should not be viewed as the simplistic production and maintenance of a Western-style homosexual identity through the constitutional discourse. While it might seem inevitable that the sexual orientation clause in the Constitution will contribute to the creation and maintenance of a seemingly stable and homogenous homosexual subject before the law, the heterogeneous nature of our society will invariably create a tension between this legal fiction and the lived reality of people's lives. In this lived reality, our own racial, sexual, gender, cultural, social, religious or other identities will influence the way in which we construct our own sexual identities and how we are constructed by others. However, there is a danger that the legal discourse around homosexuality will contribute to the marginalization of individuals who do not fit the standard Western concept of homosexual identity. It is therefore imperative that those who engage with the law challenge the notion that the bearer of the right not to be discriminated against on the basis of sexual orientation has a stable and fixed homosexual identity.

14

QUEERING INTERNATIONAL HUMAN RIGHTS LAW

WAYNE MORGAN

INTRODUCTION

International human rights law on sexuality is a relatively new development. It is only really in the last two decades that questions of sexuality and rights have been on the agenda of international institutions, courts and non-governmental organizations (NGOs). In those two decades, important battles have been fought and, to some extent, the privileging of heterosexuality, which is an inherent part of international human rights law, has been challenged. Yet, the challenges made by sexual outsiders[1] have been (and still are) vigorously contested by most governments who participate in the international human rights system. We have won some victories, but I doubt anyone would dispute the proposition that sexuality remains a marginalized and contested field in the international legal arena.

This contestation which surrounds sexuality takes place in a wider context of argument concerning basic values in international relations and international law. In other words, the human rights field itself is a contested and shifting one. Human rights law envisages a particular type of subject and a particular model of that subject's relationship to government. The essence of human rights law is found in enlightenment notions of the rational subject who has natural or inherent rights, protected by government under a social contract which enshrines the rule of law. Yet, this model is highly contested within the human rights field. It is questioned by countries who do not share the Western European tradition upon which the model is based. It is also questioned by critical theorists who see fundamental flaws in this description of the subject and governmentality. Dealing with these questions of law based on values which are somehow self-evident or shared, usually leads to a debate between 'universality' and 'cultural relativity' with these being put forward as the only two bases on which to build a theory of rights.[2]

Despite the uncertainty and shifting nature of the human rights terrain, human rights law is usually analysed as holding great promise for sexual outsiders. For example, human rights law gives legitimacy to our claims to be treated equally. It also can be used as a mechanism to (attempt to) force recalcitrant domestic governments to deal with a sexuality issue. Indeed, the idea of human rights and the language of human rights now permeates the arguments made by activists and lawyers when discussing sexuality issues. 'Gay rights are human rights' has become a common slogan.

Given our reliance on such ideas, a pressing question both at a theoretical and practical level concerns what human rights law has to offer sexual outsiders. Can it help us overcome oppression which manifests itself in a range of ways from violence and murder through to unfair treatment in day-to-day life? These are questions of strategy which are vital to any engagement with international human rights law and questions of law reform.

I want to explore the promise of human rights law by examining the legal texts (judicial, institutional and academic) which make up the human rights discourses concerning sexuality. First, I describe the sexuality/human rights field by examining the legal texts and the academic analysis which has been applied to those texts. I then examine this same field from a different point of view. I examine what strategies may be suggested if we attempted to *queer the field* of international human rights law. In other words, what might be achieved if we focused on the disruption of heteronormativity[3] rather than on our inclusion in a heteronormative system?

A BRIEF DESCRIPTION OF THE SEXUALITY AND HUMAN RIGHTS FIELD

Human rights law has developed (one might even say exploded) in the last 50 years,[4] while keeping issues of sexuality firmly in the closet. Literally, human rights law for much of this century has done no more than increase the 'silence' surrounding non-hetero desire, refusing to acknowledge the abuse suffered by sexual outsiders around the world. But the last few decades have seen inroads begun. There is now international human rights 'law' concerning sexuality. Human rights courts have addressed the issue, and international NGOs have been formed. Even Amnesty International, that most respectable of NGOs, finally decided to recognize sexuality as an issue of political imprisonment (but only after a long battle).[5] Human rights conferences, like the 1993 Vienna Conference on Human Rights, have been forced to confront demands for the recognition of non-hetero desire. And 'learned texts' are now written on the subject.[6] There are still no treaties or resolutions within the UN system addressing sexuality as a human rights issue, although there have been some resolutions within the institutions of Europe (particularly the Parliament).[7]

The most prominent battles over sexuality and human rights law have been fought within the human rights institutions of the European community. Although the issue had come before the European Commission as early as 1955,[8] judicial examination of sexuality issues did not begin until the case of *Dudgeon v UK* in 1981.[9] Mr Dudgeon was a gay man from Belfast. He alleged that the criminal laws then in force in Northern Ireland (repealed in England after the Wolfenden Report), breached his rights to privacy and equality under the European Convention. He also claimed that the age of consent should be the same for homosexual and heterosexual acts. The European Court of Human Rights held by a majority of 15–4 that Dudgeon's right to privacy had been breached. The Court refused to deal with the discrimination claim and stated that age of consent issues should be left to the national authorities 'in the first instance'.

The case of Dudgeon was followed by *Norris v Ireland* in 1989 and *Modinos v Cyprus* in 1993, both also dealing with the criminalization of homosexual acts.[10] The decision in *Norris* is virtually identical to *Dudgeon*, although with a much reduced judicial majority of 8–6. The dissenting judgments did not think Mr Norris could be described as a 'victim' because he had not been prosecuted under the impugned laws (an argument also made by the dissenters in *Dudgeon*). *Modinos* concerned the same issue (the Cypriot laws deriving from English provisions). In *Modinos*, the only dissent in the 8–1 judgment came from the *ad hoc* judge appointed by Cyprus, and only on the basis that the Cypriot Constitution had already rendered the impugned law inoperative. Note that no argument about equality or age of consent seems to have been made in either *Norris* or *Modinos*. In 1997, the European Human Rights Commission decided that the UK age of consent laws also breached the right to privacy.[11] This case, along with other age of consent cases, then went before the European Court of Human Rights.[12]

More recently, the European Court of Justice has added to these decisions in the context of equality in employment, in the cases of *P v S and Cornwall County Council* and *Grant v SWT*.[13] In 1996 in the case of *P*, the European Court decided that dismissing a post-operative transsexual because of her sex change was prohibited by the Community directive prohibiting discrimination on the basis of sex. In *Grant*, however, the Court ruled that the same directive did not prohibit discrimination against same-sex couples. Lisa Grant had been refused travel concessions for her female partner by her employer, when such concessions were available for opposite-sex couples. The court explicitly stated that nothing in EC law made discrimination on the basis of sexual orientation unlawful. The Court did note, however, that the Council will have the power to make policy regarding such discrimination under Article 13 of the Treaty of Amsterdam, when that enters into force.

Apart from activity in the European courts, the most active institution has been the European parliament. The parliament has passed a series of resolutions since 1984.[14] The most comprehensive resolution was passed in 1994: Equal Rights for Homosexuals and Lesbians in the EC.[15] These resolutions by the parliament have not been acted upon by the Commission or the Council.[16] Currently, the most promising opportunities for gay and lesbian rights within Europe lie under Article 13 of the Treaty of Amsterdam. This Article will give the Council power to adopt measures to address sexual orientation discrimination in member states, although doubt surrounds whether any appropriate action will be taken. In any event, there can be no doubt that Article 13 opens up the field for argument considerably. This makes strategic considerations even more vital.

Apart from developments within Europe, the United Nations (UN) has also seen increasing activity in the last two decades. In 1987–8, male homosexuality was addressed within a UN working group on Slavery and Slavery-Like Practices, because of a perceived link with the topic under discussion: prostitution.[17] A major battle over sexuality and human rights was fought in 1993–4 when the International Lesbian and Gay Association (ILGA) was finally accredited as an NGO within the Economic and Social Council (ECOSOC) system. After a long battle to gain NGO status (which gives access to the major human rights bodies within the UN), ILGA's victory was short-lived. Under pressure from homophobic lobbyists, the US brokered a deal to have ILGA expelled in 1994, because of alleged links with paedophile groups.[18] There has been a lesbian and gay presence at the two major UN human rights conferences held in the 1990s: the 1993 Vienna Conference on Human Rights and the 1995 Beijing Conference on Women, but lesbian and gay concerns have not been reflected in the final documents of these Conferences.[19]

In 1994, the *Toonen* case[20] was decided by the UN Human Rights Committee (HRC) and has been read as an example of the UN catching up with Europe on sexuality rights. Mr Toonen was a gay man from Australia, whose home state Tasmania retained the same British provisions attacked by Dudgeon. A challenge was lodged on the basis of privacy and equality rights set out in the International Covenant on Civil and Political Rights. The HRC, like the European Court, gave its decision on the basis of the right to privacy and largely adopted the same analysis.

Thus, at least from a liberal, positivist point of view, we have had some successes. We have made some gains in being included in the heteronormative system. But, as I argue below, we have not been very successful at breaking down that system. We have not managed, in human rights law, to challenge the heteronormative assumptions upon which the system is based (this task has hardly begun in domestic systems). We will not experience the sort of liberation the radicals envisioned in the early 1970s and the queers revived in the 1990s, unless we adopt strategies which challenge heteronormativity. To challenge heteronormativity, we must subtly analyse the different forms of power exercised by the law, so that we know where and how our efforts should be directed. Yet it is exactly this type of analysis of power which is absent from the major academic texts on human rights law and sexuality.

ACADEMIC ANALYSIS OF THE SEXUALITY AND HUMAN RIGHTS FIELD

Challenging heteronormativity requires an understanding of the ways in which heteronormativity is inscribed in law. This in turn entails understanding the various ways in which law exercises power over individuals and communities. It is now largely accepted by critical scholars that law exercises different forms of power: juridical and disciplinary.[21] *Juridical* power refers to the enforcement of norms of behaviour and *disciplinary* power refers to the normalizing, production and colonization of forms of identity. As Foucault discussed, legal institutions are often taken to be the paradigm of juridical power: the location of prescription and enforcement.[22] But, increasingly, legal institutions adopt mechanisms of disciplinary power to better *know* and regulate the subject.[23] And this legal *will to know* applies doubly to sexualized subjects, who perform upon the body acts of desire seen as dangerous not only to themselves and other individuals but to the polity as a whole. Indeed, the whole genus of human rights law can be read as examples in the exercise of disciplinary power. Human rights law *normalizes*. It takes the abuses suffered by those who assert difference, and colonizes their experiences to make them conformable to the structures and imperatives of the mythological nation state. And along the way, it usually exonerates governments of any wrong-doing.

Yet the legal literature on sexuality and international human rights law is largely silent on the issue of disciplinary forms of power and the law's complicity in oppression. Instead, the literature (largely) adopts a liberal, humanist framework which accepts the image of benign point-of-viewlessness which legal institutions hold out.[24] Through the work of theorists like Carol Smart,[25] we have been made aware of the seductive dangers of law, of the violence done by the gaze of legal authority (like the gaze of the House of Lords in *Brown*).[26] Yet the human rights literature largely fails to analyse these dangers, this false promise of solutions. Instead, it proceeds on the basis of dubious assumptions about law's power and place. It sees the law in juridical terms and *benign* juridical terms at that! The importance of law's disciplinary function is missed entirely.

As exemplars of the liberal, positivist framework adopted in literature dealing with sexuality and human rights, we need look no further than two major works published in 1995: Eric Heinze's *Sexual Orientation: A Human Right* and Robert Wintemute's *Sexual Orientation and Human Rights*.[27] Both these books examine human rights law on sexuality. Heinze concentrates on the international arena, examining UN and European treaties and cases. He also engages squarely with theoretical questions concerning the place and value of human rights law, which leads him to adopt a particular form of liberal legal logic in his methodology (discussed below). In true liberal tradition, Heinze ends his book with a 'Model Declaration of Rights Against Discrimination on the Basis of Sexual Orientation'. Wintemute's book is a comparative study of rights under the US Constitution, the Canadian Constitution and the European Convention. It might be called a classic 'black letter' text and does not engage explicitly with any question of human rights theory.

Heinze explores the jurisprudential basis for rights of sexual orientation. He does not attempt to ground this exploration in the experience of sexual outsiders, but rather seeks to derive a corpus of rights from extant human rights law.[28] His study is thus 'disembodied'. It does not deal with the diversity of claims made by sexual minorities and the fundamental challenges these pose to our human rights system. Heinze lets the law define the people and the 'problem' rather than seeking to question the assumptions upon which the law's definitions are based. Like an article of faith, he states the basic 'tasks' of human rights law: to *articulate* rights, *identify* violations, *create* the conditions for rights and *enlighten* people about rights.[29] Although accepting that 'deficiencies exist at all four levels' he states:

> Yet, for all its shortcomings, international human rights law is, today, the best existing framework not only for attempting to implement, but also for understanding and debating the proper relationships between governments and their citizens.[30]

Such a faith in law is a view of which we should be wary. It overlooks the fact that human rights law is largely shaped by governments and suits their interests rather than the interests of 'citizens'. It overlooks the fact that human rights law is shaped in particular ways and privileges the interests of some over the interests of others (it defines 'citizens' worthy of 'rights'). It also needlessly curtails debate about possible systems of human rights law which may be more open to diversity than the one we already have. It allows law to define us, when experience has shown that the law's definitions are usually oppressive.

Heinze's examination of the international human right to a family life is a good example of where his reliance on legal logic leads him. Because he centres the law and does not challenge its assumptions, he adopts a justification for rights, not based on experience but instead based on positivist ideology: a process of derivation from existing law. This is his principle of 'extant rights': that rights of sexual orientation must only be drawn and be consistent with rights recognized and developed within international law. This principle is used by Heinze to limit the field of rights of sexual orientation. He states that 'family' rights: relationship recognition, adoption etc. cannot be derived from existing law.[31] Although he recognizes the validity of such claims as a matter of social change, he can find no basis for them in the existing corpus. This is because Heinze sees a fundamental distinction between rights such as those to privacy, freedom of expression etc. and rights to family and marriage. He asserts that the latter always assumed a normative-heterosexual paradigm whilst the others did not. Although this may be true in a literal sense, its implications for strategy are far from clear. Rather than capitulating to the logic of the normative-heterosexual paradigm (as Heinze does here) an alternative strategy is to challenge the fundamentally discriminatory assumptions of human rights law which place heterosexuality at its core.

It should be noted, however, that Heinze is not saying that rights based on a heterosexual-normative paradigm should not be challenged, just that they cannot be used to derive rights of sexual orientation. This positivist's distinction is not one which makes a great deal of sense from an activist/strategist point of view. Properly valuing diversity, ensuring respect for sexual outsiders, requires a challenge to heterosexism in all its manifestations and, in this sense, there is little point in drawing distinctions between privacy rights, expression rights and relationship rights. Heinze has allowed a positivist strategy to limit the 'legitimate' field of gay and lesbian engagement with law:

> [o]nly rights ensuing from a one-step derivation of fundamental rights, directed towards sexual orientation as such, should be pursued. Broader changes in institutions such as the military or ... marriage, unrelated to sexual orientation per se, should be undertaken as distinct initiatives, and not as part of a platform of rights of sexual minorities.[32]

The point Heinze misses here is that sexual orientation '*per se*' is far from unrelated to our concepts of the military and of marriage. Rather, our concepts of both militarism and marriage are *constructed by* our notions of sexuality and gender.

By letting the logic of the law define the logic of his project, Heinze accepts a conclusion which excludes gay men and lesbians from the international human rights law definition of 'family'. I would argue we should not be so readily complicit in law's *will to define* us in ways which so clearly entrench the normative power of heterosexuality. Instead, we should be seeking to disrupt this very heteronormativity.[33] Heinze does not question it. Although noting in Chapter 2 that we live under a 'normative-heterosexual paradigm of social organization', he proceeds to validate that paradigm in the fixed boundaries he draws around questions of homo/hetero desire. He reinforces the homo/hetero binary which is the root cause of the law's categories of sexual oppression.

A combination of the factors explored above, the adoption of law's logic together with a minoritizing discourse of fixed and universalized homo/hetero identity, leaves Heinze's conclusion – his model declaration – a somewhat impoverished list of rights. It hardly meets queer demands for much more fundamental re-imagining and re-ordering of the system.[34] A number of goals might be pursued, based on queer concerns, that avoid the pitfalls present in Heinze: goals based on breaking down heteronormativity, on building respect for diversity through active coalitions. Such a project might result in a model declaration based on rights of sexual freedom[35] rather than a more circumscribed model pleading to be 'free from discrimination'.

Wintemute's analysis of law and sexuality is similarly circumscribed. His book compares three Western legal jurisdictions, largely on the basis of case analysis. He refers to the 'globalization' of sexuality rights,[36] but does not examine the content of what is being globalized, i.e. a specific Western concept of sexuality rights. He defines his concept of 'sexual orientation' in two senses: the direction of a person's attraction (emotional/sexual, not necessarily involving conduct); and the direction of a person's conduct (emotional/sexual, not necessarily involving attraction). That both desire and action are products of discourse does not enter the analysis.

Like Heinze, Wintemute distinguishes 'sexual orientation discrimination' from other interferences with 'sexuality' or 'sexual freedom'. Again here, we see a minoritizing discourse of fixity:

It is important to remember that sexual orientation (as I have defined it) is just one aspect (the direction, as between the sexes) of sexuality or sexual freedom. As a result, sexual orientation discrimination may be prohibited without having to address every controversial aspect of sexual freedom, and without necessarily precluding legal regulation of aspects other than sexual orientation (e.g. the parties' ages or relatedness, consensual use of force, commercial sexual activity), each of which can be considered on its own merits.[37]

The point here is that our freedom from oppression may not be possible without addressing wider questions of 'sexual freedom' and the relationships amongst gender discourses, the sexual economy and the general patterns of dominance and subordination which structure the international community and international law (in particular the relationship between discourses of sexuality and the North/South, developed/developing dichotomies). The homo/hetero binary plays into these discourses in ways left unexamined by Wintemute.

Wintemute's unacknowledged acceptance of the naturalness of the homo/hetero binary also leads him to adopt a position of formal neutrality which overlooks the dynamics of power in a heteronormative world. He explicitly adopts a (negative) concept of sexual orientation discrimination, rather than a (positive) concept of gay, lesbian and bisexual rights, to emphasize that prohibitions on discrimination should be 'symmetrical' protecting heterosexual people as well. This, according to Wintemute, also emphasizes the importance of thinking of sexual orientation as a 'neutral, universal characteristic ...'.[38] As I have argued elsewhere, adopting formal equality in matters of discrimination rarely has an impact on breaking down systemic heteronormativity.[39]

Following the positivist project in a methodology similar to Heinze, Wintemute examines existing non-discrimination law to derive certain principles he then uses to produce a normative set of values to be applied in the area of sexual orientation. The referent is always already the law and the search is one for coherent foundations across specific incidences of oppression. The principles he derives are that governments should not make distinctions based on immutable status, governments should not interfere with fundamental choices, and governments should not make distinctions based on sex.[40] He uses these three principles to structure his discussion of claims made in the three jurisdictions he examines: claims made on the basis of immutable status, fundamental choice and sex discrimination arguments.

Using as his criterion the argument which provides 'the most comprehensive protection against sexual orientation discrimination while requiring the least innovation', Wintemute concludes that strategies based on sex discrimination arguments are the most effective.[41] His analysis is valuable in reminding us that the networks of power which produce and define relations among men and women are also implicated in the networks which produce notions of same-sex desire and regulate same-sex expression. I would maintain, however, that the identity categories produced in the law regulating same-sex desire perform different ideological functions to the identity categories based on gender. They overlap, but do not occupy the same field. Oppression because one does not identify as heterosexual has as much to do with a pervasive fear of all aspects of sexuality as it has to do with gender. Yet, as noted above, both Heinze and Wintemute explicitly distinguish sexual orientation discrimination from more general questions concerning the regulation of desire.

The only explanation that Wintemute can offer as to the different treatment of sexuality in the different regimes is that the larger and more diverse populations of the USA and Europe lead to a slower development of the law.[42] While this may well be a factor, what also needs analysing is the ideological role of sexuality in each jurisdiction. Issues of sexuality, particularly homosexuality, play an important function in the political life of the US. Fundamentalist Christianity has a direct power base in the US Congress and homosexuality is often used as a rhetorical site to muster support and increase power and influence for the extreme right.[43] This sort of analysis – of the way in which homosexuality is used and produced in law and politics – seems to me fundamental in any analysis of human rights and sexuality.

Despite the lack of progress in both the US and Europe, Wintemute maintains his faith in human rights law. He concludes his book by stating:

> Protection against sexual orientation discrimination under constitutional and international human rights law has begun. Its extension and completion is a matter of time.[44]

This conclusion may be true if our goal is to seek inclusion in the heteronormative system, but again, if our goal is to break down that system (as I would argue it must be), we have not adopted the right strategies and our task has hardly begun.

The review above makes clear that both these texts are based on implicit theories of law reform as positive progress. Both argue that international human rights law can achieve positive change for sexual outsiders. They both centre law and its ability to come to the rescue. Neither show much recognition of, nor analyse, law's complicity in the policing of desire. They accept the positive value of the major discourses which structure human rights law on sexuality: legal progress, privacy, tolerance and equality, without examining the tendency of these discourses to assimilate and colonize as they speak from a position of liberal objectivity. Indeed, both authors themselves have a tendency to speak in a universalizing discourse, not just about human rights law, but also about sexual subjectivity and identity. They pay little attention to the considerable work on the social construction of sexuality and their treatment of sexual identity is thus simplistic.[45]

If we are to avoid reproducing and repeating the mythologies, if we are to avoid being trapped by the dichotomies which structure current discourse and produce heteronormativity, if we are to understand the *will to know and define* which legal institutions exhibit, we must have the ability to analyse a structure in terms of its disciplinary effects. This is necessary in understanding the ideological relations between the individual, community and structures of government. Understanding these relations is largely a question of identity formation and position. The identity you claim (or with which you are labelled) defines your subjectivity as a citizen and hence your relationship to government. Attempting to strategize law reform involves intervening in the subordination that these rigid identity categories produce.

QUEERING THE SEXUALITY AND HUMAN RIGHTS FIELD

It is not my intention here to give an outline of what 'queer' means (an almost impossible task in any event).[46] But it is possible to say that a paramount queer concern is with questions of identity. Adopting queer theory as a critical practice involves consideration of the ways in which 'identity' as a general concept and individual identities are used in various discourses to locate and regulate the individual. Applied to questions of law, queer practice entails examining the assumptions about identity and identities which are built into legal systems. It involves questioning the place of the subject/citizen in liberal democratic theory and hence in law. It means rejecting some of the assumptions about identity upon which legal texts (institutional, judicial, academic) are based.

In the legal and academic texts described above which expound human rights law on sexuality, identity is taken as a given. Each individual has a fixed identity which can be categorized according to a set of logical terms whose meaning is relatively clear (gender, race, class, sexual orientation and so on). These categories correspond to attributes of individuals which pre-exist the labels attached to them. Pursuing legal strategies based upon human rights notions means validating this theory of identity (at least, when such strategies are pursued without analysing their potential discursive effects). These notions of fixed identity are usually produced by the deployment of a series of binary oppositions: self/other; male/female, Western/non-Western, heterosexual/homosexual etc. These oppositions ascribe value (or non-value) to the subject positions they reference. Thus, in relation to sexuality, the possibilities of subject position are polarized into hetero/homo with the former being the dominant, normative category. In other words, heteronormativity is established and becomes a premise, not only of the law, but of Western liberal government itself.

In contrast to these notions of fixed identity which lie at the heart of Western law (including human rights law) is the notion put forward by queer theorists that identity is performative.[47] The individual never pre-exists, nor can be located outside, the discursive field. We come to understand who we are through the re-iteration or performance of identity. In this sense, identity is not about fixed attributes possessed by individuals, but is instead constructed in a variety of ways at a variety of levels. We participate in the construction of our own identity as individuals (we do have some agency, although it is circumscribed by our history/context). But identity formation is also outside our control in that the possibilities for self-definition are limited by the discourses which hold privileged knowledge-positions in Western systems of society. Law is one of those discourses. Identity is performed and constructed in the legal texts which structure jurisprudential fields (like human rights).

I therefore want to re-read the human rights and sexuality field described above through the queering lens of these identity questions. I wish to examine how sexual identity is performed in international human rights law and what the consequences of such performance are in the relations between the subject and government. I then want to examine questions of strategy: how do we intervene in the performance of identity in law and how do we reconstruct the meaning of community, nation and human rights.

THE PERFORMANCE OF IDENTITY IN INTERNATIONAL HUMAN RIGHTS LAW

How is sexuality performed in international human rights law? Answering this question entails a different sort of analysis than that performed by Heinze and Wintemute. It entails examining the discourses which structure the texts of decisions, resolutions, treaties and academic writing in the field. This is not simply a theoretical exercise, as I hope to show that such analysis is intimately connected with any self-reflective engagement with international law reform, as well as with subversion of the current hierarchies of heteronormativity.

When we examine human rights law on sexuality we find a number of discourses contending. These range from denials that sexuality is a human rights issue, through to religious and moral concerns and assertions that homosexuality is a Western disease. When human rights authorities have recognized the claims of sexual outsiders, their justifications have been based on discourses of 'legal neutrality' and 'emancipatory progress', of 'privacy' and 'tolerance', although claims to 'equality' and assertions of 'difference' are becoming harder to ignore. The issues of legal neutrality and supposed progress have been examined in the critique of academic work above. The ways in which 'privacy' and 'tolerance' contribute to the maintenance of heteronormativity are examined here.

Before I critique them, I should note that these two discourses have produced some positive outcomes for sexual outsiders, mainly in the European system as described above. Yet, even while appeals to privacy and tolerance are used as a basis to recognize gay rights, they help to maintain the dominance of the hetero norm. An analysis of *Dudgeon*, *Norris* and *Modinos*[48] shows this to be the case.

In *Dudgeon*, the majority gives a narrow legal opinion, without explicitly dealing with issues of the social construction and role of 'homosexuality': Nevertheless (as Judge Walsh points out), the majority does rely on a concept of homosexuality which implies innateness. Sexuality is a fundamental aspect of personhood which is neither shifting nor fluid. According to the majority, sexuality is such a fundamental aspect of personhood that the right to privacy protects it, regardless of homo/hetero. Tolerance is a value which should be respected by the heterosexual majority. Drawing such strict boundaries between homo/hetero and attempting to validate the former by appeals to innateness or naturalness (like the latter) inevitably plays in to the hands of opponents, like the dissenting judges in *Dudgeon*. These opponents find it all too easy to build on the binary distinction to produce a demonized, mythological and subordinating description of the differences between homo/hetero and the reasons why the law is entitled to regulate the two differently. This is seen clearly in the four dissenting judgments, which paint much more vivid pictures of homosex than does the majority judgment. By appealing to discourses which have strong claims to 'truth' and 'knowledge' status, the minority paints a demonized and threatening picture. Minority judgments variously deploy religious discourse (good/evil), discourses on innocence/corruption (especially concerning youth), and medical discourse (curable/incurable pathologies of homosex), to perform or re-iterate what homosexuality *is*. These demonized pictures are used to deploy fear. Homosexuality, always already associated with dangerous desire, is presented as threat to self, other and the state.

If we view the judgment in this light, it can hardly be said to be one which transmits positive images about homosex, let alone one which in any way disrupts the power of heterosex. Far from it, both majority and minority validate the hierarchy which privileges heterosex. This privileging is explicit in the minority judgments, whose powerful images are not counteracted by the majority. The majority can do no more than compare and assimilate Mr Dudgeon and thus all homos to our hetero other, thereby confirming heterosexuality's normative status and giving homos the status of minoritized victim.

And we should not forget that the outcome of *Dudgeon* was merely a call for the extension of the UK 1967 *Sexual Offences Act* to Northern Ireland. Given the homophobia which is still inscribed in the 1967 reforms, we may question the value of *Dudgeon* in breaking down heteronormativity.[49] The same criticisms can be made of the jurisprudence which builds on *Dudgeon*: *Norris*, *Modinos*, *Sutherland* and the UN HRC decision in *Toonen*.

The more recent interventions by the European Court of Justice into sexuality issues further shows how heteronormativity is preserved in human rights law. The case of *P v S and Cornwall County Council*[50] may amount to a victory of sorts, but this is undercut by the fact that the judgment reinforces notions of strictly enforced gender norms and boundaries. It goes no further than recognizing the claim to be regarded as female, by a post-operative transsexual, after the 'mistake' of being born with the wrong biological sex characteristics has been corrected. It does not disrupt the binary opposition of male/female, merely asserting that the claimant was born on the wrong biological side of that opposition. It does not disrupt the notion that we must be one or the other. It was only because the claimant was prepared to adhere to these norms and boundaries that she was successful in the case.

Grant v SWT[51] clearly shows the continued hierarchy which values hetero nuclear families above all others. It also shows that claims to equality by lesbians and gay men are still outside the cannon of human rights that governments and courts are prepared to grant us. The victories we have won (in terms of case outcomes) have been restricted to those claims based on privacy. And 'privacy' discourse (jurisprudence) is a very weak weapon when it comes to disrupting heteronormativity.

The continuous performance and validation of heteronormativity is also evident in the UN's dealings with sexuality outlined above. It is most clearly seen in the experiences of the ILGA, but is also present in the experiences of sexual outsiders at the 1993 Vienna Conference on Human Rights and the 1995 Beijing Conference on Women. These examples show continuing, extreme stigma associated with sexual outsiders.[52] Homosexuality (usually male) is most often represented or performed in UN discourse by the deployment of negative imagery productive of fear. Hysteria concerning paedophilia, myths of predation and proselytizing, discourses of Western corruption and disease are usually brought to the fore. At best, the UN like the EC, participates in a minoritizing discourse which locates the homosexual as a misunderstood victim.

The *Toonen* case[53] decided by the UN HRC has been heralded as a major victory for lesbian and gay rights within the UN system. As the equivalent to *Dudgeon*, the *Toonen* case largely adopted similar discourses of privacy and tolerance. *Toonen's* value is thus just as double-edged as its European forbears. Within Australia, the decision did finally lead to the repeal of the anti-gay laws, which is no small achievement, but *Toonen* also further entrenched heteronormativity. We need to understand the way in which discourses like 'privacy' and 'tolerance' can have such contradictory effects.

Although they can be used to advantage in a limited sense, the notions of privacy and tolerance do not disrupt, but I would argue, *strengthen* discourses of heteronormativity which construct sexual difference as 'other'. They do no more than plead for our inclusion in a heteronormative system. The predominating notion of 'tolerance' in the human rights field is a common technology of liberalism, effective in maintaining an 'otherizing' and 'subordinating' hierarchy at the same time as it grants 'rights' from its position of passionless neutrality.[54] The very notion of 'tolerance' implies subordination: you don't 'tolerate' something which is good (you celebrate it), you only 'tolerate' things you would rather didn't exist.[55] 'Tolerance' is thus a practice of oppression. In the area of sexuality, at the very moment 'tolerance' is deployed to justify the recognition of rights, it sends the message that hetero is good and non-hetero is bad. 'Tolerance' is thus also a technology for extending the panoptic gaze. It opens up new terrains of subjectivity for the state to colonize (those being tolerated) whilst maintaining the disciplinary effects of heteronormativity (because those being tolerated are *merely* that).

The discourse of 'privacy rights' which still lies at the heart of human rights law on sexuality can be similarly analysed as producing heteronormativity.[56] Think of 'the closet'. Think of the role which 'privacy' discourse plays in the maintenance of a notion of respectable, good citizen who keeps sexual matters hidden. This silences sexual difference. In sum, a sexual rights discourse based on tolerance and privacy amounts to no more than hetero law makers simultaneously assimilating a perceived threat by extending 'rights' (tolerance), whilst maintaining the subordination of those perceived as the threat (by validating heteronormativity).

Not only are they practices of heteronormativity, but 'privacy' and 'tolerance' also have very strict limits. 'Privacy' cannot deal with the type of discrimination experienced in *Grant* (it was never meant to) and, as yet, we have been unsuccessful in winning claims based on equality. 'Tolerance', apparently, does not extend to recognizing non-hetero relationships and the offspring we produce as forms of family, again as is evidenced by *Grant*.

Analysing international human rights law on sexuality with identity questions in mind shows how difficult strategizing law reform can be. If our goal is challenge rather than inclusion, how do we intervene in the law's performance of sexual hierarchy?

INTERVENING IN THE PERFORMANCE OF IDENTITY

Having re-read some of the texts of international human rights law with queer points about identity in mind, the question arises as to strategies. How do we intervene in the discourses of human rights law so as to displace the normative character of the category 'heterosexual'?

This is a question which has different answers according to the context. The practice of queering has implications for academic analysis, political lobbying and litigation. We are always located in a context of multiple identity performance, with different discourses competing to establish truth and knowledge claims. We cannot control these discourses and we cannot always predict what identity-effects our strategies may produce. But we can engage in a reflective, contingent sexual politics in academic and activist work, which avoids minoritizing discourses, attempts to disrupt heteronormativity and forges coalitions around questions of power and hierarchy.

The question of queer strategies has only recently begun to be debated in legal circles. Although I would maintain that queer questions about identity have practical implications in all areas of life, critics of queer practice usually characterize such ideas as impractical or worse: apolitical and threatening to lesbian and gay rights.[57] Recently, Nicholas Bamforth has assessed the queer ideas put forward by Carl Stychin against their 'utility' in law reform strategy at the domestic level.[58] His assessment is worth commenting on, because it so clearly highlights the differences in modernist (à la Heinze and Wintemute) and queer practice.

According to Bamforth, Stychin's theorizing involves 'a series of loose ends..., which ultimately make Stychin's theory unsatisfactory.'[59] In particular, the reactive nature of queer (the continual deconstruction of identity categories) cannot provide justifications for the *practical* questions involved in law reform. We must have arguments based on more than just reaction to existing social norms. Further, Stychin's theory, says Bamforth, is at risk of becoming internally inconsistent because the assertion of queerness itself relies on categorizations it claims to reject.[60]

From a queer point of view, Bamforth has missed the point. The criticisms listed above reflect a hunger after the very myths queer attempts to expose: a desire for metanarrative, for coherent, consistent theories which can justify and explain the relations between sexuality and law (a project pursued by Bamforth as well as Heinze and Wintemute). If our postmodern world has taught us anything, surely it has taught us that this is not possible. The best we can do, indeed *all* we can do, is be reactive. But my use of 'reactive' here is not meant to imply that we cannot take the initiative, that we cannot be proactive in our strategizing of non-hetero existence. We can, and should. But our strategies will always be reactive in the sense that none of us can ignore the context of hetero-normativity in which we operate. The imperative question in terms of strate-gizing law reform does not involve the search for coherent justifications for gay rights (a fruitless and unnecessary search), but rather the question of which approaches will best disrupt heteronormativity.[61] And contradiction, specificity, indeed reactivity are often useful in such disruption.

Bamforth uses the binary opposition of practice/theory, to delegitimize the 'theoretical' deconstructive project. The notion deployed by this dichotomy is that queer theory isn't helpful, isn't practical, as if theory isn't always already a part of practice, especially when it is hidden under a guise of point-of-view-lessness, and as if the two sides of this binary didn't already define each other. We misunderstand the way this binary functions if we think that queer ideas don't have practical effects. Indeed, the practical effects in terms of strategy are enormous (though not uniform, nor necessarily coherent).

In terms of academic work, these practical effects include paying attention to the ways in which identity is constructed in legal texts and to our own assumptions, continuously made, concerning identity. In terms of lobbying and litigation strategies, it means attempting to refuse the fixity of sexual cate-gories, to argue about identity borders, and to refuse to define what sexuality and any sub-category of it *is*. Instead of focusing on these 'status' questions concerning individuals labelled gay or lesbian, focus could be placed on questions of power, i.e. how the law regulates differently individuals who claim 'outsider' identities, how the law assumes and privileges hetero nuclear families, and so on.

I think that this would lead to the re-assessment of some strategies sexual outsiders currently adopt. For example, as mentioned above, Heinze concludes his text with a *Model Declaration of Rights of Sexual Orientation*. Disrupting heteronormativity may be better achieved by arguing for rights to sexual self-determination[62] which address a number of concerns, like sex work and women's control over their sexuality and reproductive capacity, rather than buying into a minoritizing 'homo' discourse which merely confirms the current hierarchy. Disrupting heteronormativity may also imply a different approach to the recog-nition of relationship rights in international human rights law. Arguing for the abolition of marriage as a state-sanctioned contract and a more fluid interpretation of 'family' in human rights treaties than a positivist would allow may be a more ambitious but ultimately more successful strategy in dealing with our oppression. Again, such a strategy also avoids a minoritizing discourse and opens the field for diverse claims to family status.

Opening the discursive field so that hierarchies of oppression are laid bare can be a goal in any academic, lobbying or litigation enterprise. In other words, avoiding minoritizing discourses involves strategies of coalition. Queer practice thus has wider implications than simply the rights of sexual outsiders. Questions of identity and how we approach them are obviously fundamental to any re-imaging of what international community and human rights might be like without the tyranny which rigid identity categories produce.

RECONSTRUCTING IDENTITY: COMMUNITY/NATION/ INTERNATIONAL HUMAN RIGHTS

Queer theory forces us to examine our own complicity in the normalizing strategies of human rights law which serves the purposes of the 'nation state'. In questioning the exclusionary practices of identity politics, in showing the incoherence of categories like 'gay' and 'lesbian', 'homo' and 'hetero', in re-orienting us to questions of power and hierarchy, queer theory points us towards coalition. Opening up the discursive field so that diversity may exist without assimilation entails being conscious of the ways in which different discourses and hierarchies of subordination work together to produce conceptions of international community and international relations. Patterns of dominance are organized by discourses of global capitalism, free trade, development etc., which are intimately connected to discourses of race, gender and sexuality.

A fundamental assumption upon which current hierarchies depend is the assumption of 'the nation state'. Taken as a given, the discursive structures which maintain 'the nation state' are rarely examined in legal texts. Yet the nation state is a contingent concept. In its modern bureaucratic form, it has a *will to define* and *colonize* any assertion of identity, especially those it perceives as deviant and threatening. The maintenance and reproduction of the 'nation state' depends upon such colonization and is surely the ultimate example of identity construction writ large. The ideas which control our conception of any given country are produced in a variety of ways, some by the positive exercise of agency by state actors, some totally outside their control: random and eclectic. But the one thing these constitutive ideas have in common is that they all involve an assertion of borders, of 'us' and 'them', of 'inside' and 'out'. The narrative of nation, regarded in this light, functions according to the same binary logic which produces the homo/hetero opposition.

Adopting queer questions about identity allows us to trace the genealogies of sexuality which figure in constructing the international law concept of 'the nation state',[63] as well as the role of sexuality in constructing any one country's narrative of 'nation'.[64] Such archaeologies have much in common with other deconstructive discourses of 'otherness', orientalism, post-colonialism and feminism,[65] although this commonality has not been used to advantage by gay and lesbian individuals and groups.

The role of sexuality in constructing the various meanings of 'nation' is obviously not a constant. It has various strands, ranging from silence to heteronormativity and the privileging of masculinity, to a more 'progressive' (though certainly *not* queer) championing of tolerance by some Western governments.[66] As mentioned above, one of the most disturbing strands in the narrative of sexuality and nationhood in international fora is the continued construction of sexual otherness as a white, Western 'disease' and as a product of corrupt capitalism. To some extent, 'we' (relatively privileged sexual outsiders from the 'first' world) have been complicit in the construction of this identity. Our claims have been formulated in Western, individualist, civil rights language. Many of us have not bothered to form coalitions with other groups who are interested in disrupting the hierarchies which produce global economic oppression, environmental destruction and racist notions of the international community. Is it any wonder then, that sexual rights are seen as a Western luxury?[67]

The discourses which structure narratives of nation – masculinity, heteronormativity and Western privilege – are technologies of identity. They represent sites of conflict in the local/national/international structures of identity policing. Yet, very little work has been done in excavating the role that 'sexuality' plays in international identity construction.[68] The sexuality of international law remains in the closet: the borders involved here maintain an illusion of impenetrability. Further work is needed by both activists and scholars in forging the types of theoretical and lobbying coalitions which are necessary to challenge the nation state and the international legal system based upon it.

Queering entails coalition in circumstances of non-assimilated difference. Diversity and self-determination depend on such practice. Our goal of disrupting heteronormativity is best seen as part of a wider critical politics interested in exposing the hierarchies of domination upon which the current 'nation state' depends.

CONCLUSIONS

The assimilating tendencies of law must be guarded against. The fundamental question remains: do we want to be included in a system of heteronormativity or do we want to challenge that system?

By using human rights language, we contribute to its influence and to its export of Western ideas around the world. I do not want to be taken as arguing that gay and lesbian activists should eschew the human rights field. Far from it. Engagement is vital at a number of levels. But I want to sound a few warning bells about what it is we are doing when we adopt a human rights framework for the articulation of lesbian and gay oppression. We should not forget that human rights discourse is the paradigm example of law based on core enlightenment values: respect for the individual, a faith in the rationality and objectivity of law which is a necessary part of the (fictional) social contract to which all people in the world are increasingly subject.

I like to think that by adopting queer strategies like those outlined above, we can begin to break down the hierarchies of oppression in international human rights law. We make human rights law queer by interrogating and refusing the notion of borders, by existing in the necessary contradictions that identity deconstruction entails. We queer it by analysing the role which sexuality plays in the narrative of nation, and by trying to intervene in the discourses which construct sexuality as a 'Western, first world' concern. Finally, we make it queer by focusing on questions of disciplinary power, and by deploying our own power in joining the network of critical coalitions that attempt to disrupt the ultimate real-fiction of international law: the narrative of the nation state.

CONCLUDING THOUGHTS

The essays which make up *Sexuality in the Legal Arena* have explored numerous questions and tracked many legal developments from around the world. However, the dynamic character of legal struggle means that questions and debates are continuously raised, and new controversies emerge. We end, then, with a series of questions produced by work in this field:

- Given the relationship between the nation state and the construction of sexual identities and practices, what are the implications of transnational and globalizing economic, political and legal processes for the politics of sexuality?
- To what extent is 'sexual orientation', a legal construct, itself becoming 'globalized', and how is that process being resisted at the level of the nation state and below?
- How will the discourse of international human rights, as it becomes increasingly focused on sexual identity issues, respond to the challenges of cultural relativism?
- What are the wider political implications of struggles for same-sex recognition, especially in terms of issues of gender, race and social class?
- What is the relationship between these recognition struggles and the downsizing of the welfare state?
- With the increasing presence of lesbians in popular cultural discourses, how will that visibility manifest itself in terms of legal, literary and film representations of the relationship between lesbianism and criminality?
- What is the relationship between the 'gay marriage' debates and the increasing surveillance of, and political attacks upon, single mothers?
- Given the critique of essentialism and immutability, can we say particular demands or interests are specifically gay or lesbian?
- What does lesbian and gay equality mean? Does it assume a particular, perhaps exclusive, conception of sexuality?
- To what extent are lesbian and gay identities legal constructs?
- Is there a contradiction between analyses that focus on discourse and representation and those which emphasize the economic dimensions to inequality?
- Can the 'heterosexuality of law' ever be successfully transcended? How might this be achieved?

NOTES

CHAPTER 1: A POST- WITHOUT A PAST?: SEXUAL ORIENTATION AND THE POST-COLONIAL 'MOMENT' IN SOUTH AFRICA

1. I would like to thank Palesa Beverley Ditsie, Zolani Noonan-Ngwane, Elizabeth Povinelli and Graeme Reid for their valuable insights and comments on previous drafts.
2. See Carusi, A., 'Post, Post and Post, or, Where is South African Literature in All This?', in I. Adam and H. Tiffin, eds, *Past the Last Post* (Calgary: University of Calgary, 1990); Jolly, R., 'Rehearsals of Liberation: Contemporary Postcolonial Discourse and the New South Africa', *PMLA* 110(1) (1995): 17.
3. African National Congress, 'Nation formation and nation building: the national question in South Africa', 1997 National Conference discussion document; see also Pechey, G., 'Post-apartheid narratives', in F. Barker, P. Hulmet and M. Iversen, eds, *Colonial Discourse, Postcolonial Theory* (New York: Manchester University Press, 1993).
4. See also Pechey, 'Narratives', p 55.
5. Shohat, E., 'Notes on the "post-colonial"', *Social Text* 31/32 (1992): 104; see also McClintock, A., 'The angel of progress: pitfalls of the term "post-colonialism"', *Social Text* 31/32 (1992): 84.
6. Shohat, 'Notes', p 104.
7. See Ibid, pp 109–110; Hall, S., 'When was "the post-colonial"? Thinking at the Limit', in I. Chambers and L. Curti, eds, *The Post-colonial Question: Common Skies, Divided Horizons* (New York: Routledge, 1996); Carusi, A., 'The postcolonial as a problem for political action', *JLS* 7(3/4) (1991): 228.
8. Frankenberg, R. and Mani, L. 'Crosscurrents, crosstalk: race, "post-coloniality" and the politics of location', *Cultural Studies* 7(2) (1993): 292–310 at 301.
9. Shohat, 'Notes', p 110.
10. Bravmann, S., *Queer Fictions of the Past: History, Culture and Difference* (Cambridge: Cambridge University Press, 1997): 4.
11. Beth Povinelli and Zolani Noonan-Ngwane were especially helpful in developing this element.
12. Shohat, 'Notes', p 101; Hall, 'Thinking', p 253.
13. See Phillips, O., 'Zimbabwe', in D. West and R. Green, eds, *Sociolegal Control of Homosexuality* (New York: Plenum, 1997). Unfortunately, the role of missionization and Christianity in the colonial project and in colonial and post-colonial constructs of sexuality require far more attention than I can possibly provide here.
14. *Capital Gay*, 18 September, 1987.
15. *Work in Progress* (incorporating *New Era*) 82 (1992): 13.
16. Coalition for Gay and Lesbian Equality, Submission to the Truth and Reconciliation Commission (TRC), December, 1997. For further discussion of the Winnie Mandela trial see Holmes, R., 'De-segregating sexualities: sex, race, and the politics of the 1991 Winnie Mandela trial', *Passages* 3(5) (1993): 10.
17. *Outright* 2(10) (1995): 14; see also Dunton, C. and Palmberg, M., Human rights and homosexuality in southern Africa', *Current African Issues* 19 (1996): 8.
18. *The Star*, 12 June, 1996, Letters.
19. *Mail and Guardian*, 8–14 September, 1995, p 27.
20. *Exit*, Issue 71, 1995, p 3.
21. Gevisser, M., 'Cry freedom', *Attitude*, July, 1995, p 47.
22. See Aarmo, M., 'How homosexuality became "un-African": the case of Zimbabwe', in E. Blackwood and S. Wieringa, eds, *Same-Sex Relations and Female Desires: Transgender Practices Across Cultures* (New York: Columbia University, 1999); Gevisser, M., 'A different fight for freedom', in Gevisser, M. and Cameron, E. *Defiant Desire* (New York: Routledge, 1995); Hoad, N., 'Tradition,

modernity and human rights: an interrogation of contemporary gay and lesbian rights claims in Southern African nationalist discourses', *Development Update: The Right to Be: Sexuality and Sexual Rights in Southern Africa* 2(2) (1998): 32; Phillips, O., 'Zimbabwean law and the production of a white man's disease', *Social and Legal Studies* 6(4) (1997): 471; Stychin, C., *A Nation by Rights* (Philadelphia: Temple University, 1998).

23. For assertions of homosexuality as a Western, colonial importation in other contexts see Alexander, J., 'Not just (any)body can be a citizen: The politics of law, sexuality, and postcoloniality in Trinidad and Tobago and the Bahamas', *Feminist Review* 48 (1994): 5; Altman, D., 'The emergence of "modern" gay identities and the question of human rights' paper presented at the *Beyond Boundaries: Sexuality Across Culture Conference*, Amsterdam, The Netherlands, July, 1997; Thadani, G., *Sakhiyani: Lesbian Desire in Ancient and Modern India* (London: Cassell, 1996).

24. See Gevisser, 'Fight', pp 72–3; *Mail and Guardian*, 23–29 May, 1997, p 25.

25. *Outright*, 2(10) (1995): 14.

26. *Sowetan*, 8 December, 1994, p 7.

27. *Outright*, 2(10) (1995): 14–15.

28. Coalition, TRC Submission.

29. Placard at 1995 Johannesburg demonstration against Mugabe.

30. Placard at 1995 Johannesburg demonstration against Mugabe.

31. National Coalition for Gay and Lesbian Equality, flyer announcing 11 August, 1995 protest; *Outright*, 2(10) (1995): 15.

32. See Kelly, J., *A Politics of Virtue: Hinduism, Sexuality and Countercolonial Discourse in Fiji* (Chicago: University of Chicago Press, 1991).

33. See Chatterjee, P., *The Nation and its Fragments: Colonial and Post-colonial Histories* (Princeton: Princeton University Press, 1993).

34. *Exit*, Issue 106 (1998), p 5.

35. Hall, 'Thinking', p 247.

36. *Outright*, 2(10) (1995): 14.

37. *Exit*, Issue 104 (1998), p 9.

38. *Mail and Guardian*, 23–29 May, 1997, p 25.

39. 'Equality for All', *Constitutional Talk*, no. 4, February–March, 1995.

40. Hall, 'Thinking', p 248.

41. Shohat, 'Notes', pp 106–7.

42. Hall, 'Thinking', pp 247–8.

43. Placard at 1993 Johannesburg Gay Pride Parade.

44. Coalition, 8 May, 1998 press release (emphasis added).

45. Note also that the men were tried and convicted by the Court of Justice – housed in the Castle.

46. 10 May, 1998, p 3 (emphasis added).

47. Goldberg, J., 'Bradford's "ancient members" and "A case of buggery ... amongst them"', in A. Parker, M. Russo, D. Sommer and P. Yaeger, eds, *Nationalisms and Sexualities* (New York: Routledge, 1992).

48. Stoler, A., *Race and the Education of Desire* (Durham: Duke, 1995).

49. Sedgwick, E., *Epistemology of the Closet* (Berkeley: University of Californian Press, 1990): 47.

50. Phillips, 'Disease', p 475.

51. Hall, 'Thinking', p 250.

52. Comaroff, J.L. and Comaroff, J., *Of Revelation and Revolution: The Dialectics of Modernity on a South African Frontier*, vol II (Chicago: University of Chicago Press, 1997): 365.

53. Edwin Cameron is currently Justice on South Africa's Labour Court. When he was originally appointed to the Supreme Court he was South Africa's only openly gay judge. Cameron, E., 'Sexual orientation and the Constitution: a test case for human rights, *SALJ* 110 (1993): 455.

54. Stevan Cohen is a South African queer artist who frequently interjects his imagery into public events through performance. This poster references two silkscreens of his, *I'm A Crime* and *Pope Art*.

55. Carusi, 'Post'.

56. Comaroff and Comaroff, *Revelation*, p 368.

57. *In the matter between The National Coalition for Gay and Lesbian Equality and The Minister of Justice*, High Court of South Africa, WLD (1997), Applicants Heads of Argument, para 3.8.

58. *Ibid*, para 3.11.

59. *Ibid*, para 13.7.

60. *Hansard* (S.A.), 21 April, 1967, pp 4707–8.

61. *Ibid*, p 4708.

62. *Hansard* (S.A.), 5 May, 1969, pp 2300–1.

63. *National Coalition for Gay and Lesbian Equality and The Minister of Justice*, p 22.
64. See Stychin, C., *A Nation by Rights* (Philadelphia: Temple University Press, 1998) p 70; Gevisser, 'Fight', p 31. Gevisser also notes that this coincided with anti-semitic Afrikaner panic over 'Jewish corruption' of Afrikaner boys and broader 'Jewish conspiracies'.
65. Pechey, 'Narratives', p 157.
66. *National Coalition for Gay and Lesbian Equality and The Minister of Justice,* p 7. Carl Stychin observed the contradiction of relying on Wolfenden in a decision affirming gay equality as the Report was hardly a model of gay affirming discourse. The crux of the contradiction is evident in the circumstance that the most notorious of the South African provisions (Section 20A, 'men at a party', which prohibits acts calculated to stimulate sexual passion committed between men at an occasion where more than two persons are present) is based on section 1(2)(a) of the British Sexual Offences Act of 1967 which liberalized the law concerning sex between men – while criminalizing male/male sex between or in the presence of more than two persons. *Ibid*, pp 5–6.
67. *Ibid*, p 8.
68. *National Coalition for Gay and Lesbian Equality and The Minister of Justice*, p 6.
69. Jara, M. and Lapinsky, S., 'Forging a representative gay liberation movement in South Africa', *Development Update: The Right to Be: Sexuality and Sexual Rights in Southern Africa* 2(2) (1998): 53.
70. Read: not making a claim about apartheid.
71. Gay and Lesbian Organization of the Witwatersrand Newsletter (*Glowletter*), AGM issue, 1996.
72. Darian-Smith, E., 'Postcolonialism: a brief introduction', *Social and Legal Studies* 5(3) (1996): 291.
73. Shohat, 'Notes', p 110..
74. *Ibid*, p 105.
75. *Ibid*, p 110.
76. Stychin, *Nation*, p 67; Gevisser, 'Fight', pp 72–3.
77. Antonio, E., 'Homosexuality and African culture', in P. Germond and S. de Gruchy, eds, *Aliens in the Household of God: Homosexuality and Christian Faith in South Africa* (Cape Town: David Philip, 1997); Epprecht, M., 'The "unsaying" of indigenous homosexualities in Zimbabwe: mapping blindspot in an African masculinity', *Journal of Southern African Studies* 24(4) (1998): 631.
78. *Glowletter*, March, 1990, p 9.
79. *Ibid*.
80. *Glowletter*, October 1992, p 14.
81. *Drum*, November, 1992, p 23.
82. Reid, G., 'Coming home: visions of healing in a Gauteng church', in Germond, *Aliens*, p 109.
83. See also Achmat's assertion that 'contemporary historiography' and the 'search for the origins of exploitation and oppression' have obstructed 'local memories' of both homosexuality and the 'struggles of history', Achmat, Z., ' "Apostles of civilized vice": "immoral practices" and "unnatural vice" in South African prisons and compounds, 1890–1920', *Social Dynamics* 19(2) (1993): 106.
84. Interview with Palesa Beverley Ditsie, November, 1998.
85. Reid, 'Home', p 109.
86. *Glowletter*, September 1995, p 3.
87. *Sunday Tribune*, 1 December, 1996, p 14.
88. Glowletter, October 1992, p 14.
89. *Drum*, November, 1992, p 24.
90. Ditsie, interview; Luphodwana, N., 'Talk at will, with Tim Modise', SAfm, 24 November, 1997.
91. Donham, D., 'Freeing South Africa: the "modernization"of male–male sexuality in Soweto', *Cultural Anthropology* 13(1) (1998): 14.
92. *ibid*, pp 14–15.
93. Ditsie, interview.
94. *City Press*, July 23, 1995, p 3.
95. A 'traditional leader' who 'keeps' multiple wives. See Gevisser, 'Fight', p 72.
96. 'Traditional healers'.
97. Gevisser, 'Fight', p 72; *Drum*, November, 1992, p 23.
98. *Capital Gay*, September, 1987.
99. *Work in Progress*, p 13.
100. *Glowletter*, March 1990, p 9; *Saturday Star*, 21 October, 1995.
101. Achmat, 'Apostles', p 105.
102. Partner assuming the 'passive' role in male/male sex,
103. Usually derogatory slang denoting 'hermaphrodite', literally, 'person with two (sexual) organs'.
104. This is somewhat akin to D'Emilio's argument that the emergence of gay men and lesbians is 'associated with the relations of capitalism', although the politics inherent in the South African case

produces a stronger assertion of a pre-capitalist gay identity. D'Emilio, J., 'Capitalism and gay identity', in H. Abelove, M. Barale and D. Halperin, eds, *The Lesbian and Gay Studies Reader* (New York: Routledge, 1993); see also Achmat, 'Apostles', arguing that the capitalist compound system 'partially freed the male body . . . creating a network of new pleasures and desires' (p 106).

105. GLOW collection, Gay and Lesbian Archives of South Africa, University of the Witwatersrand.
106. *Glowletter*, Pride 1991 Issue, p 7.
107. *Glowletter*, September 1995, p 3.
108. Epprecht, 'Unsaying', pp 636–7.
109. *Sowetan*, 4 April, 1996, p 12.
110. Partner assuming the 'active' role in male/male sex,
111. Reid, 'Home', p 114.
112. *Tribune*, 1 December, 1996, p 14.
113. Ditsie, interview.
114. Achmat, 'Apostles', pp 104–5.
115. Shohat, 'Notes', p 109.
116. Norval, A., 'Decolonization, demonization and difference: the difficult constitution of a nation', *Philosophy and Social Criticism* 21(3) (1995): 31.
117. *Glowletter*, October, 1992, p 14.
118. Loosely, 'brideprice'.
119. *Glowletter*, September, 1996, p 1.
120. Hall, 'Thinking', p 250.
121. Mongia, P., 'Introduction', in P. Mongia, *Contemporary Postcolonial Theory: a Reader* (New York: Oxford University Press, 1996): 1.
122. Hall, *Thinking*, pp 253–4.
123. Norval, 'Decolonization', p 43.
124. Darian-Smith, 'Introduction', p 292.
125. Shohat, 'Notes', p 108.
126. *Ibid*, p 104.
127. Derrida, J., 'The laws of reflection: Nelson Mandela, in admiration', in J. Derrida and M. Tlili, eds, *For Nelson Mandela* (New York: Seaver Books, 1987).
128. Prakash, G., 'Introduction: after colonialism', in G. Prakash, ed., *After Colonialism: Imperial Histories and Postcolonial Displacements* (Princeton: Princeton University Press, 1995): 3.
129. Carusi, 'Post'.
130. Carusi, 'Action', p 235.
131. Hall, 'Thinking', p 252.
132. Norval, 'Decolonization', p 31.
133. During, S., 'Waiting for the post: some relations between modernity, colonization, and writing', in Adam, *Last Post*, p 28.
134. Note the Coalition's latest campaign – 'Recognize Our Relationships'.
135. Kelly, *Virtue*, p 229.
136. On the Christian ideal of love and same-sex coupling in South Africa see Openshaw, V., 'Homosexuals and the right to marry' in Germond, *Aliens*.

CHAPTER 2: CONSTITUTING THE GLOBAL GAY: ISSUES OF INDIVIDUAL SUBJECTIVITY AND SEXUALITY IN SOUTHERN AFRICA

1. In 1998 the Botswana government, fearful that its prohibition of sex between men would be challenged on the grounds of sexual discrimination, passed legislation that prohibited sex between women; in the same year, the Lesbian and Gay Botswana Association was formed. In 1997, Namibian President Sam Nujoma said homosexuality 'should be uprooted totally' from Namibia, calling it 'a hideous deviation of decrepit and inhuman sordid behaviour' (*Weekly Mail and Guardian* 14 February, 1997); the Rainbow Coalition was founded earlier that same year. In March 1997, the newly formed Gays and Lesbians of Swaziland (GaLeSwa) was refused recognition by the Prime Minister of Swaziland, although there appears to be no existing legal prohibition against homosexual acts. In August 1998, the Lesbians, Gays, BiSexual and Transgender Persons Association (LEGATRA) of Zambia was formed, amid uproar from government and press (see *The Daily*

Mail of Zambia 20 September, 1998). For information on South Africa, see Gevisser, M. and Cameron, E., eds, *Defiant Desire: Gay and Lesbian Lives in South Africa* (London: Routledge, 1995).

2. Association for the Lesbian and Gay Movement – see Pinkerton, S.D. and Abramson, P.R., in D. West and R. Green, *The Socio-legal Control of Homosexuality: a Multi-nation Comparison* (New York: Plenum, 1977): 81–2.

3. For an analysis of how AIDS transformed Bolivian *genie de ambiente* ('people of the atmosphere') into 'gay' people, see Wright, T. and Wright, R., in West and Green, *Socio-legal Control*, pp 97–108.

4. See Kon, I., in West and Green, *Socio-legal Control*, pp 221–42.

5. Quoted in Kendall, ' "When a woman loves a woman" in Lesotho: love, sex, and the (Western) construction of homophobia', in S.O. Murray and W. Roscoe, eds, *Boy Wives and Female Husbands: Studies of African Homosexualities* (New York: St Martin's Press, 1998): 229.

6. See Jeater, D., *Marriage, Perversion and Power: the Construction of Moral Discourse in Southern Rhodesia 1894–1930* (Oxford: Clarendon Press, 1993).

7. Section 89 of the Constitution of Zimbabwe.

8. 1889 Charter of the British South Africa Company.

9. 'After Mzilikazi's flight to Matabeleland, [Reverend Robert] Moffat was the first European to visit him there in 1854, and five years later he established the London Missionary Society in Matabeleland', in D. Martin and P. Johnson, *The Struggle for Zimbabwe: the Chimurenga War* (London: Faber and Faber, 1981): 40.

10. See Bullock, C., *The Mashona and the Matabele* (Cape Town: Juta & Co., 1950): 45 and 50. See more generally Phillips, O., 'Zimbabwean law and the production of a white man's disease', *Social and Legal Studies* 6(4) (1987): 475–6.

11. See generally, Caplan, P., *The Cultural Construction of Sexuality* (London: Tavistock, 1987); and Greenberg, D., *The Construction of Homosexuality* (Chicago: University of Chicago Press, 1988).

12. The nineteenth century saw the beginnings of a 'scientific' approach to 'sexuality'; to varying degrees, the works of Krafft-Ebbing, Sigmeund Freud, Havelock Ellis, etc. were premised on the belief that a methodologically structured approach to sex would reveal the 'truth' about sex, and hence the 'truth' about life. Similarly, it was in the nineteenth century that the terms homo/heterosexual were first used. See Foucault, M., *The History of Sexuality: an Introduction* (London: Peregrine, 1978); and Weeks, J., *Sex, Politics, and Society, the Regulation of Sexuality since 1800* (Harrow: Longman, 1989) and Plummer, K., ed., *The Making of the Modern Homosexual* (London: Hutchinson, 1981).

13. For an account of stereotypes of race and sex from the middle ages to the twentieth century (but with 'a primary focus on the turn of the century', (p 11) see Gilman, S., *Difference and Pathology: Stereotypes of Sexuality, Race, and Madness* (New York: Cornell University Press, 1985).

14. See Burke, T., *Lifebuoy Men, Lux Women: Commodification, Consumption and Cleanliness in Modern Zimbabwe* (London: Leicester University Press, 1996).

15. Prior to the 1982 Legal Age of Majority Act, black African women in Rhodesia/Zimbabwe had no legal subjectivity, and were subject to the control of their male guardian (father/brother/husband/uncle), though certain legislative efforts did specifically prohibit women from certain acts, lending them a *de facto* subjectivity but only in so far as to restrict their behaviour, rather than empower them (e.g. the Native's Adultery Punishment Ordinance, 1916).

16. For a summary of these various attempts see Botha, K. and Cameron, E., 'South Africa', in West and Green, *Socio-legal Control*, pp 5–38. For an analysis more relevant to contemporary Zimbabwean interpretations, see Propotkin, P., 'Getting to the bottom of sodomy' (University of Zimbabwe, unpublished article, 1997).

17. For a contemporary Zimbabwean example of this specificity see *S v Meager* RLR 2 (1977) 327 and see the discussion of this case in Phillips, O., 'Zimbabwe' in West and Green, *Socio-legal Control*, pp 43–55.

18. Moran, L., 'The homosexualisation of English law', in D. Herman and C. Stychin, *Legal Inversions: Leshians, Gay Men and the Politics of Law* (Philadelphia: Temple University Press, 1995): 9–10.

19. Jeater, *Marriage*.

20. Therapeutic treatments and rehabilitative programmes for (sexual or ordinary) offenders held in custody are extremely rare in Zimbabwe, and the sentence of custody is predicated on the belief that punishment of the individual is a suitable mechanism of retribution for anti-social acts. Traditionally, restitution would be made through lineage structures (for example the paying of damages in the form of livestock which would not simply belong to one person but to the family, or more specifically, the male head of that family) rather than being embodied in the custody of the individual.

21. For discussion of this see Phillips, 'Zimbabwean law'.

22. Under the LAMA, consent is not required for a civil law marriage, into which any adult may freely enter – however, it would seem that the consent of a guardian is still required when a woman enters

into a marriage under Customary Law; Jacobs, S.M. and Howard, T., 'Women in Zimbabwe: stated policy and state action', in H. Afshar, ed., *Women, State, and Ideology Studies from Africa and Asia* (London: Macmillan, 1987): 75.

23. *Ibid*, p 32; and Folbre, N., 'Patriarchal social formations in Zimbabwe', in S.B. Stichter and J.L. Parpart, eds, *Patriarchy and Class: African Women in the Home and the Workforce* (Boulder: Westview Press, 1988): 75.

24. Zimbabwe African National Union – in 1980 it became the ruling party.

25. Seidman, G.W., 'Women in Zimbabwe: post-Independence struggles', *Feminist Studies* 10(3) (Fall 1984): 432.

26. *Ibid.*

27. 'Consideration of Reports Submitted by States Parties Under Article 40 to the Covenant', United Nations Human Rights Committee 1651st Meeting, 26 March, 1998 (CCPR/C/74/Add.3, HRI/CORE/1/Add.55).

28. UN Human Rights Committee – Summary record of the 1651st meeting released 28 July, 1998 (CCPR/C/SR.1651@31).

29. In this chapter, for reasons of space, I shall assume but not critically address this understanding of the creation of ethnic identities, and for an exposition of more direct relevance to the history of ethnicities in Zimbabwe, I suggest Beach, D.N. *The Shona and Zimbabwe, 900–1850* (London, 1980); and Ranger, T., 'Missionaries, migrants, and the Manyika: the invention of ethnicity in Zimbabwe', in Vail, L., ed., *The Creation of Tribalist in Southern Africa* (London: James Currey, 1989).

30. See Hobsbawm, E. and Ranger, T., eds *The Invention of Tradition* (Cambridge: Cambridge University Press, 1983).

31. Butler, J., *Gender Trouble* (Routledge: London 1990): 24.

32. The *Native Adultery Punishment Ordinance* (NAPO) of 1916 was intended to strengthen African marriages by making adultery a criminal offence, punishable by up to a year's imprisonment. While this referred to both men and women, the fact that African marriages were polygynous meant that its application was persistently gender bound. For a married woman to sleep with any man other than her husband would be committing adultery, while a married man could be convicted of adultery only if he slept with another man's wife. Thus, he could sleep with any woman who was not-married to another man. So while the NAPO was superficially symmetrical in its design, in effect it penalised only married women and the men they slept with.

33. The requirement of penile–vaginal penetration and the impunity with which a man could rape his wife are both symbolic of this preoccupation.

34. Stychin, C., *Law's Desire* (London: Routledge, 1995): 30.

35. This increase is seen to be reflected in the growth of the organization GALZ and the fact that black members of GALZ are now the most numerous, and the most active executive positions are occupied by black Zimbabweans.

36. In June 1998, at the trial of ex-President Canaan Banana, the first interpreter had to be replaced as she could not cope with the translation of such clinical terms as 'erections' and 'semen' (Matyszak, D., personal communication Faculty of Law, University of Zimbabwe).

37. See Pattman, 'Discourses of sex, Aids, and sex/Aids education in Zimbabwe' (Unpublished Ph.D. thesis, Institute of Education, University of London, 1995).

38. Misihairambwi, P., 'The WASN Youth Programme in Zimbabwe', unpublished paper given at conference on *Community Responses to HIV in Southern Africa* (Sheffield, October, 1997).

39. A substantial number of marriages are still polygynous, and even where the marriage is not officially polygynous, many men appear to believe that fidelity is an obligation which falls only to a wife.

40. Foucault, M., *The History of Sexuality: an Introduction* (London: Penguin, 1978): 127.

41. Stychin, C., *A Nation by Rights* (Philadelphia: Temple University Press, 1998): 198.

CHAPTER 3: 'I'D RATHER BE AN OUTLAW': IDENTITY, ACTIVISM AND DECRIMINALIZATION IN TASMANIA

1. I would like to thank Rodney Croome, Richard Hale and Nick Toonen for giving their time so generously as I conducted the research on which this chapter is based, and Richard Bootle, Jenny Morgan and Carl Stychin for their thoughtful and thought-provoking comments and discussions as I wrote it.

2. Rodney Croome, TGLRG, interview with the author, 29 November, 1997.

3. For further, see Emma Henderson, 'Of signifiers and sodomy: privacy, public morality and sex in the decriminalisation debates' *Melbourne University Law Review* 20 (1996): 1023.

4. For example, the airplay given to the One Nation Party, a political party based on the personal following of its leader, Pauline Hanson, provides a more recent Australian example. Hanson attributes political instability and unemployment to the dangers of multiculturalism and advocates a reversion to the White Australia immigration policies of the 1950s and the absolute denial of the validity of the Aboriginal rights movement; her party achieved almost 10% of the vote in the 1998 federal election (although receiving only one senate seat), and in the 1997 Queensland state elections attracted almost a quarter of the vote. The controversy that Hanson created during 1997–8 worked to allow mainstream Australia to distance itself from racism through the 'I would never say such things so I can't be a racist' phenomenon, and allowed conservative political parties and government policies to attain a centrist impartial positioning through the simple act of remaining silent.

5. Rodney Croome, Tasmanian Gay and Lesbian Rights Group, interview with the author, 25 November, 1997.

6. 'I was recently on the mainland, following that *60 Minutes*, and every Tasmanian now has the redneck label of the majority of people on that program. That is the response we got everywhere we went...'; Mr White, Tasmanian Legislative Assembly, Parliamentary Debates, *Hansard,* 14 September, 1994 at 2098.

7. For example, where in New South Wales or Victoria advertisments promote the 'buy Australian' made brand, in Tasmania the theme is 'buy Tasmanian made'.

8. Rodney Croome, see, note 2.

9. *Ibid.*

10. Richard Hale, Tasmanian Gay and Lesbian Rights Group, previously coordinator of Tasmanian AIDS Council, interview with the author, 28 November, 1997.

11. Their descendants now form the centre of small but vocal evangelical Christian movements in small rural communities of Tasmania, such as St Helen, host to one of the more vehement but quiet anti-gay rallies in 1990.

12. Rodney Croome, see note 2.

13. George Brookes, Tasmanian Legislative Council, Parliamentary Debates, *Hansard*, 2 July, 1991 at 1244–6.

14. 'Surely our task is to build a bulwark which will defy evil influences which are seeking to undermine the very foundations of our national character ... I have heard that such practices are allowed in France and other NATO countries We are not French, we are not other nationals. We are British thank God!' see Viscount Montgomery of Alamein, House of Lords, Parliamentary Debates, *Hansard,* 24 May, 1965 at 648.

15. Note that doing this silences a Tasmanian past where convict homo-sex was endemic and publicly acknowledged until massive and vicious clampdown in the 1840s; see Rodney Croome, 'At the crossroads: may and green politics', in Cassandra Pybus and Richard Flanagan, eds, *The Rest of the World is Watching: Tasmania and the Greens* (Sydney: Pan MacMillan, 1990): 107; see also Rodney Croome, 'Out and about: the public rights of lesbians and gays in Tasmania', *Australian Gay and Lesbian Law Journal* 6 (1992): 63 at 69.

16. George Brookes, Tasmanian Legislative Council, Parliamentary Debates, *Hansard*, 2 July, 1991 at 1246.

17. *Sydney Morning Herald,* 17 October, 1988, p 3.

18. Rodney Croome and Nick Toonen, interview with the author, 28 November, 1997; for discussion of the trade boycott, see Mr Watson MLC, Tasmanian Legislative Council, Parliamentary Debates, *Hansard,* 8 December, 1994 at 4325.

19. Briefly, the TGLRG sought permission to set up a stall at the Third National AIDS Conference in 1988. The organizers of the conference refused the application, considering that in aiming to network with other community groups around the law reform issue, the TGLRG would be acting in a consciously political manner inconsistent with the aims of the conference. Lengthy negotiations led to the group running both a stall and a very influential workshop on gay law reform which was attended by over 100 organizations and individuals. The lesson learned by the group itself came not from the workshop but from the reaction caused by its intention to ask the Tasmanian Minister for Health why his government did not support law reform. The response of conference participants to this decision was swift and extremely hostile: the organizers, other (non-gay) activist groups and the AIDS Council were all afraid that such a move would embarrass the government, unduly 'politicize' the conference, and consequently jeopardize AIDS funding and support.

20. See Miranda Morris, *Pink Triangle: the Gay Law Reform Debate in Tasmania* (Sydney: UNSW Press, 1995) for further details.

21. The 1989 election, which saw the birth of the Green movement as a significant force in Tasmanian politics, followed several extremely contentious decisions regarding the Tasmanian environment: hydro-electric schemes which had flooded Lake Pedder and attempted to dam the Franklin River and attempts to build a Pulp Mill in Wesley Vale. Five independent Green candidates went on to win 18% of the vote and hold the balance of power; they spent 6 weeks following the election settling on the terms of the Accord under which they would govern with the minority Labour Party, one of the conditions of which, as Item W, was gay law reform.

22. Note, however, that they were more closely related to the American counterparts in other ways – namely in the fact the the primary constituents of Tasmanian anti-gay groups were more likely to see themselves (and to be seen by others) as economically and socially vulnerable: 'We didn't look at the anti-gay groups and think that they were particularly privileged ... they weren't traditional high brow conservatives at all. They were resented by traditional high brows as low brow and they saw themselves as low brow, they were there shoulder by shoulder with the working man ... very much like, in fact a precursor, of the Pauline Hanson thing', Rodney Croome, interview with the author, 28 November, 1997.

23. *The Mercury,* 30 September, 1988, reported in Miranda Morris, see note 17 at 27.

24. By denying that HIV was anything other than a medical issue (and thus refusing to fund 'safe sex' programmes which rather than treating HIV symptoms, aimed to encourage safer (gay) sex practices), the government turned such programmes into private concerns. This can be seen in a similar light to American government initiatives to view abortion as a private matter – allowable but not fundable from public monies.

25. Miranda Morris, see note 17 at 32.

26. *Examiner,* 26 April, 1989.

27. Interestingly, CRAMP was made up of members of a group called CROPS (Concerned Residents Oppose Pulp Sites) which had been set up to oppose the development of a NW coastal site for the Wesley Vale Mill; they had voted Green against their traditional Liberal sympathies but were now hostile to the merging of Green with Labour concerns. Approximately 35 attended their first meeting in Devonport (the city closest to Wesley Vale), and the meeting emphasized the regional specificity of their group: 'The south might be too corrupt for us but if there's anyone down there who wants to form a group they'd have our blessing'. Reported in Morris, see note 17, at 41. See also Letter to the Editor, *The Mercury,* 12 November, 1988.

28. The creation of 'shadow' parliamentary positions is part of the Westminster tradition of government as practised in Australia, New Zealand and Britain. For each government Minister there exists a 'shadow' opponent politician from the ranks of the official parliamentary opposition.

29. There were three rallies, the smallest at St Helens, a meeting that excluded TV cameras and reporters. The meeting held in Burnie on 8 November, 1989 was attended by 600 people (a staggering total for a town of only 3000) and three motions were passed: calling for the establishing of a government sponsored counselling service to help homosexuals revert to heterosexuality, ensuring that sex education in schools covers only monogamous husband/wife relationships, and supporting research into the causes of homosexuality. Although it was advertised as a debate, no pro-gay speaker was invited nor was any gay law reformer allowed a right of reply. Councillor Cooper ended the evening with the statement that 'tonight we have woken up the slumbering masses. We will now turn the tables and show the powers in Hobart that they are our servants'. At the next Ulverstone Council meeting, a motion was passed congratulating Cooper 'in recognition of his contribution to health and hygiene'. The following week the rally was repeated in St Helens and for the first time there were as many gay supporters as anti-gays, and it was quite vocal – grass roots rather than stage managed. MP Chris Miles spoke about anal insertion of lightbulbs and Beeston spoke about the need for compassion. Rodney Croome describes the St Helen meeting as empowering because there were no cameras so the TGLRG members who had gone to protest at the meeting did not have to be respectable or polite. See Rodney Croome, 'At the crossroads'.

30. The members of FACT and CRAMP often had a stronger allegiance to the anti-gay movement than they did to their respective faiths; although there were increasing numbers of church leaders involved, there was little reference to religious sources or arguments for maintaining the laws.

31. Howard Carter, the leader of the Tasmanian Pentecostal Church and a former Baptist Minister. Quoted in Miranda Morris, see note 17 at 38.

32. The gay and lesbian community in Ulverston initiated a letter writing campaign and several weeks later the resolution was revoked by the council. See Rodney Croome, 'Out and about', at 67 for further details. Wynyard Council passed resolutions against reform soon after Ulverston.

33. The clauses were removed in the Lower House, after an extremely bitter debate, in a failed attempt to make other provisions (such as needle exchanges and privacy of testing) more palatable to the

Upper House. Although a re-introduced 1992 Bill (without the decriminalization provisions) eventually succeeded in passing through the Upper House, the Bill still met with an unprecedented level of animus.

34. Section 122 of the Criminal Code Act 1924 (Tas) states:

> Any person who –
> (a) has sexual intercourse with any person against the order of nature;
> (b) has sexual intercourse with an animal; or
> (c) consents to a male person having sexual intercourse with him or her against the order of nature, is guilty of a crime.
> Charge: unnatural sexual intercourse.
> Section 123 provides:
> Any male person who, whether in public or private, commits any indecent assault upon, or other act of gross indecency with, another male person, or procures another male person to commit any act of gross indecency with himself or any other male person, is guilty of a crime.
> Charge: indecent practice between male persons.

Thus the only clearly excluded form of sexual expression is heterosexual vaginal penetration by a penis. The maximum penalty for these offences rose from 21 to 25 years imprisonment in 1996.

35. With the exception of the Individual Opinion appended by the Swedish Member, the UNHRC declined to examine the issue in the light of the equality provisions of the ICCPR. See Wayne Morgan, 'Identifying evil for what it is: Tasmania, sexual perversity and the United Nations' *Melbourne University Law Review* 19 (1994) 740 for further details.

36. Voted on 19 October, 1994: 70 for, 55 against.

37. Clause 4 of the Bill defined arbitrary interferences with privacy as those defined 'within the meaning of Article 17 of the International Covenant on Civil and Political Rights'.

38. Given the 1990 Director of Public Prosections directive that no criminal charges be brought against the kind of sex covered by the Act, it was unlikely there would be such a case. The fact that the court granted standing was the subject of much rancour within conservative ranks in Tasmania: 'it has always been my understanding that you have no standing in the High Court unless you have been convicted but here you have the incredible situation where the High Court indicated that they were prepared to hear the case ... they would rule on a hypothetical situation', George Brookes MLC, Tasmanian Legislative Council, Parliamentary Debates, *Hansard,* 15 April, 1997 at 7.

39. UNHRC UN Doc CCPR/C/50/D/488/1992 (13 March, 1993).

40. George Brookes, Tasmanian Legislative Council, Parliamentary Debates, *Hansard,* 2 July, 1991 at 1244.

41. I have discussed elsewhere the costs involved in the efforts of the Homosexual Law Reform Society (HLRS) in England in the 1950s–60s to achieve law reform; the fact that England continues to have a discriminatory age of consent is due in large part to the on-going effect of the Wolfenden Report and the HLRS; see note 3. In Western Australia (WA), following a series of inflammatory and hostile debates, a law reform bill comprising a discriminatory age of consent (a five year age differential: 16 for hetero, 21 for homo), an anti-proselytizing measure and a preamble that reinforces many disturbing stereotypes and prejudices, was enacted. The Law Reform (Decriminalization of Sodomy) Act 1989 (WA) begins:

> WHEREAS the Parliament does not believe that sexual acts between consenting adults in private ought to be regulated by the criminal law;
> AND WHEREAS the Parliament disapproves of sexual relations between persons of the same sex;
> AND WHEREAS the Parliament disapproves of the promotion or encouragement of homosexual behaviour;
> AND WHEREAS the Parliament does not by its action in removing any criminal penalty for sexual acts in private between persons of the same sex wish to create a change in community attitude to homosexual behaviour;
> AND WHEREAS in particular the Parliament disapproves of persons with care supervision or authority over young persons urging them to adopt homosexuality as a lifestyle and disapproves of instrumentalities of the State so doing.

42. In sticking to this principle, the group was at times alienated from and risked total exclusion from all political decisions regarding law reform attempts; politicans often expressed themselves to be bewildered by the attitude of the group and used as evidence of a hidden agenda the fact that the TGLRG would not support their attempts to change the law.

43. Nick Toonen, interview with the author 25 November, 1998.

44. Witness the age of consent that still governs English homosex, 40 years after the Wolfenden Committee privately conceded that while 16 or 18 was the only legitimate age of consent, it would be best to wait for the furore of law reform to settle before further reform.

45. The Australian Government was requested to submit a defence and requested information from the Tasmanian Government as part of its preparation. The Tasmanian Government reiterated the objections it had made at the Admissibility stage (namely that Nick Toonen was not a victim as he had not been, and would not be, prosecuted under the criminal laws, and that he had not exhausted all domestic remedies before applying to the UNHRC), and added that the federal government should make reference to moral and health grounds as justification for the criminal laws as well as acknowledging that criminal laws form part of the democratic process and thus should not be open to review in the international arena. The federal government declined to make these arguments, and, after accepting that the laws were an arbitrary interference with Toonen's privacy, requested the UNHRC's guidance as to whether the Criminal Code Act (Tas) breached the equality provisions of the ICCPR. The Government refused, however, to accept the TGLRG argument that the stories of discrimination and violence outlined in the Communication could be directly traced to the existence of the unnatural sex provisions in the Act.

46. Egypt, Jordan, Senegal, Yugoslavia and Venezuela (this point was taken from Freedom House). Technically members of the UNHRC are not there as representatives of their countries but in their own rights as legal or human rights advocates. Opponents of the *Toonen* decision argued that a member has to be selected by his own government to be appointed to the Committee and that members do not have tenure (as, for example, politically appointed judges in Australia or the United States do) to guarantee their non-partisanship. For an example of this type of argument, see Mr Truss, Federal House of Representatives, Parliamentary Debates, *Hansard*, 13 October, 1994 at 1960–62.

47. Those countries being UK, USA, Japan, Egypt and Jordan.

48. In the face of strong criticisms of privacy, the TGLRG justified their recourse to privacy through utilization of a distinction between privacy as a result and privacy as a strategy.

> [The criticisms of privacy] do not invalidate the pursuit of privacy rights as a gay and lesbian rights strategy. It is possible to challenge a legal system which refuses to recognise our right to privacy within a context which affirms rather than denies gay and lesbian identity and sexuality and which sees the recognition of the right to privacy as just one part (albeit an important part in Tasmania) of an overall strategy for gay and lesbian rights. This is the strategy that has been pursued by the TGLRG and while many of our 'allies' in the campaign for criminal law reform still maintain a Wolfenden approach to the issue some of them are being won over to a broader and more affirmative perspective on the issue.

> See Rodney Croome, 'Australian gay rights case goes to the United Nations' *Australian Gay and Lesbian Law Journal* 6 (1992): 55.

49. As Wayne Morgan sums up, 'the text might transmit the truth through the stories it tells but without the endorsemement of the committee or Australian government', see note 35.

50. See *Dudgeon v United Kingdom* (1982), a decision of the Court of the European Convention of Human Rights.

51. Rodney Croome, interview with the author, 25 November, 1997.

> There are some very deeply essentialist older gay men around, as you can imagine and for some reason in rural Tasmania in particular there are a lot of people who have some views and are very vocal about them and they support gay law reform but have some old fashioned, incredibly old fashioned views, about homosexuality. I have been to meetings in country areas about gay law reform where people talk about third sex theories, and hormonal stuff from the fifties – it's bizzare.'

52. Mr Wilkinson MLC, Tasmanian Legislative Council, Parliamentary Debates, *Hansard*, 17 June, 1996 at 3.

53. Mr Shaw MLC, Tasmanian Legislative Council, Parliamentary Debates, *Hansard*, 17 June, 1996 at 9.

54. Mr Loone MLC, Tasmanian Legislative Council, Parliamentary Debates, *Hansard*, 17 June, 1996 at 12.

55. Mr Harris MLC, Tasmanian Legislative Council, Parliamentary Debates, *Hansard*, 16 April, 1997 at 22.

56. See Legislative Council debates in Committee on 24 April and 1 May 1997; the preamble, which would have contained references to the prevention of promotion of homosex and the desire that there not be a Mardigras or other celebrations in Tasmania, was rejected, again by a vote of one – albeit a different combination than that which accepted reform.

57. Consider also the issue raised by Wayne Morgan and Hillary Charlesworth, for example, that, as the rhetoric of international law is directed at holding the state accountable for breaches of human rights, the extent that this process helps to stop private abuses, must be questioned. See Hillary Charlesworth, 'Equality and non-discrimination under the optional protocol', unpublished paper, Melbourne University Law School, at 6.

58. Nick Toonen, see note 1.

59. Mr Fletcher MLC, Tasmanian Legislative Council, Parliamentary Debates, *Hansard*, 17 June, 1966 at 14.

60. Mr Aird MLC, Tasmanian Legislative Council, Parliamentary Debates *Hansard*, 17 June, 1996 at 34.

61. Richard Hale, interview with the author, 28 November 1997. Of course, it was not only the straight public who thought this was the case. One of the most powerful headlines following decriminalization in June 1997 was that of the *Melbourne Star Observer*, a prominent gay community paper, which covered its front page (literally) with the text: 'IT'S ALL OVER NOW'.

62. [You will be] hard pressed to find anything about assimilation in the Tasmanian debates. We always pushed that we wanted reform to acknowledge difference in the community. Most who supported us could see it was a diversity issue rather than a sameness thing ... and that's different than elsewhere ... diversity has not been the point elsewhere. Here gay law reform debate in the minds of most people who supported us is a symbol of a break from a really homogenised past.

Rodney Croome, supra note 2.

CHAPTER 4: REWRITING DESIRE: THE CONSTRUCTION OF SEXUAL IDENTITY IN LITERARY AND LEGAL DISCOURSE IN POST-COLONIAL IRELAND

1. This is a somewhat revised version of an article which first appeared in *Social and Legal Studies* 7 (1998): 409.

2. Eve Darian-Smith, 'Postcolonialism: a brief introduction', *Social and Legal Studies* 5 (1996): 291 at 297.

3. See e.g. Alpha Connelly, *Gender and the Law in Ireland* (Dublin: Oak Tree Press, 1993); Leo Flynn, 'Cherishing all her children equally': the law and politics of Irish lesbian and gay citizenship', *Social and Legal Studies* 6 (1997): 493; and Mary Robinson, 'Women and the law in Ireland'. *Women's Studies International Forum* 11 (1988): 351.

4. Julia Kristeva, *Powers of Horror: an Essay on Abjection* (New York: Columbia University Press, 1982).

5. Elizabeth Grosz, 'The body of signification', in Julia Fletcher and Andrew Benjamin, eds, *Abjection, Melancholia and Love: The Work of Julia Kristeva* (London: Routledge, 1990): 88–9.

6. Anne McClintock, *Imperial Leather: Race, Gender and Sexuality in the Colonial Contest* (New York: Routledge, 1995): 72.

7. The idea of a national narrative is captured by Donald Pease, ed., *National Identities and Post-Americanist Narratives* (Durham, NC: Duke University Press, 1994): 3: 'The term national narrative itself refers to the process whereby the discourse of the Enlightenment produced particulars – nation states – out of universal norms: Reason, Equality, Social Justice, Liberty. Acting as agents of the state, these national narratives constructed imaginary relations to actual sociopolitical conditions to effect imagined communities called national peoples.'

8. Homi K. Bhabha, ed., *Nation and Narration* (London: Routledge, 1990): 3.

9. E. Ann Kaplan, *Looking for the Other: Feminism, Film and the Imperial Gaze* (New York: Routledge, 1997): 32.

10. Joseph Valente, *James Joyce and the Problem of Justice: Negotiating Sexual and Colonial Difference* (Cambridge: Cambridge University Press, 1995): 34.

11. Declan Kiberd, *Inventing Ireland: The Literature of the Modern Canon* (London: Jonathan Cape, 1995).

12. Jeffrey Prager, *Building Democracy in Ireland: Political Order and Cultural Integration in a Newly Independent Nation* (Cambridge: Cambridge University Press, 1986): 31.
13. *Ibid*, p 42.
14. Julia Kristeva, *Nations Without Nationalism* (New York: Columbia University Press, 1993): 44.
15. Kiberd, *Inventing*, p 301.
16. Representations of homosexuality in Irish literature have been largely hidden in texts. Thus, while homosexuality has figured in Irish literature, it has largely been overlooked. One source of such repression was the strict censorship legislation introduced in the early years of the state which was used as means of excluding discussion of sexual difference. See, e.g., Keith Hopper, *Flann O'Brien: a Portrait of the Artist as a Young Postmodernist* (Cork: Cork University Press, 1995): 56–107; John R. Quinn, 'The lost language of the Irish gay male: textualization in Ireland's law and literature (or the most hidden Ireland)', *Columbia Human Rights Law Review* 26 (1995): 553; and Eibhear Walshe, ed., *Sex, Nation and Dissent in Irish Writing* (Cork: Cork University Press, 1997).
17. See, e.g., O'Brien's novels *Mary Lavelle* (London: Heinemann, 1936) and *As Music and Splendour* (London: Heinemann, 1958); and Eibhear Walshe, *Ordinary People Dancing: Essays on Kate O'Brien* (Cork: Cork University Press, 1993).
18. See, e.g. Brian Finnegan, ed., *Quare Fellas: New Irish Gay Writing* (Dublin: Basement Press, 1994); and Walshe, *Dissent*.
19. Geraldine Moane, 'A psychological analysis of colonialism in an Irish context', *The Irish Journal of Psychology* 15 (1994): 250.
20. Trevor Fisher, *Scandal: The Sexual Politics of Late Victorian Britain* (Stroud: Alan Sutton, 1995): 140.
21. See, e.g., Eve Kosofsky Sedgwick, *Epistemology of the Closet* (New York: Harvester Wheatsheaf, 1991): 2.
22. Cathy Honan, 137 *Seanad Debates* 29 June, 1993, 307, col 301.
23. David Beriss, 'If you're gay and Irish, your parents must be English', *Identities – Global Studies in Culture and Power* 2 (1996): 189, at 194.
24. Thomas Hofheinz, *Joyce and the Invention of Irish History: Finnegans Wake in Context* (Cambridge: Cambridge University Press, 1995): 37–8.
25. See, e.g., Eibhear Walshe, 'Sexing the shamrock', *Critical Survey* 8 (1996): 159.
26. *Ibid*, p 160.
27. McClintock, *Imperial Leather*, p 25.
28. See Colin Graham, 'Subalternity and gender: problems of post-colonial Irishness', *Journal of Gender Studies* 5 (1996): 363.
29. Vincent Cheng, 'Of canons, colonies, and critics: the ethics and politics of postcolonial Joyce studies', *Cultural Critique* 35 (1997): 81, at 85.
30. Derek Hand, 'Points of departure', *The Irish Literary Supplement* 18 (1999): 21, citing Gerry Smyth, *The Novel and the Nation: Studies in the new Irish Fiction* (London: Pluto Press, 1998).
31. See e.g., Jennifer Levine, 'James Joyce, tattoo artist: tracing the outlines of homosocial desire', *James Joyce Quarterly* 31 (1994): 277.
32. David Norris, 'The "unhappy mania" and Mr. Bloom's cigar: homosexuality in the Works of James Joyce', *James Joyce Quarterly* 31 (1994): 357.
33. See e.g., Leo Flynn, ' "Cherishing all her children equally": the law and politics of Irish lesbian and gay citizenship', *Social and Legal Studies* 6 (1997): 493.
34. Padraic Pearse, 'Little lad of the tricks', in Padraic Pearse *Plays, Stories, Poems* (Dublin: Maunsel, 1917): 316–17.
35. Lilis O'Laoire, 'Dearg dobhoghta chain/The indelible mark of Cain: sexual dissidence in the poetry of Cathal O'Searcaigh', in Walshe, *Dissent*, pp 221–34.
36. Emma Donoghue, ' "How could I fear thee and hold thee by the hand": the poetry of Eva Gore-Booth', in Walshe, *Dissent*, pp 16–42.
37. Jonathan Dollimore, *Sexual Dissidence: Augustine to Wilde, Freud to Foucault* (Oxford: Clarendon Press, 1991), p 62.
38. John Hutchinson, *The Dynamics of Cultural Nationalism: the Gaelic Revival and the Creation of the Irish State* (London: Allen and Unwin, 1987): 321.
39. Dominic Manganiello, *Joyce's Politics* (London: Routledge and Kegan Paul, 1980): 185.
40. Paul Ricoeur, 'The creativity of language', in Richard Kearney, *States of Mind: Dialogues with Con-tem orary Thinkers on the European Mind* (Manchester: Manchester University Press, 1995): 29–30.
41. See, e.g., Valente, *Problem of Justice*, p 34.
42. Kiberd, *Inventing*, p 391.
43. Carl Stychin, 'Queer nations: nationalism, sexuality and the discourse of rights in Quebec', *Feminist Legal Studies* 5 (1997): 25.

44. *Norris v Attorney-General* [1984] IR 36, 64.
45. Kenji Yoshino, 'Suspect symbols: the literary argument for heightened scrutiny for gays' *Columbia Law Review* 96 (1996): 1753, 1789.
46. Thomas O'Higgins, *The Irish Times*, 14 October, 1991, 8.
47. Ronald Dworkin, *Life's Dominion: an Argument About Abortion and Euthanasia* (London: HarperCollins, 1993): 119.
48. *Ibid*.
49. *Ibid*.
50. See, e.g., Roderick O'Hanlon, 'Natural rights and the Irish Constitution', *Irish Law Times* 1 (1993): 8.
51. Walter Murphy, 'An ordering of constitutional values', *Southern California Law Review* 51 (1980): 703.
52. Glenn Bowman, "'A country of words": conceiving the Palestinian nation from the position of exile', in Ernesto Laclau, ed., *The Making of Political Identities* (London: Verso, 1994): 144.
53. Cass Sunstein, 'Social norms and social roles', *Columbia Law Review* 96 (1996): 903, at 953.
54. *Ibid*, p 912.
55. Chris Robson, 'Anatomy of a campaign', in Ide O'Carroll and Eoin Collins, eds, *Lesbian and Gay Visions of Ireland: Towards the Twenty-first Century* (London: Cassell, 1995): 47–59.
56. Valente, *Problem of Justice*, p 80.
57. Leo Flynn, 'No gay people need apply', *Dublin University Law Journal* 16 (1994): 180.
58. Bruce Smith, *Homosexual Desire in Shakespeare's England* (Chicago: University of Chicago Press, 1991): 13–15.
59. Kiberd, *Inventing Ireland*, p 301.
60. Smith, *Desire*, p 22.
61. Ailbhe Smyth, '"And nobody was any the wiser": Irish abortion rights and the European Union', in Rebecca Elman, ed., *Sexual Politics and the European Union* (Providence, RI: Berghahn, 1996): 109–30.
62. Walshe, 'Sexing the shamrock', p 166.
63. Cited in O'Laoire, 'Indelible mark of Cain', p 232.
64. Lance Petit, 'Pigs and Provos, prostitutes and prejudice: gay representation in Irish film, 1984–1995', in Walshe, *Dissent*, p 254.
65. Anne Fogarty, 'The ear of the other: dissident voices in Kate O'Brien's *As Music and Splendour* and Mary Dorcey's *A Noise from the Woodshed*', in Walshe, *Dissent*, p 193.
66. Fogarty, 'Ear of the other', pp 195–6.
67. William Eskridge, 'Gay legal narratives', *Stanford Law Review* 46 (1994): 607, at 626.
68. Richard Kearney, *Poetics of Modernity: Toward a Hermeneutic Imagination* (Atlantic Highlands, NJ: Humanities Press, 1995): 105.
69. *Ibid*, p 100.

CHAPTER 5: THE DEVIANT GAZE: IMAGINING THE HOMOSEXUAL AS CRIMINAL THROUGH CINEMATIC AND LEGAL DISCOURSES

1. This piece of writing owes a great deal to those people whose suggestions and comments helped me refine and clarify my ideas as this work evolved. My heartfelt thanks and appreciation to Peter Rush, Carl Stychin, Alison Young and Leslie Moran for providing inspiration, motivation and much practical guidance. I also offer special thanks to my friends Rebecca Bray and Danielle Tyson for sharing ideas during our 'tea and sympathy' sessions.
2. Austin Sarat spoke of the similarities between law and cinema at the 9th Annual *Law and Literature Conference* in Beechworth, Australia, February, 1999. Films, he said, resemble law in that they invite judgment. By doing so films create a juridical space that is ripe for exploration.
3. Denvir, J., *Legal Realism, Movies as Legal Texts* (Chicago: University of Illinois Press, 1996): xii.
4. Denvir, *Legal Realism*, p xvi.
5. Alison Young's article, 'In the eyes of the law: the look of violence', *Australian Feminist Law Journal* 8 (1997): 9–26, reads law as it appears in the films *Psycho* and *The Silence of the Lambs*. Young's comparative analysis emphasizes the films' implications for a theory of legal identity given their fascination with subjectivity in law. It represents essential reading for anyone interested in theories of legal subjectivity, spectatorship and the thematics of law and order in film.

6. Millbank, J., 'From butcher to butcher's knife: film, crime and lesbian sexuality', *Sydney Law Review* 18 (1996): 451 at 452.

7. Elena Loizidou uses the cinematic text *Heavenly Creatures* to shed light on the processes that the criminal law uses to define bodies that come before it. See Loizidou, E. 'Intimate queer celluloid: heavenly creatures and criminal law' in L.J. Moran, D. Monk and S. Beresford, eds, *Legal Queeries: Lesbian, Gay and Transgender Issues* (London: Cassell, 1998).

8. Rosenberg cited in Denvir, 1996, *Legal Realism*, p xvii.

9. My thanks to Peter Rush for his insights into the complexities of *Cruising*'s narrative structure. To further understand the narrative structures and nuances of the detective genre (in particular detective fiction) and the pleasures associated with detecting vicariously see Chapter Four 'The scene of the crime: reading the justice of detective fiction' in Alison Young's *Imagining Crime* (London: Sage, 1996).

10. Despite the empirical fact that most violence against gay men is instigated by straight men, the film fails to canvass the possibility that the criminal is a heterosexual. Men who display leather are construed as homosexual and therefore become the sole focus of the film's investigation.

11. Paul Burston charts the notoriety surrounding the release of *Cruising*, arguing that 'reactions to *Cruising* say as much about the time when they were written as the film itself'. He asserts that the film's reputation, as one of the most homophobic films ever to come out of Hollywood, is undeserved; Burston, P., 'So good it hurts', in *Sight and Sound* 11 (1998): 24.

12. Tomsen, S., 'Was Lombroso a queer? Criminology, criminal justice and the heterosexual imaginary', in G. Mason and S. Tomsen, eds, *Homophobic Violence* (Sydney: Hawkins Press, 1997): 39. Such cases include: *R v M* (Supreme Court of Victoria, May, 1992); *Stiles v R* (1990) 50 A Crim R 13, 15; *R v Dunn* (Supreme Court of New South Wales, Grove J, 14 July, 1994); *R v O'Connor* (Supreme Court of Western Australia, 17 February, 1994) and *R v Bonner* (Supreme Court of New South Wales, Dowd J, 19 May, 1995). For a detailed list of cases involving anti-gay violence refer to Johnston, P., 'More than ordinary men gone wrong: can the law know the gay subject?', *Melbourne University Law Review* 20 (1996): 1153.

13. Peter Rush terms the killing of homosexuals in *Cruising* as 'an affair of homosexuality' (whether that of the victim, of the criminal, and often both). The film's narrative works towards attaching a homosexual intention to the death of gay men. The distinction between 'innocent' victim and 'guilty' criminal is blurred by the fact that each resembles the other. Both wear leather and are drawn to the scenes of the murders for a common pursuit (to engage in sex).

14. *Cruising* (1980), this disclaimer is presented in subtitles before the film commences.

15. Interestingly, adorning oneself in leather in *Cruising* imitates the law of contracts. A man clad in leather is framed as visually sending out a signal to those who gaze at him; his appearance mimicking the provision in contract law of 'an invitation to treat'. Indeed, the spectator comes to see the wilful display of leather in this film as flaunting with the risk of death.

16. The cinema has often made links between homosexuality and vampirism. Such films include *The Hunger* (1983, dir. Tony Scott), *Interview With The Vampire* (1994, dir. Neil Jordan) and *Nadja* (1994, dir. Michael Almereyda). Vampires have often been linked with the languid aesthete rather than the heavily physical type as depicted in *Cruising*. In regard to *Cruising* the vampire coding is related to the nocturnal world of the gay man being presented as analogous with vampires searching for victims at night – both operate under a veil of secretive darkness. The vampires' exchange of fluids (blood) is taken to be similar to the exchange of bodily fluids, which occur during homosexual sex. Both gay sex and vampire feeding on blood are bound up in notions of death and infection being linked to sexuality.

17. Twenty years after its initial release, some critics are reassessing the importance of *Cruising*'s depiction of this exotic underworld. Kermode argues that the film should be recognized as 'some kind of dark triumph' for its bold depiction of a world unseen elsewhere in modem cinema; Kermode, M., 'Cruise control: was cruising ever lethal to gays?' *Sight and Sound* 11 (1998): 22.

18. Russo, V., *The Celluloid Closet: Homosexuality in the Movies* (New York: Harper & Row, 1987): 237.

19. Stychin, C., *Law's Desire* (London: Routledge, 1995): 117. The idea of epidemic is applied in two ways: first to the risk of infection in regard to HIV/AIDS; and second to the notion that homosexuality is a contagion that can cause heterosexual men to be drawn into the ways of homosexuality (through seduction).

20. Friedkin arranged for the film's editor to 'drop in frames from a hardcore pornographic film each time a knife enters flesh', reinforced this connection between the violence and sex of the story (Kermode, 'Cruise control'). The effect of these inserted frames is extremely subliminal. The shots of anal penetration intercut with the murder scenes appear and disappear with such rapidity that many viewers don't consciously register having seen these images.

21. Redhead, S., *Unpopular Cultures: the Birth of Law and Popular Culture* (Manchester: Manchester University Press, 1995): 30; Redhead argues that popular culture and the formal discipline of cultural studies 'impinges on jurisprudential thinking as never before' and that legal theorists must necessarily devote their energies to the ways in which law and popular culture intersect.

22. In sentencing Koeleman, Cummins J spoke of the murdered man, Francis Arnoldt, as an 'inevitable and anonymous victim, another homosexual'. Such a description seems to imply that homosexual identity is attributed with a fatalistic propensity to victimhood. Cummins J contributes to the mythologizing of homosexual encounters as monstrous events by utilizing a generic trope to begin his narration of the murder events in passing sentence – 'And so it was that, on a dark and rainy night ... you took a large knife and went to a well-known homosexual beat....'

23. *The Age*, 'Movie linked to gay killing', 2 September, 1998.

24. An application to appeal the sentence and conviction has been lodged by Koeleman. Some media commentators are alleging that the Koeleman verdict represents a gross miscarriage of justice. Koeleman's confession, they claim, was merely a fanciful story told to arouse an ex-boyfriend. The manner in which Koeleman was coaxed into retelling this 'story' over lunch and drinks at a restaurant (a conversation which was covertly tape recorded) will be a matter raised in the course of his appeal. See 'Jamie Koeleman's story', in *Brother/Sister*, 13 May, 1999, p 11.

25. *Herald Sun*, '19 years for "Cruising" gay murder', 27 March, 1999.

26. *The Director of Public Prosecutions v Jamie Koeleman (Sentence)*, Supreme Court of Victoria, 119, 26 March, 1999.

27. *The Director of Public Prosecutions v Jamie Koeleman (Sentence)*, Supreme Court of Victoria, 119, 26 March, 1999.

28. *Herald Sun*, '19 years for "Cruising" gay murder', 27 March, 1999.

29. The jury were shown various excerpts from *Cruising* and it was argued that the murder was a sexually inspired killing modelled on the killings that are depicted in the film. It was argued that Koeleman sought to emulate the killer in the film by stabbing his victim in, or at least related to, the act of orgasm.

30. These so-called 'raft of different factual scenarios' relate to the fact that the killer in *Cruising* murders some victims before intercourse, others after intercourse, and that he sometimes ties the victims up.

31. Ruling no. l in the matter of *DPP v Koeleman*, 1 March, 1999, at 36.

32. *Ibid.*

33. *The Director of Public Prosecutions v Jamie Koeleman (Sentence)*, Supreme Court of Victoria, 119, 26 March, 1999.

34. Young, A., *Imagining Crime* (London: Sage, 1996): 22.

35. In an interview with Kermode ('Cruise control'), Friedkin stresses that the men in the club scenes aren't extras. Rather, they are the guys who frequented clubs like Manhattan's Ramrod (featured in the film) and Mineshaft. Friedkin said of their behaviour in the film – 'they did their own thing'.

36. Freeman-Greene, S., 'A night to remember', in *The Age – Good Weekend Magazine*, Saturday 29 November, 1997, p 19. During the drag queen's rendition of a song called 'Dirty Money', balloons were burst causing fake money to rain down on patrons. The symbolism of the fake money in the balloons was clear. It alluded to the notoriety of an official investigation called Operation Bart into Victorian Police Officers receiving 'kickbacks' from window shutter companies as payment for directing business their way.

37. Another film which frames homosexual desire as a precipitator of death is *Apartment Zero* (1989, dir. Martin Donovan) in which the serial killer Jack Carney exchanges a desiring gaze with a young man at an airport concourse. This scene is immediately followed by the gruesome image of the young man lying dead on a bed in a Buenos Aires hotel room, having been murdered by Carney as the culmination of their sexual encounter.

38. Howe, A., 'More folk provoke their own demise homophobic violence and sexed excuses – rejoining the provocation law debate, courtesy of the homosexual advance defence', *Sydney Law Review* 19 (1997): 336 at 338.

39. Supreme Court of New South Wales Criminal Division, nos 70372–70377 of 1990, 15.4, p 21. For a particularly original analysis of strategic stories told to, by and of the courts in relation to acts of violence directed at gay men see: Kiley, D. 'Real stories: true narratology, false narratives and a trial', *Australian Journal of Law and Society* 12 (1996): 37–48.

40. This case arose after a police investigation code-named 'Operation Spanner', which led to the arrest of a group of approximately 40 gay male sadomasochists in the United Kingdom. Many of these men were charged with and eventually convicted of various counts of assault and wounding. Despite the fact they raised the defence that they had consented to the performance of these acts on each other in private, their appeals to the House of Lords were dismissed.

41. *R. v Brown* (1993) 2 All ER 75 (HL).
42. Stychin, *Law's Desire*, p 129.
43. *Cruising* suggests that Stuart is driven by a need to literally kill his own desire. In a disturbing fantasy sequence within the film Stuart imagines meeting with his cold, detached father (later revealed to be long dead) who tells him 'You know what you have to do'. Thus Stuart's murderous rampage is seen to partly emanate from his father's express wish that he 'do' something about his homosexuality.
44. Russo, *The Celluloid Chart*, p 259.
45. Glass, 1997, p 36.
46. *Swoon* utilizes a fractured narrative and experimental format – involving scripted dramatic narrative, archival footage from the 1920s and contemplation on the use of photography and phrenology to construct criminal and sexual deviants.
47. Jones, C., 'Lesbian and gay cinema', in J. Nelmes, ed., *An Introductin to Film Studies* (London: Routledge, 1996): 285.
48. Francke, L., '*Swoon*', *Sight and Sound* 2 (September, 1992): 59. Despite its signification of history and memory, the film incorporates anachronistic details (such as touch tone telephones) to resituate the story in a perpetual present.
49. Taubin, A., 'Beyond the sons of Scorsese: *Swoon*, feminism and the limits of the new cinema', *Sight and Sound* 2 (September 1992): 37.
50. Burston, P., 'Killing time', in *What are you looking at: Queer Sex, Style and Cinema* (London: Cassell, 1995): 136.
51. *Swoon* presents the exchange of sex for crime through narrated extracts from Nathan's diary accompanied by images of the men passionately making love. The entries trace the gradual increase in severity of the crimes committed and serves to remind the spectator that this is the basis of their 'marriage'.

> March 4th 1923: Dickie threw a brick through the window of the Paul Syn drug store window.
> Sept 9th 1923: We burned a building near the train station. We watched the firemen extinguish it.
> Sept 28th 1923: We broke into a frat house and stole a typewriter. Dick says we can use it for the ransom letter.
> October 13 1923: I've waited 6 weeks since our last crime. He's letting me down again.
> May 20th 1924: Nathan bought a chisel and 30 feet of rope. I'm afraid he'll ruin everything.
> Dec 25th 1924: Dick and I argued about the boy. He wants to kidnap his brother and collect the ransom from his father. He wants to be a pallbearer at the funeral.

52. This pact in the film of Nathan participating in criminal acts in exchange for Richard engaging in sexual acts functions as a classic SM configuration of dominance and submission. But it is not so simple as Richard being in control of Nathan, as the film suggests that they were both the master and slave depending on whether either party was demanding crime or sex. The film uses the sound of a whiplash to signify that either man was exerting dominance over the other. Similarly, the sound of bird wings fluttering signified some aspect of submissive behaviour.
53. Busch, F., *Notable American Trials: Prisoners at the Bar* (New York: Bobbs Merrill, 1952): p 169. [As extracted from the judgement of *People of the State of Illinois Nathan Leopold, Jr, and Richard Loeb*.]
54. Peter Rush's notes in Hocquenghem's text *Homosexual Desire* first alerted me to the distinction that the term 'desire' in part derives from the term 'sire' – to father, breed and in archaic form – to 'beget'. This distinction is a reminder that the process of desiring entails reproductive, spawning potential. Interestingly, the 'marriage' in *Swoon* will not beget children, but rather will herald the conception and execution of criminal plans. Leopold and Loeb are thus presented as veritable 'bad seeds'.
55. This sets up a two-fold structure that facilitates the following readings. The heterosexual coupling of male and female produces a child. Conversely, the homosexual coupling of Leopold and Loeb produces crimes. Thus child and crime are presented as the binding agents that are characteristic of heterosexuality and homosexuality respectively. In this sense crimes are held to naturally belong to homosexuals in the same way that children naturally belong to heterosexuals.
56. Richard and Nathan's identities seem to become intertwined after the murder. It is as if the murder has made them one. When giving evidence to the police Richard confuses himself with Nathan – 'I' becomes 'he'.
57. Kalin (text from Connoisseur video film notes accompanying the video release), 1992.
58. Busch, *Notable American Trials*, p 187.

59. Murray, R., ed., *Images in the Dark: an Encyclopaedia of Gay and Lesbian Film and Video* (Philadelphia: TLA, 1994): 392. This novel was adapted and made into the film *Compulsion* (1959, dir. Richard Fleischer). The homosexuality of the men was inferred due to the operation of the production code, however the inferences were sufficient enough for critics at the time to characterise the two 'dirty little degenerates' as homosexual lovers.
60. Russo, *The Celluloid Closet*, p 309.
61. *Ibid*, p 309.
62. Sedgwick, E. K., *Epistemology of the Closet* (Berkeley: University of California Press, 1990): 23.
63. Hundley, J., 'The dark side: Todd Verow gets frisky' (interview with Todd Verow (http://www.phx.com).
64. In an erotically charged fantasy scene in *Swoon,* Richard and Nathan are depicted having sex in a huge bed in the middle of the courtroom while the courtroom audience fails to notice what is going on. The scene suggests the paradox of law's ambivalent relationship to the (in)visibility of homosexuality. For at times the law is highly anxious to see and identify homosexuals (e.g. to exclude gay men from the military), yet at other times the law is wilfully blind to their presence.

CHAPTER 6: HOMOSEXUAL ADVANCES IN LAW: MURDEROUS EXCUSE, PLURALIZED IGNORANCE AND THE PRIVILEGE OF UNKNOWING

1. The author wishes to thank Samantha Fradd for helping her formulate the ideas in this chapter.
2. Malcolm Green quoted by Kirby J in *Green v the Queen* (1997) 148 ALR 659, 700.
3. Tom Molomby, '"Revisiting lethal violence by men" – a reply', *Criminal Law Journal* 22 (1998): 116.
4. Molomby was responding to Graeme Coss, 'Lethal violence by men', *Criminal Law Journal* 20 (1996): 305.
5. Adrian Howe, '*Green v The Queen* – the provocation defence: finally provoking its own demise?' *Melbourne University Law Review* 22 (1998): 466.
6. *Ibid*, p 488. See also Adrian Howe, 'Provoking comment: the question of gender bias in the provocation defence – a Victorian case study', in Norma Grieves and Ailsa Burns, eds *Australian Women: Contemporary Feminist Thought* (Melbourne: Oxford University Press, 1994); and Adrian Howe, 'More folk provoke their own demise: homophobic violence and sexed excuses – rejoining the provocation law debate, courtesy of the homosexual advance defence', *Sydney Law Review* 19 (1997): 336.
7. Susan Edwards, 'Provoking their own demise: from common assault to homicide', in Jalna Hanmer and Mary Maynard, eds, *Women, Violence and Social Control* (London: Macmillan Press, 1987). For a recent feminist critique of gender-bias in the operation of the provocation defence in Australia see Jenny Morgan, 'Provocation law and the facts: dead women tell no tales, tales are told about them', *Melbourne University Law Review* 21 (1997): 237.
8. Eve Sedgwick, *Epistemology of the Closet* (Berkeley: University of California Press, 1990): 1.
9. *Ibid*, pp 4–5.
10. Sedgwick, E., 'Privilege of unknowing: Diderot's *The Nun*', in Eve Sedgwick, *Tendencies* (Durham: Duke University Press, 1993): 23.
11. See, e.g., Sagri Dhairyam, 'Racing the lesbian, dodging white critics', in Laura Doan, ed., *The Lesbian Postmodern* (New York, Columbia University Press, 1994) and Mary Eaton, 'Homosexual unmodified: speculations on law's discourse, race and the construction, sexual identity', in Didi Herman and Carl Stychin, eds, *Legal Inversions: Lesbians, Gay Men and the Politics of Law* (Philadelphia: Temple University Press, 1995).
12. 'Privilege of unknowing', pp 24–5.
13. *Ibid* (her emphasis).
14. Adrian Howe, 'Fictioning consent in (sexual) assault cases: bridging the gap between judicial and feminist understandings of sexuality and the law (or: "pigs might fly")', *Critical Inqueeries* 1(3) (1997): 35.
15. Linda Alcoff and Laura Grey, 'Survivor discourse: transgression or recuperation?', *Signs* 18 (1993): 268.
16. 'Privilege of unknowing', pp 24, 27–8 and 39.
17. Coss, 'Lethal violence by men', p 305.

18. See, e.g. Gary Comstock, 'Dismantling the homosexual panic defence', *Law and Sexuality* 2 (1992): 81; Joshua Dressier, 'When "heterosexual" men kill "homosexual men": reflections on provocation law, sexual advances and the "reasonable man" standard', *Journal of Criminal Law and Criminology* 85 (1995): 726; Robert Mison, 'Homophobia in manslaughter: the homosexual advance defence as insufficient provocation', *California Law Review* 80 (1992): 133. This literature is critically discussed in Howe, 'More folk provoke their own demise.'

19. Anthony Bendall and Tim Leach, '*Homosexual Panic Defence' and Other Family Values* (Sydney: Lesbian and Gay Anti-Violence Project, 1995): 9.

20. Supreme Court of Victoria, Teague J, 28 May, 1992.

21. For an excellent analysis of this case see Peter Johnston, ' "More than ordinary men gone wrong": can the law know the gay subject?,' *Melbourne University Law Review* 20 (1996): 1152.

22. Unreported, New South Wales Supreme Court, Studdard J, 24 November 1993.

23. Barbara Farrelly, 'Roll a fag and go free', *Sydney Star Observer*, 10 December, 1993, p 1.

24. See New South Wales Attorney-General's Working Party on the Review of the Homosexual Advance Defence, *Review of the Homosexual Advance Defence* (Sydney: Government Printer, 1996).

25. See, e.g. Howe, 'More folk provoke their own demise' which is cited in support of the recommendation to abolish the defence of provocation in the Model Criminal Code Officers Committee of the Standing Committee of the Attorney-Generals, 'Chapter five: fatal offences against the person', *Discussion Paper: Model Criminal Code* (Canberra: MCCOC, 1998): 69, 99.

26. *Green*, p 676.

27. Unreported, New South Wales CCA, Priestley JA, 8 November, 1995, pp 10–11.

28. *Ibid*, pp 13–15, 26–8.

29. *Green*, p 660.

30. *Ibid*, p 662.

31. *Ibid*, p 664.

32. For a queer theory reading of the use of stereotypes such as the representation of the victim as predator and the defendant as prey in the majority judgments in *Green* see Nathan Hodge, 'Transgressive sexualities and the homosexual advance', *Alternative Law Journal* 23 (1998): 30.

33. *Green*, p 665.

34. New South Wales, CCA, 8 November, 1995, Smart J, pp 22–3.

35. *Green*, p 665.

36. *Ibid*, pp 675–6.

37. *Ibid* (my emphasis).

38. 171 CLR (1990) 312.

39. *Green*, p 65.

40. *Ibid*, p 663 (my emphasis).

41. See Hilary Allen, 'One law for all reasonable persons?', *International Journal of the Sociology of Law* 16 (1987): 419.

42. *Green*, p 696.

43. *Ibid*, p 665.

44. On 'sexual provocation' see Ian Leader-Elliot, 'Passion and insurrection in the law of sexual provocation', in Ngaire Naffine and Rosemary Owens, eds, *Sexing the Subject of Law* (North Ryde, NSW: LBC Information Services, 1997).

45. Leslie J. Moran, *The Homosexual(ity) of Law* (London: Routledge, 1996): 121.

46. *Stingel v R* (1990) 171 CLR 312, 332.

47. *Green*, p 674.

48. *Ibid*, pp 674–5.

49. *Ibid*, p 682.

50. *Ibid*, p 683.

51. *Ibid*, p 683 (my emphasis). McHugh J's argument is marred by the same conceptual flaws as that of his source, Joshua Dressier, 'When "heterosexual" men kill', Dressler's narrative of 'justifiable indignation' is critiqued in Howe, 'More folk provoke their own demise'.

52. 'Privilege of unknowing', p 50 (her emphasis).

53. Justice Kirby has since outed himself in *Who's Who in Australia,* xxxvth ed. (1999): 969.

54. *Green*, pp 693–4.

55. *Ibid*, pp 694–5.

56. *Ibid*, pp 696–7.

57. *Ibid*, p 698.

58. *Ibid*, pp 700–1.

59. *Ibid*, p 704.

60. *Ibid*, pp 707–8
61. *Ibid*, p 712.
62. *Ibid*, p 714.
63. *Ibid*.
64. *Ibid*, p 718.
65. *Ibid*, p 719.
66. *Ibid*.
67. Molomby, 'Revisiting lethal violence', p 116.
68. New South Wales, CCA, 8 November, 1995, Priestley JA, p 26.
69. Judith Butler, 'Melancholy gender/refused identification', in Maurice Berger, Brian Wallis and Simon Watson, eds, *Constructing Masculinity* (New York: Routledge, 1995): 24–5, 27.
70. Sedgwick, 'Privilege of unknowing', p 51.
71. Molomby, 'Revisting lethal violence', p 118.

CHAPTER 7: PERVERTING LONDON:
THE CARTOGRAPHIC PRACTICES OF LAW

1. Sir J. Nott-Bower, Memorandum by Sir John Nott-Bower KVCR, Commissioner of the Police of the Metropolis, *Homosexual Offences* (London: Public Records Office, 1954), HO 345/7.
2. Sir J. Wolfenden, *Report of the Departmental Committee on Homosexual Offences and Prostitution*, Cmnd 247 (London: HMSO, 1957).
3. At the time of the memorandum this offence was to be found in section 1 of the Vagrancy Act of 1898. It was replaced by the Sexual Offences Act 1956, section 32, which reads as the following: 'It is an offence for a man persistently to solicit or importune in a public place for immoral purposes.'
4. At the time of the memorandum the offence of gross indecency was to be found in section 11 of the Criminal Law Amendment Act 1885. It was re-enacted in section 13 of the Sexual offences Act 1956 which reads as follows: 'It is an offence for a man to commit an act of gross indecency with another man, whether in public or in private, or to be a party to the commission by a man of an act of gross indecency with another man, or to procure the commission by a man of an act of gross indecency with another man.'
5. See also: Blomley, N.K., *Law, Space and the Geographies of Power* (London: Guilford Press, 1994) for an examination of the relationship between law and space.
6. See also McMullan, J.L., 'Social surveillance and the rise of the "police machine"', *Theoretical Criminology* 2(1) (1998) 93–117; Lowman, J., 'The geography of social control: clarifying some themes', in D.J. Evans and D.T. Herbert eds, *The Geography of Crime* (London: Routledge, 1989): 229–59.
7. Public Records Office, MEPO 8/2.
8. Bourdieu, P., *Outline of a Theory of Practice* (Cambridge: Cambridge University Press, 1977): 2.
9. See note 1, para 28, p 12.
10. *Ibid*.
11. *Horton v Mead* [1913] 1 KB 154.
12. *Ibid*, at 154–5.
13. Foucault, M., *The History of Sexuality, Vol. 1: an Introduction* (London, Penguin 1981): 18.
14. All extracts are to be found in *Horton v Mead*, at 155.
15. This is not a characteristic peculiar to the specific offence of soliciting or importuning for immoral purposes, cf. (1990) CrAppR 157 which deals with the common law offences of acts outraging public decency.
16. *Horton v Mead*, at 158.
17. See also Moran, L.J., *The Homosexual(ity) of Law* (London: Routledge, 1996).
18. Public Records Office, MEPO 3/990.
19. The accused appeared at Tower Bridge Police Court (a court of summary jurisdiction) the following day, before W.H.S. Oulton, Esq., Magistrate, and was remanded on bail. No evidence was given as the accused requested to be legally represented.
20. Humphreys, L., *The Tearoom Trade* (London: Duckworth, 1970).
21. *Ibid*.
22. Butler, J., 'Gendering the body: Beauvoir's philosophical contribution', in A. Garry (ed.) *Women, Knowledge and Reality* (New York: Routledge, 1989): 253–62, at 256.

23. Bell, D., 'Perverse dynamics, sexual citizenship and the transformation of intimacy', in D. Bell and G. Valentine, eds, *Mapping Desire* (London: Routledge, 1995): 304–17.
24. Bell, D., 'Pleasure and danger: the paradoxical spaces of sexual citizenship', *Political Geography* 4/2 (1995): 145–53, at 147.
25. D. Woodhead, 'Surveillant gays: HIV space and the constitution of identity', in D. Bell and G. Valentine, eds, *Mapping Desire* (London: Routledge): 231–45, at 238.
26. Turner, V., *The Ritual Process* (New York: Cornell University Press, 1977): 95.
27. Shields, R., *Places on the Margin* (London: Routledge, 1991): 84.
28. Bell, 'Pleasure and danger', 24, at 147.
29. Bell, 'Perverse dynamics'.
30. Bakhtin, M., *Problems of Dostoevsky's Poetics*, trans. R.W. Rotsel (USA: Ardis, 1973); Shields, *Places on the Margin*.
31. Dollimore, cited in Bell, 'Pleasure and danger'.
32. Lord Devlin, in his Maccabean lecture (1958), describes society as being entitled to be protected by laws which protect it not only from dangers from 'without' but also from the corrupting dangers from 'within' our society: Devlin, P., *The Enforcement of Morals* (Oxford: Oxford University Press, 1965): 13.
33. Fox, N.J., *Postmodernism, Sociology and Health* (Milton Keynes: Open University Press, 1993): 62.

CHAPTER 8: 'MAKING A MOCKERY OF MARRIAGE': DOMESTIC PARTNERSHIP AND EQUAL RIGHTS IN HAWAI'I

1. An expanded version of this chapter appears as 'The Status of Status: Domestic Partnership and the Politics of Same-Sex Marriage', *Studies in Law, Politics and Society* 19 (1999): 3–38.
2. (1993) 74 Haw 530.
3. (1996) Civil no. 91-1394, Circuit Court, State of Hawai'i.
4. (1996) 28 USCS section 1738c DOMA also defines marriage as the union of one man and one woman and permits states to ignore marriages from any states not comporting with this model. This is in spite of federal constitutional admonitions to grant 'Full faith and credit' to 'each state to the public acts, records and judicial proceedings of every other state' (Article IV, section 1) and to prevent states from 'impairing the obligation of contracts'. (Article I, section 10, p 1).
5. For a discussion of Fordism from this institutional perspective, see Gramsci, A., *Selections from the Prison Notebook of Antonio Gramsci* (New York: International Publishers, 1971): 277–318; Harvey, D., *The Condition of Postmodernity* (Oxford: Blackwell, 1989); Lipietz, A., 'Post-Fordism and democracy', in A. Amin, ed., *Post-Fordism: a Reader* (Oxford: Blackwell, 1994); Rupert, M., *Producing Hegemony* (Cambridge: Cambridge University Press, 1995).
6. The amendment, which reads 'The legislature shall have the power to reserve marriage to opposite-sex couples', was ultimately passed by a 69.2% affirmative vote of the electorate in November, 1998. I address the significance of this vote in the conclusion of this chapter.
7. (1997) Hawai'i Revised Statutes section 572C.
8. (1997) *Ibid*, section 572C-2.
9. *Ibid*.
10. These included inheritance rights and survivorship benefits; health-related rights including hospital visitation, family and funeral leave, private and public employee health insurance, mental health commitment approvals; motor vehicle insurance coverage; jointly held property rights such as tenancy in the entirety and public land leases; legal standing for wrongful death, crime victims' rights and domestic violence family status; and some minor benefits related to the use of state facilities and state properties. Left unavailable, but attainable through marriage, were mutual support, divorce, child custody, and federal and state tax advantages and liabilities associated with marriage, most precluded by the Defense of Marriage Act.
11. (1997) Hawai'i Revised Statutes section 572C-6.
12. See Progress non-profit organization publication (Domestic Partner Listing http://www.bayscenes.com/np/progress/dpb.htm) and National Lesbian and Gay Journalists Association publication (Domestic Partner Benefits http://www.nlgja.org/programs/DP/Dpother.htm).
13. Exceptions include Hawai'i, which eliminated medical insurance benefits after a legal challenge, and the cities of Austin, Texas, where voters passed an ordinance in 1994 nullifying the extension of benefits to city employees, Minneapolis, Minnesota, where a court invalidated domestic partner

benefits, and the District of Columbia where Congress has refused to fund a domestic partnership law passed in 1992. In the private sector, only one high-profile company has rolled back benefits: Perot Systems in 1998.

14. Ed Vitagliano, 'Why Boycott Disney?' *American Family Association Journal* (1997) reprinted at http://www.otherside.net/disnebct.htm.

15. *Perot Nixes Gay Partner Insurance*, AP News services, 9 April, 1998.

16. Written testimony of Tom Humphreys, Secretary of Alliance for Equal Rights, submitted to the Hawai'i House Judiciary Committee, 21 January, 1997, dated 20 January, 1997.

17. As one advocate of domestic partnership recalls in a letter submitted for testimony before the Hawai'i Commission on Sexual Orientation and the Law considering same-sex marriage, 'Back in the late 1980s, I was one of the vocal advocates within Lambda's [Legal Defense and Education Association] civil rights roundtable for bringing marriage litigation. Now I am much less ardent on this score, since I am convinced that the marriage issue (like, probably, the military issue) can only be resolved in the realm of politics, not adjudication'. Testimony of Arthur S. Leonard, submitted 29 November, 1995.

18. (1998) Louisiana Revised Stamtes 9:272A.

19. Grossberg envisions this connection between family and state in his study of nineteenth century domestic relations law in the following manner:

> Under the sway of republican theory and culture, the home and the polity displayed some striking similarities. These included a deep aversion to unaccountable authority and unchecked governmental activism, the equation of property rights with independence, a commitment to self-government, a belief that individual virtue could prevent the abuse of power, and a tendency to posit human relations in contractual terms that highlighted voluntary consent, reciprocal duties, and the possibility of dissolution. Most important, the American family, like the republican polity, suffered from the uncertainties of sovereignty and from the pressures of democratization and marketplace values unleashed by the Revolution's egalitarian and laissez faire ideology' (Grossberg, M., *Governing the Hearth: Law and the Family in Nineteenth-century America* (Chapel Hill: University of North Carolina Press, 1985): 6–7.

20. Author's interview with Father Marc Alexander, Co-Chair, *Hawai'i's Future Today*, March, 1998. Hereinafter, 'Alexander'.

21. Author's interview with Diane Kurtz, Spokesperson for *Save Traditional Marriage '98*, March, 1998. Hereinafter, 'Kurtz'.

22. In American equal protection law, protected class status acknowledges the social characteristics of age, race, gender, and national origin around which remedial and protective mechanisms can be asserted in the interest of social integration. Sexual orientation is not an included characteristic for these purposes. The lack of protected status along with the liberalization of laws pertaining to 'containment' has meant gays and lesbians occupy a liminal territory within the law, with implications for radical identity formation challenging liberal boundaries, see Bower, L., 'Queer problems/straight solutions: the limits of a politics of "Official recognition", in S. Phelan, ed., *Playing with Fire: Queer Politics, Queer Theories* (New York: Routledge, 1997): 267. This has amplified the significance of political discourses about rights, such as those I discuss here, for new conceptions of sovereignty.

23. Testimony of William Woods, Executive Director of Gay and Lesbian Education and Advocacy, before the Hawai'i House Judiciary Committee, 21 January, 1997.

24. Author's interview with Bill Paul, Spokesperson for *Save Traditional Marriage '98*, February, 1998. Hereinafter, 'Paul'.

25. Author's interview with Debi Hartmann, Co-Chair, *Hawai'i's Future Today*, February, 1998. Hereinafter 'Hartmann'.

26. Written testimony of Frederick Rohlfing II, before the Commission on Sexual Orientation and the Law, 25 October, 1995, p 11.

27. Written testimony of Jim Hochberg, minority member of the Governor's Commission on Sexual Orientation and the Law, submitted to the Hawai'i House Judiciary Committee, 21 January, 1997, dated 19 January, 1997.

28. Because the RBA was enacted to cover more than just gay and lesbian relationships the Governor refused to sign the bill, allowing it to become law without his signature. His act of refusal also symbolizes the claim that the RBA has leapt beyond its proper bounds.

29. Testimony of Mike Gabbard, Chairman, Alliance for Traditional Marriage, before the Hawai'i House Judiciary Committee, 21 January, 1997.

30. Testimony of Rick Lazor before the Hawai'i House Judiciary Committee 21 January, 1997.

31. Written testimony of Tom Ramsey submitted to the Hawai'i House Judiciary Committee, 21 January, 1997, dated 20 January, 1997.
32. Written testimony of Owen-Pahl Greene, submitted to the Hawai'i House Judiciary Committee, 21 January, 1997.
33. Written testimony of Wayne Akana submitted to the Hawai'i House Judiciary Committee 21 January, 1997, dated 20 January, 1997.
34. Written Testimony of Tracey Bennett submitted to the Hawai'i House Judiciary Committee, 21 January, 1997.
35. Letter from Governor Pete Wilson to California Assembly dated 11 September, 1994.
36. Testimony of Marie Sheldon, member of the dissenting minority on the Governor's Commission on Sexual Orientation and the Law, before the Hawai'i House Judiciary Committee, 21 January, 1997.
37. Archbishop John Quinn of San Francisco, *San Francisco Catholic,* October, 1989, p 7.
38. Testimony of Bishop Richard Lipka, before the Hawai'i House Judiciary Committee, 21 January, 1997.
39. Mike Gabbard, Chair of Alliance for Traditional Marriage, Hawai'i, *Honolulu Advertiser,* 30 November, 1998, p B2.
40. Press Release of Mike Gabbard, Chair of Alliance for Traditional Marriage, Hawai'i, 5 November, 1998.
41. Mary Polly, Letter to the Editor, *Honolulu Star Bulletin* 13 November, 1998, on-line version.
42. Randy Obata, Communications Director for Governor Benjamin Cayetano, Letter to the Editor, *Honolulu Star Bulletin,* 18 November, 1998, p A21.

CHAPTER 9: HOW TO DO THINGS WITH SEX

1. Thanks to Carol Johnson, Barry Hindess and Barbara Sullivan for their valuable suggestions for improvements to this paper. Thanks also to the staff and students of the Centre for Women's Studies at the Australian National University for their generous response to this work while it was very much 'in progress'. Special thanks to Rod Butlin, Rebecca Stringer and Meredith Walsh for ceaseless good humour and helpfulness. My greatest debt, however, rests with the late Sarah Zetlein, whose many conversations (and disagreements) with me continue to inspire and provoke. I dedicate this essay to her memory.
2. In this paper, I limit my remarks to heterosexual vs 'homosexual' (that is, gay and lesbian) relationships. There is much more to be said about transgender/transsexual politics and marriage; see Bates, F., 'When is a wife . . .?', *Australian Journal of Family Law* 7 (1993): 274–82; Mountbatten, J., 'Transsexuals and social security Law: the return of Gonad the Barbarian', *Australian Journal of Family Law* 8(2) (1994): 166–77 Sharpe, A.N., 'The transsexual and marriage: law's contradicting desires', *Australian Gay and Lesbian Law Journal* 7 (1997): 1–14; Ottowski, M., 'The legal status of a sexually reassigned transsexual: R v Harris and McGuiness and beyond', *Australian Law Journal* 640–2 (1990): 67–74; Mackenzie, R., 'Transsexuals' legal status and same sex marriage in New Zealand: M v M', *Otago Law Review* 7(4) (1992): 556–77; Smith, D.K., 'Transsexualism, sex reassignment surgery, and the law', *Cornell Law Review* 56 (1971): 963–1009; Finlay, H.A. and Walters, W.A.W., *Sex Change: Medical and Legal Aspects of Sex Reassignment* (Box Hill, Victoria: H.A. Finlay, 1988); Califa, P., *Sex Changes: The Politics of Transgenderism* (San Francisco: Cleis Press, 1997). However, I cannot hope to do justice to this debate in the limited space available here.
3. Austin, J.L., in J.O. Urmson, ed., *How to do Things with Words,* The William James Lectures delivered in Harvard University in 1955 (London: Oxford University Press, 1962): 5; Warnock, G.J., 'Some types of performative utterance', in Berlin *et al., Essays on J.L. Austin* (London: Clarendon Press, 1973): 69–89, at 70; Day, L., 'Who authorizes speech acts? Woolf's *Orlando* responds', occasional paper no 21 (Clayton: The Centre for Women's Studies, Monash University, 1996): 5; Forguson, L.W., 'In pursuit of performatives,' in K.T. Fann, ed., *Symposium on J.L. Austin* (London: Routledge and Kegan Paul, 1969): 412–9, at 415; Searle, J.R., 'How performatives work', *Linguistics and Philosophy* 12 (1989): 535–58, at 554; Parker, A. and Sedgwick, E.K., eds, 'Introduction: performativity and performance', in *Performativity and Performance* (New York: Routledge, 1995): 1–18, at 9.
4. In fact, as Austin's editor also notes (Austin, *How to do Things with Words,* p 5, note 2), 'I do' is not an utterance normally required in wedding ceremonies. In Australia, the Marriage Act 1961 outlines the prescribed utterances, which include both bride and groom saying 'I, [name], take thee, [name], to be my lawful wedded husband/wife' (among other utterances, including, usually 'I will'). Using

'I do' as an example of performance utterance in wedding remains, however, a convenient (though inaccurate) shorthand.

5. I prefer to use 'authorized/unauthorized' rather than Austin's 'happy/unhappy' terminology to mark the success or failure of a performative utterance. At issue is the conventional success or failure of the performative rather than its 'mood'.

6. Butler also connects speaking subjectivities to the regulation of speech, but draws her conclusions from a different and more abstract context.

7. In Australia, the relevant legislation is the Marriage Act 1961.

8. As noted above, performative utterances cannot be measured against truth-values: they are neither true nor false, but rather 'succeed' or 'fail'.

9. What changes, for example, when an already cohabiting couple marries can hardly be understood as anything other than a discursive shift. Murphy's laws and race-fixing aside, placing a bet has no impact on the outcome of a race; a promise is a promise whether or not it is fulfilled.

10. Butler's 'politics of the performative' is quite different; Butler, J., *Excitable Speech: a Politics of the Performative* (New York: Routledge, 1997).

11. See Holcombe, L., *Wives and Property: Reform of the Married Women's Property Law in Nineteenth Century England* (Oxford: Martin Robertson, 1983); Brook, H., 'The troubled courtship of Gladys and Mick', *Australian Journal of Political Science* 32 (1997): 419–36.

12. Such that 'sex' in these discourses, where it is not otherwise qualified, comes to mean heterosexual, penis-in-vagina sex.

13. Parker *et al.* state that in Australia, even today:

> Only in the Northern Territory can spouses be convicted of criminal conspiracy when they are the only alleged conspirators. Elsewhere, there needs to be a third conspirator. The derivation of the standard position from the doctrine of unity is easily seen (Parker, S., Parkinson, P. and Behrens, J., *Australian Family Law in Context: Commentary and Materials* (Sydney: The Law Book Co., 1994: 340.)

In the ACT, it remains the case that if a wife acts criminally as an accomplice to her husband, or even commits a crime in the presence of her husband, it should be presumed that she has acted under her husband's coercion.

14. Sybil Wolfram argues that the conjugal unity of coverture is overstated. She is right to question the *ontological* unity of husband and wife, but misses the point, I think, by privileging marriage as a *kinship* rather than *sexual* relationship; Wolfram, S., ' "Husband and wife are one person: the husband" (nineteenth-century English aphorism)', in A.-J. Arnaud and C. Kingdom, eds, *Women's Rights and the Rights of Man* (Aberdeen: Aberdeen University Press, 1990).

15. Scutt cites the trial judge (in part) as follows:

> There is, of course, nothing wrong with a husband, faced with his wife's initial refusal to engage in intercourse, in attempting, in an acceptable way, to persuade her to change her mind and that may involve a measure of rougher than usual handling. It may be, in the end, that handling and persuasion will persuade the wife to agree. (Scutt, J.A., 'Judicial bias or legal bias?: Battery, women and the law', *Journal of Australian Studies* 43 (1995): 130–43, at 139.

16. I refer, here, to that transition from rule of law to governmentality described by Foucault, M., 'Governmentality' in G. Burchell, C. Gordan and P. Miller, eds, *The Foucault Effect: Studies in Governmentality* (London: Harvester Wheatsheaf, 1991): 87–104; and taken up in various ways by political theorists such as Burchell and Hindess; Burchell, G., 'Liberal government and techniques of the self,' in A. Barry, T. Osborne and N. Rose, eds, *Foucault and Political Reason: Liberalism, Neo-liberalism and Rationalities of Government* (London: UCL Press, 1996); Hindess, B., 'Liberalism, socialism and democracy: variations on a governmental theme', in *Foucault and Political Reason*. See also collections edited by, Burchell *et al.*, *The Foucault Effect*; and Barry *et al.*, *Foucault and Political Reason*.

17. A couple might be deemed 'married' according to social security regulations, for example, but (simultaneously) 'single' under the terms of a superannuation policy.

18. New South Wales Lesbian and Gay Legal Rights Service.

19. The somewhat disingenuous counter is that one rejects the misogynist history of marriage by rejecting heterosexuality – which nevertheless leaves the heterosexual stability of marriage undisturbed.

20. The article is based on her more detailed Honours thesis; Zetlein, S., 'Lesbian bodies before the law: intimate relations and regulatory fictions', Honours thesis, Department of Politics and Department of Women's Studies, University of Adelaide, Australia, 1994. All citations are from the Honours thesis.

21. Zetlein notes that the phrase 'theatrical militancy' is Butler's; Butler, J., 'The body you want: Liz Kotz interviews Judith Butler', *Artforum* 31 (1992): 82–9, at 83, in Zetlein.
22. The range of meanings attaching to these sorts of performances is myriad. One has only to read the kinds of homophobic diatribes launched against the Mardi Gras in the tabloid press, for example, to see that a float full of trannie brides by no means *necessarily* destabilizes heterosexual norms at all. For a more detailed exposition of the political limitations of a queer aesthetic, see Brook, H., 'Queer football: feminism, sexuality, corporeality', *Critical inQueeries* 1(2) (1996): 25–45.
23 See Baird, R.M. and Rosenbaum, S.E., eds, *Same-Sex Marriage: the Moral and Legal Debate* (Amherst, NY: Prometheus Books, 1997; Sullivan, A., *Virtually Normal: an Argument about Homosexuality*, 2nd edn (London: Picador, 1996); Sullivan, A., *Same-Sex Marriage: Pro and Con: a Reader* (New York: Vintage, 1997); Sherman, S., ed., *Lesbian and Gay Marriage: Private Commitments, Public Ceremonies* (Philadelphia: Temple University Press, 1992); Eskridge, W.N. Jr, *The Case for Same-Sex Marriage: from Sexual Liberty to Civilized Commitment* (New York: The Free Press, 1996).

CHAPTER 10: 'AGING AND RETIREMENT ARE NOT UNIQUE TO HETEROSEXUALS': *ROSENBERG V CANADA*

1. Many thanks to Nicole Todosichuk for her excellent research assistance and to Susan Boyd for her comments on an earlier draft. The financial support of the Social Sciences and Humanities Research Council of Canada by way of strategic grant under the Women and Change program is also gratefully acknowledged. The quotation in the title comes from the judgment of Abella J. in (1998) *Rosenberg v Canada (Attorney-General)* 98 DTC 6286 (Ont. C.A.) at 6290.
2. (1998) 98 DTC 6286 (Ont. C.A.).
3. John Fisher, Executive Director of Equality for Lesbians and Gay Men Everywhere (EGALE), as reported by the Canadian Press, 23 June, 1998.
4. RSC 1985, clause 1 (5th Suppl.) [hereinafter the Act]. Section 252(4) reads in part:

   252(4) In this Act,
   (a) words referring to a spouse at any time of a taxpayer include the person of the opposite sex who cohabits at that time with the taxpayer in a conjugal relationship and
      (i) has so cohabited with the taxpayer throughout the 12-month period ending before that time, or
      (ii) is the parent of a child of whom the taxpayer is a parent.

5. Charter of Rights and Freedoms, Part 1 of the Constitution Act, 1982, being Schedule B to the *Canada Act 1982* (UK), 1982, clause 11 [hereinafter the Charter]. Section 15(1) reads in part:

   15(1) Every individual is equal before and under the law and has the right to equal protection and equal benefit of the law without discrimination and in particular, without discrimination based on race, nationality or ethnic origin, colour, religion, sex, age, or mental or physical disability.

6. Section 1 of the Charter reads as follows:

   The Canadian Charter of Rights and Freedoms guarantees the rights and freedoms set out in it subject only to such reasonable limits prescribed by law as can be demonstrably justified in a free and democratic society.

7. For a discussion of this Bill, see Susan B. Boyd, 'Expanding the family in family law: recent Ontario proposals on same-sex relationships', *Canadian Journal of Women and the Law* 7(2) (1994): 545.
8. RSBC 1996, c. 128, section 1, as amended by the Family Relations Amendment Act, SBC 1997 clause 20.
9. The definition of spouse now includes a person who 'lived with another person in a marriage-like relationship for a period of at least 2 years ... and for the purposes of this Act, the *marriage-like relationship* may be between persons of the same gender' (emphasis added).
10. RSBC 1996 clause 5, sections 5 and 29. Previously only an 'adult husband and his adult wife' were able to apply to adopt a child together or to adopt the child of their partner. See Adoption Act, RSBC 1979, clause 4, section 3(1) and (2).

11. M. v H. (1996) 142 DLR (4th) 1 (Ont. C.A.), heard and reserved by the Supreme Court of Canada on 18 March, 1998.
12. *Buist v Greaves* [1997] O.J. no. 2646 (Ont. Ct Gen. Div.).
13. (1992) 16 CHRR D/184 (Ontario Board of Inquiry) [hereinafter *Leschner*].
14. [1996] 8 CHRD (Can. Human Rights Tribunal) [hereinafter *Moore*].
15. *Ibid* at D/224. This kind of plan is referred to as an 'offside plan'.
16. Revenue Canada, Technical Interpretation 9637385, dated 15 November, 1996.
17. [1995] 2 SCR 513 [hereinafter *Egan*].
18. RSC 1985, clause 0–9.
19. *Ibid.* at 576. As I shall discuss, the question of the 'novelty' of considering lesbian and gay relationships to be spousal relationships was an issue in *Rosenberg.*
20. Section 147.2(1) and (4) of the Act.
21. Section 149(1) (o.1) of the Act.
22. Government of Canada, *Tax Expenditures 1997* (Ottawa: Department of Finance, 1997) at 28.
23. Section 8501 of the Income Tax Regulations.
24. (1996) 27 CHRD D/1 (Can. Human Rights Tribunal).
25. (1996) 27 CHRR D/108 (Ont. Bd Of Inquiry).
26. (1995) 127 DLR, (4th) 738 at 748.
27. As noted earlier in this chapter William Dwyer had been unsuccessful in persuading a human rights tribunal to order his employer to establish a separate RPP for its lesbian and gay employees. Rather than appeal that decision, Dwyer sought and was granted leave to intervene in *Rosenberg.*
28. Realistic, Equal and Active for Life Women (REAL women) is a conservative organization which intervenes in cases such as this to argue that lesbians and gay men should not be entitled to spousal benefits because to grant such benefits would undermine the 'traditional' family.
29. The Appellants' Factum in *Rosenberg* [hereinafter Appellants' Factum] at para 19.
30. *Ibid* at para 21.
31. The Respondent's Factum in *Rosenberg* [hereinafter Respondent's Factum] at para 66.
32. *R v Oakes*, [1986] 1 SRC 103 identified two central criteria in determining whether a limitation on a right or freedom is justified under section 1 of the Charter. First, the objective of the limiting measure must be of sufficient importance to warrant overriding the right. Second, the means chosen to achieve that objective must be proportional to the ends. The limiting measure must be rationally connected to the objective, minimally impair the Charter right in question, and not so severely trench on an individual or group that legislative objective is outweighed by the abridgment of rights.
33. Respondent's Factum at para 64.
34. *Ibid* at para 29.
35. (1998) 156 DLR (4th) 385.
36. RSA 1980, clause I-2. After Vriend had commenced his legal action the legislation was amended and renamed the Human Rights, Citizenship and Multiculturalism Act, R.S.A. 1980, clause H-11.7.
37. *Ibid* at 6289.
38. *Ibid* at 6292.
39. *Ibid* at 6290.
40. *Ibid* at 6291
41. [1992] 2 SCR 679 at 709.
42. This point is discussed later in this chapter when the issue of cost is examined in more detail.
43. 'N. S. extends same-sex rights', *Globe and Mail*, 26 May, 1998, p A1.
44. 'Reform seeks curbs on judicial activism,' *The Globe and Mail*, 11 June, 1998, p A4.
45. *Ibid.*
46. B.C. expands same-sex rights', *The Globe and Mail*, 23 June, 1998, p A1 at A9.
47. *Ibid.*
48. 'Civil Service to get Same-Sex Benefits', *The Globe and Mail*, 16 March, 1999 at A1.
49. Bill C-386, *An Act to Amend the Income Tax Act and the Canada Pension Plan (definition of spouse)*, 1st Session, 36th Parliament, 1998.
50. *Ritchie and Gavel v Canada*, The Supreme Court of British Columbia, Victoria registry no. 964815.
51. Foundation for Equal Families, Press release, http://www.ffef.ca/chal.htm.
52. *The Globe and Mail*, 20 January 1999, p A7.
53. 'PM waffles on same-sex equality', Press Release of EGALE (Equality for Gays and Lesbians Everywhere) at http://www.egale.ca/pressrel/990120.htm.
54. Claire F. L. Young, 'Taxing times for lesbians and gay men: equality at what cost?' 17 Dalhousie Law Journal (1994) 534.

55. Canada, Department of Finance, 'Budget papers supplementary information', 25 February, 1992, at 138–9.
56. *Ibid.*
57. Space does not permit a full analysis of the reasons for this outcome, but see Young, 'Taxing times', *supra* at 548–553.
58. *Ibid.*
59. *Ibid.*
60. *Ibid.*
61. (1998) 152 DLR (4th) 738 (Ont. Gen. Div.).
62. *Supra.* In this line of reasoning she drew on *Schachter v Canada*, [1992] 2 SCR 679.
63. *Ibid.* at 572.
64. *Ibid.* at 434.
65. Margot Young, 'Change at the margins: *Eldridge v British Columbia (A.G)* and *Vriend v. Alberta'*, *Canadian Journal of Women and the Law* 10 (1) (1998) 244–63.

CHAPTER 11; STRAIGHT FAMILIES, QUEER LIVES?: HETEROSEXUAL(IZING) FAMILY LAW

1. This poststructuralist reading of the self is usefully summarized by Sandland, J., 'Between "truth" and "difference": poststructuralism, law and the power of feminism', *Feminist Legal Studies* 3 (1995): 3–47.
2. For a critical discussion of the work of both Giddens and Beck and Beck-Gernsheim, see further Smart, C. and Neale, B., 'Good enough morality? Divorce and postmodernity', *Critical Social Policy* 17(4) (1999): 3–27.
3. Note, for example, in the UK context: implementation of the Working Time and Part-Time Work Directives and the National Minimum Wage: the Out of School Child Care Initiative; consultation papers on Early Education and Day Care; the establishment of the 'National Child Care Strategy' and, of particular significance, the implementation of the EU Parental Leave Directive (no. 96/34) and the White Paper *Fairness at Work* (1998). See, more generally, the 1998 consultation paper *Supporting Families* (especially Chapter 4 'Strengthening Marriage').
4. Although, according to the 1995 *Social Trends* analysis of lifestyle and expenditure, traditional divisions of domestic labour remain deep rooted: 'New Man fails to survive into the nineties', *The Independent,* 25 January, 1996.
5. Note, for example, the *Sunday Express,* 14 February, 1999 'Lesbians can make better parents' and Editorial 'Lesbian parents give everyone a valuable lesson in equality'.
6. In theory, many of the social characteristics associated with heterosexuality could be, and have been, applied to gay and lesbian relationships. To reductively attach to heterosexuality the qualities of routine, unimaginative, exploitative relations is not only to idealize that which is already constituted as Other; it is to purge human sexuality itself of its ineluctable entwining with power and resistance.
7. This echoes the argument made by Brown in relation to feminist engagements with criminology; Brown, B., 'Reassessing the critique of biologism', in L. Gelsthorpe and A. Morris, eds, *Feminist Perspectives in Criminology* (Buckingham: Open University Press, 1990): 41.
8. I was thinking, in writing this, of the diverse, complex and contradictory representations of heterosexuality, power and desire, contained in the Report to the US Congress by Independent Counsel Kenneth Starr (1998) (The Starr Report).

CHAPTER 12: TREADING ON DICEY GROUND: CITIZENSHIP AND THE POLITICS OF THE RULE OF LAW

1. Laurence H. Tribe, *Constitutional Choices* (Cambridge: Harvard University Press, 1985): p vii–viii.
2. See for example Keith Banting and Richard Simeon, eds, *And No One Cheered: Federalism, Democracy and The Constitution Act* (Toronto: Methuen, 1983).
3. See M. Elizabeth Atcheson, Mary Eberts and Beth Symes, *Women and Legal Action: Precedents, Resources and Strategies for the Future* (Ottawa: Canadian Advisory Council on the Status of Women,

1984); Thomas R. Berger, 'The judicial rule in interpreting the equality provisions of the charter', in E. Diane Pask, Kathleen E. Mahoney and Catherine A. Brown, eds, *Women, the Law and the Economy* (Toronto: Butterworth, 1985) at 315; Mary Eberts, 'Making use of the Charter of Rights', in E. Diane Pask, Kathleen E. Mahoney and Catherine A. Brown, eds, *Women, the Law and the Economy* (Toronto: Butterworth, 1985) at 327.

4. Gwen Brodsky and Shelagh Day, *Canadian Charter Equality Rights for Women: One Step Forward or Two Steps Back?* (Ottawa: Canadian Advisory Council on the Status of Women, 1989); Elizabeth M. Schneider, 'The dialectic of rights and politics: perspectives from the women's movement', *New York University Law Review* 61 (1986): 589.

5. Mary Ann Glendon, *Rights Talk: the Impoverishment of Political Discourse* (New York: The Free Press, 1991); Michael Mandel, *The Charter of Rights and the Legalization of Politics in Canada*, revised edn (Toronto: Thompson Educational, 1994).

6. Joel Bakan, *Just Words: Constitutional Rights and Social Wrongs* (Toronto: University of Toronto Press, 1997).

7. On the persistence of dominant heterosexist frameworks of meaning, and the ways in which those frameworks may shape and reconstitute the actors and communities who seek to harness rights discourses, see Didi Herman, *Rights of Passage: Struggles for Lesbian and Gay Legal Equality* (Toronto: University of Toronto Press, 1994). A review of early historical roots of this discrimination is traced in John Boswell, *Christianity, Social Tolerance, and Homosexuality: Gay People in Western Europe from the Beginning of the Christian Era to the Fourteenth Century* (Chicago: University of Chicago Press, 1980).

8. Indeed, one needs to keep in mind the comments of scholars pointing out the irony that rights have been devalued as a tool at the moment that historically disadvantaged groups have begun using them. As one scholar put it, 'Only those who least need rights in order to secure their existence have the luxury of abandoning rights as an organizing jurisprudential principle.' Monica J. Evans, 'Stealing away: Black women, outlaw culture and the rhetoric of rights', *Harvard Civil Rights-Civil Liberties Law Review* 28 (1993): 263 at 292. A similar argument runs as a theme through Patricia Williams, *The Alchemy of Race and Rights* (Cambridge: Harvard University Press, 1991).

9. James S. Hans, *The Fate of Desire* (New York: State University of New York Press, 1990): p 210.

10 *Ibid., p 133*

11. [1998] 1 SCR 493.

12. A national organization comprising the 13 Canadian statutory human rights agencies, CASHRA is the public face of the human rights commissions of the country. As a result of its federal structure, Canada's human rights law is bifurcated between the federal and the provincial jurisdictions. Each province, as well as the federal and territorial jurisdictions, have enacted human rights legislation. These statutes ensure that the rights of all citizens and residents of Canada are enjoyed free of discrimination based on grounds including race, religion and ancestry. Although the details of the particular legislative regimes may differ, their overall structure and contour is sufficiently similar that one can speak of a common human rights law regime in Canada. Typically, complaints are filed with the relevant human rights commission which, after investigation, attempts to mediate the issue, failing which it is referred to an independent quasi-judicial administrative tribunal for resolution. Upon referral to a tribunal, a full hearing is held at which evidence is led and argument made. A decision is rendered on a complaint and if it is in favour of the complainant, consequential relief is granted by way of an order. The decision of the tribunal and its order are subject to review before the ordinary courts of superior jurisdiction.

13. *Seneca College v Bhadauria* [1981] 2 SCR 181.

14. Although both human rights codes and the Charter speak of prohibited forms of discrimination, there are important distinctions to be made between the two documents. First, although human rights codes are sometimes spoken of as having a unique 'quasi-constitutional' nature, they are not constitutionally entrenched. They can be modified by legislative fiat. The Charter, however, is part of the Canadian Constitution. The Constitution (including the Charter) is the supreme law of Canada. Any law that is inconsistent with its provisions is to the extent of that inconsistency of neither force nor effect. Second, the Charter applies to the federal, provincial and territorial governments in Canada with respect to all of the actions of those governments, whether they be legislative, executive or administrative. The guarantee of equality in section 15 the Charter, provides protection from discriminatory government action. It does not prohibit discrimination between private individuals. Discriminatory conduct between individuals is regulated under human rights codes. Vriend could not argue that his employer had violated section 15 of the Charter. He could, however, argue that the Alberta government had violated the Charter by drafting human rights legislation which denied protection based on sexual orientation.

15. *Andrews v Law Society of British Columbia*, [1989] 1 SCR 13. Here, the court concluded that the ground of citizenship was analogous to forms of discrimination enumerated in section 15 of the Charter.

16. *Egan v Canada*, [1995] 2 SCR 513.

17. Those supporting Vriend included: CASHRA, The Alberta Civil Liberties Association, The Canadian Jewish Congress, the Alberta and Northwest Conference of the United Church of Canada, the Canadian Labour Congress, The Women's Legal Education and Action Fund (LEAF), The Canadian Bar Association – Alberta Branch, the Canadian Human Rights Commission, the Attorney General of Canada, The Foundation for Equal Families, and Equality for Gays and Lesbians Everywhere (EGALE). Those intervening in support of the Alberta government included: the Evangelical Fellowship of Canada, the Christian Legal Fellowship, the Focus on the Family (Canada) Association, and the Alberta Federation of Women United for Families. The Attorney General of Ontario took no position on the facts, and argued only that provincial human rights legislation did not need to mirror the Charter.

18. Alberta defended its action on a number of grounds. Amongst them, it asserted that the Charter did not apply since the government had not acted: it had simply been silent. They did not 'say' gays were excluded, they simply did not add them to the list, and could not be found guilty of discrimination for a failure to act. Given the Court's attention to substance over form, it seemed unlikely that this argument would prove persuasive. See Dianne Pothier, 'The sounds of silence: Charter application when the legislature declines to speak', *Constitutional Forum* 7 (1996): 113. See also chapter 4, 'Construing the sounds of congressional and constitutional silence', in Tribe, *Constitutional Choices*. Alberta also argued that its decision to leave sexual orientation off the list was based on the demands of freedom of religion: religious groups should not be required to provide services against their consciences. Given the structure of human rights codes, this argument also seemed unlikely to be persuasive. Even had sexual orientation been protected, there was no necessary violation of religious freedom. The 'bona fide occupational requirement' clauses in human rights codes provided internal mechanisms for balancing the needs of conflicting rights. The issue here was that the government was preventing gays and lesbians from even having access to a forum in which their needs could be balanced against the desires of those whose religious views included a religious-based affirmation of heterosexuality.

19. The Court set out guidelines for the operation of section 1 in *R v Oakes* [1986] 1 SCR 103. In order for the government to justify a violation of a Charter right, the government must establish that the legislation advances a pressing and substantial objective, that the law is rationally connected to the objective, that the law impairs the right no more than necessary to accomplish the objective, and that the law does not have a disproportionately severe effect on the persons to whom it applies. For a general discussion of section 1 of the Charter, see Chapter 35, 'Limitation of rights' in Peter Hogg, *Constitutional Law of Canada*, 4th edn (Toronto: Carswell, 1998).

20. *Supra*, note 16. In *Egan*, five judges concluded that the same-sex requirement in the pension benefit scheme violated section 15's guarantee of equality. A four-judge minority (Lamer CJ, La Forest, Gonthier, Major) found that there was no violation of section 15 because the same-sex requirement was a 'relevant' distinction. This relevancy distinction is somewhat of a newcomer to the Court's approach to equality questions. Generally, questions of relevance emerge during discussions of justification, rather than in the context of the section 15 analysis itself.

21. Justice Sopinka said that 'government must be accorded some flexibility in extending social benefits and does not have to be proactive in recognizing new social relationships'. He added, 'This Court has recognized that it is legitimate for the government to make choices between disadvantaged groups and that it must be provided with some leeway to do so.' The legislative decision to extend the benefit from married couples to unmarried heterosexual couples should be seen not as discrimination against same-sex couples, but rather 'a substantial step in an incremental approach to include all those who are shown to be in serious need of financial assistance due to the retirement or death of a supporting spouse.' *Egan, supra*, note 16 at 572, 573 and 575.

22. Peter Russell suggests that section 33 has the power to democratize constitutional politics by forcing governments to explain to their citizens precisely why it is necessary to exercise the override – to enter into a conversation with their citizens and to be accountable for the decision taken. See his comments in *The Toronto Star*, 4 June, 1989, p B3. On a comparative examination of the boundary between legislative and judicial sovereignty, see Calvin R. Massey, 'The locus sovereignty: judicial review, legislative supremacy, and federalism in the constitutional traditions of Canada and the United States' *Duke Law Journal* 1 [1990] 1229.

23. The most controversial use of section 33 resulted from the Supreme Court's decision to strike down Quebec's legislation mandating French-only commercial signs. See *Ford v Quebec (Attorney-General)*

[1988] 2 SCR 712. As a political statement of its refusal to recognize the legitimacy of the Charter on federalism grounds (Quebec opposed repatriation of the Constitution in 1982), all Quebec legislation is enacted, the Charter notwithstanding, by a blanket invocation of the section 33 override – SQ 1982 clause 21. Outside Quebec, the clause has been used only once – by Saskatchewan in the mid 1980s to protect a piece of back-to-work legislation that had been struck down by the Saskatchewan Court of Appeal as a violation of the Charter's section 2(d) guarantee of freedom of association in *RWDSE v Government of Saskatchewan,* [1985] 5 WWR 97. The Supreme Court later upheld the legislation, thus the use of section 33 of the Charter had been unnecessary. See [1987] 1 SCR 460.

24. This possibility was even articulated in the dissenting reasons of Justice Major (appointed from Alberta) in *Vriend, supra,* note 11, at p 587: 'the Legislature may choose to override the Charter breach by invoking s. 33 of the Charter . . . it should lie with the elected Legislature to determine this issue.' Following the decision of the Supreme Court of Canada in *Vriend,* the newspapers were full of reports that the Klein government was threatening to use the notwithstanding clause. A sample of newspaper articles referring to the debates about invoking section 33 of the Charter include Ted Morton, 'Tory ranks divided – government buys time on the issue of judicial promotion of gay rights', *The Calgary Sun,* 15 November, 1998, p C6; Neil Waugh, 'Vriend "fences" collapse – gay ruling fundamentally changing Alberta society, despite Klein's words', *The Calgary Sun,* 12 July, 1998, p C6; Rachel Giese, 'The judges just doing their jobs', *The Toronto Star,* 31 August, 1998; Neil Waugh, 'Look what happened, Ralph', *The Edmonton Sun,* 12 July 1998, p C18; Ray Martin, 'Four Tories may join Socreds', *The Edmonton Sun,* 3 June, 1998, p 11.

25. See *McKinney v University of Guelph,* 3 SCR [1990] 229.

26. Again, Justice Major suggested such an outcome in his dissent reasons in *Vriend.* He argued against the remedy of reading in, saying: 'The issue may be that the Legislature would prefer no human rights Act over one that includes sexual orientation as a prohibited ground of discrimination', *Supra,* note 11 at p 586.

27. Dicey, A.V. *The Law of the Constitution,* introduction by E.C.S. Wade, 10th edn (London: Macmillan, 1959).

28. *Reference re Alberta Statutes,* [1938] SCR 100 (the *Alberta Press* case).

29. *Saumur v City of Quebec,* [1953] 2 SCR 299 (the *Jehovah's Witnesses* case).

30. *Switzman v Elbling,* [1957] SCR 285 (the *Padlock Act* case).

31. *Ibid.* See Justice Abbott at p 328, and Justice Rand at p 307.

32. *Saumur, supra,* note 29 at p 329.

33. The robust tradition was rejected by Justice Beetz in *A.G. Canada and Dupond v Montreal,* [1978] 2 SCR 770 at 776, but later embraced by the same judge in *OPSEU v Ontario,* [1987] 1 SCR 2 at 57.

34. Dicey, *supra,* note 27 at p 141.

35. *Union Colliery Company of British Columbia v Bryden,* [1899] AC 580.

36. This progressive decision was not necessarily a function of anti-racist values. Four years after *Bryden,* the Privy Council released its reasons in *Cunningham v Tomey Homma,* [1903] AC 151. Here, they upheld Saskatchewan legislation prohibiting the employment of any white woman by any 'Chinaman', The judgment makes explicit reference to the need to protect white women from 'Chinamen', whether naturalized citizens or not. On nineteenth-century moral panics about the purity of the white race, see Mariana Valverde, *The Age of Light, Soap and Water: Moral Reform in English Canada, 1885–1925* (Toronto: McClelland & Stewart, 1991). See also James W. St. G. Walker, *'Race', Rights and the Law in the Supreme Court of Canada: Historical Case Studies* (Toronto: Waterloo, 1997). The progressive result in *Bryden* is perhaps best understood as the result of concerns about nation building, rather than concerns about racial discrimination.

37. *Winner v SMT (Eastern) Ltd,* [1951] SCR 887, per Justice Rand at 919.

38. *Ibid.*

39. See *Black and Co. v Law Society of Alberta,* [1989] 1 SCR 591, per Justice La Forest at 610–614, 612–623; also, *Hunt v T&N PLC,* [1993] 4 SCR 289, per Justice La Forest at 319–326.

40. *United States of America v Cotroni,* [1989] 1 SCR 1469, per Justice La Forest at 1480–83.

41. See Dicey, *supra,* note 27, at pp 24, 39, 71, 76, 79 and 145. The Diceyan construct continues to exercise a powerful hold on the Canadian judicial mind, strengthened no doubt by entrenchment of the 'rule of law' (together with the Supremacy of God) as an informing value of the Charter. See for example *Reference Re Manitoba Language Rights,* [1989] 1 SCR 721, and *Canadian Council of Churches v Canada (Minister of Employment and Immigration),* [1992] 1 SCR 236. Academic critique of Dicey has been fierce. For example, Harry Arthurs, 'Rethinking administrative law: a slightly Dicey business', *Osgoode Hall Law Journal* 17 (1979): 1. There are indications that Canadian courts are prepared to address the rule of law rubric in a more nuanced fashion, for

example, the reasons of decision of Justice Wilson in *National Corn Growers Association v Canada (Import Tribunal)*, [1990] 2 SCR 1324.

42. *Re Resolution to Amend the Constitution*, [1981] 1 SCR 753 at 800–84, 888. The Court adopted a framework for analysis to determine whether a convention had been established, the three-fold enquiry postulated by Sir Ivor Jennings in *The Law, and the Constitution*, 5th edn (London: University of London Press, 1959), namely: what are the precedents; did the actors treat the rule as binding; and, is there a reason for the rule.

43. At the time the *Vriend* case was argued, legislation extending the protective embrace of human rights legislation to gays and lesbians had been enacted by Parliament and the legislatures responsible for nine of 13 Canadian jurisdictions, comprising over 90% of the population of Canada.

44. *Taylor v New Zealand Poultry Board*, [1984] NZLR 394 at 398; and see as well, *Keenan v A.G.* [1986] 1 NZLR 241 at 244.

45. *New Zealand Herald,* 26 December, 1985, p 3, as cited by B.V. Harris in 'Parliamentary Sovereignty and Interim Injunctions: *Factortame v New Zealand', New Zealand Universities Law Review* 15 (1992): 55 at 65. And see his 'The law-making power of the judiciary', in Joseph, ed., *Essays on the Constitution* (1995) 265 at 269f. We are indebted to Megan Richardson of the University of Melbourne for these references.

46. *RWDSU v Dolphin Delivery Ltd* [1986] 2 SCR 573.

47. See for example, Dale Gibson, 'The charter of rights and the private sector', *Manitoba Law Journal* 12 (1982): 213, disapproved by the Court in *Dolphin Delivery, supra.* See also Allan Hutchinson and Andrew Petter, 'Private rights/pubic wrongs: the liberal lie of the Charter', *University of Toronto Law Journal* 38 (1988): 278.

48. See Catherine Swinton, 'Application of the Canadian Charter of Rights and Freedom', in Walter S. Tarnapolsky and Gerald A. Beaudoin, eds, *Canadian Charter of Rights and Freedoms: Commentary* (Toronto: Carswell, 1982), 41 at p 44–45:

> The purpose of a Charter of rights is to regulate the relationship of an individual with the government by invalidating laws and governmental activity which infringe the rights guaranteed by the document, while relationships between individuals are left to the regulation of human rights codes, other statutes, and common law remedies.'

In *Dolphin Delivery, supra,* note 47 at p 58, Justice McIntrye cited with approval this passage from Professor Swintons's analysis of the issue.

49. See for example the dissenting judgment of Justice McLachlin in *R. v Keegstra*, [1990] 3 SCR 697 at 861.

50. Justice Major refused to read sexual orientation into the legislation. See *supra* notes 24 and 26.

51. For example, consider the (in) famous minority reasons of Justice La Forest in *Egan, supra*, note 16. He concluded that support for (elderly) heterosexual couples was justifiable. Marriage was 'fundamental to the stability and well-being of the family'. While it could be legally possible to add same-sex couples to the determination of marriage, this would not change the underlying reality that 'the heterosexual family is the fundamental unit in society'. Same-sex couples, he argued, could not 'meet the fundamental social objectives thereby sought to be promoted by Parliament' (p 538). They simply don't serve the social purposes for which Parliament made the distinction (p 539).

52. A judicial emergence of both anti-Charter animus and a dismissal of minority concerns can be seen in Justice McClung's reasons in the Court of Appeal in *Vriend v Alberta* (1996) 132 DLR (4th) 595. Provinces, he says, should not be forced to 'march to the Charter drum' (p 605). He argues that 'The Charter is not everyone's' system. It belongs to Canada's minorities' (p 614). Judges, he claims, are descending into 'collegial bodies that meet regularly to promulgate "desirable" legislation'. This should be avoided since 'Few social fissures are healed by stamping judicial solutions into them' (pp 614–15). He argues against 'right-restless judges' and says that reading up is 'a Trojan horse' (p 616). Constitutional principles and formative resources 'stand suspended when rights-restless judges pitchfork their courts into the uncertain waters of political debate' (p 618). 'None of our precious and historic legislative safeguards are in play when judges choose to privateer in parliamentary sea lanes' (p 621). Further, 'In the search for the just Canadian equilibrium it was not expected that majority rights and interests would curtsy, endlessly, to minority rites' (p 621). For an examination of Justice McClung's reasons, see William Black, 'Vriend, Rights and Democracy' *Constitutional Forum* 7 (1996): 126. See also F.C. de Coste, '*Vriend v Alberta*: sexual orientation and liberal polity', *Alberta Law Review* 34 (1996): 950.

53. Martha R. Mahoney, 'Exit: power and the idea of leaving in love, work, and the confirmation hearings', *Southern California Law Review* 65 (1992): 1283 at 1317.

54. Oddly enough, the majority of the Court used an argument very much like the one CASHRA explicitly sketched out in *Vriend* in a case heard the same year, *Reference re Remuneration of Judges of the Provincial Court (P.E.I.)*, [1997] 3 SCR 3. Justice Lamer used arguments about citizenship and the implied bill of rights to find an extended constitutional protection for an independent judiciary. He did so in a context where the parties themselves had not made these arguments. It is interesting that the majority chose to use arguments similar to those made by CASHRA in a context where the issue was the possible reduction of judicial salaries. However, they were silent on these arguments in *Vriend*, a context which seemed much more apposite (the legislative disenfranchisement of a whole category of citizens).

CHAPTER 13: THE CONSTITUTION MADE US QUEER: THE SEXUAL ORIENTATION CLAUSE IN THE SOUTH AFRICAN CONSTITUTION AND THE EMERGENCE OF GAY AND LESBIAN IDENTITY

1. Michel Foucault, *Power/Knowledge: Selected interviews and other writings 1972–77* (London: Harvester Press, 1980): 97.
2. Ferial Haffajee, 'Gay couple tie the knot', *Mail & Guardian*, 5–11 September, 1997, p 11.
3. See Diana Fuss, 'Inside/Out', in Diana Fuss, ed., *Inside/out: Lesbian Theories, Gay Theories* (New York: Routledge, 1991): 7.
4. See Judith Butler, *Gender Trouble: Feminism and the Subversion of Identity* (New York: Routledge, 1990): 3.
5. For an excellent narrative of the events surrounding the Book Fair, see Chris Dunton and Mai Palmberg, 'Zimbabwe – the book fair drama,' in Chris Dunton and Mai Palmberg, eds, *Human Rights and Homosexuality in Southern Africa* (Uppsala, Sweden: Nordiska Afrikainstituet, 1996): 7–17. See also Carl Stychin, A *Nation by Rights: National Cultures, Sexual Identity Politics and the Discourse of Rights* (Philadelphia: Temple University Press, 1998): 62–3.
6. See for example the remarks by Pan Africanist Congress member, Bennie Alexander (who later renamed himself !Khoisan X) quoted in Mark Gevisser, 'A different fight for freedom: a history of South African lesbian and gay organisations', in Edwin Cameron and Mark Gevisser, eds, *Defiant Desire: Gay and Lesbian Lives in South Africa* (Braamfontein: Ravan Press, 1994): p 71:

   [H]omosexuality is un-African. It is part of the spin-off of the capitalist system. We should not take the European leftist position on the matter. It should be looked at in its total perspective from our own Afrocentric position.'

   See also remarks made by Kenyan President Daniel arap Moi to the Daily Nation newspaper, according to the Sapa-Panos news agency only 14 August 1998: 'Kenya has no room or time for homosexuals and lesbians. Homosexuality is against African norms and traditions, and even in religion it is considered a great sin.' Also President Robert Mugabe, as reported in Chris Dunton and Mai Palmberg, *Human Rights and Homosexuality in Southern Africa* (Uppsala, Sweden: Nordiska Afrikainstituet, June 1996): 13: 'Let the Americans keep their sodomy, bestiality, stupid and foolish ways to themselves, out of Zimbabwe .... Let them be gay in the US, Europe and elsewhere. They shall be sad people here.'
7. Stychin, *Nation*, pp 62–3. See also Rachel Holmes, 'White rapists make coloureds (and homosexuals): the Winnie Mandela Trial and the politics of race and sexuality', in Cameron and Gevisser, *Defiant Desire*, pp 289, 292.
8. Stychin, *Nation,* pp 64–5.
9. Andrew Pantazis, 'The problematic nature of gay identity', *South African Journal on Human Rights* 12 (1996): 299. Pantazis writes:

   there may be some truth in the assertion that homosexuality in South Africa is a white European imposition. While same-sex desire is a transcultural phenomenon ... it would be missing the point of constructivism not to be careful about universalising conditions which go to the making of a gay identity.

10. See generally R. Bleys, *The Geography of Perversion* (London: Cassell, 1996).

11. E.E. Evans-Pritchard, 'Sexual Inversion Among the Azande', *American Anthropologist* 72 (1970). This report, of course, falls exactly in the trap of viewing practices in another culture through the lens of the European idea of homosexuality. It is nevertheless a valuable document on sexual practices among the Azande people. See also Gilbert Herdt, *Same Sex, Different Cultures: Exploring Gay and Lesbian Lives* (Boulder: Westview Press, 1997): 37–8.

12. Zackie Achmat, ' "Apostles of civilised vice" "Immoral practices" and "unnatural vice" in South African prisons and compounds, 1890–1920', *Social Dynamics* 19 (1993): 107.

13. Stychin, *Nation*, p 66.

14. J. Comaroff and J. Comaroff, *Ethnography and the Historical Imagination* (Boulder: Westview Press, 1992): 160.

15. Achmat, 'Apostles of civilised vice', p 96.

16. Oliver Phillips, 'Zimbabwean Law and production of white man's disease', *Social and Legal Studies* 6 (1997): 474.

17. Phillips, 'Zimbabwean Law', p 483.

18. Constitution of the Republic of South Africa, Act 200 of 1993, section 8(2).

19. Constitution of the Republic of South Africa, Act 108 of 1996. Because the 1993 Constitution was negotiated before the first democratic election by unelected representatives of the various parties at the negotiations, the 1993 Constitution provided for the establishment of a democratically elected Constitutional Assembly to draw up a 'final' Constitution in accordance with a set of Constitutional Principles negotiated by the parties in 1993.

20. Thus far, the Constitutional Court has only had the opportunity to deliver two judgements based on a claim of discrimination based on sexual orientation in *National Coalition for Lesbian and Gay Equality and Another v Minister of Justice and Others* 1998 12 BCLR 1517 (CC) and *National Coalition for Lesbian and Gay Equality and Others v Minister of Home Affairs and Others* 1 BCLR 2000 39 (CC). There have been four High Courts judgements on this issue. These were: *S v K* 9 (1997) BCLR 1283 (C) (common law crime of sodomy declared unconstitutional); *Langemaat v Minister of Safety and Security* (1998) 4 BCLR 444 (T) (police medical aid scheme discriminated against police captain in refusing to register her female partner on the scheme); *National Coalition for Lesbian and Gay Equality and Another v Minister of Justice and Others* (1998) 6 BCLR 726 W (common law crime of sodomy, as well as other sexual offences declared unconstitutional); and *National Coalition for Gay and Lesbian Equality and Others v Minister of Home Affairs and Others* (1999) 3 BCLR 280 (C) (immigration law providing special arrangements for legally married partners declared unconstitutional).

21. See Alan Hunt and Gary Wickham, *Foucault and Law: Towards a Sociology of Law as Governance* (London: Pluto Press, 1994): 60–61.

22. Michel Foucault, *Discipline and Punish: The Birth of the Prison*, translated by Alan Sheridan (New York: Pantheon, 1977): 194.

23. Michel Foucault, 'Two Lectures', in Colin Gordon, ed., *Power/Knowledge: Selected Interviews and Other Writings 1972–1977* (Brighton: Harvester Press, 1980): 107.

24. Jerry D. Leonard, 'Foucault: genealogy, law, praxis', *Legal Studies Forum* 14 (1990): 11.

25. Michel Foucault, *The History Sexuality Volume One, An Introduction* (London: Penguin Books, 1990): 144.

26. Foucault, 'Two lectures', p 106. I would argue that one can see this merely as a way of saying the repressive aspect of the law should be deemphasized in favour of an analysis of its constructive functions as discipline, surveillance, normalization, and a discourse of power/knowledge.

27. Foucault, *History of Sexuality*, pp. 101–2.

28. I am in no way claiming that individuals can somehow miraculously take control of their own destinies and mould their own identities at will, as if, somehow, they are placed outside the power/knowledge matrix. On the contrary, I am claiming that individuals are part of the currents of power and hence are constituted by these power relations while, at the same time, being able to contribute to their own formation.

29. See Janet E. Halley, 'Reasoning about sodomy: act and identity in and after *Bowers v Hardwick*', *Virginia Law Review* 79 (1993): 1729.

30. It is interesting to note that the phrase 'sexual orientation' is often used as synonymous with 'gay' or 'lesbian'. This is perhaps because of the entrenched nature of heterosexuality as the sexual norm in society. This allows heterosexuality to go almost completely unchallenged and unquestioned and thus allows almost exclusively for a view that any talk of sexual orientation must be talk of homosexuality. Thus, the inclusion of the sexual orientation clause has not, as might have been hoped, begun to problematize heterosexuality, but seems, on the contrary, to merely assist in the policing of the boundaries of heterosexuality. For description of the way in which heterosexuality secures its self-identity, see Fuss, *Inside/out*, p 2.

31. *Vermank v Van der Merwe* (1981) 3 SA 78 (N). In this case a certain Mrs Vermeak phoned Mr Van der Merwe and asked whether she could speak to his wife, and received the reply: 'Het jy nie gehoor dat sy bly by daardie donnerse lesbian nie? (Haven't you heard that she is staying with that bloody lesbian?). Mrs Vermaak did not know what a lesbian was and later asked her husband what it meant and he told her. The issue was whether such ignorance could thwart a defamation claim on grounds that it was not published.

32. Edwin Cameron, 'Sexual orientation and the Constitution: a test case for human rights', *South African Law Journal* 110 (1993): 450; and Labuschage, J.M.T., 'Dekrimalisasie van Homo- en Soofilie', *Tydskrif vir Regswetenskap* 11 (1986): 167.

33. See for example, Pierre de Vos, 'The right of a lesbian mother to have access to her children: some constitutional issues', *South African Law Journal* 111 (1994): 687; Divya Singh, 'Discrimination against lesbians in family law', *South African Journal on Human Rights* 11 (1995): 571; Visser, P.J., Enkele gedagtes oor fundamentele regte in die familiereg', *Tydstrif vir Hedendaags Romeins-Holalndse Reg* 58 (1995): 702; Craig Lind, 'Sexual orientation, family law and the transitional Constitution', *South African Law Journal* 112 (1995): 481; Frans Viljoen, 'Signs of the times: changing attitudes under the new constitution', *Stellenbosch Law Review* 3 (1995): 232; Elsje Bonthuys, 'Awarding access and custody to homosexual parents of minor children: a discussion of *Van Rooyen v Van Rooyen* ', *Stellenbosch Law Review* 2 (1994): 298; Pierre de Vos, 'On the legal construction of gay and lesbian identity and South Africa's transitional Constitution', *South African Journal on Human Rights* 12 (1996): 265; Pierre de Vos, '*S v Moses*: criminal capacity, provocation and HIV', *South African Criminal Law Journal* 11 (1996): 354; Labuschagne, J.M.T., 'Eengeslaghuwelike: 'n Menseregtelike en Regsrevolusionere perspektief', *South African Journal on Human Rights* 12 (1996): 534; Tshepo L. Mosikatsana, 'The definitional exclusion of gays and lesbians from family status', *South Arican Journal on Human Rights* 12 (1996): 549; Brenda Grant, 'Homosexual marriage and the constitu- tion', *South African Journal on Human Rights* 12 (1996): 568; Bradley Silver, 'Till deportation do us part: the extension of spousal recognition to same-sex parnerships', *South African Journal on Human Rights* 12 (1996): 575; Tshepo L. Mosikatsana, 'Comment on the adoption by K and B, Re', *South African Journal on Human Rights* 12 (1996): 582; Angelo Pantazis, 'The problematic nature of gay identity', *South African Journal on Human Rights* 12 (1996): 291; Michael P. Katz, 'Close encounters of the third kind: privacy, equality and the expression of homosexual preference', *South African Journal on Human Rights* 12 (1996): 308; Labuschangne, J.M.T., 'Sexual orientation, sexual autonomy and discrimination in definition of crime', *South African Journal on Human Rights* 12 (1996): 321.

34. See for example, Prakash Naidoo, 'Gay man to challenge dismissal in landmark court case', *Sunday Independent,* 26 October, 1997; Swapna Prabhakaran, 'End of willy-nilly willy', *Mail & Guardian,* 17–23 October, 1997; 'Single women win right to insemination', *Cape Times,* 14 October, 1997; 'Slow coming out for black lesbians', *The Star,* 26 November, 1997; Melanie-Ann Feris, 'A day to come out and be yourself', *The Star,* 4 October, 1996; Elissa Goodman, 'Omar leaves gays in the lurch', *Cape Times,* 24 September, 1997; 'Good signs for gays', *The Star,* 20 April, 1998; Gumisai Mutume, 'Gay rights are guaranteed, but laws and attitudes still have to change', *The Star,* 4 August, 1996; Hug Robertson and Jennaine Craig, 'Marriage rights for gay couples', *Cape Argus,* 13 March, 1997; Nikki Whitfield, 'New SA makes life easier for gays who "come out" ', *The Star,* 5 July, 1996; 'SA comes out of the closet', *Saturday Star,* 24 November, 1997; 'Lesbian couple gets first official adoption', *Mail & Guardian,* 11 August, 1995.

35. Haffajee, 'Gay couple tie the knot', p 2.

36. Officers of the police force have proven to be at the forefront of challenging the status quo with an explicit or implicit reliance on the legal protection provided by the sexual orientation clause in the South African Constitution. It was, after all, Jolande Langemaat, a captain in the police force, who sued the police medical aid scheme to get them to register her partner, thereby coming out to the whole nation. See *Langemoat v Minister of Safety and Security* (1998) 4 BCLR 444 (T).

37. Fatima Schroeder, 'Discrimination drove 300 gay SA police to suicide last year', *Cape Times,* 5 August, 1997, p 3.

38. For a more extensive discussion on the police culture, see Pierre de Vos, 'Policing', in Ronald Louw, ed., *South African Human Rights Yearbook 1995*, vol. 6 (Durban: Oxford University Press, 1996): 193–212. The extreme homophobia in the police force is well illustrated by the fate of Corrie van Niekerk. In 1985 Corrie van Niekerk was a constable, working with two other lesbians at the front desk of a police station in Johannesburg. She was harassed at the time by her commanding officer and had to leave the SAP to work for a privately run force in Soweto. Today she is a captain in the police. 'SA comes out of the closet', *Saturday Argus,* 24 November, 1997.

39. Schroeder, 'Discrimination drove 300 SA police to suicide last year', p 3.

40. David Halperin, *Saint=Foucault: Towards a Gay Hagiography* (Cambridge: Oxford University Press, 1995): 30.
41. See Judith Butler, 'Decking out: performing identities', in Diana Fuss, ed., *Inside/out: Lesbian Theories, Gay Theories* (New York: Routledge, 1991): 15.
42. On South African descriptive terminology for gay men and lesbians, see Shaun de Waal, 'Etymological note On "moffie"', in Mark Gevisser and Edwin Cameron, eds, *Defiant Desire: Gay and Lesbian Lives in South Africa* (Johannesburg: Raven Press, 1994): x.
43. Butler, *Gender Trouble*, p 2.
44. Butler, *Gender Trouble*, p 3.
45. See for example, 'SA comes out of the closet', *Saturday Argus*, 24 November, 1997; Nikki Whitfield, 'New S.A makes life easier for gays who "come out"', *The Star*, 5 July, 1996; Thami Ngidi, 'Poverty forces black gays into the closet, says activist', *Sunday Argus*, 6 May, 1997.
46. 'Slow coming out for black lesbians', *The Star*, 26 November, 1997. See also 'SA comes out of the closet,' *Saturday Argus*, 24 November, 1997. Busi Kheswa, chair of a black gay organization in Soweto relates the story of how she was dancing with her girlfriend at a nightclub when a stranger started shouting at her 'He said my parents had not performed the proper rituals when I was born, and that's why I was abnormal, she recalled.' And Zanele Mphika, a policewoman, was walking with her girlfriend in a township when a thug drew a gun on them. 'He told me he knew who I was, and he was going to rape my girlfriend in front of me to teach us what happens to people like us.' Caught without her own weapon, she fought him off barehanded. There is also very often an explicit gender connotation made. For example, Bev Ditsie, a gay activist from Soweto recalls how, when she was 10 years old, she began acting in children's television series, but: 'The weird thing is, I was always given boys roles. Maybe they knew something.' See Nikki Whitfield, 'New SA makes life easier for gays who "come out"', *The Star*, 5 July, 1996.

CHAPTER 14: QUEERING INTERNATIONAL HUMAN RIGHTS LAW

1. Although my focus will be on gay men and lesbians, I mean this term in a broader sense, to also encompass the transgendered and those whose appearance and proclivities make them gender and sexuality ambiguous.
2. See Dianne Otto, 'Rethinking the "universality" of human rights law', *Columbia Human Rights Law Review* 29 (1997): 1.
3. See Lisa Duggan 'Queering the state', *Social Text* 39 (1994): 1. By heteronormativity, I mean a world view in which the framework, points of reference and assumptions are all heterosexual. Heteronormativity is thus different from homophobia, which is the irrational fear or hatred of lesbians and gay men.
4. On the development of Human Rights Law generally, see, Henry Steiner and Philip Alston *International Human Rights in Context: Law, Politics, Morals* (Oxford: Clarendon Press, 1996), Chapters 2–5.
5. See Amnesty International 1991 ICM Report (ORG 52/01/92), Decisions of the 1991 Council (1991). Amnesty has been increasingly active on sexuality issues. See, e.g., Amnesty International, *Breaking the Silence: Human Rights Violations Based on Sexual Orientation* (London: Amnesty UK, 1997).
6. E.g. Eric Heinze, *Sexual Orientation: a Human Right* (Dordrecht: Martinus Nijhoff, 1995); Robert Wintemute, *Sexual Orientation and Human Rights* (Oxford: Clarendon Press, 1995). These texts are discussed below.
7. See Kees Waaldjik and Andrew Clapham, eds, *Homosexuality: a European Community Issue* (Dordrecht: Martinus Nijhoff, 1993).
8. See Wintemute, *Sexual Orientation and Human Rights*, pp 92–97. Even when the Commission began to accept such cases as admissible, a breach was rarely found.
9. (1981) 45 Eur Ct HR (ser A).
10. (1988) 142 Eur Ct HR (ser A); (1993) 259 Eur Ct HR.
11. *Sutherland v UK* Application no. 25186/94 (1/7/97).
12. Helmut Graupner, 'Update on Austria', in ILGA-Europe, *ILGA Euroletter* 65 (November 1998).
13. *P v S and Cornwall County Council* (1996) C-13/94 ECR, [1996] All ER (EC) 397; *Grant v SWT* ECR C-249/96 (17 February, 1998).
14. See Waaldjik and Clapham, *Homosexuality*.

15. Document A3-0098/94.
16. Note that the European Parliament adopted an urgency resolution on *Equal Rights for Gays and Lesbians* in September 1998. See ILGA-Europe, *ILGA Euroletter* 63 (September 1998).
17. See Heinze, *Sexual Orientation*, p 12.
18. See further, Dianne Otto, 'Non-government organisations in the United Nations system: the emerging role of international civil society', *Human Rights Quarterly* 18 (Pt 1) (1996): 107–141.
19. The UN World Conference on Human Rights held in 1993 in Vienna was the first UN Conference to have a visible lesbian and gay presence, amidst some hostility; see ILGA, *The Start of a Process: Report of the ILGA Committee on the UN Conference on Human Rights* (July 1993). On Beijing see Dianne Otto, 'Sexualities and solidarities: some thoughts on coalitional strategies in the context of international law', *Australasian Gay and Lesbian Law Journal* 8 (1999): 27–38.
20. *Toonen v Australia* UN Doc CCPR/C/50/D/488/1992 (31 March, 1994). For history of the Tasmanian campaign see Miranda Morris, *The Pink Triangle* (Sydney: University of NSW Press, 1995); Rodney Croome, 'Australian gay rights case goes to the United Nations', *Australasian Gay and Lesbian Law Journal* 2 (1992): 55; Wayne Morgan, 'Identifying evil for what it is: Tasmania, sexual perversity and the United Nations', *Melbourne University Law Review* 19 (1994): 740.
21. For a useful description of these different forms of power, see Sheila Duncan, 'Law's sexual discipline: visibility, violence and consent', *Journal of Law and Society* 23 (1995): 326.
22. See generally Michel Foucault *Discipline and Punish* (New York: Vintage Books, 1979); Michel Foucault, 'Power and sex', in L.D. Kritzman, ed., *Michel Foucault, Politics Philosophy Culture* (New York: Routledge, 1990): pp 110–24.
23. Investigation of the exercise of these forms of power is rare in the legal context, although growing, e.g. Leslie Moran, *The Homosexual(ity) of Law* (London: Routledge, 1996); Dianne Otto, 'Rethinking'.
24. Most law review articles on human rights and sexuality can be so characterized, in my opinion; see the bibliographies in Heinze, *Sexual Orientation*, and in Wintemute, *Sexual Orientation and Human Rights*.
25. Carol Smart, *Feminism and the Power of Law*, especially Chapter 1 (London: Routledge, 1990).
26. *R v Brown* [1994] AC 212; *Laskey, Jaggard and Brown v United Kingdom* (109/1995/615/703-705) 19 February, 1997.
27. Heinze, *Sexual Orientation*, and Wintemute, *Sexual Orientation and Human Rights*.
28. This process of derivation is justified in Chapters 7 and 8. Heinze argues that the goals and assumptions behind human rights law justify and necessitate the derivation of new rights from the exiting corpus. His project is thus presented as non-threatening, rational and coherent with the status quo.
29. *Ibid*, at p 11.
30. *Ibid*, at pp 11–12.
31. *Ibid*, at pp 137–41.
32. *Ibid*, at p 148.
33. Duggan, 'Queering the state'.
34. See, e.g. Anonymous Queers, 'Queers read this', in William Rubenstein, ed., *Lesbians, Gay Men and the Law* (New York: The New Press, 1993).
35. Kris Walker, 'Capitalism, gay identity and international human rights law', unpublished paper delivered at the American Society of International Law Annual Meeting, April, 1999.
36. Wintemute, *Sexual Orientation and Human Rights*, p 5.
37. *Ibid*, pp 11–12.
38. *Ibid*, pp 12–13.
39. Wayne Morgan, 'A queer kind of law: the Senate inquires into sexuality', *International Journal of Law and Discrimination* 2 (1997): 317.
40. Wintemute, *Sexual Orientation and Human Rights*, pp 16–17.
41. *Ibid*, pp 245–6.
42. *Ibid*, p 249.
43. See Cindy Patton, 'Tremble hetero Swine', in Michael Warner, ed., *Fear of a Queer Planet* (Minneapolis: University of Minnesota Press, 1993); Didi Herman, *The Antigay Agenda* (Chicago: University of Chicago Press, 1997).
44. Wintemute, *Sexual Orientation and Human Rights*, p 254.
45. See Heinze, *Sexual Orientation*, Chapter 2; Wintemute, *Sexual Orientation and Human Rights*, pp 6–10. Heinze pays more attention to this issue, but still represents sexual orientation as a fixed category of identity. Wintemute shows no recognition of the debates on sexual identity construction, relying on dictionary definitions for his discussion of this 'concept'.

46. A definition or description of 'queer theory' is not possible (at least, not a succinct one). Queer is a set of disruptive practices, academic and otherwise, aimed at unsettling fields of knowledge we accept as given. Queer(ing) is a process, rather than a theory. Disrupting the way we think about identity construction (sexual and other) has been one area of profound interest to queer theorists. Although it is impossible to pin down 'queer theory', there are, nevertheless, some important (one is tempted to write 'foundational') texts in the queer cannon, e.g. Eve Kosofsky Sedgwick, *Epistemology of the Closet* (Berkeley: University of California Press, 1990); Michael Warner, ed., *Fear of a Queer Planet* (Minneapolis: University of Minnesota Press, 1993); Judith Butler, *Bodies that Matter* (New York: Routledge, 1993); Judith Butler, *Gender Trouble* (New York: Routledge 1990); Lisa Duggan, 'Making it perfectly queer', *Socialist Review* 22 (1992): 11. For an excellent introduction to queer ideas, see Anna Marie Jagose, *Queer Theory* (Melbourne: Melbourne University Press, 1996). In the legal context, see Carl Stychin, *Law's Desire* (London: Routledge, 1996); Wayne Morgan, 'Queer law: identity culture, diversity, law', *Australasian Gay and Lesbian Law Journal* 5 (1995): 1; Frank Valdes, 'Coming out and stepping up: queer legal theory and connectivity', *National Journal of Sexual Orientation Law* 1.1 (1995) (http://sunsite.unc.edu/gaylaw).
47. See Butler, *Bodies that Matter*.
48. *Supra*, notes 9 and 10.
49. See Moran, *The Homosexual(ity) of Law*, p 175.
50. *Supra*, note 13.
51. *Ibid*.
52. *Supra*, note 19.
53. *Supra*, note 20.
54. Dianne Otto, Wayne Morgan, and Kris Walker, 'Rejecting (in)tolerance: critical perspectives on the United Nations Year for Tolerance', *Melbourne University Law Review* 20 (1995): 190.
55. Joseph Raz, *The Morality of Freedom* (Oxford: Clarendon Press, 1990): 401–2 states:

> Toleration implies the suppression or containment of an inclination or desire to persecute, harrass [sic], harm or react in an unwelcome way to a person. But even this does not yet capture the essence of toleration... [A] person is tolerant if and only if he [sic] suppresses a desire to cause to another a harm or hurt which he thinks the other deserves.

56. See further, Morgan, 'Identifying evil'.
57. Sheila Jeffreys, *The Lesbian Heresy* (Melbourne: Spinifex, 1993); Richard Mohr, 'The perils of post-modernity for gay rights', *Canadian Journal of Law and Jurisprudence* 8 (1995): 5.
58. Nicholas Bamforth, *Sexuality, Morals and Justice: a Theory of Lesbian and Gay Rights Law* (London: Cassell, 1997).
59. *Ibid*, p 228.
60. *Ibid*, p 229.
61. See Duggan, 'Queering the state'.
62. See also Walker, 'Capitalism'.
63. Much feminist work has exposed the masculinist and heterosexist foundations of the 'nation state', e.g. Hilary Charlesworth *et al.*, 'Feminist approaches to international law', *American Journal of International Law* 85 (1991): 613.
64. Perhaps the most obvious recent example of sexuality figuring publicly in the construction of national identity is the trial of Anwar Ibrahim in Malaysia in 1998–9. The former Deputy Prime Minister was charged with treason and sodomy. The borders between these two offences were frequently blurred so that the two terms together became virtually oxymoronic. Other notorious examples from twentieth century history include the periods of 'McArthyism' in both USA and Australia. The links between sodomy and the construction of national identity are traced in such works as Moran, *The Homosexual(ity) of Law*, and Carl Stychin, *A Nation By Rights* (Philadelphia: Temple University Press, 1998).
65. See, e.g. Ranajit Guha and Gayatri Chakrovorty Spivak, eds, *Selected Subaltern Studies* (Delhi: Oxford, 1988); Dianne Otto, 'Subalternity and International Law: the Problems of Global Community and the Incommensurability of Difference', *Social and Legal Studies* 5 (1996): 337.
66. Some of these strands of discourse are explored above. It seems trite but necessary to remark that 'sexuality' receives very little attention as a constitutive discourse in international relations (hence silence). The 'championing' of sexuality rights by governments is a 1990s phenomenon, restricted largely to Nordic countries, Canada and Australia; see Doug Sanders, 'Getting lesbian and gay issues onto the international human rights agenda', *Human Rights Quarterly* 18 (1996): 67.
67. See further Otto, 'Sexualities and solidarities'.

68. Some notable exceptions to this silence include: M. Jacqui Alexander, 'Not just (any)body can be a citizen: the politics of law, sexuality and postcoloniality in Trinidad and Tobago and the Bahamas', *Feminist Review* 48 (1994): 5; Peter Drukert, 'In the tropics there is no sin: sexuality and gay–lesbian movements in the third world', *New Left Review* 218 (1996): 74; Lenore Manderson and Margaret Jolly, eds, *Sites of Desire/Economies of Pleasure: Sexualities in Asia and the Pacific* (Chicago: University of Chicago Press, 1997). See also Rachel Rosenbloom, ed., *Unspoken Rules: Sexual Orientation and Women's Human Rights* (London: Cassell, 1996).

REFERENCES

Amin, A. 1994. *Post-Fordism: A Reader*, Oxford: Blackwell.

Arditti, J. and Allen, K. 1993. 'Distressed fathers' perceptions of legal and relational inequities post-divorce', *Family and Conciliation Courts Review* 31:461–76.

Arendell, T. 1995. *Fathers and Divorce*, London: Sage.

Auchmuty, R. 1997. 'Last in, first out: lesbian and gay legal studies', *Feminist Legal Studies* 5(2): 235–53.

Austin, J.L. 1962. *How To Do Things With Words*, the William James Lectures delivered in Harvard University in 1955, edited by J.O. Urmson, London: Oxford University Press.

Baird, R.M. and Rosenbaum, S.E., eds. 1997. *Same-Sex Marriage: the Moral and Legal Debate*, Amherst, NY: Prometheus Books.

Barry, A., Osborne, T., Rose, N., eds. 1996. *Foucault and Political Reason: Liberalism, Neo-liberalism and Rationalities of Government*, London: UCL Press.

Bates, F. 1993. 'When is a wife...?' *Australian Journal of Family Law* 7:274–82.

Beach, D.N. 1980. *The Shona and Zimbabwe, 900–1850*, London: James Currey.

Beck, U. and Beck Gernsheim, E. 1995. *The Normal Chaos of Love*, Cambridge: Polity.

Bell, D. and Valentine, G. 1995. 'The sexed self: strategies of performance, sites of resistance', in *Mapping the Subject: Geographies of Cultural Transformation*, edited by S. Pile and N. Thrift, London: Routledge.

Bergman, M. 1991. 'Status, contract, and history: a dialectical view', *Cardozo Law Review* 13: 171.

Berlant, L. and Freeman, E. 1993. 'Queer nationality', in *Fear of a Queer Planet: Queer Politics and Social Theory*, edited by M. Warner, Minneapolis: University of Minnesota Press, p 193.

Bernard, J. 1973. *The Future of Marriage*, Souvenir Press, New York.

Berotia, C. and Drakich, J. 1993. 'The fathers' rights movement: contradictions in rhetoric and practice', *Journal of Family Issues* 14(4): 592–615.

Blackstone, Sir W. 1765. *Commentaries on the Laws of England*, 4th edn, edited by J. DeWitt Andrews (1899). Chicago: Callaghan and Co.

Blankenhorn, D. 1995. *Fatherless America: Confronting our most Urgent Social Problem*, New York: Basic Books.

Botha, K. and Cameron, E. 1997. 'South Africa', in *Socio-Legal Control of Homosexual Behaviour*, edited by R. Green, and D.J. West, London: Plenum.

Bower, L. 1997. 'Queer problems/straight solutions: the limits of a politics of "official recognition"', in *Playing with Fire: Queer Politics, Queer Theories*, edited by S. Phelan, New York: Routledge, p 267.

Briggs, S. 1994. 'Domestic partners and family benefits: an emerging trend', *Labor Law Journal* 1994:749.

Brook, H. 1996. 'Queer football: feminism, sexuality, corporeality', *Critical inQueeries*, 1(2): 25–45.

Brook, H. 1997. 'The troubled courtship of Gladys and Mick', *Australian Journal of Political Science* 32(3): 419–36.

Brown, B. 1990. 'Reassessing the critique of biologism', in *Feminist Perspectives in Criminology*, edited by L. Gelsthorpe and A. Morris, Buckingham: Open University Press.

Brown, B. 1994. 'Pleasures untold: heterosexuality, power and radicalism', *Feminism and Psychology* 4(2): 322–25.

Brown, J. and Day Sclater, S. 1999. 'Divorce: a psychodynamic perspective', in *Undercurrents of Divorce*, edited by S. Day Sclater and C. Piper, Aldershot: Ashgate Dartmouth.

Bullock, C. 1950. *The Mashona and the Matabele*, Cape Town: Juta & Co.

Burchell, G. 1996. 'Liberal government and techniques of the self', in *Foucault and Political Reason: Liberalism, Neo-liberalism and Rationalities of Government*, edited by A. Barry, T. Osborne and N. Rose, London: UCL Press.

Burchell, G., Gordon C. and Miller, P., eds. 1991. *The Foucault Effect: Studies in Governmentality*, Chicago: University of Chicago Press.

Burgess, A. 1997. *Fatherhood Reclaimed*, London: Vermillion.

Burgess, A. and Ruxton, S. 1996. *Men and Their Children: Proposals for Public Policy*, London: Institute for Public Policy Research.

Burghes, L., Clarke, L. and Cronin, N. 1997. *Fathers and Fatherhood in Britain*, London: Family Policy Studies Centre.

Burke, T. 1996. *Lifebuoy Men, Lux Women: Commodification, Consumption, and Cleanliness in Modern Zimbabwe*, London: Leicester University Press.

Butler, J. 1988. 'Performative acts and gender constitution: an essay in phenomenology and feminist theory', *Theatre Journal* 40(4): 519–31.

Butler, J. 1990. *Gender Trouble: Feminism and the Subversion of Identity*, New York: Routledge.

Butler, J. 1991. 'Imitation and gender insubordination', in *Inside/out: Lesbian Theories, Gay Theories*, edited by D. Fuss, New York: Routledge.

Butler, J. 1992. 'The body you want: Liz Kotz interviews Judith Butler', *Artforum* 31(3): 82–9.

Butler, J. 1993. *Bodies That Matter: On the Discursive Limits of 'Sex'*, New York: Routledge.

Butler, J. 1994. 'Against proper objects', *Differences* 6(2 and 3): 1–26.

Butler, J. 1995. 'For a careful reading', in *Feminist Contentions*, edited by L. Nicholson, New York: Routledge.

Butler, J. 1996. 'Sexual inversions', in *Feminist Interpretations of Michel Foucault*, edited by S.J. Hekman, University Park, Pennsylvania: Pennsylvania University Press.

Butler, J. 1997. *Excitable Speech: a Politics of the Performative*, New York and London: Routledge.

Butler, J. 1998. 'Merely cultural', *New Left Review* 227: 33.

Califia, P. 1997. *Sex Changes: the Politics of Transgenderism*. San Francisco: Cleis Press.

Canberra Times. 1995. 'Nats say no to rights for gay families', 11 September, 1995, p 1.

Caplan, P., ed. 1987. *The Cultural Construction of Sexuality*, London: Tavistock.

Carabine, J. 1996a. 'Heterosexuality and social policy', in *Theorising Heterosexuality: Telling it Straight*, edited by D. Richardson, Buckingham: Open University Press

Carabine, J. 1996b. 'A straight playing field or queering the pitch? Centring sexuality in social policy', *Feminist Review* 54 (Autumn): 31–64.

Casey, C. 1995. *Work, Self, and Society after Industrialism*, London: Routledge.

Christensen, C. 1998. 'If not marriage? On securing gay and lesbian family values by a "simulacrum of marriage"', *Fordham Law Review* 66: 1699.

Coleman, T. 1995. 'The Hawaii legislature has compelling reasons to adopt a comprehensive domestic partnership act', *Law & Sexuality* 5: 541.

Collier, R. 1992. '"The art of living the married life": representations of male heterosexuality in law', *Social and Legal Studies* 1(4): 543–63.

Collier, R. 1996. '"Coming together?": post-heterosexuality, masculine crisis and the new men's movement', *Feminist Legal Studies* 4(1): 3–48.

Collier, R. 1995. *Masculinity, Law and the Family*, London: Routledge.

Collier, R. 1998. *Masculinities, Crime and Criminology*, London: Sage.

Collier, R. 1999. 'From women's emancipation to sex war? Men, heterosexuality and the politics of divorce', in *Undercurrents of Divorce*, edited by S. Day Sclater and C. Piper, Aldershot: Ashgate Dartmouth.

Comaroff, J. 1997. 'The discourse of rights in colonial South Africa: subjectivity, sovereignty, modernity', in *Identities, Politics and Rights*, edited by A. Sarat and T.R. Kearns, Ann Arbor: University of Michigan Press.

Connolly, T. 1994. *Speeches in the ACT Legislative Assembly*, 21st April and 19th May 1994, Australian Capital Territory, Parliamentary Debates.

Connolly, W. 1991. *Identity/Difference: Democratic Negotiations of Political Paradox*, Ithaca, NY: Cornell University Press.

Cooper, D. 1994. *Sexing the City: Lesbian and Gay Politics Within the Activist State*, London: Rivers Oram Press.

Currah, P. 1997. 'Politics, practices, publics: identity and queer rights', in *Playing with Fire: Queer Politics, Queer Theories*, edited by S. Phelan, New York: Routledge, p 231.

Day Sclater, S. 1998. *The Psychology of Divorce: a Research Report to the ESRC* University of East London.

Day Sclater, S. 1999. *Divorce: a Psycho-social Study*, Aldershot: Ashgate.

Day Sclater, S. and Piper, C. 1999. *Undercurrents of Divorce*, Aldershot: Ashgate Dartmouth.

Day Sclater, S. and Yates, C. 1999. 'The psycho-politics of post divorce parenting', in *What is a Parent? A Socio-Legal Analysis*, edited by A. Bainham, S. Day Sclater and M. Richards, Oxford: Hart Publishing, pp 271–93.

Day, L. 1996. 'Who authorises speech acts? Woolf's *Orlando* responds', occasional paper no 21, Clayton, Victoria: The Centre for Women's Studies, Monash University.

Dench, G. 1996. *Exploring Variations in Men's Family Roles: Joseph Rowntree Foundation Social Policy Research Findings No 99*, London: Joseph Rowntree Foundation.

Dewar, J. 1996. 'Family, law and theory', *Oxford Journal of Legal Studies* 16(4): 725.

Dewar, J. 1998. 'The normal chaos of family law', *Modern Law Review* 61 (Pt 4): 467–85.

Diduck, A. 1995. 'The unmodified family: the Child Support Act and the construction of legal subjects', *Journal of Law and Society* 22(4): 527-48.

Diduck, A. 1998. 'In search of the feminist good mother', *Social and Legal Studies* 7 (1): 129–36.

Donzelot, J. 1979. *The Policing of Families*, New York: Pantheon Books.

Eskridge, W.N. Jr. 1996. *The Case for Same-Sex Marriage: from Sexual Liberty to Civilized Commitment*, New York: The Free Press.

Esser, J. 1996. 'Institutionalizing industry: the changing forms of contract', *Law & Social Inquiry* 21: 593.

Ewald, F. 1990. 'Norms, discipline and the law', *Representations* 30: 138–161.

Feinman, J. and Gabel, P. 1990. 'Contract law as ideology', in *The Politics of Law: a Progressive Critique*, edited by D. Kairys, New York: Pantheon Books, p 373.

Fineman, M.A. 1991. *The Illusion of Equality: the Rhetoric and Reality of Divorce Reform*, Chicago: University of Chicago Press.

Fineman, M.A. 1995. *The Neutered Mother, the Sexual Family and Other Twentieth Century Tragedies*, New York: Routledge.

Fineman, M.A. and Karpin, I., eds, 1995. *Mothers in Law: Feminist Theory and the Legal Regulation of Motherhood*, New York: Columbia University Press.

Finlay, H.A. and Walters, W.A.W. 1988. *Sex Change: Medical and Legal Aspects of Sex Reassignment*, Box Hill, Victoria: H.A. Finlay.

Folbre, N. 1988. Patriarchal social formations in Zimbabwe, in *Patriarchy and Class: African Women in the Home and the Workforce*, edited by S.B. Stichter and J.L. Parpart, Boulder: Westview Press.

Forguson, L.W. 1969. 'In pursuit of performatives', in *Symposium on J.L. Austin*, edited by K.T. Fann, London: Routledge & Kegan Paul, pp 412–9.

Fortin, A. 1995. 'AIDS, surveillance, and public policy', *Research in Law and Policy Studies* 4: 173.

Foucault, M. 1978. *The History of Sexuality: an Introduction*, London: Penguin Books.

Foucault, M. 1979a. *Discipline and Punish: the Birth of the Prison*, London: Peregrine.

Foucault, M. 1979b. *The History of Sexuality, vol 1*, London: Allen Lane.

Foucault, M. 1991. 'Governmentality', in *The Foucault Effect: Studies in Governmentality*, edited by G. Burchell, C. Gordon and P. Miller, London: Harvester Wheatsheaf, pp 87–104.

Fraser, N. 1997. *Justice Interruptus: Critical Reflections on the "Postsocialist" Condition*, New York: Routledge.

Gabin, N. 1990. *Feminism in the Labor Movement: Women and the United Auto Wokers, 1935–1975*, Ithaca, NY: Cornell University Press.

Gerson, K. 1993. *No Man's Land: Men's Changing Commitment to Family and Work*, New York: Basic Books.

Gevisser, M. and Cameron, E., eds. 1995. *Defiant Desire: Gay and Lesbian Lives in South Africa*, London: Routledge.

Giddens, A. 1991. *Modernity and Self-Identity*, Cambridge: Polity.

Giddens, A. 1992. *The Transformation of Intimacy*. Stanford, California: Stanford University Press.

Giddens, A. 1998. *The Third Way*, Cambridge: Polity.

Gilman, S.L. 1986. *Difference and Pathology: Stereotypes of Sexuality, Race, and Madness*, Ithaca: Cornell University Press.

Gramsci, A. 1971. *Selections from the Prison Notebooks of Antonio Gramsci*, New York: International Publishers.

Greenberg, D.F. 1988. *The Construction of Homosexuality*, Chicago: University of Chicago Press.

Grossberg, M. 1985. *Governing the Hearth: Law and the Family in Nineteenth-century America*, Chapel Hill: University of North Carolina Press.

Hambly, D. and Turner, J.N. 1971. *Cases and Materials on Australian Family Law*, Sydney: The Law Book Company Ltd.

Harvey, D. 1989. *The Condition of Postmodernity*, Oxford: Blackwell.

Hawkes, G. 1996. *A Sociology of Sex and Gender*, London: Macmillan.

Hearn, J. 1996. 'Is masculinity dead? A critique of the concept of masculinity', in *Understanding Masculinities*, edited by M. Mac an Ghaill, Buckingham: Open University Press.

Herman, D. 1994. *Rights of Passage: Struggles for Lesbian and Gay Equality*, Toronto: University of Toronto Press.

Herman, D. 1997. *The Antigay Agenda: Orthodox Vision and the Christian Right*, Chicago: University of Chicago Press.

Herman, D. and Stychin, C., eds, 1995. *Legal Inversions: Lesbians, Gay Men and the Politics of Law*, Philadelphia: Temple University Press.

Hindess, B. 1996. 'Liberalism, socialism and democracy: variations on a governmental theme', in *Foucault and Political Reason: Liberalism, neo-liberalism and rationalities of government*, edited by A. Barry, T. Osborne, N. Rose, London: UCL Press.

Hoad, N. 1998. 'Tradition, modernity and human rights: an interrogation of contemporary gay and lesbian rights' claims in southern African nationalist discourses', in *Development Update* 2(2): 32–43.

Hobsbawm, E. and Ranger, T., eds. 1983. *The Invention of Tradition*, Cambridge: Cambridge University Press.

Holcombe, L. 1983. *Wives and Property: Reform of the Married Women's Property Law in Nineteenth-Century England*, Oxford: Martin Robertson.

Hollway, W. 1993. 'Theorising heterosexuality: a response', *Feminism and Psychology* 3(2): 412–17.

Hollway, W. 1995a. 'A second bite at the heterosexual cherry', *Feminism and Psychology* 5(1): 126–30.

Hollway, W. 1995b. 'Feminist discourses and women's heterosexual desire', in *Feminism and Discourse*, edited by S. Wilkinson and C. Kitzinger, London: Sage.

Hollway, W. 1996. 'Recognition and heterosexual desire', in *Theorising Heterosexuality: Telling it Straight*, edited by D. Richardson, Buckingham: Open University Press.

Hughes, H. 1998. 'Same-sex marriage and simulacra: exploring conceptions of equality', *Harvard Civil Rights – Civil Liberties Law Review* 33: 237.

Jackson, S. 1996. 'Heterosexuality and feminist theory', in *Theorising Heterosexuality: Telling it Straight*, edited by D. Richardson, Buckingham: Open University Press.

Jacob, H. 1988. *Silent Revolution: the Transformation of Divorce Law in the United States*, Chicago: University of Chicago Press.

Jacobs, S.M. 1984. 'Women and land resettlement in Zimbabwe', in *Review of African Political Economy* 27/28: 33–50.

Jacobs, S.M. and Howard, T. 1987. 'Women in Zimbabwe: stated policy and state action', in *Women, State, and Ideology: Studies from Africa and Asia*, edited by H. Afshar, London: Macmillan.

Jeater, D. 1993. 'Marriage, perversion and power: the construction of moral discourse in southern Rhodesia 1894–1930', Oxford: Clarendon Press.

Jefferson, T. 1994. 'Theorizing masculine subjectivity', in *Just Boys Doing Business? Men, Masculinities and Crime*, edited by T. Newburn and E.E. Stanko, London: Routledge.

Johnson, R. 1997. 'Contested borders, contingent lives', in *Border Patrols: Policing the Boundaries of Heterosexuality*, edited by D.L. Steinberg, D. Epstein and R. Johnson, London: Cassell.

Kann, M. 1991. *On the Man Question: Gender and Civic Virtue in America*, Philadelphia: Temple University Press.

Kendall. 1998. '"When a woman loves a woman" in Lesotho: love, sex, and the (Western) construction of homophobia', in *Boy Wives and Female Husbands: Studies of African Homosexualities*, edited by S.O. Murray and W. Roscoe, New York: St Martin's Press.

Kitzinger, C. and Wilkinson, S. 1994. 'Re-viewing heterosexuality', *Feminism and Psychology* 4(2): 330–6.

Kon, I. 1997. 'Russia', in *Socio-Legal Control of Homosexual Behaviour: a Multi-Nation Comparison*, edited by R. Green and D.J. West, London: Plenum.

Lesbian & Gay Legal Rights Service (LGLRS). 1994. *The Bride Wore Pink: Legal Recognition of Our Relationships. A Discussion Paper*, 2nd edn, Darlinghurst, NSW: Lesbian & Gay Legal Rights Service, a project of the Gay and Lesbian Rights Lobby.

Lipietz, A. 1994. 'Post-Fordism and democracy', in *Post-Fordism: a Reader*, edited by A. Amin, Oxford: Blackwell, p 338.

Locke, J. 1980 <1690>. *Second Treatise of Government*, Indianapolis, Indiana: Hackett.
Lord Chancellor's Department. 1998. *Court Procedures for the Determination of Paternity: the Law on Parental Responsibility for Unmarried Fathers – Consultation Paper*, London: Lord Chancellor's Department.
Luhmann, N. 1986. *Love as Passion: the Codification of Intimacy*, Cambridge, Massachusetts: Harvard University Press.
Lupton, D and Barclay, L. 1997. *Constructing Fatherhood: Discourses and Experiences*, London: Sage.

MacDougall, D.J. 1966. 'Proposals to reform the law of condonation', *Australian Law Journal* 39: 295–301.
Mackenzie, R. 1992. 'Transsexuals' legal status and same sex marriage in New Zealand: M v M', *Otago Law Review* 7(4): 556-77.
Maine, Sir H. 1917. *Ancient Law*, London: J. M. Dent & Sons.
Martin, D. and Johnson, P. 1981. *The Struggle for Zimbabwe: the Chimurenga War*, London: Faber and Faber.
Marx, K. 1978 <1848>. 'On the Jewish question', in *The Marx–Engels Reader*, 2nd edn, edited by R. Tucker, New York: W.W. Norton, p 26.
Maynard, M. and Purvis, J. 1995. *(Hetero)Sexual Politics*, London: Taylor & Francis.
Midgley, M. and Hughes, J. 1997. 'Are families out of date?', in *Feminism and Families*, edited by H.L. Nelson, London: Routledge.
Misihairambwi, P. 1997. 'The WASN Youth Programme in Zimbabwe', unpublished paper given at conference on *Community Responses to HIV in Southern Africa*, Sheffield.
Mitchell, J. and Goody, J. 1997. 'Feminism, fatherhood and the family in Britain', in *Who's Afraid of Feminism? Seeing Through the Backlash*, edited by A. Oakley and J. Mitchell, London: Hamish Hamilton.
Moran, L. 1995. 'The homosexualization of English law', in *Legal Inversions: Lesbians, Gay Men, and the Politics of Law*, edited by D. Herman, and C. Stychin, Philadelphia: Temple University Press.
Morgan, D. 1996. *Family Connections: an Introduction to Family Studies*, Oxford: Polity Press.
Mountbatten, J. 1994. 'Transsexuals and social security law: the return of Gonad the Barbarian', *Australian Journal of Family Law* 8(2): 166–77.
Myerson, A. 1998. 'Perot ends benefits for partners of newly hired gay workers', *New York Times*, 10 April.

New Ways to Work. 1995. *Balanced Lives: Changing Work Patterns for Men*, London.

O'Donovan, K. 1985. *Sexual Divisions in Law*, London: Weidenfeld & Nicolson.
O'Donovan, K. 1993. *Family Law Matters*, London: Pluto.
Oerton, S. 1996. *Beyond Hierarchy*, London: Taylor & Francis.
Oliver, M. and Shapiro, T. 1995. *Black Wealth/White Wealth: a New Perspective on Racial Inequality*, New York: Routledge.
Otlowski, M. 1990. 'The legal status of a sexually reassigned transsexual: R v Harris and McGuiness and beyond.' *Australian Law Journal* 64(1–2): 67–74.

Parker, A. and Sedgwick, E.K., eds. 1995. 'Introduction: performativity and performance', in *Performativity and Performance*, New York and London: Routledge, pp 1–18.
Parker, S., Parkinson, P. and Behrens, J. 1994. *Australian Family Law in Context: Commentary and Materials*, Sydney: The Law Book Co.
Pashukanis, E. 1978. *Law and Marxism: a General Theory*, London: Ink Links.
Pateman, C. 1988. *The Sexual Contract*, Stanford, California: Stanford University Press.
Pattman, R. 1995. 'Discourses of Sex, Aids, and Sex/Aids Education in Zimbabwe', unpublished Ph.D. thesis, Institute of Education, London.
Patton, C. 1995. 'Refiguring social Space', in *Social Postmodernism: Beyond Identity Politics*, edited by L. Nicholson and S. Seidman, Cambridge: Cambridge University Press, p 216.
Patton, C. 1997. 'Queer space/God's space: counting down to the apocalypse', *Rethinking Marxism* 9: 1.
Phelan, S. 1995. 'The space of justice: lesbians and democratic politics', in *Social Postmodernism: Beyond Identity Politics*, edited by L. Nicholson and S. Seidman, Cambridge: Cambridge University Press, p 332.
Phelan, S. 1998. 'Bodies, passions and citizenship', paper presented at 1998 American Political Science Association Meetings, Boston.
Phillips, O.C. 1997a. 'Zimbabwe', in *Socio-Legal Control of Homosexual Behaviour: a Multi-Nation Comparison*, edited by R. Green and D.J. West, London: Plenum.

Phillips, O.C. 1997b. 'Zimbabwean law and the production of a white man's disease', *Social and Legal Studies* 6(4): 471–92.

Pinkerton, S.D. and Abramson, P.R. 1997. 'Japan', in *Socio-Legal Control of Homosexual Behaviour: a Multi-Nation Comparison*, edited by R. Green and D.J. West, London: Plenum.

Plummer, K., ed. 1981. *The Making of the Modern Homosexual*, London: Hutchinson.

Posner, R. 1992. *Sex and Reason*, Cambridge, Massachusetts: Harvard University Press.

Pound, R. 1909. 'Liberty of contract', *Yale Law Jounal* 18: 454.

Prendergast, S. and Forrest, S. 1997. 'Hieroglyphs of the heterosexual: learning about gender in school', in *New Sexual Agendas*, edited by L. Segal, London: Macmillan.

Probyn, E. 1993. *Sexing the Self: Gendered Positions in Cultural Studies*, London: Routledge.

Ramazanoglu, C. 1994. 'Theorizing heterosexuality: a response to Wendy Hollway', *Feminism and Psychology* 4(2): 320–21.

Ramazanoglu, C. 1995. 'Back to basics: heterosexuality, biology and why men stay on top', in *(Hetero)Sexual Politics*, edited by M. Maynard and J. Purvis, London: Taylor & Francis.

Ranger, T. 1989. 'Missionaries, migrants, and the Manyika: the invention of ethnicity in Zimbabwe', in *The Creation of Tribalism in Southern Africa*, edited by L. Vail, London: James Currey.

Regan, M. 1993. *Family Law and the Pursuit of Intimacy*, New York: New York University Press.

Reinhold, S. 1994. 'Through the parliamentary looking glass: "real" and "pretend" families in contemporary British politics', *Feminist Review* 48: 61–79.

Rich, A. 1980. 'Compulsory heterosexuality and lesbian existence', *Signs* 5(4): 631–60.

Rich, A. 1981. *Compulsory Heterosexuality and Lesbian Existence*, London: Onlywomen Press.

Richardson, D., ed. 1996. *Theorising Heterosexuality: Telling it Straight*, Buckingham: Open University Press

Robinson, V. 1996. 'Heterosexuality and masculinity: theorising male power or the wounded male psyche?', in *Theorising Heterosexuality*, edited by D. Richardson, Buckingham: Open University Press.

Robson, R. 1992. *Lesbian (Out)Law: Survival Under the Rule of Law*, Ithaca, NY: Firebrand Books.

Robson, R. and S. Valentine. 1990. 'Lov(H)ers: lesbians as intimate partners and lesbian legal theory', *Temple Law Review* 63: 511.

Rose, N. and Valverde, M. 1998. 'Governed by law?', *Social and Legal Studies* 7(4): 541–53.

Rupert, M. 1995. *Producing Hegemony*, Cambridge: Cambridge University Press.

Samuels, A. 1997. 'Therapy as think tank: from a man's internal family to new political forms', *New Sexual Agendas*, edited by L. Segal, London: Macmillan.

Sandland, J. 1995. 'Between "truth" and "difference": poststructuralism, law and the power of feminism', *Feminist Legal Studies* 3(1): 3–47.

Schacter, J. 1997. 'Skepticism, culture and the gay civil rights debate in a post-civil-rights era', *Harvard Law Review* 110: 684.

Scutt, J.A. 1995. 'Judicial bias or legal bias?: Battery, women and the law', *Journal of Australian Studies* 43: 130–43.

Searle, J.R. 1989. 'How performatives work', *Linguistics and Philosophy* 12(5): 535–58.

Sedgwick, E. 1990. *Epistemology of the Closet*, Berkeley: University of California Press and Hemel Hempstead: Harverster Wheatsheaf.

Segal, L. 1994. *Straight Sex: the Politics of Pleasure*, London: Virago.

Segal, L. 1997. 'Feminist sexual politics and the heterosexual predicament', in *New Sexual Agendas*, edited by L. Segal, London: Macmillan.

Seidman, G. 1984. 'Women in Zimbabwe: post-independence struggles', in *Feminist Studies* 10(3): Fall.

Sevenhuijsen, S. 1998. *Citizenship and the Ethics of Care: Feminist Considerations about Justice, Morality and Politics*, London: Routledge.

Sharpe, A.N. 1997. 'The transsexual and marriage: law's contradictory desires', *Australasian Gay and Lesbian Law Journal* 7: 1–14.

Sherman, S., ed. 1992. *Lesbian and Gay Marriage: Private Commitments, Public Ceremonies*, Philadelphia: Temple University Press.

Showalter, E. 1992. *Sexual Anarchy*, London: Virago.

Silva, E., ed. 1996. *Good Enough Mothering? Feminist Perspectives on Lone Motherhood*, London: Routledge.

Smart, C. 1984. *The Ties That Bind*, London: Routledge and Kegan Paul.

Smart, C. 1989. *Feminism and the Power of Law*, London: Routledge.

Smart, C. 1996a. 'Collusion, collaboration and confession on moving beyond the heterosexuality debate', in *Theorising Heterosexuality: Telling it Straight*, edited by D. Richardson, Open University Press: Buckingham.

Smart, C. 1996b. 'Desperately seeking post-heterosexual woman', in *Sex, Sensibility and the Gendered Body*, edited by J. Holland and L. Adkins, London: Macmillan.

Smart, C. 1997. 'Wishful thinking and harmful tinkering? Sociological reflections on family policy', *Journal of Social Policy* 26(3): 301–21.

Smart, C. and Brophy, J., eds, 1985. *Women in Law: Explorations in Law, Family, Sexuality*, London: Routledge and Kegan Paul.

Smart, C. and Neale, B. 1997. 'Good enough morality? Divorce and postmodernity', *Critical Social Policy* 17(4): 3–27.

Smith, D.K. 1971. 'Transsexualism, sex reassignment surgery, and the law', *Cornell Law Review* 56: 963–1009.

Social Focus on Men and Women. 1998. *Social Focus on Men and Women: Report*, London: HMSO.

Soper, K. 1995. 'Heterosexual utopianism', *Radical Philosophy* 69: 5–15.

Speilman, S. and Winfeld, L. 1996. 'Domestic partner benefits: a bottom line discussion', in *Sexual Identity on the Job: Issues and Services*, edited by A. Ellis and E. Riggle, New York: The Haworth Press, p 53.

Stacey, J. 1996. *In the Name of the Family: Rethinking Family Values in the Postmodern Age*, Boston: Beacon Press.

Steinberg, D.L., Epstein, D. and Johnson, R., eds. 1997. *Border Patrols: policing the boundaries of Heterosexuality*, London: Cassell.

Stoler, A.C. 1995. *Race and the Education of Desire: Foucault's History of Sexuality and the Colonial Order of Things*, London: Duke University Press.

Stychin, C.F. 1995. *Law's Desire: Sexuality and the Limits of Justice*, London: Routledge.

Stychin, C.F. 1998. *A Nation by Rights: National Cultures, Sexual Identity Politics, and the Discourse of Rights*, Philadelphia: Temple University Press.

Sullivan, A. 1996. *Virtually Normal: an Argument About Homosexuality*, 2nd edn, London: Picador.

Sullivan, A. 1997. *Same-Sex Marriage: Pro and Con: a Reader*, New York: Vintage Books.

Sullivan, A. 1998. 'Going down screaming', *New York Times Magazine*, 11 October 1998, p 47.

Sunstein, C. 1994. 'Homosexuality and the constitution', *Indiana Law Journal* 70: 1.

Supporting Families: a consultation document', 1998. London: HMSO.

Swindello, J. 1993. 'A straight outing: what exactly is heterosexuality and what causes it?', *Trouble and Strife* 26 (Summer): 40–43.

'Thomas'. 1992. *Interview*. Balancing Rocks, Epworth, Harare, 15 November.

Thompson, D. 1994. 'Retaining the radical challenge: a reply to Wendy Hollway', *Feminism and Psychology* 4(2): 326–9.

Unger, R. 1987. 'False necessity: anti-necessitarian social theory in the service of radical democracy', Cambridge: Cambridge University Press.

United Nations Human Rights Committee. 1998a. 'Summary record of the 1651st meeting', released 28 July 1998, CCPR/C/SR, 1651.

United Nations Human Rights Committee. 1998b. 'Consideration of reports submitted by states parties under Article 40 to the Covenant', 1651st Meeting, 26 March 1998, CCPR/C/74/Add.3, HRI/CORE/1/ADD.55.

Utting, D. 1995. *Family and Parenthood: Supporting Families, Preventing Breakdown: Social Policy Summary 4*, London: Joseph Rowntree Foundation,

Vaid, U. 1995. *Virtual Equality: the Mainstreaming of Gay & Lesbian Liberation*, New York: Anchor Books.

Waldby, C. 1995. 'Destruction: boundary erotics and refigurations of the heterosexual male body', in *Sexy Bodies: the Strange Carnalities of Feminism*, edited by E. Grosz and E. Probyn, London: Routledge.

Wallbank, J. 1997. 'The campaign for change of the Child Support Act 1991: Reconstituting the "absent" father', *Social and Legal Studies* 6(2): 191–216.

Warner, M., ed. 1993. *Fear of a Queer Planet*, Minneapolis, University of Minnesota Press.

Warnock, G.J. 1973. 'Some types of performative utterance', in Berlin *et al.*, *Essays on J.L. Austin*, London: Clarendon Press, pp 69–89.

Weeks, J. 1989. *Sex, Politics and Society: the Regulation of Sexuality since 1800*, Harlow: Longman.

Westwood, S. 1996. '"Feckless Fathers" masculinities and the British state', in *Understanding Masculinities*, edited by M. Mac an Ghaill, Buckingham: Open University Press.

Weyland, I. 1997. 'The blood tie: raised to the status of a presumption', *Journal of Social Welfare and Family Law* 19(2): 173–88.

Wilkinson, S. and Kitzinger, C., eds. 1993. *Heterosexuality: a Feminism and Psychology Reader*, London: Sage.

Wittig, M. 1992. *The Straight Mind and Other Essays, Brighton: Harvester Wheatsheaf.*

Wolfram, S. 1990. ' "Husband and wife are one person: the husband" (nineteenth-century English aphorism)', in *Women's Rights and the Rights of Man*, edited by A.-J. Arnaud and E. Kingdom, Aberdeen: Aberdeen University Press.

Wolfson, E. 1994. 'Crossing the threshold: equal marriage rights for lesbians and gay men and the intra-community critique', *Review of Law and Social Change* 21: 567.

Wright, T. and Wright, R. 1997. 'Bolivia', in *Socio-Legal Control of Homosexual Behaviour: a Multi-Nation Comparison*, edited by R. Green, and D.J. West, London: Plenum Press.

Young, A. 1993. 'The authority of the name', in *Heterosexuality: A Feminism and Psychology Reader*, edited by S. Wilkinson and C. Kitzinger, London: Sage.

Zetlein, S. 1994. 'Lesbian Bodies Before the Law: Intimate Relations and Regulatory Fictions', Honours Thesis, Department of Politics and Department of Women's Studies, University of Adelaide, South Australia.

Zetlein, S. 1996. 'Lesbian bodies before the law: chicks in white satin', *Australian Feminist Law Journal* 5: 49–63.

ABOUT THE EDITORS

CARL STYCHIN is Professor of Law and Social Theory at the University of Reading, UK. His publications include *Law's Desire: Sexuality and the Limits of Justice* (London: Routledge, 1995), *A Nation by Rights: National Cultures, Sexual Identity Politics, and the Discourse of Rights* (Philadelphia: Temple University Press, 1998), and he was co-editor (with Didi Herman) of *Legal Inversions: Lesbians, Gay Men, and the Politics of Law* (Philadelphia: Temple University Press, 1995). He is currently vice-chair of the Socio Legal Studies Association and an editor of the journal *Social and Legal Studies*.

DIDI HERMAN is Professor of Law and Social Change at Keele University, UK. Her publications include *Rights of Passage: Struggles for Lesbian and Gay Equality* (Toronto: University of Toronto Press, 1994), *The Antigay Agenda: Orthodox Vision and the Christian Right* (Chicago: University of Chicago Press, 1997) and, with Doris Buss, *Globalising Family Values: The Christian Right's International Campaign Against Feminism and Gay Rights* (Chicago: University of Chicago Press, forthcoming, 2001). She is currently Head of Keele University's Law Department and an editor of the journal *Social and Legal Studies*.

ABOUT THE CONTRIBUTORS

HEATHER BROOK teaches Women's Studies at Flinders University and Cultural Studies at the University of South Australia. Her research interests include feminist theory, indigenous Australia, the government of 'private life' (especially through marriage and marriage-like relationships), the politics of sport, and drug law reform. Her work has appeared in *Critical inQueeries* and the *Australian Journal of Political Science*.

RICHARD COLLIER is a Professor of Law at the University of Newcastle Upon Tyne, UK. He has published widely in the area of gender and law and is the author of *Masculinities Crime and Criminology* (London: Sage, 1998) and *Masculinity, Law and the Family* (London: Routledge, 1995).

DEREK DALTON is undertaking doctoral research in the Criminology Department at the University of Melbourne, Australia. His thesis, 'Homocriminality: the legal and cultural imagination of the gay male subject', interrogates the ways in which homosexuality is articulated through Australian cultural (cinematic, literary, legal) texts. Additionally, the project seeks to examine strategies gay men adopt to defy regulation of their desire.

PIERRE DE VOS is an associate professor in the Department of Public Law at the University of the Western Cape, South Africa where he teaches Constitutional Law and International Human Rights Law. He has recently completed an LLD thesis entitled 'Sexual orientation, the right to equality and South Africa's 1996 Constitution' and has written widely on sexuality and the new constitutional order in South Africa.

JONATHAN GOLDBERG-HILLER holds degrees from the University of Wisconsin and Reed College and is a member of the political science faculty at the University of Hawai'i at Manoa. He has published on the political and legal dynamics of same-sex marriage in the United States and on labour law. His forthcoming book on the same-sex marriage issue is entitled *The Limits to Union* (Michigan: University of Michigan Press).

PATRICK HANAFIN is a lecturer in the Department of Law at Birkbeck College, University of London, where he teaches courses in criminal law, media law and culture, and medical law and ethics. His research interests lie in the areas of law and postcoloniality, law and bioethics and law and psychoanalysis. His publications include *Last Rights: Death, Dying and the Law in Ireland* (Cork: Cork University Press, 1997), and *Identity, Rights and Constitutional Transformation* (co-edited with Melissa Wiliams, Aldershot: Ashgate, 1999).

EMMA M. HENDERSON teaches law at La Trobe University, Melbourne Australia. Her Ph.D. (University of Melbourne, 1999) and publications to date revolve around a comparison of decriminalization struggles in England, Canada and Australia.

ADRIAN HOWE teaches critical criminology at La Trobe University. Her publications include *Punish and Critique: Towards a Feminist Analysis of Penality* (London: Routledge, 1994), and the edited collection, *Sexed Crime in the News* (Sydney: Federation Press, 1998).

REBECCA JOHNSON is an assistant professor in the Faculty of Law at the University of New Brunswick, Canada, where she teaches constitutional law, criminal law, feminist advocacy, and law and popular culture. Her doctoral dissertation, 'Power and wound: the intersection of privilege and disadvantage in *Symes v Canada*' (S.J.D., University of Michigan), explores the ways in which individual lives are marked by different combinations of privilege and disadvantage through the intersection of gender with class, race, and sexual orientation.

THOMAS KUTTNER has been on the Faculty of Law at the University of New Brunswick, Canada, since 1979 where he teaches and engages in research in the fields of administrative, constitutional and labour law. In addition he sits as a Vice-Chair of the New Brunswick Labour and Employment Board, and is active in labour arbitration and mediation. He has acted as Counsel pro bono in several human rights cases before the Courts of New Brunswick and the Supreme Court of Canada.

DEREK McGHEE is a Lecturer in the Department of Sociology and Social Policy at Southampton University, UK. His research interests lie in socio-legal studies, the sociologization of queer theory, the body and Foucauldian institutional and insurrectional politics. Publications include articles in *Feminist Legal Studies, Law and Critique, Body and Society*, and *Space and Culture*. He is currently working on a monograph on contemporary case studies including the British armed forces' homosexual exclusion policy, homosexual refugees, and the age of consent.

LESLIE J. MORAN is Reader in Law at Birkbeck College, University of London, where he teaches courses on Gender, Sexuality and Law. He has written extensively on sexuality and law. He is author of *The Homosexual(ity) of Law* (London: Routledge, 1996), was co-editor of *Legal Queeries* (London:

Cassell, 1998), and has written a collection of essays on lesbian, gay and transgender issues in law. In 1997, he edited 'Legal perversions', a special issue of the journal *Social and Legal Studies*. He is currently engaged in the UK's largest multidisciplinary empirical study of homophobic violence: 'Violence, sexuality, space'. He is also a member of the London Metropolitan Police Lesbian, Gay, Bisexual, Transgender Community Advisory Group. He is currently working on a book entitled *Critiques of Hate*.

WAYNE MORGAN is Lecturer in Law at Flinders University, Australia. He teaches courses in both law and sexuality, and human rights law. He has also litigated Australian gay and lesbian rights cases at the state, national and international level.

OLIVER PHILLIPS is a Lecturer in Law at Keele University, UK. Having grown up in Zimbabwe and South Africa, he completed his Ph.D. at the Institute of Criminology, Cambridge, on 'Sexual offences in Zimbabwe: fetishisms of procreation, perversion, and individual autonomy'. He has published a number of articles out of this research. He was for a long time active in the organization of the Gays and Lesbians of Zimbabwe (GALZ).

JENNIFER SPRUILL is a doctoral candidate in the Department of Anthropology, University of Chicago, and a candidate for a graduate degree in law, University of the Witwatersrand, South Africa. She is a graduate in law from the University of Chicago, and also holds degrees from Bryn Mawr College, USA. Her research concerns issues of sexuality, law, nationalism and postcolonialism in South Africa.

CLAIRE F.L. YOUNG is a Professor of Law at the University of British Columbia, Vancouver, Canada. She teaches, researches and writes on all aspects of tax law and policy, including the impact of tax policies on lesbians and gay men. She is currently working on a major study for the Canadian government which will examine the impact on women of delivering social programs through the tax system.

ACKNOWLEDGMENTS

Our first acknowledgment is to our contributors. We thank them for their superb essays. Most of these chapters were presented at the Gender, Sexuality and Law Conference held at Keele University in June, 1998. As two of the organizers of that Conference, we thank all of the participants, the rest of the organizing group, and we acknowledge the financial support of Keele University and the British Academy. Many thanks to Davina Cooper for all of her help; to Kitty Cooper for the use of her photograph; and also to Tristan Palmer at Athlone Press.

Finally, we acknowledge permission to reprint the following previously published works: Patrick Hanafin. 1998. 'Rewriting desire: the construction of sexual identity in literary and legal discourse in postcolonial Ireland', *Social and Legal Studies* 7(3): 409; and Leslie J. Moran and Derek McGhee. 1998. 'Perverting London: the cartographic practices of law', *Law and Critique* 9(2): 207.

INDEX